DATE DUE

GAYLORD	PRINTED IN U.S.A.

MODERNIZATION IN THE MIDDLE EAST
The Ottoman Empire and its Afro-Asian Successors

**Studies on Modernization
of the Center of International Studies
at Princeton University**

*The Modernization
of Japan and Russia* (1975)

The Modernization of China (1981)

The Modernization of Inner Asia (1991)

*Modernization in the Middle East,
The Ottoman Empire and its Afro-Asian Successors* (1992)

MODERNIZATION IN THE MIDDLE EAST

THE OTTOMAN EMPIRE AND ITS AFRO-ASIAN SUCCESSORS

Written under the auspices of the
Center of International Studies
and
The Program in Near Eastern Studies,
Princeton University

Cyril E. Black and L. Carl Brown, Editors

THE DARWIN PRESS, INC.
Princeton, New Jersey USA

Library of Congress Cataloging in Publication Data

Modernization in the Middle East: the Ottoman empire and its Afro-Asian successors / Cyril E. Black and L. Carl Brown, editors.
    p.   cm.
    "Written under the auspices of the Center of International Studies and the Program in Near Eastern Studies, Princeton University."
    Includes bibliographical references and index.
    ISBN 0–87850–085–5 (alk. paper)
    1. Middle East—History—1517–   2. Africa, North—History—1517–1882.   3. Africa, North—History—1882–   I. Black, Cyril Edwin, 1915–1989. II. Brown, L. Carl (Leon Carl), 1928–   .
III. Woodrow Wilson School of Public and International Affairs. Center of International Studies.   IV. Princeton University. Program in Near Eastern Studies.
DS62.4.M64   1991
956'.015—dc20   91–44788
                                     CIP

The paper in this book is acid-free neutral pH stock and meets the guidelines for permanence and durability of the Committee on Production Guidelines for Book Longevity of the Council on Library Resources.

Published by
The Darwin Press, Inc.
Box 2202
Princeton, NJ 08543 USA

Printed in the United States of America

To the Memory of Cyril E. Black (1915–1989)
Colleague and Co-Editor of this book and
Modernization Studies Pioneer

CONTENTS

Maps

CONTRIBUTING AUTHORS

Karl K. Barbir, Professor of History at Siena College, Loudonville, New York, received the Ph.D. in Near Eastern Studies from Princeton University. He is the author of *Ottoman Rule in Damascus, 1708–1758* (1980); of a forthcoming biography of Muhammad Khalil al-Muradi (1760–1791), historian and notable of Damascus; and of several articles and reviews.

Cyril E. Black (1915–1989) at the time of his death was James S. McDonnell Distinguished University Professor of History and International Affairs Emeritus at Princeton University, where he also served as director of the Center of International Studies for 17 years. A major part of his long scholarly career was devoted to the study of modernization. His *The Dynamics of Modernization: A Study in Comparative History* (1966) set an agenda for the many scholars who followed his lead. He was as well the individual who brought together the four volumes that have appeared in this series, *The Modernization of Japan and Russia* (1975), *The Modernization of China* (1981), *The Modernization of Inner Asia* (1991), and the present work.

L. Carl Brown is Garrett Professor in Foreign Affairs and Director of the Program in Near Eastern Studies at Princeton University. He is the co-author of *Tunisia: The Politics of Modernization* (1964) and author of *The Tunisia of Ahmad Bey* (1974) and *International Politics and the Middle East, Old Rules, Dangerous Game* (1984).

Carter Vaughn Findley is professor of history at Ohio State University. He is the author of *Bureaucratic Reform in the Ottoman Empire: The Sublime Porte, 1789–1922* (1980) and co-author with John Rothney of *Twentieth-Century World* (2nd edition, 1990).

Charles Issawi, Bayard Dodge Professor of Near Eastern Studies Emeritus at Princeton University, has written extensively on the economics, economic history, and cultural history of the Middle East. His most recent books are: *An Economic History of the Middle East and North Africa* (1982), *The Fertile Crescent* (1988), and *Issawi's Laws of Social Motion* (Enlarged Edition, 1991).

ix

Norman Itzkowitz is professor of Near Eastern Studies at Princeton University. He is the author of *Ottoman Empire and Islamic Tradition* (1973), co-author of *Mubadele: An Ottoman Russian Exchange of Ambassadors* (1970), and *The Immortal Atatürk: A Psychobiography* (1984).

Samir Khalaf, on leave from the American University of Beirut, is currently visiting professor of sociology at Princeton University. He is the author, among others, of *Persistence and Change in Nineteenth-Century Lebanon* (1979), *Hamra of Beirut* (1973), and *Lebanon's Predicament* (1987).

Ergün Ozbudun is professor of Constitutional Law and Comparative Politics at Ankara University Law School in Turkey. Currently he is also the President of the Turkish Political Science Association and the Vice-President of the Turkish Democracy Foundation. He has been a visiting professor at numerous other institutions, including Columbia University and the Woodrow Wilson School at Princeton. Among his extensive writing on democratic politics both in Turkey and in comparative perspective are three books, including *Social Change and Political Participation in Turkey*. Among the works he has edited are *The Political Economy of Income Distribution in Turkey* (with Aydin Ulusan), *Atatürk: Founder of a Modern State* (with Ali Kazancigil), and *Competitive Elections in Developing Countries* (with Myron Weiner).

Joseph S. Szyliowicz is professor of Middle East Studies at the Graduate School of International Studies, University of Denver. He is the author of *Politics, Technology and Development* (1991), *Education and Modernization in the Middle East* (1973), *A Political Analysis of Student Activism: The Turkish Case* (1972), *Political Change in Rural Turkey* (1966), and co-author and co-editor of *The Contemporary Middle East* (1965).

A NOTE ON TRANSLITERATION

Arabic and Turkish words have been transliterated in a simplified fashion consistent with standard English orthography. In a few cases, the customary Arabic spelling for a word appears in certain places with the Turkish spelling for the same word used elsewhere (e.g., ulama-ulema, Muhammad Ali-Mehmed Ali, madrasa-medrese). Since modern Turkish is written in the Latin script, it would be arbitrary to impose a spelling different from that appearing in standard Turkish sources. At the same time, Turkish usage should not be imposed on Arabic or on Arabists. In any case, this does serve to alert readers to the different spellings that they are likely to come across in other sources. These few differently spelled words are cross-listed in the Index.

PREFACE

This book was written as a group project with the contributing authors reviewing and providing suggested changes to all the different chapters. Primary responsibility for writing the different chapters was as follows:

The Introductions and Chapters 1, 2, 8, 9, and 15	Cyril E. Black and L. Carl Brown
Chapter 3, and 10, and the Bibliographical Essay	L. Carl Brown
Chapter 4	Norman Itzkowitz and L. Carl Brown
Chapters 5 and 12	Charles Issawi
Chapter 6	Karl K. Barbir
Chapter 7	Carter Vaughn Findley
Chapter 11	Ergün Ozbudun
Chapter 13	Samir Khalaf
Chapter 14	Joseph S. Szyliowicz

MAPS

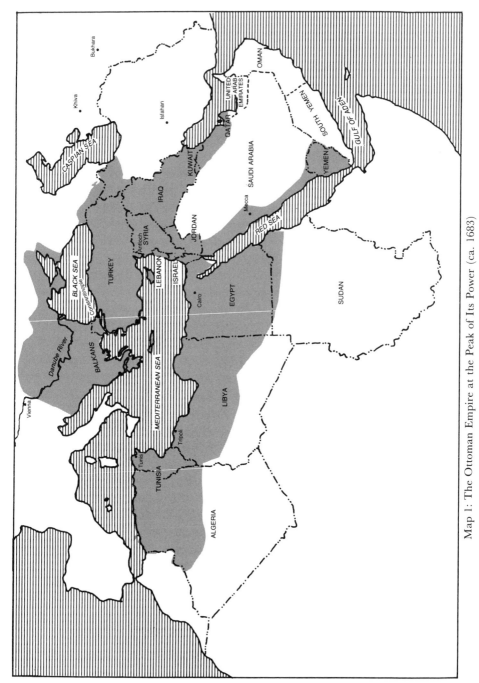

Map 1: The Ottoman Empire at the Peak of Its Power (ca. 1683)

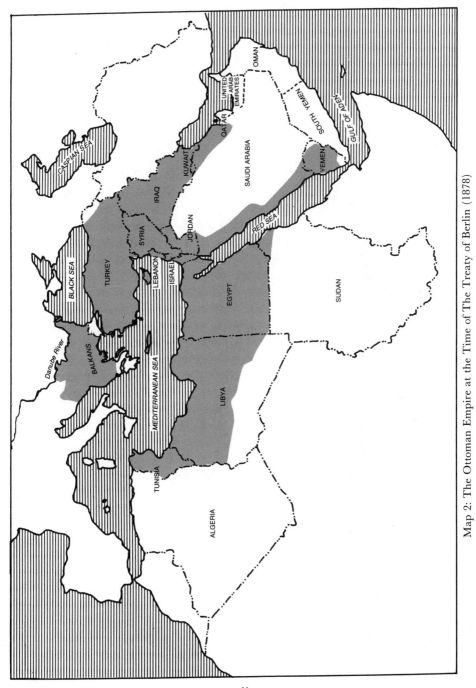

Map 2: The Ottoman Empire at the Time of The Treaty of Berlin (1878)

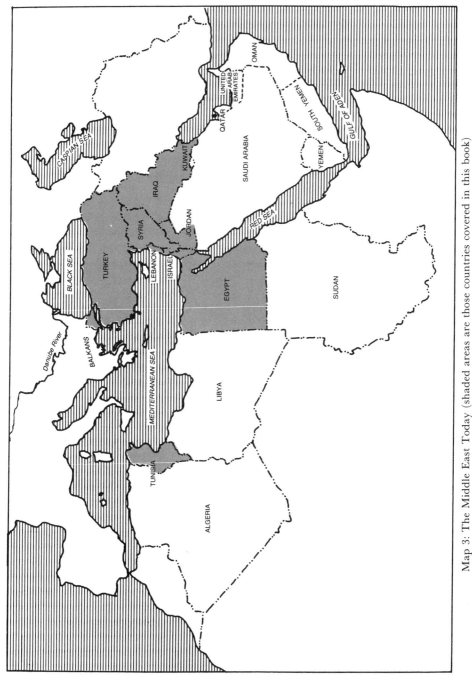

Map 3: The Middle East Today (shaded areas are those countries covered in this book)

CHAPTER ONE

General Introduction

THIS BOOK TAKES its place in a series of modernization studies including *The Modernization of Japan and Russia* (1975), *The Modernization of China* (1981), and *The Modernization of Inner Asia* (1991).

We have followed the basic methods, assumptions, and goals of the other books, and especially the first two, in order to assure the broadest possible scope for comparability.

At the same time, the subject of the present book dictates certain departures. Japan, Russia, and China all have remained distinctive state systems and political communities to the present day. No such continuity characterizes the Middle East.

Russia has vastly increased its territory over the last two centuries, becoming in the process much more of a multilanguage, multiethnic, and multireligious country, but it remains possible to trace this development within the framework of a single state. By the turn of this century, China was virtually dismembered as a result of internal weakness and external interference, but the sense of a single China was never abandoned by China's elites or masses. The last seven decades have witnessed a major reassertion of China's political presence. For all the vicissitudes of modern Japanese history, there was never a moment when the question of Japanese political identity was in doubt. To study the distinct paths to modernization of these three states thus seems as natural as to study that of the early modernizers— Britain, France, and the United States, for example.

The decision concerning the appropriate unit (or units) of analysis is not so natural as regards Ottoman Afro-Asia. Here the beginnings of modernization are roughly contemporary with the beginnings of a long period of imperial disintegration under outside pressure. Unlike the situation in China, this imperial disintegration was not later reversed. Instead, it led to the emergence of a number of Western-style nation states.

Given this historical development, one possible approach is to focus on the Ottoman Empire until its demise after the First World War and then trace how the emergent Republic of Turkey modernized. Since the Ottoman imperial capital—Istanbul—remains a part of Turkey (although no longer the capital), since the language of imperial administration was Ottoman Turkish for which modern Turkish is the successor language,

1

and since Turkey more than any other successor state to the Ottoman Empire accepts much of the Ottoman heritage as its own, such a choice would seem reasonable. This accords also with the conventional approach among students of modern Middle Eastern history.

One general study, for example, is entitled *A History of the Ottoman Empire and Modern Turkey,* and a classic study, with many insights put to use in this book, is entitled *The Emergence of Modern Turkey.*[1] The author of this latter book situates the roots of Turkey in the Ottoman past and traces its development from the late eighteenth century onward, that is, from the time when the Ottoman Empire lost its earlier self-sufficiency and became the prey of the European state system. Other works, whether textbooks or monographs, follow the same basic line.

That the Republic of Turkey is a successor state to the Ottoman Empire is beyond dispute. That in terms of cultural continuity it is the most important single successor state to the Ottoman Empire is also a fact. Turkey is not, however, the only state in today's Middle East whose existing political culture is largely explained in terms of the Ottoman past. Indeed, in certain important respects Atatürk's Turkey represents a sharper break with the Ottoman past than what transpired in the Arab lands formerly under the Ottomans.

To consider only Turkey after the fall of the Ottoman Empire is to miss the majority of the people of Ottoman Afro-Asia who shared centuries of experience under Ottoman rule. Moreover, such an approach serves to keep alive, however unintentionally, the anachronistic notion that Turkish nationalism and Arab nationalism have existed for centuries instead of being, each, a slowly emerging regional response to new politico-military challenges coming from Europe.

This point is especially important in the study of the modern Arab world. As so often happens in history, the Arabs have tended to adopt the thought-patterns of their tormentors. Having borrowed nineteenth-century European Romanticism, liberal and then not-so-liberal nationalism to create Arab nationalism, they now are inclined to read back into earlier times the existence of this new ideology. In this European version of modern Arab history, the Arabs become a colonized people struggling to be free of the Turks. And the four centuries of Ottoman rule in the Arab lands become four centuries of darkness and oppression, which can

---

[1] The books cited are written by Stanford J. Shaw and Ezel Kural Shaw and by Bernard Lewis, respectively.

then be used to explain existing contemporary deficiencies or "backwardness."

In fact, the Ottoman ruling elite did not think of themselves as "Turks" (although Europeans had long called them by that name). To the cosmopolitan Ottoman official, "Turk" was a pejorative term best translated as "bumpkin." Moreover, "Arab" to most urbanites and sedentary rural folk in the Arab world meant the bedouin.

Subjects of the vast Ottoman Empire on the eve of modern times used other than nationalist forms of identification. There were rulers and the ruled. There were different religious communities, occupational loyalties, tribes, families, attachments to specific localities, memberships in religious brotherhoods, and the differences distinguishing peasants, urbanites, nomads, and mountaineers. Slowly, over roughly the last two centuries, European-style nationalism emerged in the Middle East, not replacing these older forms of identification but merging and at times conflicting with them in an untidy fashion. Turkish and Arab nationalisms as they exist today are among the results, but both began in a common political culture that has been subject to continued modification in modern times under the combined onslaught of outside pressures and internal responses. There was no state of Turkey in 1800, nor for that matter a Syria or an Iraq. Such entities were then quite literally unthinkable. In Ottoman Afro-Asia, the process that changed the reality as well as the ideologies of politics, like the process of modernization itself, starts from the Ottoman matrix.

From the one extreme of studying modernization in the Ottoman Empire and the one successor state of Turkey, it would be possible to move to the other extreme of studying the Ottoman Empire and all its successor states—in Europe, Asia, and Africa. Such an approach must also be rejected. It is, quite simply, unwieldy. One can count as many as twenty-six Ottoman successor states. Even this figure is open to debate, so different are the means of defining the Ottoman imperial system and the modern state system. For example, should Hungary be included? Much of what is now Hungary was under Ottoman domination from roughly 1526 to 1699. Or the tiny states of the Persian Gulf that came under loose Ottoman control as early as the sixteenth century, but by the early nineteenth century had fallen to British rule? Even the most modest enumeration of successor states presents too great a number for effective treatment.

An entirely different approach would be to study a cultural area rather than any political community or communities (whether an empire or several states). Then roughly the same territory and the same peoples could be studied over time without the awkward expanding or contracting of the focus of attention according to changing political boundaries. The term already introduced—Ottoman Afro-Asia—presupposes just such a cultural area, for it is a region that is overwhelmingly Muslim in religion (roughly 90 percent of today's total population), contains the homeland and heartland of Islam, has constituted a universe to itself for at least a millennium (and for several millennia in certain parts), has been linked together for centuries by two major languages—Arabic and Turkish—and has shared a common Ottoman political heritage for some four centuries.

To study Ottoman Afro-Asia as an entity in itself also avoids the problem of considering those parts of southeastern Europe that long formed part of the Ottoman Empire. Since formerly Ottoman Europe is overwhelmingly Christian—its peoples speak different languages (which serve as well to tie them to other Europeans), it broke away earlier from the Ottoman Empire and has since been involved almost exclusively in the European or Eurasian cultural world—there is every reason to treat this region separately. The Ottoman legacy in Europe would still deserve more attention than it usually receives, but the resulting cultural area would be demonstrably different from Ottoman Afro-Asia.

Using a cultural area instead of one or more political entities as the unit of analysis also facilitates the study of these aspects of modernization that transcend political boundaries (such as technology, economic forces, religious institutions, ideologies, and even distinctive ecological areas). Such an approach avoids the possible trap of implicitly assuming that the state is always the major dynamic variable in the modernization process, yet it is able to take note of the state or of states within the framework of the larger unit of analysis.

Too much emphasis on the cultural area approach with a concomitant downgrading of the state as the chosen unit of analysis would, however, draw this modernization study away from its aims of following the methodology of and be comparable to *The Modernization of Japan and Russia* and *The Modernization of China*. This consideration brings us back to the need to work within the context of explicit political units—in a word, of states.

Yet, even after putting aside formerly Ottoman Europe, too many states remain. The Ottoman Empire in Afro-Asia embraced virtually all of today's Arab world, Anatolia, and portions of Turkic lands controlled by the former Soviet Union. Of the Arab states, only Morocco and what later became Mauritania totally escaped Ottoman control. Leaving aside the Central Asian territory absorbed by Russia (and then the Soviet Union), Ottoman Afro-Asia has since divided into some twenty successor states.

The solution adopted here is to proceed on the working assumption that Ottoman Afro-Asia does constitute a coherent cultural area, but to single out for study in this book only certain parts of the larger whole. Accordingly, while speaking throughout of Ottoman Afro-Asia, the countries actually considered are, in terms of present-day states, Turkey, Tunisia, Egypt, and the states of the Fertile Crescent—Lebanon, Syria, Iraq, Jordan, and Israel.

Two criteria dictated the choice made. First, to maximize comparability with Japan, Russia, and China, only those lands within Ottoman Afro-Asia having a long historical record of independence or de facto independence have been selected. This means, first of all, that the imperial state apparatus ruling from Istanbul must be considered until the last days of the Ottoman Empire.

Even so, two important parts of Ottoman Afro-Asia deserve to be singled out for having experienced political autonomy from at least the beginning of the modernization process in the Middle East. These two parts are Egypt and Tunisia. Juridically, both were provinces of the Ottoman Empire, but in fact each had its own local (but not native) ruling dynasty, its own bureaucracy, and its own army. Tunisia, or the beylik of Tunis, to use the older, prenational name, had an autonomous ruling dynasty from 1705 until 1957. Egypt, after being controlled by different Mamluk factions, came under the sway of the Muhammad Ali dynasty from 1805 until 1952, when the Nasserist Free Officers sent King Faruq into exile.

This gives us three separate political entities—(1) the central Ottoman Empire, including those areas under Istanbul's more-or-less direct control; (2) Egypt; and (3) Tunisia, the latter two being Ottoman provinces in law but in fact autonomous to the point of virtual independence.

All three shared a common Ottoman political culture. They also faced common problems of outside interference, and their political elites came forward with similar responses to those challenges. Moreover, all three continued as distinctive political units after the Ottoman period (deeming the Republic of Turkey as the legal and ideologically preeminent successor to the Ottoman Empire).

The second criterion for deciding which territories of Ottoman Afro-Asia were to be included was the degree of involvement in Ottoman political culture. By this criterion, Algeria, on the western fringe of the

Ottoman Empire, was a less likely candidate, since the French conquest of Algeria began as early as 1830. Equally, most of the Arabian Peninsula was never really controlled by the Ottomans. The Ottoman rulers monitored the bedouin of Arabia but made no effort to govern them. Even the invasion of Arabia by Egypt's Muhammad Ali, beginning in 1812 (at the behest of Ottoman Sultan Mahmud II), did not lead to Egyptian or Ottoman control in central Arabia. Muhammad Ali's forces did overthrow the first Wahhabi regime (the second created Saudi Arabia a century later), but within roughly a generation Egyptian forces had withdrawn. Saudi Arabia's political legacy is largely to be found in other than the Ottoman background.

Essentially the same can be said for the other states around the perimeter of the Arabian peninsula. Ottoman rule was somewhat stronger in the lowlands of Yemen, but never so consistently nor intensely as in Anatolia or the Fertile Crescent. Aden passed into British hands in 1839, and British sea power controlled the Persian Gulf littoral beginning in the 1820s.

Aside from Anatolia, the Fertile Crescent is the area par excellence of consistent and intensive Ottoman presence (from the early sixteenth century until the end of the empire after World War I). Moreover, the Fertile Crescent—now divided into five sovereign states—was ruled directly from the Ottoman center and did not enjoy the de facto independence of Tunisia or Egypt. Provincial governors were posted from Istanbul, regular Ottoman army units (in addition to local irregular forces) served tours of duty there, and edicts emanating from the imperial capital were applied in the Fertile Crescent.

Including the Fertile Crescent in the part of Ottoman Afro-Asia considered in this book offers several advantages. First, it facilitates the study of early modernization outside the context of a single state. Because it consisted of a group of provinces ruled from Istanbul, the Ottoman Fertile Crescent as a region had no single political voice as did Egypt or Tunisia. Yet, the Fertile Crescent, like other parts of the empire, was exposed to new technologies, new economic forces, and new ideologies coming from the West. In certain respects, exposure to these influences was more intensive in the Fertile Crescent than it was elsewhere in Ottoman Afro-Asia, especially those concerning trade and education, both of which served to challenge existing occupational patterns as well as existing ideologies.

At the same time, the Ottoman Fertile Crescent served as an arena of intra-Ottoman political struggles (especially Muhammad Ali's challenge to his nominal sovereign, the Ottoman sultan, during the 1830s), of Great Power competition, and of governmental reformist efforts radiating from Istanbul. For all these reasons, the Ottoman Fertile Crescent offers an interesting set of comparisons and contrasts with what occurred elsewhere in Ottoman Afro-Asia. Lacking political unity and independent political initiative, the Ottoman Fertile Crescent was a complex human laboratory in which most of the stimuli to change came from outside and stimulated diverse responses. Yet, the Fertile Crescent was very much a part of the Ottoman world, having been linked to the Ottoman Empire since the early years of the sixteenth century.

Placing the politically disparate Fertile Crescent alongside the political unity that characterizes Egypt, Tunisia, and the Ottoman Empire (followed by the Republic of Turkey) makes it possible to compare the importance of political unity and continuity throughout different phases of the modernization process. In a sense, we suggest that this, the third book in our modernization series, may serve both to clarify the modernization process in Ottoman Afro-Asia and to establish a framework for the study of the other parts of the world that entered modern times without political unity or that cannot look back on long periods of political continuity.

A few other points concerning the parts of Ottoman Afro-Asia included (or excluded) in this book are in order. What is now Libya was part of the Ottoman world for as long as Tunisia. Libya was colonized and settled by Europeans as was Tunisia. Libya, in addition, is one of the oil-rich states of the Middle East (having quickly gone from penury to theretofore undreamed-of wealth beginning in 1959 with the discovery of oil in commercial quantities). Libya could therefore have exemplified a developmental experience distinguishing several Middle Eastern countries—a society moving almost overnight from virtually no internal sources of capital to almost embarrassing wealth. We decided not to consider Libya for two reasons. First, the number of different units to be considered even in the restricted format arrived at remains intimidatingly large. There are four in the Ottoman period: central Ottoman Empire, Egypt, Tunisia, and the entire Fertile Crescent; and double that number for the post Ottoman period: Turkey, Egypt, Tunisia, Lebanon, Syria, Iraq, Jordan, and Israel. The addition of even one more example might have proved unnecessarily burdensome.

Second, it may be useful in a later book to bring together in a modernization study Libya, Saudi Arabia, and the Persian Gulf states, all examples of states with tiny populations (even Saudi Arabia and Libya having only some 5 to 10 persons per square mile) of a largely bedouin background that are now faced with the boon and the curse of fabulous oil wealth.

Sudan, a huge country one-third the size of the continental United States, was passed over largely because it was much less a part of the Ottoman world. Until Sudan was conquered by Egypt's Muhammad Ali, beginning in the 1820s, that vast country could look back on centuries of political and cultural history largely different from that of Egypt and the Muslim Mediterranean. Even after the 1820s, the modern Sudanese political experience came in an Egyptian and, later, Anglo-Egyptian context.

Finally, the question of Zionism and Israel remains. It cannot be claimed that the roots of Zionism lie in the Ottoman Middle East. Zionism grew up in Europe (especially Eastern Europe and Russia) as a European Jewish response to distinctively European experiences. It is true that a majority of Israel's Jewish population today are Oriental Jews (overwhelmingly Jews from the Arab lands of the Middle East and North Africa), but Zionism as an ideology came late to Jews of the Arab world, and Jews from the Arab world came late to Palestine or (after 1948) to Israel. Moreover, the developments that brought into existence the state of Israel and the standing of Israel in the region and the world are all so manifestly unique that one could easily justify excluding Israel from consideration in this book.

On the other hand, modernization is not a process taking place apart from prevailing political and military realities. The Arab-Israeli confrontation is too much a part of that reality to be ignored. In a sense, if Israel had been politically accepted by its neighbors and become simply a small Middle Eastern state enjoying normal relations with its neighbors, then the argument for not taking Israel into account in this modernization study would have been stronger. Since, instead, Arab-Israeli relations are a major determinant of ideologies and policies in the entire area under consideration (with the partial exception of Turkey), this important factor must be given its due.

For purposes of this study, Ottoman Afro-Asia and the Middle East are used interchangeably to embrace the area from Algeria's border with Morocco to the Persian Gulf and from Anatolia to the southern end of the Arabian peninsula. At the same time, the only part of that large area to be treated in detail are the present states of Egypt, Tunisia, Turkey, and the Fertile Crescent states—Lebanon, Syria, Iraq, Jordan, and Israel. This is not an effort to advance yet another definition of that protean term, the Middle East, in the belief that it is preferable to many others already in use. It is, rather, a pragmatic decision taken in order to give historical and cultural coherence to our chosen subject.

Nor is this particular definition of the Middle East as the states evolving out of Ottoman Afro-Asia intended to imply that Morocco or Iran share few of the same cultural characteristics. Cultural boundaries are always imprecise. We believe those we have chosen are less so than many. Our major purpose, in any case, is not to define cultural areas, but to isolate a region of sufficient historical and cultural coherence to serve the purposes of this modernization study.

The decision to concentrate on specified regions within Ottoman Afro-Asia is not honored to the point of foolish consistency. If an illustration from some other part of the Middle East helps to demonstrate a point, it is used. Even more, where adequate study of an area requires a more global treatment, this is done. This is all the more pertinent since we sincerely believe that the interpretation presented here concerning modernization in Egypt, Tunisia, Turkey, and the Fertile Crescent is applicable to other parts of the Middle East as well. The testing of that applicability must, however, be left to another occasion and to other authors.

II

Turning now to the conceptual framework of this study, it is important to define the approach on which this study is based. To quote from the first study in this series: "By modernization the authors mean the process by which societies have been and are being transformed under the impact of the scientific and technological revolution. In this study we view modernization as a holistic process affecting all aspects of society . . . we have been concerned especially with the international environment, political structures (patterns of coordination and control), economic growth, general social interdependence, and knowledge and education because we think these are the strategic areas for making comparisons and for examining their significance."[2]

Any comparative study of modernization is concerned in particular with two basic problems: (1) preconditions (on the basis of its premodern

---

[2] *The Modernization of Japan and Russia, A Comparative Study,* ed. by Cyril E. Black, New York, The Free Press, New York.

heritage, what assets and liabilities does a society bring to the problems of modernization?); and (2) the process of transformation (how has the society in question coped with the problems of the advancement of knowledge, political development, economic growth, and social mobilization?). There is also a third state of advanced modernization, sometimes referred to as the "postindustrial society," but this is not yet a concern of the countries of the Middle East.

In considering the premodern heritage of a society, the primary concern is to identify those elements that are easily convertible to the requirements of modernization, and also those that present particular obstacles. The implication of this concen is that some societies may have a much greater capacity than others for taking advantage of the opportunities offered by the scientific and technological revolutions, and that those lacking such capabilities may need to find substitutes for them.

The premodern capabilities that we have thus far found to be particularly conducive to subsequent modernization include a continuity of territory and population under a government with a capacity to undertake significant mobilization of human and material resources; an agrarian economy sufficiently productive to provide a surplus for investment in other sectors; a network of markets permitting society-wide commerce in raw materials and manufactures; and levels of urbanization, literacy, and specialized education sufficient to provide a basis for the development of a highly integrated modern society.

Among the socieities that have been studied from this point of view, not only those that underwent predominantly indigenous modernization (Britain and France, and their offshoots in the New World), but also such latecomers as the countries of Central Europe and Japan and Russia, where foreign influences played a major role—few were relatively well endowed with these capabilities. Most others were not.

A further precondition of strategic importance for latercomers is their capacity to borrow from the earlier modernizers, and to make effective use of such borrowing. Societies vary greatly in this respect. Some, such as Japan and Russia, were particularly well prepared by historical experience to be receptive to foreign influences. Similarly, the countries of Central Europe, as constituted in the nineteenth and twentieth centuries, were accustomed to borrowing from abroad. The numerous colonial peoples, for very different reasons, were likewise open to foreign influences.

Others, of which China is a prime example, were until the end of the nineteenth century particularly resistant to foreign influences. So strong was their belief in the inherent superiority of their culture that it took very extensive exposure to more modern societies, involving humiliating military defeats over many decades, before their leaders came to recognize the political, economic, and social opportunities offered by modern knowledge. One of the important questions raised by the present study is the receptivity of Ottoman society to foreign influences.

Study of the transformation from relatively nonmodernized to relatively modernized societies is concerned with two basic problems: the conversion of premodern capabilities to modern uses; and the introduction of new techniques and institutions—either developed indigenously, in the case of the early modernizers, or borrowed and adapted, in the case of the latecomers.

To judge from the experience of those societies that have gone farthest along this road, this transition calls for a number of fundamental changes. Modern knowledge must be accepted as superseding earlier conceptions of the human environment. In varying degrees of specialization, large segments of the population become involved in the production and distribution of knowledge. Transformation requires not only a political leadership capable of instituting the necessary economic and social change, but also a much greater society-wide coordination based on political participation in a variety of forms.

Policies designed to promote modern economic growth are called for by the state directly or indirectly through legal and institutional changes designed to encourage savings and investment. In the realm that particularly affects the individual and the family, a vast process of internal migration, universal education, and provisions for health and welfare must be administered on an unprecedented scale.

This process of transformation is more difficult for latecomers than for early modernizers because of the expectations aroused by the example of the latter. It is even more difficult for those latecomers lacking in some or even all of the desirable preconditions. More often than not, national territories must be consolidated and defended; and systems of national administration established at the same time that the disruptive processes of economic growth and social integration are in progress. Those societies lacking in essential preconditions must seek substitutes. Where no common language exists, as in India and many African states, a foreign language must be adopted. The failure of political leaders to establish stable administration often leads to military rule. Where a reservoir of administrative and technical personnel and infrastructure is lacking, as with many of the oil-producing countries, these must be imported wholesale from abroad.

The study of the process of change in the modern era must be set in a framework that is both global and multidisciplinary. The comparative study of modernization starts with the observation that unprecedented changes have taken place in the modern era in the advancement of knowledge, political development, economic growth, social mobilization, and individual change. It seeks to understand these changes, to evaluate the results of different policies of change in the various societies of the world, and to study the assets and liabilities brought to the process of change by the differing institutional heritages. It is an approach that seeks to reduce ethnocentric bias through the application of the comparative method, and it does not assume that any of the current patterns of policy in the advanced societies are necessarily applicable to other societies or are themselves immune to drastic change.[3]

As regards the advancement of knowledge, for example, the comparative study of modernization is concerned with the world views of pre-modern and modernizing leaders, the modes and structures of intellectual controversy, the share of society's resources that is devoted to basic and applied research, the proportion of the population that is engaged in primary, secondary, and higher education, and the extent and natures of its communications network. In the case of less developed societies, crucial considerations include their capacity for borrowing from the more advanced societies, their employment of foreign specialists, and their interest in sending students abroad for specialized training. All these concerns are to some degree measurable, and all change over time.

In the political realm, the comparative study of modernization focuses on the relations between the central structures of coordination and control and the individuals and groups that make up a society. Size and specialization is one indication of the level of development of a state bureaucracy; this level may also be measured by how much money the central bureaucracy spends in relation to the regional and local bureaucracies. A political system may be gauged, too, by the effectiveness of its performance, that is, by its capacity to maintain order, to endure without violent change, and to command the loyalty of citizens. The participation of individuals in government decision-making may be judged both in terms of a society's formal institutions (such as elected local, regional, and national representative bodies) and in terms of its informal institutions (such as political

---

[3] The five paragraphs that follow draw on C. E. Black, "Modernization as an Organizing Principle for World History," *1982 World History Teaching Conference*, ed. by J. C. Dixon and N. D. Martin (Colorado, 1983), pp. 58–60.

parties and special interest groups) and the means by which political, economic, ethnic, and other social interest groups influence political decision-making. Societies may also be compared with regard to their prevailing political ideologies, especially as they relate to the role of the public and private sectors.

In the economic realm, both the changing structure of economic activity and the rate of growth may be compared. It is customary to think of economic activity as divided into three main sectors: agriculture, industry, and the services. It is also customary to consider each of these sectors in relation to the proportion of the labor force they employ, the proportion of investments they absorb, and their contribution to the gross national product. Though such estimates are not very accurate, they reflect adequately the main distinctions among societies at different stages of development. The relationship of a society's economy to that of other societies may also be assessed by the rate of growth of foreign trade, the compositions of the foreign trade in terms of raw materials and manufactured goods, and the ratio of foreign trade to gross national product.

In many ways the most visible aspect of change as it affects human welfare is what may be called social mobilization—those changes that transform a society from one of small and relatively isolated communities to one that is tightly knit by bonds of education, communications, transportation, urbanization, and common interests. The improvement of health from the advancement of knowledge leads to an abrupt increase in births over deaths, resulting in a population explosion that does not regain stability for several generations. This factor alone can provide a barrier to human welfare, as production must rise faster than population growth if people are to benefit.

The relationship among strata within a society is also drastically altered. A modern society of managers, specialists of many kinds, industrial workers, office workers, and farmers with technical skills must be created out of a population that is normally four-fifths peasants, and such a transformation influences the life of every individual. In some degree, the sense of community and the mutual self-help characteristic of premodern villages is created at a national level in the urban way of life, in the common education and socialization of children in national school systems, and in the expanding communication system of the newspapers, radio, television, and rapid transportation. Yet even in the most advanced societies, human relationships remain less personal and cohesive than in agricultural communities, and individuals have a sense of isolation that is difficult to measure and evaluate. Further, with the drastic changes in stratification in the course of economic growth, the distribution of income tends to lag. Although the income of all strata of a population grows markedly in the long run, distribution of income has thus far remained decidedly unequal even in the most advanced societies.

The personality of an individual results from the interaction of biological characteristics with social environment—the immediate family, the community, and the larger society with which the individual comes into contact. Personalities vary as these biological attributes and environments differ, and the general process of change in the modern era has substantially transformed the environment within which individual personalities are formed.

To attempt an understanding of personality adaptation what needs to be measured, or at least evaluated, are the ability of individuals to empathize with others beyond their immediate circle of acquaintances, their acceptance of both the desirability of change and the recognition of a need for delayed gratification in the interest of future benefits, and their capacity to judge peers according to their performance rather than their status. As compared with individuals in earlier times, a modern personality may be described as more open, more tolerant of ambiguity, and more concerned with controlling the environment—and by the same token, perhaps less self-assured and stable. The psychological aspect of modernization has not been the subject of extensive research, but it has been demonstrated that modern characteristics can be measured and compared.

The process of modernization may thus be seen, at a rather abstract level, as the adaptation of a great diversity—the some 170 or more countries of the world—of historical experiences before the modern era to the challenges of modernity common to all societies.

There is no agreement whatsoever as to how this adaptation should be carried out in practice. No country has done it gracefully or without great turmoil. It is the most devastating and destabilizing experience that the human community has undergone during its entire history.

Within the setting of this abstract problem of adapting premodern institutions and values to the requirements of modernity, research on comparative modernization is thus in practice concerned with the continuing conflicts of leaders, political parties, and ideologies over how individual societies should seek to accommodate premodern belief systems to modern knowledge, establish workable political systems, promote economic growth, and deal with the many problems involved in restructuring social relations.

Much of the writing about the modern transformation of the societies of the Middle East has stressed Westernization, particularly European influence and models. This emphasis more often than not implies that Western and European institutions represent the patterns which other societies should seek to follow. Our view is rather that each society must find its own means of adapting its heritage of institutions and values to the requirements of modernity, and of borrowing where adaptation is not feasible.

Frequently leaders in the Middle East and elsewhere have sought too hastily to model their institutions on those of the West or Europe, only to find that these models are not suited to their needs. We are inclined to anticipate not convergence on the patterns of these societies that are at present most highly modernized, but rather a diversity of institutional means of achieving common levels of achievement. The differences among the institutional patterns of Japan, the United States, the countries of Western Europe, and the former Soviet Union are already sufficiently great to warrant the assumption that other societies will modernize along equally idiosyncratic lines.

Before turning our attention more specifically to the Middle East, it is also important to recognize that modernization should not be equated with "progress." The process of modernization reflects the enhancement of the human capacity to take advantage of the opportunities offered by the scientific and technological revolutions for the exploitation of the environment. This enhanced capacity can be used for any purpose. It can be used to promote political development, economic growth, and social integration, the aspects which have been of primary concern to modernization studies. This enhanced capacity can also be used, however, to destroy all humankind. Not only may many societies not have the capacity to attain the levels of achievement of those societies that are already relatively modernized, but those that are relatively modernized may not have the capacity to avoid their own destruction.

Part One

The Heritage of the Past

CHAPTER TWO

Introduction

PART ONE IS concerned with the premodern characteristics of Ottoman Afro-Asia (or the Middle East, as defined for purposes of this book) and with the early period of what can largely be described as defensive modernization directed by existing political elites. The time covered is from the late eighteenth century until the demise of the Ottoman system following the First World War.

In studying the preconditions of modernization in the Middle East we are especially interested in the characteristics of Ottoman society that were readily adaptable to change. We are also interested, of course, in those that presented significant obstacles both to indigenous adaptation and to the adoption of ideas and institutions from more modernized societies.

As regards the relation of the Ottoman Empire to its international environment, for example, we are interested in probing to what extent there was a common heritage of values and institutions within the empire that nurtured a distinctive common identity in dealing with other states. And, of course, the question of defining government and state, not juridically but sociologically, will be examined. To what extent did a common "Ottomanness" give cohesion to the entire area? Egypt and Tunisia, autonomous to the point of de facto independence, must be treated to some extent separately. Still, any tendency to "read back" into the earlier period the actual evolution of states and state boundaries following the First World War must be avoided. The reality of an Ottoman Middle East possessing not only roughly a half millennium of shared values and institutions but also shared foreign enemies—especially during the last 150 years of the Ottoman Empire—necessarily provides the organizing framework for studying the premodern characteristics of this region.

To what extent, then, were these governments—the Ottoman Empire and the areas under Istanbul's direct administration plus the autonomous governments of Egypt and Tunisia—able to initiate change within the area under their jurisdiction and also to defend themselves against intrusion by other states?

What experience did the Middle Eastern political leadership have in borrowing ideas and institutions from more developed societies, and could Middle Eastern states and societies undertake such borrowing without loss of political identity and group integrity? Both Japan and Russia, for example, had had extensive experience in borrowing long before the modern era, Japan from China and Russia from the Byzantine Empire. The idea of adopting institutions and belief systems from abroad was not new to them. China, by contrast, had had the opposite experience and had great difficulty in recognizing the need for borrowing from abroad. An important aspect of this process is the extent to which, through translations of foreign books and study of foreign institutions, a country deliberately organizes itself to gain access to knowledge coming from abroad.

Of particular concern in the Middle East is the extent to which religion may have been an obstacle to change. The Ottoman Empire was an Islamic state ruling a population of different religions—Muslims, Christian of every conceivable variety, Jews, and several others. Even so, the state was explicitly Muslim, deriving much of its legitimacy from this fact. And the majority of the subjects were Muslim, especially in the Afro-Asian parts of the empire. Since Western nationalism steadily spread to the Christian minorities of the empire, first in Greece and the Balkans and later (but never so completely) in Ottoman Afro-Asia and since, further, Christian Europe was the principal threat to the Ottoman Empire, could the Muslim rulers and their subjects be open to modernizing influences "Made in Europe"?

In view of the important role played by political control in societal transformation, we are also concerned with the ability of Middle Eastern governments to mobilize and allocate skills and resources on a regional and statewide basis. To what extent did the principal interest groups in the empire accept the leading role of the central authorities? Was the government served by bureaucratic personnel experienced in practical administration, and were there stable administrative structures from the national to the local level? Did Ottoman society possess autonomous corporate interest groups with established mechanisms for communicating with central government? Modern political systems require a greatly enhanced role for public and private central organizations, and the ability of countries to modernize is strongly influenced by the extent of their organizational experience before the advent of modernization.

Contrary to a widely held view, premodern societies vary greatly in their rates of economic growth. In the case of the Ottoman Empire, we must examine the capacity of the state to mobilize agricultural surpluses and to adopt growth-stimulating economic policies. Societies with relatively high levels of per capita production in premodern agriculture are usually more adaptable to societal transformation. Similarly, modern economic growth is also easier in societies with well-developed preindustrial craft and factory enterprises and experience in the exploitation of raw material resources. Economic institutions supporting a statewide exchange of goods and services likewise play an important role.

In the case of the Ottoman economy, to what extent were the manufacturing and service sectors in the hands of Christian and Jewish minorities, many of them living in territories that seceded from the empire in the course of the nineteenth century? What impact from an economic standpoint did the separatist nationalist challenges to Ottoman central control, causing the eventual loss of most of Ottoman Europe, have? Did the later nationalisms of Arabism and Turkism leading to the state boundaries in place after the First World War prefigure more coherent "national" economies or did these nationalisms sacrifice the earlier advantages of a larger, more integrated economic unit?

Modern societies are predominately urban, with most of their labor force in nonagricultural occupations. To what extent was the basis for modern change established during the Ottoman period by the development of administrative skills in business and government? Did family, classes, professions, and autonomous confessional communities (*millets*) represent obstacles to needed social mobility or were they assets?

Premodern societies vary widely in the level of literacy, education, and communications, and the extent that these were developed in the Ottoman Empire represents an important indicator of their readiness for societal transformation.

Were those territories most directly exposed to Western influences better able to modernize? Or did the very pace of imposed change create fissiparous forces? What on balance was the record of areas peopled by significant Christian populations in comparison with areas lacking important non-Muslim minorities? Did the Christians, more inclined to accept Western ways, serve as a modernizing vanguard? Or did the Christian attraction to these alien ways delegitimize these modernizing models in the eyes of the Muslim majorities?

It can readily be seen that most Ottoman preconditions to modernization were subject to the changing nature of the state and were subject equally to the question for which so many answers were proposed: What was the ideal state in territorial, religious, and ethnic terms? The previous studies in this series had no such additional complicating factor, Russia, Japan, and China all remaining as the core of a continuous state system. For Ottoman Afro-Asia it was as if the motto *E Pluribus Unum* was to be reversed. Instead of "From many, one" it was to be "From one, many." This question was not resolved during the period covered in Part One. The extent to which it was later resolved figures as an important theme in Part Two.

Finally, it should be emphasized yet again that Part One treats the Ottoman preconditions to modernization but within the temporal framework of that extended period of early, or defensive, modernization. To some extent, accordingly, the study of preconditions to modernization and early transformation must be joined.

CHAPTER THREE

The International Context

THE IMAGE OF the Ottoman Empire, still all too common in the West, as the "sick man of Europe" can easily lull the unwary into mistaken assumptions concerning the Afro-Asian lands once ruled by the Ottomans. While it is true that from the late eighteenth century until the end of the empire, following World War One, the Ottomans were politically and militarily subordinated to Europe, no such dependency characterized previous centuries.

Until modern times, the Ottoman Empire was not tributary to Europe or any other part of the world. Instead, the Ottoman Empire provided the political armature to a cultural area that had been self-sufficient for centuries.

The Ottoman state remained on the historical stage for six centuries. During much of that time it was a major world power. In one sense the Ottomans can be seen as heirs to the Byzantine tradition. Indeed, they saw themselves in this light. The Ottoman sultan who wrested Constantinople from the remnant Byzantine state in 1453 immediately assumed the title of Mehmed the Conqueror. Another throne title thereafter adopted by Ottoman rulers was that of "*sultan-i Rum*" (Sultan of Rome).

The Ottomans were equally heirs to the Turko-Mongol tradition of disciplined military elites capable of conquering and then organizing vast territories. Their earliest roots go back to ghazi warfare, of march warriors fighting to extend the frontiers of the state.

An Islamic state from the beginning, and after the early years of the sixteenth century the guardian of the holy cities of Mecca and Madina, the Ottoman Empire naturally built on Muslim institutions and traditions developed with the rise of Islam in the early seventh century.

With the conquest of geographical Syria in 1516 and of Egypt the following year, the Ottoman Empire became a major Arab power. Extending their sway westward across northern Africa to the borders of Morocco throughout the sixteenth century, the Ottomans brought almost all Arabic speakers within the same political tradition for the first time since the collapse of the Abbasid Empire in the mid-thirteenth century. As an Afro-Asian power dominating and giving institutional coherence to the

Middle Eastern heartland, the Ottomans emerged as heirs of the Abbasids, the Umayyads, and the early Islamic community founded by the Prophet Muhammad. Not surprisingly, the Ottoman political, religious, and cultural leadership looked to its Islamic and Middle Eastern past for guidance.

To speak of the Byzantine, Turko-Mongol, Abbasid, and Islamic heritages that combined to make up the cultural foundation of the Ottoman Empire is accurate but inadequate. The roster of influence that went into the making of the Ottoman Middle East included as well the Sassanian tradition that prevailed in the eastern part of the Fertile Crescent (and in Iran east of the Ottomans) and the many institutions and ideologies kept alive by the different Christian churches.

One could go even farther back in time and argue that a distinctive approach to political organization has characterized the Middle East since the dawn of civilization. In this light the early pharaonic and Mesopotamian empires figure as the first links in a historical chain leading through the Achaemenids, the Greeks of Alexander and his successors, the Romans, Byzantines, Sassanids, Umayyads, Abbasids, Seljuks, Mamluks, and then the Ottomans. The Middle East has for centuries, indeed millennia, been attuned to the political idea of centralized bureaucratic empires ruling over vast territories and disparate peoples while at the same time leaving considerable autonomy at local levels.

Character of the Region

Alongside this long-lived political tradition there developed many other distinctive customs that served to make the Middle East a sharply defined region. These have included, to cite only a few examples, cuisine, relations between the sexes with marked patterns of female seclusion and strict codes of female modesty, what is often called an "introverted" style of residential architecture, and a general cultural bias in favor of the cities at the expense of the countryside.

The Middle East that the Ottomans came to rule is the homeland of the three great monotheistic religions—Judaism, Christianity, and Islam. All three spread beyond the Middle East. All three remained attached in imagery and ideology to their Middle Eastern origins, none more so than Islam. Centuries before modern times, the great majority of the world's Christians and Jews looked to the Holy Land as a territory removed both physically and politically from their daily lives. Not so for

Muslims of the Ottoman Empire. Their Holy Land was at hand under the political suzerainty of the sultans. This added to the sense of Ottoman cultural self-sufficiency. In the same way, the Christian and Jewish subjects of the Ottoman Empire also had reason to feel culturally "at home."

Until modern times, the Ottoman Middle East was thus a world unto itself. Not that the Ottoman Middle East lived in a Tibet-like isolation from its neighbors. Contacts with peoples beyond its borders were constant and often intense, but they did not seriously impinge upon the internally determined rhythm of Middle East life, not at least until modern times. In roughly the first millennium of the Islamic period, the emerging Muslim polity had absorbed two major outside challenges. The first challenge was the elaborate western Asian imperial tradition itself as represented in its Byzantine and Sassanian forms, so radically different from the worldview of the Arabian Peninsula Arabs who first received Allah's message as sent through His chosen messenger, Muhammad. By the time of the later Umayyad rulers, the dialectic pitting primitive Arabian Islam (using the word as in "primitive Christianity" and not in any pejorative sense) against the elaborate Byzantine and Sassanian worldviews, embracing everything from philosophy to politics, had achieved a new synthesis destined thereafter to survive as the prevailing cultural choice of Middle Eastern society.

The other great challenge was military, that of the Mongols throughout the thirteenth century and until the last thrust of Tamerlane against the rising Ottomans. Tamerlane's crushing defeat of Sultan Bayazid at the Battle of Ankara in 1402 set back for a time the Ottoman march to empire. The Mongol incursions also left a legacy of a conquering military state. Not only did the Mongols offer an awesome model of military efficiency, but only another military regime was able to stop the Mongol advance. This was the feat of the Mamluks, then ruling Egypt and Syria, who in 1260 won the Battle of Ain Jalut (near Nazareth) against an, admittedly, greatly reduced Mongol army.

The Mongol invasion also represented an important development that had begun centuries earlier: the introduction of central Asian, largely Turkic peoples, into the Middle Eastern body politic as mercenaries, Mamluks, and eventually military rulers. What might be dubbed the "mamlukization" of the Middle East (the idea of government in the hands of an ethnically distinct military caste) had begun in the middle Abbasid Period (from the mid-ninth century) and continued thereafter, reaching its fullest development in the Ottoman Empire itself, whose officials were deemed "slaves of the sultan."

Neither the Mongols nor the Mamluks presented the Middle East with challenges in the realm of ideas or culture. They brought no new religion, no new philosophy, no different approaches to education and learning. The one great intellectual challenge (that of adapting the Greco-Persian high cultural tradition) had been met earlier by a militarily dominant, politically secure, and religiously confident early Muslim leadership. The later military challenge of the Mongols did not call into question the cultural underpinnings of Middle Eastern society. Only with the modern threat from the West did the military and the ideological challenge come in tandem.

From early Islamic times, the basic sense of Middle Eastern self-sufficiency had its theological expression. The area of Muslim control was *dar al-Islam* (the abode of Islam). All else was *dar al-Harb* (the abode of war). The theological formulation was not so much a "we-they" dichotomy as it was a way of expressing the idea "we and everyone else." A society that thinks in "we-they" terms is, after all, giving individuality if not even equality to the alien other. No such specific personality was given those beyond the pale of Islam. There was a world that mattered—dar al-Islam—wherein distinctions and nuances were properly made. Beyond that lay a world that merited neither curiosity nor concern.

This attitude was not so provincial as it might appear. The Ottoman Middle East, plus the even larger Muslim world to which it belonged, constituted a vast universe in itself. There were many pockets of parochialism, but the political and intellectual leadership possessed a cosmopolitanism seldom matched in other civilizations. A religious scholar might well pursue his studies in a number of different places, turn a pilgrimage to Mecca into a journey of several years duration in order to study with a number of scholars en route to the holy cities. A typical Ottoman bureaucrat or soldier could expect to serve in a number of posts in the Balkans, Anatolia, the Fertile Crescent, or even as far away as Yemen.

For a member of the Ottoman political or cultural elite, travel within the vast area of Ottoman suzerainty, or even to neighboring Muslim lands, was in no way unusual. Moreover, members of that elite while indifferent to non-Muslim languages or lands were interested in Arabic, Turkish, and Persian languages and literature much as earlier generations of Europeans deemed Greek and Latin the measure of the learned man.

Religion and State

In the Ottoman Empire, a restless scholar or an ambitious official could satisfy both intellectual curiosity and wanderlust within Ottoman borders or certainly within the limits of dar al-Islam. Yet, to present Middle Eastern political and cultural self-sufficiency strictly in terms of a Muslim universe—dar al-Islam—does not do justice to the region's diversity.

Unlike medieval European Christendom, in which the overwhelming majority of the people were Christians organized in a single, hierarchically structured Catholic Church, the Muslim rulers of the Middle East in the formative early centuries were a decided minority ruling over non-Muslim majorities, mainly Christian, but also Jews and smaller religious groups as well. The steady Islamization over the centuries would have made the Ottoman Empire a political system of and for Muslims but for the significant Ottoman holdings in largely Christian Europe. Instead, almost two out of every five Ottoman subjects were non-Muslim at the beginning of the nineteenth century.

The combination of these two important factors—the basic institutionalization of Middle Eastern politics and society having occurred when the Muslims were a ruling minority and the existence of a large non-Muslim population within the Ottoman Middle East—fostered and then maintained a distinctive approach to religion and the state. In theory, several approaches would have been possible. A Muslim sultan/caliph could attempt to impose a form of caesaropapism in which the state monitored religious orthodoxy and used its power to penalize those straying from orthodoxy.

Or a fully elaborated Muslim "church" hierarchy could speak for religious interests, facing both the organized state and the masses of people. This would create something like the medieval European church-state confrontation.

A third possibility was a less explicitly drawn and thus less potentially confrontational approach: The state could claim to represent the majority religious community but make no effort to impose religious doctrine. The state could honor the religious establishment but work to keep that establishment from being so institutionally autonomous that it might pose a political challenge. The majority religious establishment, in its turn, would be sufficiently a part of the state as to have no motivation to oppose it and sufficiently free of state interference in matters of dogma as to have no qualms about its links to political authority. The non-Muslim religious communities would be protected. This third possibility better describes what developed in the Ottoman Empire.

The international implications of this were several. Neither the Sunni Muslim religious leadership nor the rank-and-file had reason to challenge the state or to look beyond state borders for succor. At the same time, the sizeable Christian and Jewish minorities were given adequate religious and social autonomy to be satisfied with the political status quo. The contrast with Europe of the Reconquista or the Reformation and Counter-Reformation is striking. The Reconquista even had its direct impact on the Ottoman world, for the latter offered refuge to Spanish Muslims and Jews expelled from their homeland.

Most of the Christians within the Ottoman Empire were Orthodox. They did have coreligionists to the north, in the Austrian and Russian empires, but a common Orthodox Christian religion became politically significant only in the nineteenth century. Orthodox Christianity accepted the decentralized principle of autocephalous churches, and the Orthodox laity of the Ottoman Empire had their own religious hierarchy within Ottoman borders. No patriarch and, a fortiori, no pope beyond the Ottoman Empire could claim the loyalty of Ottoman Orthodox subjects.

As early as the latter years of the sixteenth century, Western Catholicism began a missionary drive directed against the faithful in the different Eastern Churches. These Catholic efforts picked up momentum and converts, creating in the process uniate (i.e., linked to Rome but maintaining their own liturgy and orders) Christian communities within the Ottoman Empire with potentially divided loyalties, but an offsetting result followed as well. Orthodox Christianity and the other Eastern Churches rightly saw in these years that the major threat came not from an infidel (in Christian eyes) Ottoman state but from an intrusive Christian rival. Until the nineteenth century brought to the Ottoman world the fateful mixture of religious nationalism, there was reason for the Eastern Churches to accept the political protection provided by the Ottoman system.

A very different perception of history also divided the Eastern Churches from the Western (Catholic, and, after the Reformation, both Catholic and Protestant). The former saw themselves as the true church, with roots back to the time of Christ. Antioch, Jerusalem, Constantinople, and Alexandria (all in Ottoman territory) were deemed more important than Rome. In the narrower terms of church history, the West had been hectoring the East centuries before the Eastern Question began. What to the Western Christians was often depicted as the ultimate in religious zeal against the infidels—the Crusaders—was seen quite differently by the Eastern Christians. They remembered that the Fourth Crusade rather than attack Muslim lands had conquered Constantinople, then the political capital of the Byzantine Empire and the religious capital of Eastern Orthodoxy.

The largest concentration of Catholics in the Afro-Asian lands of the Ottoman Empire was in Mount Lebanon, where the Maronites lived. The Maronites, united with Rome since the late twelfth century, were a potential pocket of religiopolitical disaffection; but as viewed by the Ottoman imperial capital, they were only one more recalcitrant group of mountain folk somewhat like the Druze, the Kurds, the Berbers of North Africa, and the Zaydi Shiites of Yemen. Since the Ottomans did not attempt to impose religious orthodoxy on either Muslim or infidel, they were content to let these mountaineers go their own way so long as they did not disturb public order in the plains and the urban areas.

The Jews had no outside sponsor, actual or potential. Scholars can dispute the precise status of Jews in the Ottoman Empire or for that matter in earlier Muslim regimes of the Middle East, but there can be no doubt that compared with Western Christendom's treatment of Jews, the Ottoman Middle East, and its predecessors, offered a favorable environment for Judaism and for Jews.

To say that most of these large non-Muslim minorities spread throughout the Ottoman Middle East were loyal subjects would be an exaggeration. Indeed, that way of posing the issue is anachronistic. The notion of political loyalty is a modern, and European, idea based on the quite different concept of the nation-state made up of citizens, not subjects, entitled and indeed expected to participate actively in politics. In the classical Ottoman political world there was no room for such a sense of loyalty to the state on the part of the subjects, Muslim or non-Muslim. The "state" was a small, distinctive group of individuals presiding over their charges according to the venerable political metaphor of the shepherd tending his sheep (*ra'aya*). This clear division between "state" and society was, moreover, acceptable to both parties, rulers and subjects.

It can be said, however, that in the long period of Ottoman control before the Western threat became obvious to all parties, there was, generally speaking, little sense of religiopolitical identification linking Ottoman Christians and Jews to their coreligionists in neighboring Europe. The Catholic missionaries and the later Protestant missionaries eventually contributed mightily to the reorientation of religious and political values in the Middle East, but neither rulers nor subjects sensed the explosive nature of this development until the Ottoman system was in the clutches of European political domination. The Ottoman rulers viewed these intra-Christian rivalries with patronizing indifference, for "infidelity constitutes a single millet."

The only significant intra-Muslim religiopolitical confrontation transcending state boundaries during the Ottoman period was the pitting of Ottomans, championing Sunni orthodoxy, against the Shi'ite Safavid state. This was a major duel in the sixteenth century, when both the Ottoman and Safavid states attained their greatest power. But with the latter's political decline in the following century, the confrontation became accordingly attenuated.

Dar al-Islam

The Ottoman state was the last imperial expression of dar al-Islam, for the only two other claimants to that role—the Iranian Safavids and Moghul India—disintegrated in the eighteenth century. The Ottoman state was, at the same time, a multireligious, multilingual, and multiethnic empire. These characteristics, the major causes of difficulties faced by the Ottoman state in the last century or so of its life, had before that time induced the Ottoman rulers to create an imperial system of striking flexibility and self-sufficiency.

By the late sixteenth century, the Ottoman Empire had reached its full growth. This is not to say that it had attained any readily apparent geographical limits. Most of its borders with Europe (including Russia), with Iran, or in northern Africa offered no clearly defined physical dividing line such as a sea or a mountain range. Moreover, several of these borders were in dispute and subject to fluctuation over time. There was, however, a certain naturalness in the late sixteenth-century borders, given the basic Ottoman military strategy. Ottoman government being by design highly centralized, especially so for a premodern state, the rulers did not keep a large part of the army or navy away from Istanbul's control. Accordingly, campaigns against the European enemy to the west or the Shi'ite Safavid enemy to the east started from near the imperial capital with the beginning of good weather in the spring. By the time the forces had reached the outskirts of, say, Vienna in the west (or the lands beyond Baghdad in the east), usually only a few weeks remained for warfare before it was necessary to begin the long march back to winter quarters.

In the same way, provinces of North Africa—especially Algeria and Tunisia and to a somewhat lesser extent Libya (to use the present-day names)—were too far away to be easily controlled or defended by the Ottoman navy operating from home waters. This was one very important reason why Algeria and Tunisia became more nearly client-states within a loose Ottoman suzerainty than controlled-from-the-center provinces such as Anatolia or the Fertile Crescent.

The situation in Tripolitania was not appreciably different. There, too, the Ottoman "governors" were autonomous rulers with their own bureaucracy and military, not officials or troops rotated periodically from one part of the empire to another, until the Ottomans, taking advantage of local disorders, restored direct administration from Istanbul in 1835— one of the few examples of successful Ottoman expansion during the age of the "Sick Man of Europe."

Egypt was in a somewhat different situation. Closer to the imperial center and accessible both by sea and by land, Egypt, with its rich Nile Valley, was a prize worthy of Istanbul's concern. That Egypt also attained virtual autonomy under the Mamluks (who after their defeat in 1516–1517 agreed to serve their conquerors) is not to be explained by Ottoman strategy or Istanbul's indifference. Rather, Egypt was sufficiently rich and the Mamluks sufficiently well organized to make their assertion of virtual autonomy hold most of the time. Sultans and their viziers in Istanbul always kept a careful eye on Ottoman Egypt and quickly moved in to reassert central government whenever division or weakness among the Mamluks made this possible at acceptable cost.

Egypt, in any case, was safely sheltered within the vast Ottoman Empire, remote enough from any border with the European enemy to be protected from a major military thrust that might upset the prevailing strategic balance in the Mediterranean. For this reason, the Ottomans could tolerate Mamluk pretensions, waiting patiently until intra-Mamluk fights in Egypt permitted an economical reassertion of Ottoman control.

Such were the rules of the game in Egypt and, indeed, throughout the Ottoman Empire until modern times. Before the late eighteenth century, no foreign enemy truly threatened the Ottoman world. Warfare was endemic, but the Ottomans were conditioned by their history to see the hostile peoples beyond their border more as an opportunity than a danger. The resulting sense of self-sufficiency shaped Ottoman views of diplomacy.

Ever since the young state recovered from the devastating defeat Tamerlane had inflicted on Sultan Bayazid (Battle of Ankara, 1402), the Ottomans had presided over a victorious, expanding empire. It is true that the age of great expansion had come to an end by the late sixteenth century and that major losses to the European enemy (Hungary, Transylvania, and Podalia) were sustained a century later. But the group psychology of a political elite who still felt capable of state expansion and who believed still ruled over a going concern remained intact well into the eighteenth century.

What might be called the "late classical" Ottoman view of the world (from roughly 1583 to 1774) can be epitomized as follows: The tradition of ghazi warfare, of serving on the borders of dar al-Islam in an effort to advance against the infidel, was still honored. There was no feeling that the state of war between dar al-Islam and dar al-Harb was ever destined to give way to detente. Yet, the Ottoman Empire was roughly as large as it could be, given the existing state of technology and the prevailing Ottoman strategic assumptions. At the level of ideology, the Ottoman Empire was still an expanding, ghazi state, but the daily management of the vast empire that earlier Ottoman energies had brought into being largely occupied the political elite. The obsessive concern with what intrusive Europe might do would have been incomprehensible to Middle Eastern political leadership before the late eighteenth century.

The Ottoman Empire and the West

Accordingly, the Ottomans in those days when the empire was strong paid little attention to diplomacy. The rulers in Istanbul took the disdainful position that if outsiders wished to negotiate they must present themselves at the imperial capital. This is just what happened. By the end of the sixteenth century, England, France, the Holy Roman Empire, and Venice had established permanent resident embassies. Most other European states, already in the habit of regularly sending special envoys to Istanbul, followed suit during the next two centuries. By contrast, the Ottomans did not establish a resident embassy until 1793—in London.

A few special Ottoman embassies did travel to Europe seemingly as early as the late sixteenth century, and roughly a century later it became customary for the returning envoy to write a *sefaratname*, or mission report. These sporadic diplomatic visits did not, however, serve to challenge the Ottoman self-image in international relations. The Ottomans did not see their empire as one state in a world of several states. Accordingly, the notion of reciprocity among states did not arise. Nor did the idea of a balance of power arrived at by ever-shifting combinations of several different states fit into the traditional Ottoman worldview. Such outlooks were to be imposed on the Ottoman Middle East later.

With a hostile, disdainful attitude toward the outside world and a belief that everything should be controlled from Istanbul, the Ottomans perferred that foreign diplomats should come to them. The same thinking prevailed in the matter of foreign trade, and this led to the capitulations system. These capitulations were special privileges that the Ottoman state chose to grant foreign merchants in order that they would govern themselves while resident in the empire. As a result, such merchants would thereby have limited contact with Ottoman subjects and would be less of a bother to the Ottoman government.

In no sense were the capitulations seen by the Ottomans as privileges won by foreign states for their subjects after hard bargaining. Even less were they regarded as having been forcibly extorted from a reluctant Ottoman state by the threatening European state system. The capitulations were throughout the long period of Ottoman strength simply a convenient way for the empire to handle a matter of no great consequence. (The European usage "capitulation" had then only the sense of "chapters" or items listed in a document. The term employed by the Ottomans— *imtiyaz*—clearly conveyed the sense of a concession or privilege granted by one in authority.)

The system of capitulations also developed in Ottoman provincial cities, even in those provinces along the Mediterranean coast of Ottoman Africa that largely escaped direct rule from Istanbul. States enjoying considerable de facto autonomy, if not virtual independence, within the Ottoman system, such as Algiers, Tunisia, and Tripoli, can be found entering into direct commercial treaties with European states from the seventeenth century onward. At times, these autonomous "states" would refuse to honor capitulatory concessions granted by the Ottoman sultan to European states or their subjects. Such, for example, was the fate of the 1604 capitulation agreement in which the Ottoman government granted French merchants fishing and trading rights in the area of Bone, Algeria. The issue was not resolved until years later, in 1628, when the French were able to obtain a treaty directly with the Algerian *beylik*.

Only with the decline of Ottoman power and self-sufficiency did the capitulations become an institutionalized pattern of abusive European extraterritoriality seriously undermining Ottoman sovereignty.

Why were trade and diplomacy between Ottoman lands and Europe such a one-way matter? A venerable tradition of Western scholarship would emphasize that the capitulations and Ottoman attitudes toward diplomacy may be traced to the general conservatism and lack of curiosity concerning the outside world among people of the Ottoman world, both rulers and ruled. From one limited perspective this is true. The people of Ottoman Afro-Asia long remained notably incurious about Europe and disinclined to consider European ways worthy of emulation or even of notice.

This Ottoman mindset can, however, be better explained in other terms. With so many opportunities for advancement within the Ottoman world, an ambitious Ottoman subject would have been perverse to have specialized in the knowledge of foreign lands. The Ottoman Empire at its peak, in the late sixteenth century, offered its subjects a vast area of political and economic opportunity larger than the present-day United States. An Arab merchant or scholar, for example, could travel the roughly 3000 miles from Tlemcen on Algeria's border with Morocco to Basra on the Persian Gulf relying solely on his native language and finding no surprises as regards customs, laws, or accommodations. Knowledge of Turkish would suffice for matters of government and politics throughout the entire empire in roughly the same way English serves as a lingua franca throughout much of today's world.

Moreover, the capitulations—while conceived as a sovereign's gracious concession rather than a bargain between sovereign equals—were not lacking in the idea of reciprocity. If Ottoman subjects trading in a state benefitting from an Ottoman capitulatory grant were deemed to have been mistreated, this was grounds for withdrawing the capitulatory privileges. Nor was this threat an empty gesture in the absence of Ottomans trading in Europe. Although the number of Ottoman Muslim traders who established themselves in Europe was always slight (but one does hear of a Muslim *funduq* or hostel-factory in Venice), Ottoman Christians and Jews did garner much of the Eastern European trade.

This brings the matter back to a fundamental point characterizing the Ottoman world in relations with lands beyond its borders. The Ottoman Empire was a multireligious and multinational empire. Just as the capitulations system may rightly be seen as an extension of the celebrated millet system according to which many governmental functions (as courts and schools) were delegated to different religious communities (the European resident communities enjoying capitulatory rights usually being referred to as *ta'ifa* or *milla*, roughly guild or religious nation), so too was there a semiautomatic division of labor according to such distinctions as religious community. Thus, most of the Ottoman subjects engaged in trade with Europe were Christians or Jews, because they knew the necessary languages and could with minimal cultural adjustments accommodate themselves to European mores.

In the same way, the many dragomans (from the Ottoman, originally Arabic, word for interpreter) of European-Ottoman commerce and diplomacy throughout the capitals and trading cities of the Ottoman world were non-Muslims. Certainly, this arrangement put the Ottoman political elite, who were Muslim, at a disadvantage when knowledge of Western ways became the key to political survival. But it grew out of an earlier, sensible division of labor along religious lines, not a congenital Muslim lack of curiosity. Muslim curiosity was, instead, drawn off in other directions. In commerce, this, seemingly, included much of the trade within the Ottoman world, all of the trade (with proselytizing to boot) between Ottoman North Africa and black Africa, and trade to the east of the Ottoman world.

Ottoman Muslim self-absorption and self-sufficiency are indicated by the number of restless Europeans who escaped the law or bad luck at home to seek a second chance in the Ottoman Empire. From the days of Ottoman strength until long after Ottoman decline vis-à-vis Europe had begun, a number of such "Turks by profession" or "renegades" (as they were called in European sources) made their fortunes in the Ottoman world, often but not always converting to Islam in the process. There was almost no such traffic in the other direction—from the Ottoman world to Europe.

In sum, the classical Ottoman view of the world was that of a long-lived imperial system embracing a sufficiently large and complex body of peoples and lands to form, and equally be seen as forming, its own universe. Relations with the peoples and lands beyond that Ottoman-Muslim-Middle Eastern universe were subordinate to the interests, attitudes, and needs developed within this vast cultural system.

An Age of Transition

By the late eighteenth century, however, Ottoman self-sufficiency and with it the Ottoman supercilious attitude toward the outside world had been shattered, never to be restored. A long period of frantic efforts to meet the threat (and also the enticements) posed by Europe ensued. This was to continue until the final dismembering of the Ottoman Empire following the First World War. And for the Afro-Asian successor states to the Ottoman Empire, efforts to adapt or resist (or some combination of the two) to outside influences have continued to the present day. This move from political and cultural self-sufficiency as regards the outside world to a diametrically opposite feeling of being obliged to change under the whip of outside pressure can, for present purposes, be sketched in a few broad themes.

First, there was no single great turning point marking the transition from one age to the next. Ottoman expansion had ended for all practical purposes by the late sixteenth century, and the Ottomans sustained appreciable losses in Europe following the second unsuccessful siege of Vienna in 1683 (the first was in 1529). Yet, in the first half of the eighteenth century the Ottoman world seemed to be holding its own against Europe.

The sense that the Ottoman world had slipped into a state of sustained weakness and thus vulnerability in the face of Europe may be more justly said to have emerged during the years from 1774 to 1829, a period begun with the fateful Treaty of Kuçuk Kaynarca following the Russian defeat of the Ottomans and the imposition of terms that involved Ottoman surrender of territories inhabited overwhelmingly by Muslims (the Crimean region). The period ends with the settlement on European terms of the Greek War of Independence in the nineteenth century. Midway in this transitional period Napoleon's 1798 invasion of Egypt had demonstrated the vulnerability not just of those Ottoman lands sharing a border with Europe but of even the Arab heartland. Napoleon's daring thrust was no sooner countered—with the help of British intervention—than the Ottomans had to face an internal challenge in the form of the Wahhabiyya bursting out of the Arabian Peninsula.

Thereafter, the political leadership within the entire Ottoman world lived in the knowledge that their once secure political structures were dangerously outmatched by Europe's still growing strength and also—because of this weakness—exposed to political threats from within the Ottoman world as well. One year after Europe had imposed the separation of Greece from the Ottoman Empire (1829), France began the conquest of Algeria, the westernmost Ottoman province. The following decade of the 1830s showed even the assertive Muhammad Ali in Egypt that military success against his nominal sovereign, the Ottoman Sultan, could be brought to nought by European intervention.

During the years between 1832 and 1833, the beylik of Tunis was involved in a dispute with Sardinia, a state that previous Tunisian rulers had confronted without hesitation. This time the bleak advice given by a minister to the bey summed up the changed power relationship between Europe and the Ottoman world: "Sardinia and Genoa are not what we used to know. They have advanced in prosperity and power just as we have declined."

A second major theme concerning this extended period of transition from Ottoman self-sufficiency to vulnerability is that the response to the new international situation came slowly and somewhat disjunctively. As long ago as the later decades of the seventeenth century, Ottoman reformers were to be found prepared to accept truces with the infidel enemy in order to direct attention to needed reforms with the Ottoman system.

Such, for example, was the argument of the celebrated Ottoman historian Naima (ca. 1665–1717), who advanced the example of the Prophet Muhammad's having accepted the truce of Hudaybiyya with the still infidel Meccans in A.D. 627.

Then the early years of the eighteenth century brought what was called the "Tulip Period" in Ottoman history, so named because of the upper class Ottoman passion for Dutch tulips. More important, the period (ca. 1718–1730) was marked by an artistic voluptuousness and—so radically different from earlier Ottoman styles—a penchant for borrowing European arts and styles. This opening to the outside world was continued in other fields under the stimulus of one Ibrahim Muteferrika (1674–1745), a European convert to Islam. He was able to establish a printing press in Istanbul to oversee the publication of some 20 volumes on the sciences, history, and geography. Muteferrika argued that the Ottomans needed to borrow knowledge of all kinds from the infidel world, a motif destined to become conventional by the time of the sustained nineteenth-century reformist efforts.

This early eighteenth-century opening to Europe, always resisted by conservatives, did not strike deep roots. Muteferrika's printing press closed soon after his death in 1745. Nor was there an equivalent to the Tulip Period or to an Ibrahim Muteferrika in the autonomous Egyptian or Tunisian provinces.

The third major theme is that the period of sustained borrowing from Europe was ushered in, not surprisingly, during the age (ca. 1774–1820s) when Europe's military superiority over the Ottoman world could no longer be ignored. Beginning in this age or soon thereafter was a pattern of conscious borrowing of European technology, first and foremost in the military field, adopted by the ruling elite not just in Istanbul but also in Egypt and Tunisia. The reformist period inaugurated by Sultan Selim III (1789–1807), and continued with greater intensity and accomplishment during the long reign of Mahmud II (1809–1839), was matched by efforts in Egypt under the driving force of Muhammad Ali, who ruled from 1805 to 1849, and in Tunisia during the reign of Ahmad Bey (1837–1855).

All three adopted similar ideologies, citing examples from the time of the Prophet Muhammad and the early Islamic community and depicting the changes not as innovation but as restoration of an earlier golden age.

All three concentrated on military westernization but found that this necessarily led to reforms in education, administration, law, and even in the state's relations to society (such as conscription and the levying of increased taxation to pay for more salaried officials).

In all three—Egypt, Tunisia, and the central Ottoman Empire—reforms were initiated from within the ruling elite in direct response to the elite's perceptions of the European threat. They were, thus, classic examples of reform-from-the-top, of enlightened despotism.

All three reformist programs eventually put such strains on governmental budgets as to cause bankruptcy, beginning in 1869 in Tunisia and in 1876 in Egypt and in the central Ottoman Empire. In all three cases, state bankruptcy led to direct intervention in the form of European-appointed financial administrators. In two of the three state systems, bankruptcy and the ensuing financial administration proved to be the last stage before direct Western imperial rule—the French protectorate in Tunisia from 1881 and the British occupation of Egypt beginning the following year.

In all three, adjustments to the new international situation brought radically different career patterns leading to political eminence. Whereas previously the Ottoman Empire had scorned the idea of sending resident ambassadors abroad and left the tedious task of interpreters for European diplomats or merchants to non-Muslim dragomans, Ottoman resident ambassadors chosen from the Ottoman political elite thenceforth became the norm. Moreover, those individuals who learned to communicate with Europe, to understand the European threat and thus to be able to confront that threat, earned a steadily increasing role in government whether in Istanbul, Cairo, or Tunis.

Fourth, the would-be enlightened despots and the ministerial westernizers they recruited represented only one possible response to Europe's challenge. At the other extreme could be found varieties of nativistic, xenophobic reactions usually taking a religious coloration. The extreme case was that of the Sudanese mahdi in the 1880s. But many examples of establishment ulama rallying conservative forces against the westernizers occur throughout the nineteenth century. Perhaps the earliest significant case was the deposing of Selim III in 1807, who fell afoul of both the Janissaries and the conservative ulama. The latter suspected the sultan's innovation as much as they deplored his ties with France. Nor were more strictly political revolts lacking against existing governments deemed to have "sold out" to foreigners, as was demonstrated by the 1864 revolt that swept much of the Tunisian countryside or Egypt's 'Urabi Pasha movement (1879–1882).

Yet another variant was what might be called Muslim religious nationalism in an effort to sustain a political base while strengthening the state (which invariably involved the continued borrowing of European technology and methods). The most famous example was the Pan-Islam movement embraced by Sultan Abdul Hamid (reigned from 1876 to 1909).

More important for the long-term and post-Ottoman developments were the various adaptations to the Ottoman world of that most explosive European import: nationalism.

All these many tendencies are held together by the common thread of a vast political culture—the Ottoman world—that having enjoyed self-sufficiency for centuries was thenceforth obliged to wrestle with a generation-after-generation problem of military, political, and economic inferiority vis-à-vis the European neighbor. In the process, the Ottoman world became an adjunct of the European states system. The 1856 Treaty of Paris following the Crimean War even explicitly admitted the Sublime Porte "to the advantages of the public law and system of Europe." Statesmen in the Ottoman world continued to cope with these "advantages" until one after another Tunisia, Egypt, and the several parts of the Fertile Crescent fell under the direct control of a European power. Moreover, what would have been the informal collective European protectorate over a truncated Ottoman Empire after defeat in the First World War was avoided only by Kemal Atatürk's adaptation of European nationalism to create a new nation-state, Turkey.

International Comparisons

The Ottoman world on the threshold of modern times possessed a centuries-old tradition of cultural self-sufficiency that accounted for its political durability but almost certainly inhibited a disposition to borrow from foreign sources. In this respect, the Ottoman world is best compared to China. Both had long accepted the idea of bureaucratic imperial rule over a vast area whose peoples shared a common cultural heritage.

China, however, presented a much greater linguistic and religio-cultural uniformity than did the multireligious, multilingual, and multinational Ottoman world. Yet, quite possibly the latter was even more resistant to outside influence, for even though its cultural diversity as compared with China gave the Ottoman world a more varied heritage, some parts of which predisposed links to peoples beyond Ottoman borders, the Ottoman self-image was ultimately based on a scriptural, revealed religion, Islam, seen by its followers as built on, but surpassing, the earlier partial divine revelations that gave rise to Judaism and Christianity.

The ruling elites of both China and the Ottoman Empire believed their way of life to be clearly the most advanced. They were thus little disposed to look for guidance beyond their borders. But for the Middle Eastern leadership any doubt concerning the superiority of their own ways raised questions of basic religious values. There was, moreover, a Muslim religious establishment capable of organizing an institutionalized resistance to alien influences in the name of Islam.

Even so, the Ottoman Empire was by no means a Muslim state in the sense that the Chinese imperial enterprise was based on a common core of Confucianism and the Chinese language. The Ottoman Empire always contained sizeable non-Muslim minorities, and certain regions, especially the Fertile Crescent, were a patchwork of different religions.

Another useful comparison is with medieval Christendom of Europe. In basic political institutions and political ideology the two had several points in common. The notion of Christendom in medieval Europe can be set alongside that of the single Islamic community (the umma), the Holy Roman Empire matching dar al-Islam, and the Holy Roman Emperor the equivalent of the sultan/caliph. The people, however, of medieval European Christendom were overwhelmingly Christian. No such Muslim uniformity characterized the Ottoman world. In the Ottoman Empire a complete identification between Islam and the state was always diluted by this practical consideration.

Politics to the Ottomans involved the delicate and necessarily inconsistent task of being an explicitly Muslim state while carefully balancing and protecting the many different religious communities under their rule. The resulting tradition of strong, centralized imperial rule mitigated by benign neglect of the subjects (the millet system, no attempt to impose religious doctrine, sharp separation between state and society) gave the Ottoman system great flexibility. Offsetting this was a limited capacity of any government in the Ottoman world to harness all the available human resources to any state-directed tasks.

Continuing the comparison with Europe, the European Renaissance, Reformation, and Counter-Reformation all worked to both reopen fundamental societal questions and to push political development in the direction of smaller, more cohesive groupings that eventually emerged as nation states.

In the Ottoman world, by contrast, no persistent religious or ideological movements provoked a reexamination of basic principles of societal organization, and no political movements fostered the creation of smaller but potentially more cohesive groupings that could become the chrysalis of nation states. The puritanical religious movements such as the Naqshbandiyya, starting in India early in the seventeenth century, or the Wahhabiyya out of the Arabian Peninsula the following century, came closest to providing a Muslim "Reformation"; but the Naqshbandiyya was domesticated within the Ottoman system and the Wahhabiyya defeated militarily early in the nineteenth century.

The very flexibility that helped make possible a long-lived Ottoman system ruling over a huge territory inhabited by peoples of such diverse languages and religions also served to neutralize challenges generated either from within or from outside. In a sense, European developments from the time of Christendom onward were marked by confrontation, those in the Ottoman world by insulation. Europe witnessed the clash of distinctive, institutionalized groups. The Ottoman approach both inhibited the drawing of such precise lines and worked to keep potentially antagonistic groups buffered from each other.

The sophisticated political flexibility that characterized the Ottoman system should be seen, however, as more a mechanical balancing of unassimilable elements rather than a protean capacity to adjust to new developments. The Ottoman-controlled civilization of the Middle East possessed none of that absorptive capacity of the Hindu civilization in India, for example. Indeed, these two major cultural areas, the Middle East and India, both representing adjustment to multilingual, multireligious, multicultural environments exemplify the two ends of the spectrum of possible approaches to neutralizing outside influences: the former by compartmentalizing and isolating, the latter by embracing and thereby absorbing. It might well be argued that both the Middle East and India paid a price for their striking success in maintaining cultural equilibrium in the face of new challenges. In both cases challenges tended to be deflected rather than confronted.

Eventually, the intensive, sustained outside challenge posed by Europe broke down the venerable Middle Eastern idea of an imperial unity serving as the armature and symbol of a cultural unity-in-diversity. This however, came very late to a region parts of which were poorly adapted to become smaller but more cohesive political entities, or—accepting the ethnocentric European terminology—to become nation states. Certain areas such as Egypt, Tunisia, and what became Turkey made the adjustment by rearranging longstanding historical, geographical, and cultural elements along nation-state lines. Even for these three the transition was not without difficulty, the strains of which persist as ongoing political problems to this day.

On this matter the Ottoman world's develoment was significantly different from comparable areas. China throughout modern times has been able to maintain its centuries-old territorial and cultural unity. India increased the centralizing political strength of roughly four-fifths of the subcontinent, while suffering only a single major partition, that which produced Pakistan (later Pakistan and Bangladesh). The Ottoman world's move from premodern empire to modern states was more nearly like that of Europe's move from Christendom to nation states, but Europe has had roughly a half millennium to work out the transition while being free from outside pressures during this time. The Ottoman move was, however, radically telescoped in time and carried out under the whip of unremitting outside pressure. The resulting disjunctures can hardly occasion surprise.

Unlike Western Europe, the Ottoman world is to be numbered among the late modernizers. Here, in comparison with China, Japan, or Russia, the Ottoman Middle East can be seen to have confronted major obstacles. Resistance to borrowing from outside was far stronger than in Japan or Russia and probably stronger even than in China. The Ottoman world must be placed at the bottom of the list in terms of possessing a traditional "national" identity that also was able to survive into the age of modernization. The question of the appropriate unit of sociopolitical organization became one of the most confusing and disputed to plague the Ottoman Middle East, whereas China, Japan, and, perhaps to a somewhat lesser extent Russia, had early resolved this vexatious issue.

CHAPTER FOUR

Political Structure

THE OTTOMANS IN the 1790s were no longer a threat to Europe. They were poised on the threshold of a new era that would be characterized by intense westernization while still carrying the political and institutional baggage left over from their long and glorious past.

Ottoman institutional concepts about the structure and nature of state and society had served well during the centuries of expansion that had witnessed the extension of Ottoman rule into the Balkans and then into the Arab Islamic heartland. The Ottoman Empire in its early and middle period had been organized for and dependent upon conquest. Constant conquest had sustained the vitality of Ottoman institutions and had helped to produce a vibrant, self-confident culture.

For a variety of reasons that include the shifting patterns of trade, the inflationary influence of new world silver that hit the Levant in the late sixteenth and early seventeenth centuries, and technological advances in the West that were slow to be introduced into the Ottoman domains, the Ottoman Empire went into a period of decline. The empire gradually dismembered, and its retreat from Europe began in serious fashion with the Treaty of Karlowitz (1699). Ottoman institutional resiliency coupled with the inability of the empire's enemies to inflict a definitive defeat upon Ottoman forces did, however, mitigate Ottoman decline.

Ottoman Islamic Traditions

Ottoman institutions and political ideas were deeply rooted in older Islamic traditions. Pre-Ottoman Islamic social theorists had posited the existence of four classes: the men of the sword, the men of the pen, the men of affairs (merchants), and the men of husbandry. Included in the men of the pen were religious dignitaries and functionaries, for in medieval Islamic times no clear distinction had yet been drawn between the bureaucracy and religious affairs. Nascent Ottoman society, however, knew a simpler division into two classes: the military (*askeri*) and the subjects (*reaya*), that is, the rulers and the ruled. The *reaya* produced the wealth from an agricultural base that supported the askeri class.

Askeri success, with its associated territorial expansion of the Ottoman domains, involved the growth of the military class and the concomitant differentiation of its functions. By the time of Suleyman the Magnificent (r. 1520–66), the askeri class had become differentiated into three
careers: the military (*seyf* = sword), the bureaucracy (*kalem* = pen), and
religion (*ilm* = religious knowledge; members were known collectively
as the *ulema*). Members of the fighting forces, the bureaucracy, and the
ulema increased in number; their power grew as increasingly they came
to represent the authority of the sultan. Status as a member of the askeri
class carried with it a number of important privileges, perhaps the most
significant of which was exemption from taxation. Also benefiting the
askeris were sumptuary laws that served to distinguish them from the
reaya. The division between the askeris and the reaya was fundamental
and was supposed to be maintained most rigorously by the sultan.

Secure behind their privileges, the *timar* holders formed the largest
constituent element among the askeris. These were the men who were
granted a share in the tax income of a particular region and a portion of
land sufficient for their own maintenance. Timar holders formed the
provincial cavalry that terrorized Europe and numbered some 40,000 in
the mid-sixteenth century. Timars were allocated on the basis of a land
survey carried out initially upon the conquest of a region, and then
subsequently as needed to update the information on tax yield and the
number of fighting men the tax base could support. Varying considerably
in the amount of yearly income, timars also varied in their requirements
of service. The greater the income, the greater the service contribution
in terms of men and materiel.

Closely intertwined with the timar system was the Ottoman provincial organization. The basic administrative unit was the *sançak* under the
command of the sançak bey who usually resided in the main town of the
sançak. In his administrative and military duties that included supervision
of tax collection and the maintenance of law and order, the sançak bey
was assisted by his lieutenants, the *subashis*. It was a tightly knit chain
of command that assured maximum military and financial returns to the
sultan while offering security, justice, and equity to the reaya.

Another group of fighting men was also at the disposal of the sultan.
These were the *kapi kullari*, the slaves of the Porte. Two main groups of
slaves deserve special attention—the products of the Palace School and
the Janissaries. Like many Muslim rulers before them, the Ottoman
sultans had large numbers of *ghulams*, or slaves, who were non-Muslim
in origin and were taken into royal service at an early age. They were

educated to become warrior/administrators. At the close of the fourteenth century, the Ottomans added an innovation to this Islamic tradition by drawing ghulam recruits from their own non-Muslim subjects through the means of a periodic levy called the *devshirme*. The best of the youths recruited in this manner were reserved for special training in the Palace School, whereas the rest were hired out to Turkish farmers, ultimately to become members of the Janissaries in their late teens.

Those who were selected for palace training received perhaps the finest education available in the Muslim world. Subjected to periodic review in the course of their training, the best students were allowed to continue, whereas the others were assigned to a variety of positions, including posts in the six divisions of the household cavalry, or leadership roles in the timar organization as subashis or sançak beys. This was the primary manner in which the Ottoman military/administrative elite was recruited, trained, and replenished in the course of the fifteenth, sixteenth, and seventeenth centuries.

Sharing askeri status with the kapi kullari and the men of the sword in general were the ulema, or members of the religious career. While the sultan's relationship with the military class was governed largely by administrative law (*kanun*), it must not be forgotten that the Ottoman Empire was an Islamic state resting on the Holy Law, the *shariah*. The administration of religious and administrative law was in the hands of judges called *kadis*. They were the products of the traditional educational system available exclusively to males; it took them through a series of schools from *sibyan mektebis* (elementary schools) or local Quran schools to the main *medreses* attached to the leading imperial mosques. This system of religious education (which was modeled on that available in the central Islamic world in medieval times) was still in effect well into the nineteenth century. Ulema produced by this system in the Ottoman Empire served not only as kadis but also as professors in the many medreses located throughout the Ottoman domains. Service as a kadi, however, was abhorred by many of the ulema, who faced with unease the prospect of diluting the strictly religious shariah law with the secular kanun and who, moreover, feared the pressures and corruption of involvement in government.

Even so, more kadis came to administer both kanun law and the shariah as Ottoman expansion accomplished by the timar cavalry and the Janissaries brought more territory under the sultan's sway. Expansion brought with it a need for a larger bureaucracy. Early Ottoman bureaucrats were generally drawn from the ulema, for they more than any others had the requisite skills, much as early European administrators had been drawn from the ranks of the churchmen. In the earlier Islamic formulations of class structure, the men of the pen, as we have noted, referred to the ulema, who also served as bureaucrats. Eventually, however, an Ottoman bureaucracy grew up staffed by professional bureaucrats. Trained by senior scribes during lengthy apprenticeships, these men continued their education in the humanistic tradition (*adab* = culture). They quickly developed a guild mentality that sought to limit access to the bureaucratic career in favor of their own offspring or other relatives.

Ottoman bureaucrats were not alone in seeking to limit career access. The ulema and the Janissaries, especially the high-ranking officials in both careers, engaged in the same practices. In this manner, they strove to maintain their status, and that of their families, as Ottomans.

The Ottomans

The term Ottoman had by the mid-sixteenth century come to be both a dynastic term and the designation for an entire governing elite. As a dynastic term it referred to the House of Osman, the *al-i Osman*, the family descended from their eponymous leader, Osman. They had risen in stages from frontier march wardens to imperial sultans resident in Istanbul at the crossroads of Europe and Asia.

As a term describing the governing elite, Ottoman designated the entire askeri class. Ottomans were those who served religion and the state (*din-u-devlet*), that is, those who were Muslims and who served in the military, the bureaucracy, or the Muslim religious establishment. As with most ruling classes, sharply distinguishing themselves from the ruled, the Ottomans came to identify themselves by a pattern of attitudes and behavior built on venerable traditions of Muslim ruling elites. For the Ottomans this included, in addition to identification with the sultan as living representation of the state and a paternalistic attitude toward the subjects (reaya), an appreciation for the Ottoman-Muslim high cultural tradition. The exemplary Ottoman would be proficient in Ottoman Turkish, that form of Turkish written in the Arabic script and highly influenced by Arabic and Persian. He would also adopt a posture of public conformity (whatever might be the behavior in private) with the canons of Islamic piety and behave in the fashion of the ruling elite.

For those not within the Ottoman circle, several avenues were open for attainment of that select status. Those born as non-Muslim members of the reaya would have to become Muslims and move from the reaya into the askeri class and obtain the education necessary to admit them to Ottoman status. This was most easily acomplished through the devshirme. Those youths who made it into the Palace School would be converted to Islam early in their training. Ultimately, they would move into positions that would assure them of Ottoman status. Muslim-born youths had only to cross the educational barrier and find a position in the askeri class—no mean feat for those without connections. Upward mobility usually involved finding an Ottoman sponsor, and history is replete with examples of those who managed to do so.

Sons born to members of the Ottoman elite clearly had an advantage. Their fathers would see to their education, and they had the connections necessary to launch their sons on Ottoman careers. Sons of men who were members of the askeri class, but who were not within the Ottoman circle, such as sons of ordinary Janissaries, would have to find ways to clear the educational barrier that stood between them and the coveted Ottoman status.

From the mid-sixteenth century on, the Ottoman elite replenished its ranks largely from within. More and more sons came to follow in the careers of their fathers. Sons of bureaucrats tended to become bureaucrats, sons of military officers became military officers, and sons of ulema became ulema. This system worked well as long as new lands continued to be conquered, opening up vast areas to be populated by timar holders under the supervisions of sançak beys and subashis, with positions for kadis and opportunities for teachers in a variety of schools, and all of it administered by the bureaucracy. Incessant warfare also took its toll of trained Ottomans, who were then replaced by young products of the system.

When the Ottoman conquest began to founder on the rocks of European resistance, pressures were introduced into the system that led to instability. Poorly prepared people began to find their way into the Ottoman elite. Connections rather than training began to count heavily in the quest for places, increasing the competition for existing positions. Pressures developed within the society for fathers to seek to insure Ottoman status for their sons. Increasingly, in all three careers, sword, pen, and religion, not only did sons follow in the careers of their fathers, but it also became increasingly difficult to have a career unless one's father was already in that career. This was especially true within the bureaucracy and religion. Within the military, the devshirme gradually died out in the early eighteenth century, and the rank and file of the Janissary corps was riddled with Muslim-born sons following in the footsteps of their fathers in a corps that once had been the preserve of levied Christian youths.

Replacing the devshirme as a source of both officers and troops were the households of individual pashas. Military men of the highest rank, pashas, began to revive the practice of the earliest frontier lords. These lords had gathered large households of slaves and retainers, trained them for military service, and then brought their household troops into the sultan's service. Such households began to increase in number and size in the eighteenth century. In contradistinction to the earlier example, the most powerful pashas of the late eighteenth and early nineteenth centuries began to set up their own regional jurisdictions and became what are known as *ayan* (notables) or *derebeys* (lords of the valley). For the first time since the social dislocations of the seventeenth century, a serious threat to the sovereignty of the sultan emerged.

The Sultans

Ottoman sultans and their prerogatives had been insulated from the rash of changes that Ottoman society had experienced through good days and bad. The earliest sultans, those through Suleyman, had campaigned with their troops on both the western and eastern fronts of the empire. They spent their private lives within the confines of the Inner Palace surrounded by their slaves, who constituted the Inner Service. The palace served not only as the sultan's royal residence but also as the hub of government; it was the place where those destined for high government service were trained. Many of those whose training was considered complete passed out of the Inner Service of the palace to the Outside Service, usually as provincial governors, Janissary officers, and officers in the household cavalry. The Outside Service constituted all those who assisted the sultan in his relations with the world outside the palace—the army, the cavalry, the bureaucracy, etc.

After Suleyman, few sultans risked the hardships of large-scale rigorous military campaigns. But even while Ottoman military prowess gradually declined, the status of the Ottoman sultans remained unaffected. Ottoman society still considered the sultan as the shadow of God on earth, the repository of justice, and the source of all material well-being. Even the deposition and execution of Sultan Ibrahim in 1648 and Sultan Mustafa IV in 1808 did not diminish the authority of the sultans or tarnish their glitter. Several strong sultans, men who were in the mold of Mehmed the Conqueror and Suleyman the Magnificent, made their appearance at the end of the eighteenth century and early in the nineteenth century.

Selim III (reigned from 1789 to 1807) and Mahmud II (reigned from 1808 to 1839) acted energetically to deal with the internal and external problems of the empire, initiating serious reforms designed to restore the empire's fortunes. Perception of them as active, capable sultans certainly enhanced their aura, but it is equally true that even mediocre seventeenth-century sultans had been held in awe. That feeling of awe was expressly cultivated by the Ottoman sultans, who surrounded the rare moments when they showed themselves to their subjects with as much pomp and circumstance as possible.

Even the sultan's seclusion behind his palace walls was part of the mystique that set him apart from mere mortals. Throughout the empire's history the sultan was perceived as the font of felicity and the ultimate repository of power. He dispensed justice, favors, and munificence. His words could cause robes of honor to be draped around one's shoulders, or the sword to sever the head from one's body. To him was owed absolute obedience. The advent of nationalism in the Ottoman domains in the nineteenth century would cause non-Muslim subjects to challenge that, and the reform movement would encourage some of his Muslim subjects to question the nature of the relationship between the sultan and his flock. In the face of this corrosive dual attack, the sultan's power and authority ebbed throughout the last century of Ottoman rule.

Similar challenges would be raised to the power and authority of the Russian tsar and the Japanese emperor in the nineteenth century. As in the Ottoman Empire, these rulers were the embodiment of sovereignty. In Russia, the 1825 Decembrists had ushered in a movement that would question the absolutist nature of the tsar's authority throughout the rest of the century. The Russian autocracy would become first a European style monarchy and then, after World War I, a socialist state. Japan would move from a decentralized realm into a unified, constitutional state, impelled by the series of reforms begun in 1868 and known as the Meiji Restoration.

The Bureaucracy

Whereas the Ottoman sultan remained the locus of power, he had long ago withdrawn from the day-to-day personal exercise of authority. Authority had been delegated to the grand vezirs, chief financial officers, Janissary aghas, and others. Those highest officials who wielded the sultan's authority constituted the imperial *divan*, which met several times a week, initially in the palace, and later on in the official residence of the grand vezir. Information, complaints, and petitions were received by the divan. Actions were taken, decisions made on some matters, and other matters were referred to the sultan for his own decision.

Supporting the divan was the Ottoman bureaucracy. It consisted of two main sections. One, the bureaus of the imperial divan, dealt with the immense amount of paper work involved in the drafting, issuance, and filing of all official correspondence and decrees not relating to financial matters and the appointments to timars. The financial section dealt with the empire's income and expenditures. By the end of the eighteenth century, there were twenty-five bureaus in the financial section and four in the central administration, the bureaus of the imperial divan. The total number of scribes was slightly under a thousand. The chief officer of the central administration was the *reis ul-kuttab*, the chief of the scribes. As part of the reform movement of the nineteenth century he would become the foreign minister, whereas the head of the financial administration would become the minister of finances.

Since the beginning of the eighteenth century, the position of the reis ul-kuttab had risen in importance in response primarily to the situation that had converted the Ottoman Empire from a state engaged in holy war in the interests of expanding the dar al-Islam into a state that engaged more and more heavily in diplomacy to fend off European encroachment. In this era of diplomacy, the reis ul-kuttab became one of the sultan's leading advisers. Men who held this position were generally professional bureaucrats, educated, trained, and promoted within the bureaucracy.

In the eighteenth century, these high level bureaucrats began to be promoted outside the bureaucracy into positions previously the preserve of the elite products of the devshirme and Palace School. These bureaucrats-turned-administrators became governors of provinces and even grand vezirs. This blurring of the lines that had separated one career from another was both a symptom and an effect of the shutdown of conquest and the end of the devshirme. There was still a need for highly trained, literate, loyal Ottomans. Increasingly, the sultan found them among his high-level bureaucrats.

Change even took place within the group generally considered to be the most impervious to change, the ulema. As early as the mid-sixteenth century, commentators such as Ali Efendi pointed out that the ulema career was characterized by nepotism, favoritism, and bribery. So ingrown had the topmost levels of the ulema become that in the seventeenth century only a few families mattered. There are a number of examples of three generations—grandfather, father, and son, serving in the highest ulema office, that of *shaykh ul-Islam.*

The Janissaries

No institution experienced greater change than the Janissaries. Once the elite infantry corps whose awesome power was intensified by their use of firearms, the Janissaries were by the end of the eighteenth century a moribund group. More concerned with protecting their privileges than with fighting the enemy, the Janissaries stuck to their barracks in Istanbul and to their compounds in other cities. Over time, they became intensely involved in the economic life of those cities, as in Aleppo, where leading Janissary families married into the important local Arab elite.

The combination of Janissary privileges and local business interests undermined Janissary discipline and prowess. Steady increase in the size of the corps also put a strain on the budget. The Ottoman military system worked best when the number of troops who had to be paid in cash was kept low. Fiscal crises were exacerbated when the number of troops paid in cash increased at the same time that new sources of wealth in the form of conquests failed to materialize. To a large extent the *Celali* revolts of the seventeenth century may be seen as part of the social dislocation caused by the empire's inability to keep large numbers of salaried troops on the payroll.

A series of defeats at the hands of the Russians late in the eighteenth century forced the Ottomans to come to grips with the problem of Janissary incompetence. Sultan Selim III did not feel that the time was right for a frontal attack upon the Janissaries. He opted to organize a new corps that would be European-trained and equipped. While his reforms (which came to be known as the *Nizam-i Cedid*) were intended to be of a thoroughgoing nature, including new military schools and taxes, the term came to be applied to his new body of troops. The Nizam-i Cedid existed alongside the older Janissary corps. This tendency to allow the old to exist alongside the new would become a feature of Ottoman reform. Reaction to the reformist tendencies of Selim III was not slow to develop. In 1805, he was forced to suspend his reforms, and in 1807 the Nizam-i Cedid was disbanded, but the reaction was too strong to be stemmed. Selim III was toppled from his throne.

In all such reforms the sultan, both Selim III and thereafter his successors, drew heavily upon supporters in the military, the bureaucracy, and the ulema. Those who opposed the sultan had supporters among the same elements. Reform was never solely the work of the people in any one career, nor was reaction the work of a group drawn from a single element within the society. It would be misleading to speak of a monolithic "Janissary mentality," or "ulema mentality." Nowhere is this more evident than in the ultimate destruction of the Janissaries in 1826.

The destruction of the Janissaries was a major event in Ottoman history. After more than four and a quarter centuries of existence, the Janissaries were suppressed by Mahmud II in 1826. He had come to the throne in 1808 after the deposition of his brother, Mustafa IV, who had replaced Selim III in the upheavals of 1807. Mahmud II was forced to be circumspect in his actions after assuming the throne, for as the sole remaining Ottoman of ruling age he wished to do nothing that might endanger the continuation of the line of Osman. His political weakness emboldened the forces of decentralization, enabling them to compel the sultan to sign a document called the *Sened-i Ittifak* in 1808. It was the Magna Carta of the Ottoman *derebeys*, recognizing their claim to autonomy. And it was the nadir of central government control.

Mahmud II realized the need to reassert the central authority of the sultan over these disruptive elements, but he could not do so without a loyal army. By 1826, he had gathered sufficient support among the upper levels of the Janissaries, ulema, and bureaucracy to move against the Janissaries and their supporters. On May 28, 1826, he proposed the establishment of a new military corps to be drawn from the ranks of the Janissaries. This was in effect a revival of the Nizam-i Cedid, but it was intended to arouse the ire of the Janissaries. They reacted as anticipated and attempted to recreate the situation of 1807 when they had succeeded in deposing Selim III. This time, however, it was the Janissaries who fell. On June 15, 1826, troops loyal to the sultan cornered the Janissaries in Istanbul and bombarded them. Thousands died. On the same day a proclamation was issued disbanding the corps that had done more perhaps than any other institution to establish, expand, defend, and then weaken the Ottoman Empire. Mahmud II had achieved his first objective. He would thereafter devote himself to a program of military and administrative reform, setting the stage for the intensive westernization of the Ottoman Empire.

The Reforms of Mahmud II

Highest on the list of priorities ushered in by the destruction of the

Janissaries was the need to organize and train a new army. Mahmud II decreed a new corps of men who would be exposed to western training. These new recruits met with indifferent success under both the British and Prussian advisers who were brought to the empire. Xenophobic and anti-Christian attitudes, most pronounced in the ranks and decreasing the higher up one went in the officer cadre, contributed to this lackluster performance.

More crucial perhaps was the sad state of education in the empire, especially in the technological areas so necessary to the military. Consequently, Mahmud II devoted a great deal of attention to educational matters, seeking to provide the military establishment with a larger pool of competent officers. Despite vociferous opposition, Mahmud II sent young Ottomans in increasing numbers to Europe for training in a variety of fields, including naval affairs. Military education at home was fostered through the opening of new schools. Warfare was no longer the simple matter of sweeping cavalry charges and the clash of armies on open plains as during the fifteenth and sixteenth centuries, or the mining and countermining operations that had characterized the seventeenth and eighteenth centuries. It was a seriously professional business that required schooling. Documents on the Ottoman officer corps from 1838 show that 20 percent were literate (literacy in the society at large was under 5 percent) and the average age of lieutenants a decade after the destruction of the Janissaries was slightly over 28. Men who were the equivalent of brigadier generals were 35-years-old. The officer corps commanded an army of some 70,000 men (infantry and cavalry) that represented the serving remnant of over 150,000 who had been recruited, the rest having deserted, died, or otherwise been removed from the rolls. Institution-building was proving to be a difficult business.

Ottoman Reforms

The period beginning with the efforts of Sultan Selim III to impose military reforms in the early 1790s and ending with the death of Mahmud II in 1839 following a 31-year reign marks what might be labelled the first round of Ottoman reform. The essential characteristics of this almost half-century period were as follows:

(1) The stimulus to change came from an awareness that the Ottoman state system, once capable of successful incursions against the European enemy to the West and the Shi'ite Iran enemy to the East, had become

dangerously vulnerable in the face of Europe's obvious military superiority.

(2) It was the existing governmental elite that first realized the Ottoman vulnerability and sought ways to respond to the threats coming from Europe. Nor did everybody within the governing elite favor change. Accordingly, from the time of Selim III on, Ottoman history "at the top" can be viewed as a struggle pitting Westernizing innovators against traditionalists.

(3) Concurrent with this intragoverning elite struggle was the absorption of separatist nationalist sentiments by one after another ethnic or linguistic or religious groups from the Ottoman reaya class. Nationalist movements grew up first among the Christians in Ottoman Europe (e.g., the Serbs, then the Greeks, and later others as well). The Muslim reaya long remained resistant to innovation. Thus, the non-Muslim and Muslim reaya were both obstacles to reformist and centralizing efforts of the Ottoman Westernizers, the non-Muslims seeking to break away from the Empire, and the Muslims opposing any governmental dynamism that would modify the venerable pattern of a loose relationship between governors and the governed.

(4) Ultimately, but much later, even the Muslim population came to be attracted to forms of nationalism such as Arabism and Turkism. Pan-Islam stands out as another ideological option that arose later. All three ideologies threatened in different ways the idea of a strengthened Ottoman state capable of holding together a linguistically and religiously diverse population.

(5) Those Ottomans realizing the need to borrow from Europe sensed as well that they should attempt to line up support from certain European states as the best available way to neutralize the pressures from other European states. This meant that the Ottoman Empire became absorbed into the European diplomatic system. Thus began what Europeans came to call "the Eastern Question" which from the European perspective was the question of how to divide up the Ottoman Empire without risking conflict within the European state system. To the Ottomans, the question was rather that of how to "buy time" in order to borrow and adapt the European technology (seen at first in almost exclusively military terms) and thereafter be able to withstand European pressures.

(6) Becoming absorbed into the European diplomatic system changed the intraelite value system. Whereas previously the notion of a diplomatic profession hardly existed, and the Ottomans were satisfied to let non-Muslim subjects serve as dragomans (literally, "interpreter"), henceforth those

Ottomans able to understand European ways and negotiate successfully with European statesmen were prized. Ottoman embassies abroad had been opened in 1793, the first in London, followed in short order by Vienna, Berlin, and Paris. Young Ottoman bureaucrats were attached to these embassies expressly to learn European languages and to study European institutions. In this manner, a small cadre of officials with European experience developed within the Ottoman bureaucracy. Many of these individuals became supporters of the Ottoman reform program.

(7) The ideology of reform was not, however, presented in terms of borrowing from the infidel enemy. Rather, it was argued that the Ottoman state needed to get back to the golden age epitomized by the reign of Suleyman the Magnificent (r. 1520–66). This was an effort to depict the reforms as consistent with the best of the Ottoman and Islamic traditions, as indeed no more than a decision to return to those venerable traditions.

What Sultan Mahmud II actually achieved resulted in a centralization of power far beyond what had prevailed in the empire at any earlier time. The Sened-i Ittifak of 1808, the would-be Magna Carta of the Ottoman Empire, represented only a brief interlude of provincial strength against the center. Even though the Ottoman state lost territories in Sultan Mahmud II's time (e.g., Greece) and thereafter, the forces of change in the ever-shrinking Ottoman Empire favored centralization. It is for this reason that certain historians have called Sultan Mahmud II the "Peter the Great of the Ottoman Empire." The enlightened despot motif—the pattern of reform-from-the-top imposed upon, and only to some limited extent filtering down to and integrated by the rest of society—was destined to characterize later developments within the Ottoman Empire as well. (It would equally characterize the thrust of change of Egypt and Tunisia, as will be noted later.)

The Tanzimat Period

In conventional historical periodization, it was the age immediately after the death of Sultan Mahmud II that ushered in major westernizing reforms. This was the time of the Tanzimat (literally, "reforms" or "re-orderings"), deemed to have extended from 1839 to 1876, beginning with a dramatic imperial rescript—the Hatt-i Sherif of Gulhane—announcing major westernizing reforms and ending with the establishment of the Ottoman constitution creating a parliament (but the constitution was suspended and the parliament prorogued within a year). It is, however, more accurate to see the Tanzimat Period as a continuation of the centralizing and modernizing efforts begun by Sultan Selim III but then aborted, then begun again by Sultan Mahmud II only to continue successfully throughout his long reign (here defining "success" not in terms of growing strength to resist outside encroachments but of centralization within).

Even so, certain traits and developments do distinguish this middle period of the nineteenth century. The Tanzimat Period, first, represented the triumph for a time of the upper bureaucratic ranks. A handful of leading reformers, many themselves having first trained in the early Ottoman embassies in Europe or in the Translation Office (which became the school for fledgling diplomats and ultimately the foreign ministry), dominated affairs in this period even more than the sultans.

Second, these "men of the Tanzimat" embraced the idea that only a thoroughgoing westernization would suffice to restore the Ottoman state to strength. To this extent they went beyond the earlier notion that limited, piecemeal borrowing of military drill and technology would be enough. Accordingly, the reforms they sought to implement included western-style legal codes, an adaptation of the highly centralized French system of local government and administration, efforts to put in place a state-controlled comprehensive educational system and not just technical training for the military or bureaucrats, the growth of a more functionally elaborate system of ministries and even a European-style national bank.

Cynical European contemporaries were wont to dismiss these reformist efforts as tactical dodges to deflect European pressures for change. "The Tanzimat," so went the supercilious jibe, "stopped at the doorstep of the Sublime Porte." In fact, the men of the Tanzimat were committed to reform, and they had a good notion of what measures were required, but they remained a beleagured minority. They never totally won over the bureaucracy and made even less progress in gaining the loyalty, or at least the acquiescence, of the governed. Lacking either the power or the legitimacy to impose their will, the reformers were reduced to manipulating as best they could much stronger forces. They were obliged constantly to wheedle potential outside allies (most consistently, Great Britain) into supporting them against enemies both within the Ottoman Empire and in Europe, while pleading the limitations that traditionalist forces within the Ottoman lands imposed upon their actions.

To those very traditionalist forces at home, especially those within the ruling elite who had the power to frustrate their plans and, indeed, take their jobs, the reformers argued that the price of delaying the reforms they urged would be, in effect, even more European meddling in Ottoman affairs.

The limits of the power wielded by the men of the Tanzimat were clearly demonstrated with the advent of Sultan Abdulhamid.II in 1876, the same year in which the Ottoman constitution had been proclaimed and an Ottoman parliament elected and convened. The reformers in the upper levels of the bureaucracy hoped that the new sultan would support constitutionalism and continue westernizing reforms. Implicit in westernization ever since the first great reformist rescript of 1839 had been the idea that the inhabitants of the Empire should cease being resistant or at best acquiescent subjects and become loyal citizens actively participating in affairs of state and society. The men of the Tanzimat were not populists, however. Everything in their training—the survival of the shepherd-sheep idea of the relationship between the governors and the governed—induced them to embrace a very paternalistic notion of constitutionalism.

Sultan Abdulhamid II had no intention of reigning while letting the reformist bureaucrats rule. Constitutionalism and the new parliamentary system had not yet put down roots. The sultan's peremptory move of putting these innovations aside aroused hardly a murmur of protest outside the ranks of the all-too-vulnerable reformist bureaucrats. Moreover, the sultan demonstrated that the popular issue among the Muslim population was the defense of Islam against the threatening European infidels. And the Ottoman Empire was becoming increasingly a state with an overwhelmingly Muslim majority as more and more European territories were lost and, after the disastrous war with Russia (1877–78), as significant numbers of Muslim refugees from Europe poured into the shrunken empire. Sultan Abdulhamid II championed Pan-Islam while continuing and refining one aspect of the reformist program since Selim III— strengthening central state control over society.

Autonomy of Egypt and Tunisia

In the two autonomous governments within the Ottoman world, Egypt and Tunisia, developments during roughly the same time span serve to underscore two interrelated themes. First, most of the political institutions and ideas about government in Egypt and Tunisia were essentially provincial variants of the central Ottoman model. Or, to state the issue in more general terms, they conformed to venerable Islamic and

Middle Eastern political ideas and institutions for which the Ottoman state ruling from Istanbul represented the most fully elaborated example.

Second, the early modernizing efforts in Egypt and Tunisia followed closely that which has been outlined above as regards the Ottoman Empire. This is not so much that the governments of Egypt and Tunisia were aping the Ottomans (in fact, in several important respects Cairo preceded Istanbul with a number of reformist innovations) as it was that all three were working from an identical political legacy and facing a similar political challenge coming from Europe.

Egypt had been part of the Ottoman Empire since 1517, the year Sultan Selim I had defeated the Mamluks. The Mamluks were Turkish-speaking non-Egyptians who started their careers technically as slaves (the literal meaning of "mamluk") of one or another bey and remained very much clients of the specific bey even after manumission. The Mamluks who had been Egypt's rulers since the thirteenth century were in organization and esprit thus comparable to the traditional Ottoman political elite, technically kapi kullar, or slaves of the Porte (i.e., government). Both Mamluks and kapi kullar were taken as young boys from their families, enslaved and given special training in order to become eventually the elite military officers and top administrators. Both Mamluks and kapi kullar possessed a powerful esprit de corps (and they were in origin, training, and outlook a military body); they arrogantly deemed themselves distinctive from, and superior to, the great mass of the governed. The defeated Mamluks, given this similarity of training, function, and outlook, were easily integrated into the Ottoman system, and it was not long before later generations of Mamluks in Egypt were again wielding real power, Istanbul being able to reassert its authority only from time to time.

The Ottoman Mamluks, in turn, were again defeated by an invading army. This time it was the French army under Napoleon in 1798. Within three years, the French army was defeated and evacuated by a combined Ottoman-British force, but the post-1798 disorders gave one Muhammad Ali (Turkish: Mehmed Ali) the opportunity to found a new, autonomous dynasty that survived until Abd al-Nasir's Free Officers' revolt in July 1952 forced King Faruq, Muhammad Ali's great-great grandson, into exile.

Muhammad Ali

Born in Kavalla, in Macedonia, Muhammad Ali had come to Egypt as part of an Albanian-Ottoman contingent sent in 1801 to fight the French. Skillfully playing off the British, Ottomans, the different surviving Mamluk forces, and the ulema representing the native Egyptians, Muhammad Ali had by 1805 emerged as the leader accepted in Egypt and recognized by Istanbul. He was destined to rule Egypt autocratically for over four eventful decades. His heavy involvement in regional and Eastern Question diplomacy, the staple of most historical accounts, need only be outlined here. He intervened, unsuccessfully ultimately, on the side of his Ottoman nominal sovereign in the Greek civil war; in the 1820s he conquered the Sudan (which thereafter remained under Egyptian rule until the Mahdist revolt of the 1880s); he sent troops to defeat the first Wahhabi kingdom in Arabia (the second, begun in the first years of the twentieth century under Ibn Saud, eventually became Saudi Arabia); and he wrested Greater Syria from the Ottomans, imposing Egyptian rule in the 1830s. Twice during that same decade and as part of Muhammad Ali's venture into Greater Syria, the Egyptian army defeated the Ottomans and might well have overthrown the Ottoman dynasty itself but for European intervention.

Soon after establishing his authority, Muhammad Ali realized that the obstreperous Mamluks would seek to reassert their power at the first sign of weakness. He chose to preempt. In 1811, the Mamluk leaders were ambushed and destroyed, a bloody incident that prefigures Sultan Mahmud II's destruction of the Janissaries sixteen years later. Muhammad Ali then continued to amass power, persistently undermining any actual or potential power wielders, whether military, political, economic, or religious.

Egypt, the "Gift of the Nile," is the example par excellence of an ecosystem requiring centralized control to oversee the maintenance and distribution of an irrigation network on which the very survival of society depends. It is a country that has known authoritarian rule since the time of the pharaohs. That Muhammad Ali put into place a centralized autocracy is not, in itself, an indication of modernization. Nor is the question of his personal motivation as clear as with the men of the Tanzimat operating from Istanbul. To this day, certain historians regard him as the last of the Mamluks, whereas to others he was "the founder of modern Egypt."[1] Nevertheless, the steps he took did inaugurate modern times for Egypt. He achieved a governmental centralization beyond anything realized by the Mamluks, who in their dividing of political and economic power among the different beys and their clients may be compared to the timariots of the Ottoman Empire in earlier times.

---

[1] The title of a book by Henry Dodwell, first published in 1931.

Muhammad Ali also sought to adapt European military technology to his use, not so much to defend the state against fissiparous tendencies at home and threats from Europe (as was the case with the Ottoman rulers), but sought to achieve regional military superiority in order to advance his expansionist goals. Whatever the difference in motives between Cairo and Istanbul, the modalities were the same. He brought European military advisers to Egypt, set up new European-style schools, sent student missions abroad (mainly to France), and sought to turn Egypt economically into a state-directed command economy in order both to garner the vastly increased revenues needed and to produce the material requirements for war.

Muhammad Ali brought the ulema directly under state control by confiscating the waqfs (pious trust), whose funds, in Islamic legal theory inviolate against such actions by the state, gave the religious leadership some measure of autonomy. Thereafter, the ulema depended for their livelihood on the positions and perquisites held tightly by the state.

His expansionist plans required soldiers, and after a failed effort to garner military manpower from the newly conquered Sudan (the Sudanese forcibly brought to Egypt died in droves), Muhammad Ali turned to the native Egyptians themselves. With this step, Muhammad Ali set in motion the nationalization of the Egyptian military, reversing an over-two millennium tradition in which native Egypt had been dominated by foreign rulers and their foreign armies.

There was nothing quite like the Tanzimat Period following Muhammad Ali's reign (he died in 1849). The upper ranks of the bureaucracy had their appetites whetted for greater control, but effective power remained with the ruler, even when—as with Abbas I (1849–54) and Said (1854–63)—they were rather indecisive figures. More despotism came with Ismail (who reigned from 1863 until 1879). Ismail might be said to represent in his person an Egyptian combination of Sultan Mahmud II and the men of the Tanzimat. He was familiar with Europe, had spent three years in Paris, spoke French, and had been sent by his predecessor, Said, on several diplomatic missions to Europe. Ismail is remembered also for his bold statement, "My country is no longer part of Africa, we are now part of Europe."

The Age of Khedive Ismail

With Ismail came another round of forced-draft modernization greatly strengthening Egypt's basic socioeconomic infrastructure with an ambitious building program—railroads, telegraphs, vastly increased irrigation canals, urban planning (e.g., commissioning Ali Mubarak to adapt Baron Haussmann's urban development of Paris, with the grand boulevards, to Cairo), and massive increases in public schooling for both sexes.

Ismail also introduced a parliament in the 1860s and even announced the acceptance of cabinet government with ministerial responsibility in 1878. These moves, however, were even more a façade than such steps in Istanbul. Ismail was largely maneuveing against the increasing pressure of the European powers, who both jealously guarded their strategic interests and protected the Europeans who had invested in Ismail's ambitious developmental programs.

By the 1860s and 1870s, a small but growing group of bureaucrats wished to convert Egypt to a constitutional monarchy—that is, to a situation in which the khedive (the title bestowed by the Ottoman sultan on Ismail in 1867 in return for a handsome payment) would reign but the bureaucrats would rule. Just as with the men of the Tanzimat, these upper level administrators felt obliged to play the Eastern Question game. They sought support from selected European states against the pressures from other European states or, for that matter, from the khedive himself.

These Egyptian upper level officials, however, were even more vulnerable than the men of the Tanzimat. They did not have the same sense of political legitimacy as their peers in Istanbul, for the Muhammad Ali line in facing the sultan could with justice be seen rather like disobedient dukes frustrating the unifying efforts of a beleaguered king. This was especially the case in that most of the Egyptian officials were descendants of Mamluk or Ottoman Turkish families and did not identify with Egypt as such. Nor was it all that prudent to identify with the Muhammad Ali dynasty. After all, Europe had brought to ground the dynamic Muhammad Ali himself in 1840, forcing him to evacuate Syria. And it took only the stroke of the sultan's pen (after the necessary nod from the European powers) to send Khedive Ismail into exile in 1879.

As for the small but growing number of native Egyptians in the ruling elite, they could hardly manage to develop a bureaucratic class loyalty concerned as they were about the continuing power of the Mamluk-Ottoman ruling elite. Finally, all Egypt—khedive, officialdom, and fellahin—was more at the mercy of Europe than were the rulers in Istanbul. The early modernizing moves in Egypt thus were more mercurial than in the Ottoman Empire: extremes of dynamism and defeat marked the reigns of both Muhammad Ali and Ismail, interspersed by two less forceful rulers—the one, Abbas I, an archreactionary, and the other, Said, an uncritical and inefficient westernizer. Early modernization efforts in Egypt also remained autocratic, with little institutionalization of new groups.

Tunisia

Generally, Tunisia followed a pattern somewhat in between the Ottoman Empire and Egypt. Tunisia, unlike the Egypt of Muhammad Ali and Ismail, was not seeking to expand. On the contrary, like the rulers in Istanbul, those in Tunis sought only to hold their own against the outside world. Tunisia was in the awkward position of being a small country having infinitely more powerful immediate neighbors—France across the Mediterranean and in Algeria after 1830, Sardinia and then with unification later in the century all Italy to the north, and the Ottoman Empire, which reestablished direct administration over Tripolitania in 1835 to the east. The Ottomans also showed signs thereafter of doing the same in Tunisia when possible.

There was not the same dramatic crushing of the traditional military as with Muhammad Ali's massacre of the Mamluks in 1811 or Mahmud's destruction of the Janissaries in 1827. But the Bey of Tunis after putting down a revolt of the "Turkish" (so-called in Tunisia since they were not natives, their language of command was Turkish, and many but by no means all were native Turkish speakers) troops in 1816 slowly began to rely more on troops levied within Tunisia. This process increased in the 1830s, with the creation of European-style units dubbed Nizami, the same name associated with the earlier Ottoman and Egyptian military modernization. Tunisian authorities, however, were not following Ottoman or Egyptian models. The name Nizami was clearly used to convey a cetain intra-Islamic legitimacy, but the source of inspiration was European as were a number of its instructors.

This began a few years before the long reign of Ahmad Bey (1837–55), who presided over the most sustained effort in Tunisia's first round of reform from the top. Again, military modernization was the keystone, and this entailed bringing in a French military advisory team, the creation of a European style officer training facility, the Bardo Military School, and an effort (more modest than in Egypt) to produce locally needed material for the army.

Ahmad Bey also attempted to curry favor with the European states by such acts as a state visit to Paris, abolishing first the slave trade and then slavery and sending a Tunisian contingent (at ruinous cost) to participate in the Crimean War alongside the Ottomans, British, and French.

His reign also brought a number of steps that advanced the process of nationalizing the Tunisian political system. He equalized governmental treatment of the Maliki and the Hanafi ulema. (These are two of the four legal systems, or schools of law, in Sunni Islam. The Hanafi, the official Ottoman system, had precedence in Ottoman Tunisia; but the overwhelming majority of Tunisians were Malikis). He took steps to integrate native Tunisians into the army. Conscription was adopted just as in Egypt and resisted by the populace just like there, but the record of "Tunisifying" the officer class and the bureaucracy was in proportion to the population, probably somewhat more successful than in Egypt. He presided over a de facto Arabization of the bureaucracy and was the first Tunisian bey to write to the Ottoman sultan in Arabic (explaining that he wanted fully to understand what he was signing).

In the years following Ahmad Bey's reign, a small cadre of Westernizers rallied around a certain Khayr al-Din Pasha, of Mamluk origins. The year 1861 even saw the introduction of a constitution (the first in the Arab world), but it survived only slightly longer than the later Ottoman constitution. It was suspended following a revolt against higher taxes that swept the countryside in 1864 and came close to overthrowing the Tunisian Husaynid dynasty.

The short reformist ministry of Khayr al-Din from 1873 to 1877 marked a brief period during which the Tunisian equivalents of the Ottoman men of the Tanzimat held sway. This ministry was, however, brought down by a combination of foreign (mainly French) intrigues and resistance from the more reactionary forces within the Tunisian governing elite—yet another indication of the marginality and vulnerability of the modernizers throughout the Middle East in these years.

State Fiscal Crises

The revolt against higher taxes and the problem of raising money illustrate another common theme linking the early modernizing experience directed from Istanbul, Cairo, and Tunis. The moves away from tax farming to tax collection by regular government employees, from timariot or Mamluk (or "feudal") type military forces to a regular, standing army, the increase of government services, and the concomitant increase in the number of government bureaucrats, the purchase of technical services and equipment from Europe, and the governmental investment in basic socioeconomic infrastructure—all put severe strain on the government treasuries. With the best of timing and good fortune such additional expenses could have been borne, given a national economy expanding commensurately. Such was seemingly the case for a brief time in Egypt. There was a boom in Egyptian cotton exports during the American Civil War, when the export of Southern cotton declined. This brief period of prosperity came to a crashing end after 1865. Neither tiny Tunisia nor the more sprawling Ottoman Empire ever had even those few boom years.

The upshot was that all three states went bankrupt: first Tunisia, in 1869, Egypt and the Ottoman Empire both in 1876. With bankruptcy came European-imposed debt commissions in all three countries. Not long after, Tunisia and Egypt fell under outright colonial rule, that of France in Tunisia beginning in 1881 and the British in Egypt one year later.

Political Change: The Balance Sheet

This first period of modernization—which ended with the demise of the Ottoman Empire after the First World War—records a rather bleak political development. Political elites in Istanbul, Cairo, and Tunis, attempting to adapt what were seen as superior European ways, had managed to destroy the venerable checks and balances that characterized the traditional Ottoman political system. These reformers, however, had not succeeded in establishing themselves in power or in institutionalizing the more fundamental changes borrowed from Europe. The increased burden imposed on government in the absence of a growing economy had created a top-heavy superstructure that went bankrupt and thereby fell even more decidedly into the hands of neighboring, threatening Europe. Tunisia and Egypt lost even the façade of political autonomy with the French Protectorate over the former and the British occupation (Protectorate after 1914) of the latter.

None seemed to have made progress in bringing about what is surely the fundamental political characteristic of modernity—an integrated political community in which all inhabitants are effectively mobilized toward the achievement of group goals accepted as legitimate. The Ottoman effort to create a sense of Ottomanism—of loyalty by the diverse Ottoman population to a state that was multilingual, multireligious, and multinational—failed. The separatism of the non-Muslims was never overcome. As for the Muslim population, Sultan Abdulhamid's championing of Pan-Islam eventually faded to be replaced by the ethnolinguistic confrontation between Turkism and Arabism.

All this is true. Even so, a more positive interpretation can also be advanced. Although frustrated in their immediate goals, those political leaders favoring the kind of political integration facilitating modernization had grown in number. Their political ideology had been refined. On the eve of the First World War, political and nationalist party development was under way. A rudimentary national educational system had made some inroads into the millet mentality (the idea of organizing social life almost exclusively around the religious community). Moreover, consecutive generations of political elites gained experience in the painful process of becoming a nation state by facing the challenge coming from modernizing Europe and adjusting to that challenge. And since the driving force of what became the Republic of Turkey came from a cadre of modernizers from the Ottoman political elite, it is possible to identify three political units that strengthened their political integration—Egypt, Tunisia, and the Ottoman core that later became Turkey.

The integration of an ethnically and linguistically alien political elite with the native population had been considerable in Tunisia, less so but not insignificant in Egypt. Something of the same thing was happening in what became Turkey, for the post-Hamidian phase of Young Turk rule in the Ottoman Empire (after 1908–19) was a decisive step toward Turkish nationalism.

On balance, however, political developments as related to modernization in this period (from the late eighteenth century until the First World War) amounted mainly to the destruction of the old patterns of politics making way for something new. Whatever this was to become was not yet clear. Even less was it institutionalized and legitimized.

The Fertile Crescent

A word on the Fertile Crescent during this period is in order. This area remained under direct Ottoman administration from Istanbul except for the decade of the 1830s, when Muhammad Ali had wrested Greater

Syria from the sultan. This fact plus the existence in the Fertile Crescent—
especially in Greater Syria—of the most exuberant juxtaposition of different religious, ethnic, and linguistic communities in all of Ottoman Afro-
Asia gave a special character to developments there.

First, the peoples of the Fertile Crescent were in the position of
responding to political initiatives coming from outside, just as in previous
generations of Ottoman rule. Generally, the native political leadership
continued its venerable practice of negotiating the best possible arrangements for their small following with representatives of the more powerful
but remote Ottoman Empire. It remained a matter of urban notables,
village mukhtars, tribal shaykhs, and religious leaders of the non-Muslim
communities dealing with Ottoman (or for the crucial 1830s, with Egyptian) authority. The tendency for political networking to become broader,
more "national" to use a word that must be to a considerable extent
anachronistic in this context, was limited, even though that was the thrust
of the state-centralizing efforts emanating from Istanbul (or, again, Cairo
in the 1830s). Even the various local councils, part of the Tanzimat
reforms, made little progress in breaking down the centuries-old small
group and millet mentality.

Equally, although the Fertile Crescent became heavily involved in
intrusive European penetration associated with the Eastern Question,
this too did not generally serve to foster a pattern of ever larger political
circles. On the contrary, the European rivalries were often overlaid with
support of the most appropriate non-Muslim community in the area (e.g.,
France championing the Catholics and Uniate Christians, Russia the
Orthodox, and Britain, finding no native Protestants, the Druze).

At the same time, the Fertile Crescent received the most direct modernizing western influences of any part of Ottoman Afro-Asia. This came
by way of commercial and missionary activities, especially in education.
The greater influence received and absorbed by the non-Muslim populations disturbed the old balances of relations among the millets, thereby
exacerbating intergroup tensions. This was in the short run not integrating, but the opposite. Even so, some of the more perceptive observers
from both the Muslim and non-Muslim communities did begin to discern
the need for an integrating political ideology that would transcend religious separatism. Out of this emerged eventually Arab nationalism, but
in this period the forces making for a more sharply etched separatism
were ascendant.

Accordingly, the peoples of the Fertile Crescent experienced the
greatest impact of modernizing forces coming from Europe. A greater

proportion of this population began to absorb Western ways, but the political institutionalization of all this was less developed than in any part of the Middle East.

One partial exception to the above was Mount Lebanon. Following a short but brutal civil war in the late 1850s and 1860, this area was exposed to European intervention and the imposition of a European-monitored autonomy with an elaborate arrangement for multicommunal representation. The Lebanese, accordingly, had had by the First World War (when the Ottomans suspended the system) almost three generations of experience in limited self-government.

International Comparisons

Whereas with Japan, Russia, and even China the route to moderni-zation did not involve the breaking up of the premodern state system into several smaller units, this is just what happened in the Ottoman Middle East. The loose, flexible Ottoman administration of remote pro-vinces, which had worked so well in earlier centuries, predisposed the sundering of the Ottoman Empire.

The pattern of reform-from-the-top political modernization evokes comparison with the enlightened despots of eighteenth-century Europe. But the ruling elites in Istanbul, Cairo, and Tunis never enjoyed the margin of maneuver available to an earlier Russia, Prussia, or Austria. Nor did they enjoy the relative isolation from outside pressures of Japan. Ottoman reformers were obliged to ally with certain European states to protect themselves against the pressure of others, but this very alliance with the outside enemy weakened their ability to rally traditional forces at home or to foster increased politicization.

The Ottoman Middle East, rather like China, was also afflicted with multipower outside interference. It was not just one outside state that became dominant, as with the British in India, but several contended for influence. Even the two examples of outright colonial rule that began in this period offer two separate colonial overlords, the British in Egypt and the French in Tunisia.

Finally, the great religious, ethnic, and linguistic differences found in the Ottoman Middle East, plus the differences in life-style imposed by geography (e.g., desert nomadism, pastoralism, extensive dry farming, intensive irrigated agriculture, several mountain refuges sheltering the introverted life of mountaineers, and great cities not closely linked to their hinterland) evoke comparison with Iran, South Asia, and Central Asia—all regions where geographically and historically shaped cultures have favored the development of extensive "imperial" politics that did not, however, penetrate deeply into the daily life of the subject. To move from such wide-ranging but, in the literal sense of the word, superficial political systems to the tight-knit, integrated politics of modern nation states requires a much more revolutionary change than in the states of Western and Central Europe or Japan.

CHAPTER FIVE

Economic Structure and Growth

IN SPITE OF some diversity in its constituent parts—notably the contrast between the river valleys of the Nile and Tigris-Euphrates and the coastlands, mountains, and dry inland plains—the Near East may justifiably be treated as a whole for the purpose of economic analysis. Its geography and ecology are broadly similar, with short wet winters and dry summers. Consequently, agriculture concentrated heavily on winter cereals (viz., wheat and barley), which between them accounted for 80 to 90 percent of the cultivated area, but more valuable crops were also grown in the humid coastal zones or under irrigation. Basically the same pattern of land tenure prevailed. Compared to other regions, all its constituent parts—Turkey, Egypt, Syria, Iraq, and Tunisia—were highly urbanized. In this chapter "Egypt," "Turkey," "Tunisia," and "Iraq" refer to the areas within their present borders; "Syria" designates "Greater Syria" (i.e., the area consisting of present-day Syria, Lebanon, Israel, and Jordan).

General Characteristics

In all these countries handicrafts had been widespread and advanced, but were everywhere feeling the effects of European and Indian competition. Transport methods were practically identical, with heavy reliance on coastal shipping, caravans, and, in Egypt and Iraq, river boats—but no improvements had been made anywhere in ports, canals, or roads. Both internal and foreign trade were active, and the use of money was widespread. In 1800, internal and transit trade and the Eastern trade and shipping were mainly in Muslim hands, but trade with Europe, as well as Mediterranean shipping, had been taken over by Europeans.

The prevailing Muslim legal system, with its deep respect for property and contract, was in many ways favorable to economic activity, especially commercial. This, however, was more than offset by the attitude of the governments. For many centuries government had been in the hands of the bureaucracy and military, and their chief concerns were raising taxes and making sure that the cities were well supplied with essential goods, to avoid urban unrest. The economically productive elements of the population—the craftsmen and even more the farmers—had very little power and were in no position to influence policy to promote their interests.

Overall, taxation was probably not excessive, compared to other parts of the world, and the share of GNP accruing to the government seems to have been small. But taxes were arbitrary and very uneven in their incidence, falling particularly heavily on farmers and exempting important segments of the population. Property was insecure and liable to confiscation, a fact that discouraged accumulation and, especially, investment in long-term projects.

Traditionally, the government's economic role had been passive, extending at most to providing such infrastructure as roads and irrigation works, and little of either had been built in the modern period. Practically nothing had been done in providing social services, such as education and public health, a sphere normally left in the Near East to private charity. At the same time, even if the governments had had the desire to help, they could not have done much because of the restrictive effects of the capitulations and the commercial treaties concluded with the European states. These treaties limited customs duties paid by Europeans to 3 percent on imports and exports; they thus made it impossible either to protect domestic producers against foreign competition or to increase government revenue from the most rapidly growing sector of the economy, foreign trade. Government was therefore seen as mainly predatory. This image of government continued to prevail long after it had begun to attempt to play a more constructive part in economic development.

Very little is known about the economic history of the region in the seventeenth and eighteenth centuries, but, in contrast to the sixteenth century, which saw a revival following the establishment of Ottoman rule, these centuries seem to have been a period of stagnation. In certain areas one may go further and speak of deterioration; but this may well have been offset by progress in other areas. Population registered no increase and in certain countries may have declined (e.g., in Anatolia it went from about 8 million in 1600 to 6.7 million in 1831; it also probably declined in Egypt in the eighteenth century and in Tunisia between the 1780s and 1860). Plagues and cholera seem to have been particularly virulent in the late eighteenth and early nineteenth centuries, as may be seen from those recorded in Turkey, Iraq, Egypt, and Tunisia. Added to the other Malthusian checks of famine and war, they must have prevented any population increase except perhaps in a few restricted zones.

Urbanization showed no definite trend: tentative figures for Istanbul, the largest city, indicate that during the period 1829 to 1833 population was equal to, or slightly lower than, that of 1535. The figures for Cairo, the second largest city, show an increase from the early sixteenth century to 1660–1670 followed by an equal decline to 1800. Data for Tunis are less reliable but seem to indicate a slight decline between the beginning of the eighteenth century and the middle of the nineteenth. The population of Aleppo also seems to have decreased between the seventeenth and early nineteenth centuries. No reliable estimates are available for Baghdad, Basra, Damascus, and Mosul; their populations seem to have fluctuated sharply, in response to plagues, famines, floods, and other disasters.

Little is known about agriculture, in which 80 to 90 percent of the population was engaged. No figures are available for output, and such indirect indices as tax yields and exports of raw materials are scarce and hard to interpret. Certain parts of Syria seem to have witnessed a shrinkage in cultivated area, but this may have been offset by extension in other parts. Egypt shows no clear trend until near the end of the eighteenth century, when agriculture seems to have deteriorated; at the same time, agriculture became increasingly commercialized in the Delta. Judging from its rapidly increasing exports of produce, the Izmir region must have experienced a marked expansion. In European Turkey, agricultural output increased even more rapidly. As against that, data on prices, tax yields, and cultivated area in Tunisia show a decline in the last quarter of the eighteenth century and the first third of the nineteenth.

Throughout the region no changes took place in techniques, and the only innovation was the introduction of maize and tobacco from the New World; neither crop was extensively grown. In the nineteenth century cultivation of potatoes and tomatoes began to spread.

For the handicrafts, on the other hand, there is evidence of increasing pressure of foreign competition, mainly European but also Indian. A clear indicator is the marked decrease in the estates left by textile handicraftsmen in Egypt over the course of the eighteenth century. Another is the decline in eighteenth-century Turkey of tax yields on such handicraft products as silk and woollen and cotton cloth, accompanied by a sharp rise in the amount collected from duties on exports of raw materials. In Tunisia fezzes began to lose some of their export markets to the French in the eighteenth century. More generally, Europe's exports of textiles and other manufactured goods to all parts of the region rose, whereas its import of manufactures fell off sharply and that of raw materials greatly increased.

Intensified foreign competition does not seem to have induced the craftsmen to improve. Although a very small number of workshops and mines employed a few hundred workmen, and a somewhat larger number a few dozens, most enterprises had at most two or three hired men and apprentices. Judging from the surviving products, the quality of workmanship was no better than in the Middle Ages, and, in some cases, seems to have actually deteriorated. Craftsmen were grouped in guilds; these guilds, however, did not have the autonomy and prosperity that their European counterparts had enjoyed in previous centuries. A certain amount of territorial division of labor prevailed in some crafts. Thus, according to a Russian source of 1839, "*Kindiak* or *Bogaz* is a colored cloth used by the common people for *Kaftans*. The fabric is woven in Amasya and Malatya, dyed in Aleppo and Tokat, and glazed in Mosul."

As in the past, trade was concentrated in the bazaars (*suqs*), which sold handicraft wares, agricultural produce brought in from the countryside, and goods imported from other towns or abroad. In addition, there were daily or weekly markets in the cities and provincial towns. In European Turkey and Asia Minor, but not in the Arab provinces, annual fairs were frequent and important and seem to have become more so in the eighteenth century and early nineteenth. Transactions were settled in cash or by bills, and funds were transferred through money-changers (*sarrafs*), who also lent to the Treasury. Nearly all the leading sarrafs, including the so-called Galata bankers, were recruited from the minorities: Greeks, Armenians, Jews, and, in the Arab provinces, Arab Christians. The sarrafs also exchanged the numerous currencies, local and foreign, in use; these currencies fluctuated sharply.

It may be added that, apart from the restrictions imposed by the guilds, there were no impediments on the movement of labor into various occupations. Castes were unknown, and no stigma was attached to trade or industry. Even money-lending, though prohibited in principle by Islam, was practiced by Muslims as well as minorities, women as well as men.

Taken as a whole, Europe's trade with the Ottoman Empire rose steadily and appreciably, with interruptions caused by wars, throughout the seventeenth and eighteenth centuries. But whereas trade with Izmir and Aleppo advanced rapidly—and that with European Turkey even faster—trade with Egypt and southern Syria stagnated or declined. Tunisia's commerce decreased in the second third but rose appreciably in the last third of the eighteenth century.

Traditionally, the Middle East had a surplus in its balance of trade with Europe, partly or wholly offset by a deficit in its trade with India and the Far East. This pattern persisted until the end of the eighteenth century, even though the region was importing, from Europe and its colonies, an increasing number of goods in which it had formerly been self-sufficient or an exporter (e.g., sugar, coffee, silk and cotton textiles, glassware, and other articles).

One last economic trend may be mentioned: the constant devaluation of the currency. In the Ottoman Empire this had begun in the fifteenth century and eventually reached large proportions. The *kurush*, which in the mid-seventeenth century had been worth 5 or 6 francs, had by 1774 fallen to 2 to 4 and by 1811 was worth one franc. In Egypt, the exchange rate of the silver *para* or *medin* against foreign silver currencies fell by nearly three-quarters between 1670 and 1798. In Tunisia, the exchange rate of the piaster fell by three-fifths between 1725 and 1800. In all three countries the main cause was the debasing of the currency.

The nineteenth century saw a sharp shift in the prevailing economic trends. Some described above continued or even accelerated (e.g., the devaluation of the currency with accompanying rise in prices and the decline in handicrafts). In both respects, however, the situation stabilized or changed its course in the latter part of the period. Other trends reversed themselves. In all the countries under study, population rose at a faster and longer sustained rate than ever before, and the cities grew correspondingly. Agricultural output expanded severalfold and trade multiplied. Government revenues increased, though never fast enough to meet the rising expenditure. Taken as a whole, the economy of the region experienced greater growth and deeper change than at any time in its long history.

I. AGENTS OF CHANGE

The economic transformation of the Middle East was effected mainly by two forces: the pressures of the world market and the desire of rulers to create an economic infrastructure capable of carrying the weight of a modern state and army. Of these two forces the first was by far the more powerful, except under Muhammad Ali of Egypt in the 1820s and 1830s. In addition, the local minorities (*millets*) played a significant part in economic and social development.

World Market and Foreign Enterprise

The world market operated, in the first place, through a sustained increase in demand, interrupted by sharp declines during the periodic crises of the capitalist economy—of which the worst was the Great Depression of the 1870s—but continuing its upward course until the First World War. Expanding, but hungry, industrial Europe was an eager market for Middle Eastern raw materials such as grain, cotton, silk, wool, dried and, later, fresh fruit, olive oil, opium, dyeing and tanning materials such as madder, saffron, and valonea (until the invention of chemical dyes), and, in the latter part of the period, tobacco. This large and rising demand generated a cash flow that found its way to remote villages; simultaneously, the taste for European textiles and other manufactured goods and for sugar, tea, coffee, and other "colonial" products created a need for cash in the local populations.

A major impediment to the effective operation of European demand was soon removed. Traditionally, the governments of the region, the Ottoman included, had levied rather low duties on both imports and exports, but they also subjected many export items to monopolies or prohibitions. This antimercantilist policy, which so puzzled contemporary European observers, may be accounted for by several factors: need for revenue; anxiety about supplies, especially of food and particularly in the cities; desire to deny essential materials to "infidels"; etc. But European merchants in Turkey and elsewhere greatly resented such monopolies and prohibitions and urged their governments to press for their abolition. This coincided with the Ottoman government's pressing need for revenue and its desire to strike a blow at Muhammad Ali's monopolies in Egypt and Syria. The result was the 1838 Anglo-Ottoman Commercial Convention, which was rapidly extended to all the other Powers and was applied to Egypt in the 1840s, after Muhammad Ali's defeat. It provided for a uniform duty of 5 percent on imports, 12 percent on exports, and 3 percent on transit trade.

Between 1861 and 1862, at Ottoman request, new commercial treaties were signed, raising import duties to 8 percent and gradually reducing export duties to 1 percent. This system, which was also extended to Egypt and other Ottoman dependencies, remained in force until the eve of the First World War. The Ottoman government's attempts to modify it, in order to increase revenue and provide protection for industry and other branches of the economy, were blocked by the Powers. Only in 1907 was it allowed to raise import duties to 11 percent, and in 1914 to 15 percent, as part of an overall settlement between it and the Powers involving the granting of railway and other concessions.

The low tariff had two main effects, both stimulating trade. On the one hand, bypassing intermediaries, it raised the price of agricultural products in the villages and encouraged greater output. And on the other it made of the region one of the largest low-duty markets in the world, facilitating the export of manufactured goods to it and leaving its own industries almost totally unprotected.

The same twofold effect was produced by the development of transport to and within the region. The establishment of peace and the suppression of piracy in the Mediterranean, followed by the introduction of steam navigation in the late 1820s (and its development in the 30s and 40s), eventually led to a sharp fall in freight rates. Again, this stimulated agricultural output by reducing delivery costs and exposing domestic handicrafts to increased competition.

By the eighteenth century, the ships engaged in the Mediterranean trade were already predominantly foreign; in the nineteenth, they became overwhelmingly so. The same was also true of shipping in the Black Sea, Red Sea, and Persian Gulf. The Suez Canal, which had a profound effect, both positive and negative, on various parts of the Middle East, was also a foreign initiative, but Egypt bore a substantial portion of its cost. In addition, foreign enterprise played a large part in developing internal transport. Foreign steamboats started regular services on the Nile in Egypt and on the Tigris and Euphrates in Iraq. Foreign, privately-owned railways and ports also played a prominent part.

Starting in the 1850s, capital flows to the region were very large. By 1914, the public debt of the Ottoman Empire amounted to about $600 million, and foreign private investment to $550 million; of the latter, 60 percent lay within the present borders of Turkey and the rest mainly in Syria and Iraq. In Egypt the public debt stood at over $450 million, and private investment, including the Suez Canal, at about $550 million. In Tunisia, the public debt amounted to $70 million, and private investment to over $110 million. The regional total was therefore about $2,300 milion, or over 5 percent of total outstanding world long-term investment, a proportion distinctly higher than these countries' share of world population—about 2 percent. The impact of this capital inflow, however, was much smaller than might have been expected, since a large part of the nominal public debt was either not actually received, spent on wars, or put to other unproductive uses.

A breakdown of foreign investment shows that, in addition to transport, it had flowed into three main fields. First, banking. Commercial

banking, mainly financing foreign and domestic trade, was carried on
almost exclusively either by branches of foreign (chiefly British and
French) banks (Barclay's, Crédit Lyonnais, Comptoire d'Escompte, etc.)
or by domiciled banks founded by foreign capital (Ottoman Bank, National Bank of Egypt, etc.). In addition, mortgage banking absorbed a
large amount of capital in Egypt (Crédit Foncier) and Tunisia (Crédit
Foncier de Tunisie) but not in the other countries. British, French, and
other foreign companies also transacted all the insurance business of the
the region.

Secondly, public utilities: water, gas, electricity, and streetcars. By
1914, the main cities of the region—Istanbul, Izmir, Beirut, Damascus,
Alexandria, Cairo, Port Said, Suez, Tunis, etc.—had been provided with
some or all of these basic amenities. In this field, Belgian and French
capital were predominant.

Thirdly, mining. French and German capital predominated in Turkey's coal, chromium, and other mines; French capital in Tunisian phosphates; and British capital in Egyptian oil and phosphates. But the total
amount invested in mining was relatively small.

Apart from mortgage loans and some land development companies
in Egypt, there was little investment of capital in agriculture, except of
course for the large amounts put into the land by the French settlers in
Tunisia. Foreigners, however, were the ones who set up the necessary
processing plants for ginning cotton, reeling silk, crushing oilseeds, and
so on. In addition, they supplied much of the technical skill required to
develop improved strains of some export crops such as cotton, silk, and
tobacco. It was not, however, until two or three decades preceding the
First World War that they began to set up the few factories—textiles,
cement, food-processing, etc.—that were to constitute the nucleus of Middle Eastern industry.

Thus, apart from agriculture—and in Tunisia even in agriculture—
foreigners occupied the key positions in the economy. Thanks to the
capitulations and commercial treaties, they had extraterritorial judicial
privileges, immunity from arbitrary actions by the national governments,
and exemption from taxation. Their position was bolstered by the direct
control exercised by their governments in Egypt and Tunisia and their
considerable influence in the Ottoman Empire. They were in an excellent
position to act as the main engine of growth. The role played by foreigners
was far greater than in Japan, much greater than in Russia, and probably
greater than in China.

At the beginning of the nineteenth century, the number of Europeans in the Middle East was negligible, and it remained small over the greater part of the region. Except for Hellenes, there were probably under 20,000 foreigners in Turkey at the end of the nineteenth century. In Syria, Iraq, and Arabia, they numbered a few hundreds, again leaving aside the 80,000 Jews in Palestine in 1914. In Egypt, there were, however, 221,000 Europeans in 1907, including protégés, or 2 percent of the population; in Tunisia, some 135,000 in 1911, or 7 percent of the total, part of the large demographic colonization of North Africa.

Governments

The governments were far less well situated. First, the fact that the most dynamic sectors of the economy were in foreign hands, and outside their grasp, severely limited their scope. Secondly, until close to the end of the period, governments had neither the desire, the knowledge, nor the machinery to enforce an active economic policy like those pursued by Russia and Japan. This set of circumstances, however, applies only partly to Muhammad Ali and the British administration in Egypt and the French one in Tunisia. Thirdly, the economically most active part of their population consisted of minorities, who would gain most from development, a fact of which the governments were fully aware. This further reduced government interest in the matter.

The main contribution of the governments to economic development—apart from the imposition of security and organization of a bureaucracy capable of carrying out the minimal duties of administration—was the construction of infrastructure (specifically railways, ports, and irrigation works), the training of a very small number of technical experts, the provision of a certain amount of general education, and the promotion of agriculture by supplying improved seeds and strains. (Attempts to develop a manufacturing industry are discussed later.)

In Egypt, nearly all the infrastructure was built by the government, where necessary using foreign construction firms. This applies to the Mahmudiyya Canal; the successive improvements of the port of Alexandria in 1818, 1871–1873, and 1906–1907; the initial work on the Suez Canal; the port of Suez and other ports on the Red Sea; and the building of the large railway system starting in 1851. Foreign private enterprise laid down a substantial network of light railways, and the Suez Canal company built the harbor at Port Said. The government was also wholly responsible for Egypt's large and complex system of irrigation works, including the huge dams. Here, as with railways, foreign experts were increasingly supplemented or replaced by Egyptians trained abroad. The steady development of Egyptian cotton, making it the finest in the world, owes much to foreign agronomists, mainly British and Greek. Many of them were employed by the Egyptian government. An important role was also played by the government-supported Royal Agricultural Society, founded in 1898.

The Ottoman government did rather less for development. Starting in 1856, railways were built by foreign capital, successively British, French, and German. Almost all the lines received government guarantees of specified revenues per kilometer of line operating; the only large railway built by the government itself was the Hijaz railway, begun in 1901. All the major ports—those of Izmir, Beirut, Istanbul, and Salonica—were built by foreign companies; an ambitious program of port construction launched in 1914 was cut short by the outbreak of war. The only major irrigation works implemented were the Konya and Hindiyya dams, both completed in 1913; here again a major irrigation plan in Iraq failed to materialize because of the war. The government, however, played an important part in the development of such cash crops as silk, tobacco, and vines, supplying farmers with improved eggs, seeds, and plants and diffusing better methods of cultivation. It acted through both the Public Debt Administration and the regular bureaucracy.

Tunisia's government played a comparable part. Starting in 1876, a good railway network was built with government guarantee of a 6 percent return. In 1881, before the French invasion, the government had started work on a modern port at Tunis. Under the French, a concessionary company built the ports of Sousse and Sfax and improved that of Tunis. No major irrigation works were carried out, but agricultural development, particularly in the French sector, was helped in various ways.

One more development should be mentioned—the abortive attempts to industrialize. The most notable of these was Muhammad Ali's, part of his overall economic policy for Egypt. Government revenue was increased by compelling farmers to sell their cotton, grain, and other produce to the government at low prices; the government then resold these goods to urban consumers or to foreign buyers at high prices (a policy reminiscent of that of the Soviet Union in the 1930s). This export monopoly was accompanied by strict control over imports: 40 percent were on government account. Care was taken not to let in goods competing with Egyptian products. Factories were built to supply military and civilian needs and kept going, in the face of great difficulties, by the pasha's tireless energy and detailed supervision. Following Muhammad Ali's military defeat in

1840, the abolition of the monopoly system under the terms of the 1838 Anglo-Ottoman Convention spelled the ruin of the industries. Similar attempts, on a much smaller scale, were undertaken by the Ottoman and Tunisian governments in the 1840s and also ended in failure; an earlier unsuccessful attempt had been made by the Ottoman government in the 1720s.

Minorities

The third important agent of change was the minorities, or millets: Armenians, Greeks, Jews, Christian Arabs, and Copts. Their influence began to increase in the eighteenth century and reached its peak shortly before the First World War. It was due to many factors: their early contact with Europe and their greater familiarity with western languages, technology, and ways of doing things; the foreign protection many of them enjoyed, which safeguarded them from taxation and arbitrary action by the government; the removal by the Ottoman, Tunisian, and Egyptian governments of the disabilities from which they had previously suffered; the use made of their services by the modernizing governments; and their participation in the expanding sectors of the economy: trade with the West, finances, mechanized transport, modern industry, and export-oriented agriculture. In these fields they either played a dominant part or served as an essential intermediary between the Europeans and the Muslim population.

In Turkey, Greeks, Armenians, and Jews, in that order, dominated the urban sector. Both the traditional Galata bankers and the managers of modern European banks were members of minorities. In industry, the Greeks were predominant, but the Armenians were prominent in cigarettes and the Jews in paper; an estimate by a Turkish economist shows that 50 percent of the capital of 284 firms employing more than 5 workers was Greek; 20 percent Armenian; 5 percent Jewish; 10 percent foreign; and 15 percent Muslim. Of the labor force, Greeks constituted 60 percent, Armenians 15, Jews 10, and Muslims 15.

In agriculture, Greeks and Armenians played a crucial part in developing such cash crops as silk, cotton, and vines. Thus in Adana, of large landowners using modern methods, few were pure Turks but rather Greeks, Armenians, Syrians and so on. They handled practically all that part of trade with the West that was not in European hands and were prominent in internal trade. They played a leading role in the professions, in the technical government departments, and in certain intellectual fields.

An overall picture is provided by Table 1, according to a breakdown compiled by a Soviet scholar.

Table 1
Number and Distribution of Firms in Turkey, 1912

	Number	Turks	Percent Greeks	Armenians	Others
Internal Trade	18,063	15	43	23	19
Industry and Crafts	6,507	12	49	30	10
Professions	5,264	14	44	22	20

Source: D.G. Indzhikyan, *Buhzhuaziya Osmanskoi Imperil* (Yerevan, 1977) p. 212–14.

In Egypt, the prominent part played by minorities is shown by the fact that, as late as 1951—after thirty years of Egyptianization—of the company directors who could be identified, only 31 percent were Muslims and 4 percent Copts; 18 percent were Jews, 7 percent Greeks, 2 percent Armenians, and 11 percent Syrians or Lebanese; a further 30 percent were Europeans. Copts owned much land and formed a large part of the personnel of such ministries as finance, interior, and railways. Jews played a leading part in banking, the stock exchange, agricultural land development, department stores, and some industries, and were very well represented in medicine, law, and the foreign-language press; some reached high positions in government service. Syrians were to be numbered among large landowners, merchants, and many professional people and civil servants; the Egyptian press was, for a very long time, largely controlled by Syrians. Armenians played a leading role in the upper reaches of the bureaucracy under Muhammad Ali and his successors, thanks to their knowledge of Turkish combined with a modern education. Later, they were prominent in the cigarette and other industries. Greeks were very well represented in banking and cotton exporting; they were also responsible for developing many improved varieties of long-staple cotton, as witnessed by such names as Sakellarides, Casulli, etc. They owned many factories in the food-processing, cigarette, cotton ginning, and other industries.

In Lebanon, Christians were mainly responsible for modernizing the silk industry and soon wrested foreign trade from the Europeans. In Syria, Jews and Christians were prominent in money-lending, foreign trade, and some handicrafts. In Iraq, trade and finance were dominated by Jews to an extent unknown in other parts of the region; both the import

and export trade were largely in the hands of Jews (with such internation-
ally famous names as Sassoon and Zilkha), with operations stretching
from Britain to India or China. On the other hand, in Baghdad, Basra
and Mosul lawyers were predominantly Christians. In Tunisia, Jews were
prominent in both import-export and internal petty trade, and many
worked in handicrafts.

Thus, taken as a whole, minorities played a role that had no counterpart in Japan, China, or India (even allowing for the activity of the
Parsees); in Russia, however, Germans, Jews, Balts, and other non-Russian groups, as well as Russian dissenting sects, were also prominent in
the economy.

II. PRODUCTION OF A SURPLUS

Like other organized societies, the Middle East in the eighteenth
century produced a surplus over and above the subsistence level at which
the mass of its inhabitants lived. This maintained the soldiers, landlords,
bureaucrats, merchants, ulama, and other members of the privileged
classes and made possible its religious, intellectual, and artistic activities
and the other paraphernalia of civilization.

Agriculture

The surplus was derived almost solely from agriculture. The region
had little large-scale mining; its handicrafts, though they met the bulk
of local and regional needs, were declining and operated at a low level
of production. Trade with Europe had passed to foreign merchants and
was carried in foreign ships. Trade with Asia and Africa was active—and
in Muslim hands—and gave birth to quite considerable fortunes, but the
income so generated could not have been very large in the aggregate.
The same was true of transit trade, which had been greatly reduced from
its peak in the thirteenth and fourteenth centuries. Internal trade was
also largely in Muslim hands, but it does not seem to have generated
considerable fortunes. The only noteworthy income-earning services were
the pilgrim shrines in Mecca and Madina, Jerusalem and Najaf and
Karbala.

In the absence of data on output per worker in agriculture, perhaps
the best single measure of the extent of the surplus is the yield-to-seed
ratio and the yield per hectare of wheat, by far the most widespread crop
in both the Middle East and Europe. For Egypt in 1800, the yield-to-seed

ratio was put, by Napoleon's experts, at 14 to 15 to 1; for Turkey in the mid-nineteenth century, the figure was 5 to 6, and for Iraq at the beginning of the twentieth century, 5. In Syria, the yield must have been close to that of Turkey and Iraq, whereas for Tunisia, where the sowing of seed on a given area of land was very sparse, it may have been about 8 to 10. These figures may be compared to French yields of 5 to 6 in the eighteenth century, and to Polish and Russian yields of only 3 to 3.5 as late as the nineteenth century. They were, however, far lower than Japanese and Chinese rice yields, which, of course, are not strictly comparable.

Another measure, which does not coincide with the first because of differences in the amount of seed sown to a given area of land, is output per hectare. In Egypt, this was about 1,000 kilograms; in Turkey, Syria, and Iraq, 500 to 800; and in Tunisia about 300 to 500. These figures may be compared with nearly 2,000 in England; 1,000 in France and Germany; and 600 in Russia at the beginning of the nineteenth century. Here again, the Japanese rice figure was far higher, about 2,000 kilograms per hectare in the Tokugawa Period. Overall, it is clear that the Middle East started from a distinctly higher level of agriculture than Russia or India but at a much lower one than Japan or China; conversely, it had much more slack in its agriculture than Japan or China but far less than Russia.

In the course of the nineteenth century, there was a large increase in both total agricultural output and in the surplus generated by agriculture. Except for Egypt, no figures are available, but an indication of the expansion in the surplus available after the needs of the growing population had been met is given by Table 2. Four points should be noted regarding the figures. First, exports consisted almost entirely of agricultural produce; therefore, the increase in total trade reflects the increase in agricultural production, even though imports tended to rise a little faster than exports. Secondly, the figures are in current, not constant, prices. Since world prices fell by over 50 percent between 1820 and 1913, the increase in volume of exports and imports was much higher than is indicated by the table. Thirdly, both the Turkish and Egyptian figures seem to be undervalued, and the overall increase may have been somewhat higher. Lastly, the figures for Syria and Iraq refer to sea trade only; the land trade of both countries may have actually declined during this period, and certainly rose very little if at all. Hence, the overall growth in their trade must have been much smaller than is indicated by the table.

As a rough estimate, one can say that between the initial dates in the table and the First World War, the agricultural exports of the Ottoman

Table 2
Exports plus imports (millions of pounds sterling) and average annual growth between dates indicated

	1830s		1870–73		1900		1910–12
Ottoman Empire[a]	9	3.5%	14	−0.2%	38	+2.7%	66
Turkey[b]	5	3.5%	26	−0.5%	20	2.4%	33
	1800		1860		1901		1913
Iran	2.5	1.2%	5	2.8%	15	2.6%	20
	1810		1850		1900		1910
Egypt	1.5	3.0%	5	4.0%	36	5.3%	60
	1837–39		1861–65		1875–78		1913
Tunisia	0.5	4.8%	1.6	−2.6%	1.1	7.1%	13
	1830s		1860s		1900		1913
Morocco	1	2.4%	2	2.0%	3.5	9.0%	9
	1843–50		1875		1903		1913
Aden[c]	0.2	10.2%	3.1	3.5%	6	4.2%	9
	1845–46		1864–71		1880–87		1912–13
Iraq[c]	0.2	3.0%	0.4	8.7%	1.8%	4.6%	6.4%
	1820s		1860s		1890		1913
Syria[c]	0.5	5.6%	4.5	2.8%	9	0.5%	10
	1820		1860		1895–99		1913
World	340	3.7%	1,450	2.7%	3,900	4.9%	8,360

[a] within borders at given date.
[b] trade of Istanbul, Izmir, Trabzon, Samsun, and Adada
[c] Sea trade only
(Sources: Issawi, *Economic History of the Middle East and North Africa*, p. 24.)

Empire and Turkey may have risen by a factor of 10; of Egypt by over 50; of Tunisia by over 30; of Iraq by perhaps 30; and of Syria by perhaps 15. Available figures show a distinct improvement in the terms of trade.

Agricultural output can be increased in three ways: by extension of the cultivated area; by intensification, thus raising yields per acre; and by shifting to higher-priced crops, thus getting more value per acre. Except in Egypt, practically all the increase was achieved by extension. All over the region, cultivation had shrunk compared with former times, and there were large reserves of unutilized land. It was therefore easy to extend cultivation, and rising demand and improving transport meant that the margin of cultivation set by economics and technology was steadily being pushed back. By 1914, only Egypt and Lebanon had approached that margin. Egypt's cultivated area seems to have declined during the chaotic years following the withdrawal of the French forces. But under Muhammad Ali recovery was swift and was sustained almost uninterruptedly until the outbreak of the First World War. Between 1830–35 and 1910–14, the cultivated area increased by two-thirds.

No comparable figures are available for the other countries, but the extension of cultivation in Turkey, Syria, and Iraq must have been even larger; for in these countries the population (and therefore presumably food consumption) doubled, or more, during this period. At the same time, agricultural exports greatly increased, yet no significant rise in yields seems to have occurred. In Syria, cultivation was extended northward and eastward; in Iraq, away from the river banks; and, in Turkey, all over the country. In Tunisia, the cultivated area seems to have shrunk in 1775–1858 and output fell. But after the French conquest, there was rapid expansion. The areas planted to grain, olives, and minor crops increased 2.5 times between 1881 and the period from 1909 to 1913.

Indigenous farmers were the main driving force extending cultivation and raising output, and there were some progressive landlords. Their inducement was the prices offered by the world market and the lower transport costs gradually available.

Extension of cultivation required greater labor input, and this was supplied by the rapid growth in population. This resulted primarily from a decline in death rates, due to greater control of such epidemics as plague and the cholera thanks to quarantines and other hygienic measures; to increasing and more dependable food supplies; and to the establishment of law and order and, after about 1850, the decreasing frequency of wars. At the same time it is possible that there was a rise in the live birth rate, due to the foregoing factors, to the abandonment of abortion and other birth-control measures, and to the rapidly growing demand for labor, including child labor in the fields. At any rate, starting at various dates in the middle third of the century, population began to grow at around 1 percent per annum. Table 3 gives very tentative estimates.

Table 3
Population 1800–1914
(millions)

	1800	1830	1860	1900	1914
Egypt	3.9	4.7	5.5	10.2	12.3
Iraq			1.2	2.7	3.2
Syria		1.5	2.5	3.5	4.0
Turkey	6.5	6.7		12.5	14.7
Tunisia	1.0		1.1		2.0

(Sources: Issawi, *Economic History of Middle East and North Africa*, p. 94.)

In Turkey, Syria, Tunisia, and northern Iraq, where crops were rain-fed, available land and increasing labor were sufficient to bring about extension of cultivation once the farmers had been offered wage goods in return for their crops. In southern Iraq, simple irrigation works were required. But in Egypt much more elaborate and costly irrigation works were needed. Under Muhammad Ali and his successors, these were built by *corvée* labor, which was eventually abolished during the British occupation. By 1833, some 400 kilometers of canals had been dug. Under Ismail (1863–1879), another 13,500 kilometers were added, and some sixty million dollars were spent on irrigation. The British built many dams and barrages, including the Aswan Dam in 1902 (at that time the largest in the world), and spent over one hundred million dollars on irrigation. All this made it possible to convert most of Egypt's farmland from flood or basin irrigation, which had been practiced for thousands of years, to perennial irrigation. Two advantages followed. First, double-cropping could now be used, hence whereas the *cultivated* area rose by two-thirds, the *cropped* area doubled. Secondly, the cultivation of such valuable crops as cotton and sugar cane, which ripened in summer and therefore could not be grown under the traditional system, now became possible. Long staple cotton, introduced in the 1820s, steadily expanded and was greatly stimulated by the rise in prices caused by the American Civil War. By 1913, cotton covered 23 percent of Egypt's *cropped* area and accounted for 90 percent of its exports; in volume, cotton exports rose by a factor of 20 between 1848 and 1852 and 1908 and 1912.

In addition to double-cropping and the shift to cash crops, Egypt's agricultural output was raised by various measures of intensification. Improved seeds, better methods of cultivation, greater labor input, and, at the end of the period, increasing use of chemical fertilizers raised wheat yields and almost tripled cotton yields. The constant introduction of improved varieties of cotton also raised the value of that crop. The increase in total output between 1830 and 1835 and 1910 and 1914 has been estimated at about 17 times.

In the other countries, no significant irrigation works were built except for the Konya Dam in Turkey and the Hindiyya Dam in Iraq, both completed in 1913, at a cost of five million and three million dollars, respectively. Nor were chemical fertilizers used on a significant scale except on French farms in Tunisia. Nor, as far as can be ascertained, was there a rise in grain yields. But there was a significant shift to cash crops, and some improvement in the methods used on them, in the quality of these crops, and in their yields. In Turkey, there was cotton in the Izmir and Adana areas; silk in Bursa and elsewhere; tobacco in the Black

Sea and Izmir regions; vines and fruits in western Anatolia; and opium around Afyon Karahisar. These crops accounted for almost half of Turkey's exports, and the volume sent abroad rose greatly. In Syria, tobacco from the Latakia region, silk from Lebanon, and oranges from Palestine were important exports. In Iraq, exports of agricultural produce—wheat, barley, and dates—increased their share at the expense of pastoral products, reflecting both the shift in world demand and increasing cultivation by nomads who were settling on the land and abandoning livestock breeding. Tunisia greatly increased its exports of olive oil, produced mainly by Tunisians, and wine produced by French settlers.

These cash crops could be grafted onto traditional agriculture without any great change in either techniques or land tenure. Usually the cash crop would be grown alongside the grain and other food staples; eventually, some farmers would switch their land completely to cash crops and buy their grain from the market. The Lebanese silk-growing districts were already heavy importers of grain by the eighteenth century, and so were some silk growers in Turkey by the nineteenth. In the nineteenth century, Egyptian cotton growers were sometimes unable to meet all their food needs, and so were tobacco growers in Turkey and Syria and orange growers in Palestine. But, except for oranges in Palestine, mulberries in the silk-growing districts, and olives, none of these crops required large capital investments or fundamental changes in land tenure; they could all be raised either by peasant-proprietors or by sharecroppers working on large estates.

Nevertheless, there were some deep changes in land tenure. Traditionally, in spite of great diversity, there was a basic common pattern involving three elements: the state, the farmer, and an intermediary. The ownership (*raqaba*) of the land was vested in the state or ruler, with minor exceptions such as *milk* (freehold) and *waqf* (mortmain or endowments). The farmers who tilled the soil enjoyed usufructuary rights *(tasarruf)*, which normally descended to their heirs. In between came various intermediaries (*sipahis* and Mamluks, followed by *multazims*), who collected rents or taxes from the farmers and transferred part of the proceeds to the central treasury; they kept the balance as payment for their military or administrative services. The increase in central government control and the growth of a market economy shook the foundations of this system.

During the years 1811 to 1816, Muhammad Ali massacred the Mamluks and took over their *iltizams* (tax farms) and waqfs, becoming in effect sole owner of the country, distributing to farmers plots of 3 to 5 acres and collecting taxes directly from them. Later, he gave large tracts of uncultivated lands to notables and forced certain officials to take over some villages and be responsible for their taxes. The 1858 Land Law converted these rights and duties to almost full property rights. Egypt's land ownership took the form it was to retain for the next hundred years: a substantial proportion of land in big farms and a very large number of small peasant proprietors. The big estates were cultivated mainly by tenants recruited from among the landless or those with insufficient land, on a sharecropping or cash-rent basis. As population growth began to outstrip the extension of the cultivated area, real wages tended to stagnate, or rose very slowly, whereas rents increased sharply (i.e., the growing agricultural surplus was being appropriated mainly by the landlords).

In the Ottoman Empire, the massacre of the Janissaries (1826) was followed by the abolition of *timars* (fiefs) in 1831. The Land Code of 1858 provided for the registration of all land in individual, not collective, ownership and for the granting of usufructuary title to those who could prove continuous occupation. Its main objective was to facilitate direct collection of taxes by the state, but it also sought to encourage individual enterprise. However, different ecological, political, and social conditions led to very different outcomes. In Turkey, the bulk of the land passed to peasants, and only a small number remained landless. Rents tended to remain very low, except in such areas as the Adana and Izmir cotton fields, where they rose sharply. In Iraq and Syria, however, the new Code ran counter to prevailing communal *(musha')* or tribal ownership, which was well adapted to the lack of security, the strong communal ties, the precarious and erratic rainfall, and the consequent instability of crop yields. Moreover, bad records and poor administration, as well as distrust of the government, impeded the implementation of the Code. The result was that a large part of the land was registered in the name of tribal or village chiefs or city notables, depriving hundreds of thousands of peasants of any title and presenting a formidable obstacle to development.

In Tunisia, the most significant change was the acquisition of land by French colonists. By 1881, Frenchmen owned some 100,000 hectares. After the conquest, various measures were taken to encourage colonization, including confiscation of tribal land, sale of *habus* (mortmain), and the facilitation of registration and sale under the Land Registration Act of 1885, patterned on the Australian Torrens Act. By 1914, nearly one-fifth of the cultivated area had passed into French hands, and a larger proportion of agricultural output originated in the French sector.

Trade, Credit, and Transport

These developments in agriculture would have been impossible but for the accompanying ones in two connected sectors: trade and credit and transport. The first can be dealt with briefly. European import-export firms, located in the main seaports or in the capitals, bought produce from farmers through a network of agents—generally members of minorities—located in the provincial towns. These same agents advanced short-term loans on the security of the crops. They also sold textiles, tea, sugar, kerosene, and other consumer goods to the farmers. The necessary processing plants for ginning and pressing cotton, reeling silk, crushing oilseeds, curing tobacco, etc. were set up by foreigners or members of minorities. The import-export firms themselves relied for credit on the foreign-owned banks established after 1850; the stabilization of the currencies, in the second half of the nineteenth century, also facilitated internal and international transactions.

One of the greatest handicaps from which the Middle East suffers is the absence of navigable rivers; the two available networks—the Nile with its branches and canals and the Tigris-Euphrates—have of course been used since remotest antiquity. The Nile and almost all the waterways leading from it, which among them serve practically all the cultivated areas, are navigable the whole year round; moreover, the fact that the prevailing winds are northerly facilitates navigation, since boats can sail upstream and float downstream. The Tigris and Euphrates are much less well suited to navigation. Their currents are far swifter, their levels much more variable, and they often change their course. Moreover, neither river is navigable much further north than Baghdad.

Both Egypt and Iraq have always transported the bulk of their goods by river. Coastal navigation has also always been very important in Turkey, Syria, and Tunisia. For the rest, the region relied on caravans of mules and, especially, camels, which had taken over from wheeled traffic at the end of the Roman era. Camel loads varied, generally ranging between 250 and 300 kilograms, the speed of a caravan was 4 to 5 kilometers an hour, and the usual daily stage 25 to 30 kilometers. Caravans also differed greatly in size: in 1820, the Suez caravan had 500 camels; in 1847 the Baghdad-Damascus caravan had 1,500 to 2,000; and the Damascus-Baghdad 800 to 1,200; and, in the 1870s, 15,000 pack animals made three round trips a year on the Tabriz-Trabzon route, the carrying equivalent of 7 to 8 sailing ships each way. Boats and pack animals were adequate for the relatively small volume of traffic, but the cost of transport on the latter was high.

Mechanical transport first came to the Middle East through its rivers—steam tugs and boats on the Nile in the 1830s and on the Tigris-Euphrates in the 1860s—and played a useful part. Except in Lebanon and, to a lesser extent, Tunisia, roads carried very little traffic until the First World War. But railways were built on a fairly large scale, and, by 1914, were carrying a half or more of total freight in Egypt, Tunisia, Turkey, and Syria.

In Egypt, the first railway was begun in 1851, before those of Sweden or central Poland, not to mention China and Japan. It connected Alexandria with Cairo in 1856 and with Suez in 1858 and was built at British insistence, to speed transport on the Mediterranean-India route, and by British engineers but, like subsequent Egyptian lines, was financed by the government. In 1856, a British firm started construction on the Izmir-Aydin line, and in 1863 another began the Izmir-Kasaba line. The Ottoman government, however, wanted a railway that would serve the Anatolian hinterland and connect Istanbul with the provincial capitals of Asia Minor, Syria, and Iraq. In 1872, a master plan was drawn up for an Istanbul-Basra railway, with branches in Anatolia and Syria; and the completion of the Vienna-Istanbul line in 1888 increased the attractiveness of this project. In that same year, a concession for an Istanbul-Ankara line was granted to a German company, and in 1903 the same German interests received a concession for the prolongation of the line to Basra.

The outbreak of war interrupted operations, when only a small stretch had been built in Iraq, between Baghdad and Samarra. Connection between Anatolia and Aleppo was achieved only in 1918. The first railways in Syria were the Jaffa-Jerusalem line, begun in 1890, and the Beirut-Damascus-Muzayrib line begun in 1891. The Hijaz railway, built at the initiative of Abd al-Hamid II, with the help of subscriptions from Muslim communities all over the world, began in Damascus in 1901 and by 1908 had reached Madina, 1,320 kilometers away; its Syrian portion (about 500 kilometers) is included in Table 4. In Tunisia, a small line was built in 1876, followed by accelerated construction after the French conquest.

Except for the Egyptian State Railways, the privately owned light railways in Egypt and the Hijaz railway, almost all the lines in the region operated under guarantees by the government of revenue—usually 10,000 to 15,000 francs per kilometer open to traffic. Table 4 sums up the progress of railway building. By 1914, the region had a total of 10,300 kilometers, or about 1 percent of the world's total track of 1,100,000 kilometers.

Table 4
Length of Railways
(kilometers)

	1870	1890	1914
Egypt	1,400	1,799	4,314
Turkey	230	1,443	3,400
Syria			1,650
Iraq			132
Tunisia		416	1,785
	1,630	3,658	11,281

Railways drastically reduced traveling time. To give only one example, in 1940 the Damascus-Cairo journey took 18 hours, instead of 20 to 25 days by caravan. Railways also greatly reduced cost. Caravan freight between Ankara and Istanbul was about 10 cents per ton-mile; by 1913, the railway was charging only 1 cent per ton-mile and gave discounts of up to 50 percent for bulk orders. In Egypt, railway freights in the Delta were about one-third of those charged for pack animals.

The results of this reduction were momentous. First, it greatly promoted exports, since the cost of transport to the coast by caravan often greatly exceeded the cost of production and also the sea freight to European markets. Thus, in Syria the caravan freight of grain from Hauran to Acre (125 kilometers) was about equal to its cost of production and that to Beirut (225 kilometers away) was some three times as great. Similarly, the journey from Ankara to Istanbul (360 kilometers) by pack animals tripled the price of wheat and more than tripled that of barley. All this made it possible to extend greatly the cultivated area.

Railways, by sharply reducing costs of transport, also helped to break down the previous compartmentalization of markets characteristic of the whole region except Egypt, where cheap water transport has always been available. This had shown itself in the sharp seasonal fluctuations of prices; in the sharp price fluctuations from year to year, depending on the size of the crop; and in the vastly differing prices quoted for the same commodity at places not too distant from each other. Not until the extension of mechanical transport did the various countries of the region—again excepting Egypt—begin to have integrated national markets.

The Use of the Surplus

On the eve of the First World War the Middle East presented a paradox. Judging by the surplus it managed to generate and its overall level of output, the Middle East compared favorably with other regions. In 1913, per capita annual income in Egypt and Turkey was around $50; in Tunisia perhaps the same; and in Syria and Iraq not much less. At that date, the figure for India was about $13, for China probably not much higher, for Japan $40, and for Russia about $60. The degree of monetization of the economy was brought out by the high level of foreign trade. In 1913, exports plus imports per capita in Egypt amounted to $24.30; in Turkey, $15.20; in Syria, $15.00; in Iraq, $10.00; and in Tunisia, $31.00. These figures are far higher than those for other countries (e.g., Japan $12.60; Russia $9.20; India $4.30; and China much less). The ratio of exports to GNP for Turkey was about 14 percent and of imports 19 percent; for Egypt the figures were about 32 and 38 percent; and for Tunisia almost certainly higher—again comparing very favorably with the foregoing countries. The region also scored high marks under a third criterion, the ratio of railway mileage to population, which was distinctly higher in Egypt, Tunisia, Turkey, and Syria (but not in Iraq) than in all the foregoing countries except Russia. Except in Egypt, however, the ratio of railway mileage to the total area was not so favorable. The region's ports could also stand comparison with those of other countries.

Where the Middle East was much less successful was in the use it made of the income and surplus it had generated. More specifically, it did not raise its savings rate to the level required to sustain continued growth; it did not build a sizeable manufacturing industry; and it failed to develop its human resources. In other words, thanks to the impulsion it had received from European trade, transport, capital, and enterprise, the Middle East had greatly increased its agricultural output and expanded its exports many times over and thus had experienced much *growth*. But it had failed to achieve *development*.

Savings Rate

Throughout the region, and at all levels of society, the consumption rate was high and the savings rate low; moreover, the propensity to import was very high. The governments were large spenders and were able to indulge themselves thanks to rising revenues and massive borrowing abroad. In Egypt, government revenues rose from $7.5 million in 1818 to $25.5 million in 1861 and $88.5 million in 1913, at which date revenues amounted to about 15 percent of national income. Ottoman central revenues rose from $14 million in 1830 to $70 million in 1863 and nearly $120 million in 1913, in spite of the shrinkage of territory. By then, they amounted to about 10 percent of national income. In Tunisia, government revenues ranged between $800,000 and $1,600,000 during the period from 1800 to 1830, stood at $3million to $4 million in the early 1870s, and amounted to $8.6 million in 1907—a much lower figure per capita than in Egypt and Turkey and probably a small proportion of national income as well.

Foreign borrowing started in the 1850s and continued, at increasingly adverse terms, until bankruptcy was declared in 1869 for Tunisia and 1876 for Egypt and the Ottoman Empire. In December 1881, the Ottoman public debt stood at LT220 million (about $1,000 million), an amount reduced by the Muharrem Decree to LT124 million. In Egypt, the amount outstanding in 1876 was £92 million (about $450 million), which was consolidated at £98 million. In Tunisia, the debt in March 1870 was 160 million francs ($32 million), reduced by international agreement to 125 million. Of the net amounts received in loans (a half or less of the outstanding debt), the bulk had been spent on public works and other forms of development in Egypt, one tenth in Turkey, and probably less in Tunisia.

Much of the balance and the proceeds of taxation had been spent on wars. The direct costs of the Crimean War alone were officially put at $55–65 million, to which should be added the opportunity costs; between 1768 and 1914, Turkey engaged in major wars longer than any other country except France. Moreover, defeat in some of these wars resulted in heavy indemnities (e.g., $15 million to Russia in 1829 and $160 million in 1879). And even in times of peace, the burden of armaments, particularly navies, was heavy. In the absence of domestic heavy industry, such expenditures did not in any way stimulate the economy, as in Japan and Russia. Egypt also engaged in costly wars under Muhammad Ali and, to a lesser extent, under Ismail, but, on the whole, its military burden was lighter. Under the British, the army was drastically reduced, and military expenditure was cut down. Still, Egypt was saddled with substantial payments abroad—an annual tribute of $2.5 million to the Ottoman Sultan until 1914 and a subsidy to the Sudan amounting to $100 million (plus interest-free loans of $25 million) between 1898 and 1940. In Tunisia, too, the military burden, which in the 1840s had been quite heavy, eased thereafter.

Another form of expenditure was royal extravagance. This is witnessed by the palaces built at this time—Yildiz, Abdin, Muhammadiyya, etc.—by other monuments to royal munificence, such as the Opera in Cairo, and by the festivities inaugurating the Suez Canal, which cost some $7 million.

Starting in the 1880s, under the strict control of the French in Tunisia, the British in Egypt, and the international Public Debt Administration in Turkey, expenditure was much more restrained. Substantial amounts of foreign loans were contracted, but the bulk was spent on development—railways in Turkey, irrigation in Egypt, etc. However, the burden constituted by the servicing of the foreign debt continued to be heavy. In Egypt, interest and service charges absorbed some 40 percent of government revenues until the end of the century and over 25 percent from 1896 to 1914. As a proportion of export proceeds, the figure was almost 40 percent until around 1890, declining to about 12 percent by 1913.

In Turkey, at the beginning of this century, service charges equalled a little over 30 percent of government revenues and about the same proportion of export proceeds. In Tunisia, the figures were about 25 and 15 percent, respectively. It is clear that these payments severely reduced the region's capacity to save and invest. In the meantime, almost the whole of the ordinary revenue continued to be devoted to four items: servicing of the foreign debt, army and navy, civil administration, and maintenance of the royal family. Expenditure for development—public works, education and health—was everywhere well below 10 percent of the total.

Consumption by the upper classes, whether foreign, minority, or Muslim, was also very high. This is indicated by the growth of large new quarters in the main cities, the building of imposing country houses, the adoption of European dress, and increasing imports of luxury items. Like their counterparts in so many countries, the upper and middle classes developed a keen taste for European goods and ways of life. This shift in tastes partly explains the tendency, noted by many observers, for imports to rise somewhat faster than exports.

As regards mass consumption, only very tentative statements may be advanced. In Egypt, the level of living seems to have risen in the 1850s and 60s, and again from 1885 to 1914; this is indicated by the increase in consumption of such staples as coffee, tobacco, sugar, and textiles. In Turkey, too, conditions seem to have improved after the Crimean War, with peace, increasing agricultural production, and rising real wages; in the years before the First World War there are some indications of an increase in demand for semiluxury items like watches and bicycles. In Lebanon, conditions improved markedly from 1860 to 1914 as witnessed by, among other things, much house building in the villages, and they may also have slightly improved in Syria and Iraq. In Tunisia, there seems to have been a deterioration between 1775 and 1860 followed by a stabilization or possibly a very slight improvement.

One of the most unfortunate aspects of the recent history of the region is that unlike the Japanese, who quickly learned European production methods but kept their native patterns of consumption, the Arabs, and Turks quickly picked up European consumption habits but failed to learn European production methods. The composition of imports reflects the shift in tastes away from domestic products to European. In Turkey cotton manufactures formed about half the imports in the 1840s and 30 percent from 1910 to 1912. In Egypt, cloth accounted for a quarter to a third of imports from the 1830s to 1913; in Syria, over one third; in Iraq, two-fifths; and in Tunisia, two-fifths. Shoes and other leather products and glassware were also imported in large quantities.

Increasing imports of building materials, such as bricks, tiles, cement, and glass, reflect the change to Western-style housing. Consumption of colonial goods also rose: in Turkey, tea, coffee, and sugar accounted for 10 percent of imports. Imports of capital goods, however, remained small until the turn of the century. Just before the First World War, they amounted to about 10 percent of the total in Turkey, Egypt, and Tunisia.

This low figure reflects the low level of saving and investment in the region. Except under Muhammad Ali, even periods of relatively high investment (e.g., in Egypt under Ismail or in Iraq in the immediate prewar years, with much construction of irrigation works and railways) were accompanied by low savings rates, the gap being filled by foreign funds. During the period from 1903 to 1913, Egypt's net investment rate was about 7 percent of national income and net domestic savings were about 3.5 percent; Turkey's rates were probably comparable.

Industrialization

For most of the period, industrial output either declined or grew very slowly. With peace and security in the Mediterranean and improved transport, Europe's machine-made goods poured into the region, competing with the native handicrafts. Production of the latter was further depressed by the shift in taste to European products. Contemporary reports leave no doubt that handicrafts were severely hurt and their numbers went down sharply from 1830 to about 1870. After that, however, the situation improved. New handicrafts catering to foreign markets developed, most notably carpets. And many of the traditional ones, such as cotton and silk weaving in Egypt and Syria, changed their methods and increased their output.

The governments did next to nothing to help the handicrafts or to integrate them with what little factory industry did develop. Indeed Muhammad Ali's policy hastened their demise, not only by competing with them but by drafting craftsmen or sending them to the villages to work in agriculture. But Muhammad Ali achieved unique success in founding modern industries. By 1838, he had invested $60 million in factories employing some 30,000 workers and producing textiles, sugar, glass, paper, chemicals, ironware, arms, ammunition, and ships.

Even so, these industries operated under tremendous handicaps and were kept going only by his constant supervision and the protection provided by his monopoly system. The end of that system therefore led to a rapid decline, and, under his two successors, the factories were either liquidated or sold or leased to private individuals. In Turkey, a similar, but more limited, attempt was made in the 1840s to establish state factories, including textiles, bootmaking, sawmills, a copper-sheet rolling mill, arms, ammunition, and a small shipyard. At their peak, they employed 5,000 men. These factories too were highly inefficient; by 1849, most had been abandoned. A still feebler effort was made in Tunisia in the 1840s.

After that, there was a long pause, and, in the second half of the century, the Middle East and North Africa experienced far less industrialization than Latin America, India, or even China, not to mention Russia and Japan. In Egypt, some sugar refineries were established in the 1860s and 1870s, and, at the turn of the century, a few textile, cement, cigarette, food-processing, and other plants were built by foreign capital. By 1916, some 30,000 to 35,000 persons were employed in modern factories. In Turkey, foreigners and members of minorities set up textile and vegetable oils factories in the cotton-growing areas, and food-processing, paper, wood, ceramics, and other industries were founded in Istanbul. Still, a partial census in 1913, covering the two main centers of Istanbul and Izmir, showed only 17,000 workers in factories using steam power. In Syria, there were only some silk reeling and tobacco plants and in Palestine a few Jewish workshops. Tunisia had steam-powered oil presses and a few food-processing and building materials industries.

Mining made more rapid progress and included coal, lead, copper, boracite, and chromium in Turkey, oil, phosphates, and manganese in Egypt, and phosphates in Tunisia. After tortuous negotiations, agreement to found an Anglo-German company to exploit Iraq's oil was reached just before the outbreak of war.

This lack of industrial development is not surprising. Markets were restricted by the low purchasing power of the mass of the population and by the preference of the upper and middle classes for foreign goods. Inputs were expensive: fuel was dear, and suitable raw materials scarce. Transport was slow and expensive. Unskilled labor was, in most places, cheap, but its productivity was extremely low; skilled labor was very scarce and usually had to be imported. So were foremen, technicians, and managers. Local capital was scanty and fearful of long-term ventures, and industrial credit was practically nonexistent. Finally, a large share of blame rests with the governments; they showed very little interest in industrial development.

In this, they were continuing a long tradition, arising from their being dominated by bureaucrats, soldiers, and landlords for whom fiscal considerations came well ahead of development. They were also massively ignorant of economics, and, in so far as they had an economic policy, it was the laissez-faire preached to them by Europeans. In Egypt and Tunisia, the foreign rulers used all their influence to prevent the emergence of industries that could compete with those of the metropolis; thus Lord Cromer imposed an 8 percent excise duty on Egyptian cotton textiles to offset the 8 percent import duty.

Signs of change began, however, to appear shortly before the First World War. The Ottoman government succeeded in raising import duties and framing a differentiated tariff. After the 1908 Revolution some aid and protection was extended, including exemption of machinery from customs duties. Measures were taken to promote national shipping and to regulate foreign insurance companies. In Egypt, advocates of industrialization became much more vociferous; among these were both Muslims and members of minority groups, and there was some response on the part of local capital. The outbreak of war radically changed the situation.

Human Resources

Perhaps the greatest single weakness of Middle Eastern society in this period was its failure to develop its human resources. The region entered the nineteenth century under a heavy handicap. While health conditions may not have been worse than in other underdeveloped regions and while the Middle Easterners had acquired, in the course of their long history, a large measure of immunity against many diseases, they seem to have been susceptible to attacks of cholera. This disease caused much devastation until around 1870 and was contained only by the installation of quarantines.

In education, matters were far worse. In the early decades of the nineteenth century, the literacy rate almost certainly did not exceed 5 percent in any of these countries, a figure far below those of Japan and China and probably lower than that of Russia. Moreover, unlike Russia, the region did not have a body of administrators, officers, engineers, physicians, and scientists trained in Western methods.

This gap grew wider in the course of the century. As noted before, missions to Europe and the foundation of technical and other schools gave the governments a small but indispensable nucleus of administrators and technicians. However, as the figures given also show, no serious attempt was made to spread education widely—it continued to be regarded as a training for government service. Nor, in this respect, was British policy in Egypt or French in Tunisia different.

In all countries, matters began to improve around the turn of the century, but progress was very slow. In 1860/1861, Ottoman expenditure on civilian education was only 0.2 percent of the total; by 1911/1912, it had risen to 2.1 percent. In Egypt, in the years from 1882 to 1891, education and health combined absorbed 1.5 percent of government expenditures, but education alone rose to 3 percent just before the War. The result is best measured by the literacy rate: 4 percent for Egyptian Muslims and 10 percent for Copts in 1907, and surely not higher anywhere else except in Lebanon and Syria.

The Middle East was able to exploit its natural resources while tapping its human resources so lightly because it imported the needed skills from abroad. Foreigners and minority groups—many of them from neighboring countries, such as the Armenians and Syrian Christians in Egypt—constituted not only the upper bourgeoisie and professional classes but also large strata of the petty bourgeoisie and skilled working classes. Outside the government—and to a significant extent even inside it—all economic activity was run by them: banks, insurance, stock exchanges, mechanized transport, large-scale foreign and internal trade, the professions, etc. At a lower level, not only engineers and foremen but mechanics were usually Italians, Greeks, Armenians, or other non-Muslims. As long as this situation persisted, no true development could take place in the region, only lop-sided growth, which was bound to come to an end once the limit of easily cultivable land had been reached or when the terms of trade, which on the whole had been highly favorable to the region in the nineteenth century, began to turn. Both contingencies materialized after the First World War.

International Comparison

Comparison with China, Japan, and Russia brings out some striking differences.

First, European pressure was far greater on this region. This is indicated by the relatively high figures for trade, capital investment, railways, and number of European residents. It is not surprising in view of the Near East's proximity to Europe, its accessibility by water, and the centuries-old economic links binding the two regions. For both good and ill, the impact of Europe was very great.

By the same token, the Near Eastern governments were in a far weaker position to resist or redirect the impact than were those of Russia and Japan, though not China. This was partly, as already mentioned, because of the restrictive effects of the Capitulations and commercial treaties—though it should be pointed out that both China and Japan operated under similar disabilities. More important, the Near Eastern countries were smaller in size and population and far closer to Europe than the other three. Still more important is the fact that the Near Eastern governments had less control over their countries than did those of Russia and Japan—but this does not, of course, apply to China. Russia's earlier modernization had greatly increased its government's control; in Japan, the steady improvements of the Tokugawa Period had strengthened if not the political unity of the country then at least its cohesion and raised its economic and social level.

Lastly, the region's lower capacity to react constructively to the European challenge is to be explained by its much smaller human resource base. Two aspects should be distinguished. On the one hand the level of mass education and literacy was far lower than in the other three countries, and the gap tended to widen as regards Japan and Russia throughout the period under review. On the other hand, a disproportionately large share of the skills required for economic and social development was provided by members of the minorities, whose allegiance to their governments was by no means unqualified and who, in turn, were not fully trusted by these governments. Since these minorities controlled a significant share of the economic and social life, and stood to gain greatly from development, the governments' encouragement of many activities tended to be, at best, half-hearted.

CHAPTER SIX

Social Interdependence

BETWEEN THE FINAL decades of the eighteenth century and the years of World War I, the lands of Ottoman Afro-Asia experienced rapid changes that were deeply disturbing to the social order. Some of these changes had in fact already been underway during the seventeenth and eighteenth centuries, before pressures from the West began to be strongly felt in the nineteenth century.

The earlier changes, which took place between about 1600 and 1800, provide some sense of comparison with what was to follow during the nineteenth century and beyond, when Ottoman Afro-Asia's social formation was shaken by the demands placed upon it to achieve economic competitiveness, fiscal stability, and effective political, military, and social organization. The premodern social formation was itself dynamic; within its own bounds, it underwent significant changes almost from the peak of Ottoman power and efficiency in the sixteenth century.

The changes that occurred during the premodern period, shared more or less by all the lands of Ottoman Afro-Asia, began with the economic and social crises of the late sixteenth century. Population pressure, the strains of Ottoman warfare on several fronts (the Mediterranean, the Red Sea, southeastern Europe, and Iran), and the growing impact of New World silver on the fiscal and monetary system were factors of change. Such changes were felt directly in Ottoman Anatolia and the Fertile Crescent, less so in Egypt and Tunisia (ruled indirectly from Istanbul); yet, Tunisia became an exposed outpost on the Ottoman front in the Western Mediterranean, Egypt became far harder to govern and to exploit for its wealth. The Ottoman land regime, which had compensated *timar* cavalrymen with usufruct of agricultural land, was gradually monetized; tax-farming became a principal source of government revenues; the commercialization of agriculture continued to develop into the modern period; and the diffusion of firearms among provincial irregulars and nomads posed frequent challenges to central authority.

The state thereafter had to rely more heavily on local lords, urban notables, and provincial governors who could provide their own retainers and agents and who sought to control the sources of wealth for themselves.

101

The state gradually lost the services of the timar cavalry and had to depend on and finance a standing army composed primarily of Janissaries. The Janissaries possessed vested interests and enormous power in the imperial and provincial capitals, extending into the countryside in Anatolia and the Fertile Crescent. In Cairo and Tunis, they or their equivalent, the Mamluks, asserted themselves against the local elites, interposing themselves between provincial society and the far-away central government.

This dependence by the Ottoman state on Janissaries, irregular forces, and private armies prevented the Ottomans, had they desired to do so, from pursuing extensive technological and organizational change in the military. This latter development explains in part the Ottomans' weak performance in their military struggles with the Western powers during the seventeenth and eighteenth centuries.

In addition to this picture of decentralization of state power, and the economic and social changes associated with the transformation of the land regime, other aspects of transformation should be noted for the period after 1500, when several of the Arab lands became part of the Ottoman state. First, the process of Ottoman expansion into the Arab lands created, for the first time since the High Caliphate, a huge domestic market in Afro-Asia, now linked to Ottoman Europe. Second, as far as can be determined from surviving cadastral and taxation records, there was a substantial increase in population (during the sixteenth century, perhaps as much as 40 percent) representing in effect a delayed recovery from the demographic disaster of the great plagues of the fourteenth century. After 1600, and until the beginning of the nineteenth century, the picture is less clear, because Ottoman cadastral surveys were either nonexistent or of poor quality compared to their predecessors.

Overall population aggregates may not have increased significantly (in some areas, they almost certainly declined). There was, however, important *urban* physical and commercial growth. Studies of several Arab cities of the empire have shown evidence of new commercial and residential buildings, the former near old city centers where legal, governmental, and religious institutions were located, and the latter primarily in new suburbs outside the city walls and along the main trade routes. This evidence suggests that at least a few important Ottoman cities continued to grow right through the eighteenth century (see Table 1).

Concomitant with urban physical and commercial growth was the extension of urban control over the rural hinterland. Tax-farming was the primary reason. It tended to encourage tenancy and collective forms

Table 1
Select Population Statistics

REGIONS

(millions)	1800	1830	1860	1900	1914
Tunisia	1?		1.1?		2.0
Egypt	3.9	4.7	5.5	10.2	12.3
Iraq			1.2?		3.4?
Greater Syria		1.5?	2.5?	3.5?	4.0?
Turkey	6.5?	6.7?		12.5	14.7

CITIES

			1800	1860	1914
Tunis			100,000	80,000	200,000
Cairo	(1517: 150,000)*		250,000	300,000	700,000
Alexandria			15,000	200,000	350,000
Aleppo	(1570: 60,000)*	(1790: 120,000)*	100,000	120,000
Damascus	(1600: 52,000)*		90,000	100,000	220,000
Beirut			6,000	50,000	150,000
Baghdad		50,000–100,000?	60,000	150,000
Basra			4,000	10,000	20,000
Istanbul			400,000	500,000	1,100,000
Izmir			100,000	150,000	300,000

Sources: All figures without asterisks are taken from Charles Issawi, *An Economic History of the Middle East and North Africa* (New York: Columbia University Press, 1982), pp. 94, 101.

Figures with asterisks are from Andre Raymond, *The Great Arab Cities in the 16th–18th Centuries* (New York: New York University Press, 1984), p. 7, citing the work of the late Antoine Abdel-Nour.

of labor; after 1600, it replaced the older Ottoman hearth system of family farms that carried rights of inheritance, residence, and usufruct. The hearth system had not been applied, however, to Tunisia and Egypt; and in marginal lands of the Fertile Crescent, it was also absent. If the extraction of revenues by tax-farmers was severe enough, abandonment of the land took place. There is evidence from eighteenth-century Syria, however, of recurrent peasant debt to creditors in Damascus; this access to credit may have helped peasants through years of famine, war, and pestilence, although more often than not peasants lost their rights on the land through default on their loans. Overall conditions were therefore generally harsh for peasants.

The cities drew population from the countryside, and rural population levels declined considerably from the late sixteenth century onward in many parts of the region, prefiguring the dramatic movements of more recent times from country to city. In contrast, the exodus of urban populations during times of war was generally temporary. A prominent example was Iraq, which bordered Safavid Iran and became a battleground for much of the period from the mid-sixteenth to mid-eighteenth centuries.

Two other patterns of change in the period between approximately 1600 and 1800 may finally be mentioned. The first was a shift in control or patronage of regional trade by the eighteenth century in favor of now-stronger local rulers, such as the Egyptian military aristocracy, the princes of Mount Lebanon, the Husaynid beys of Tunisia, the rulers of Mosul (in northern Iraq), the *derebeys* of Anatolia, and others like Jazzar Pasha (died 1804), the famed governor of Sidon and Acre. Many of these rulers promoted the growth of European trade in their areas, some as early as the first quarter of the eighteenth century. Zahir al-Umar, lord of Galilee for much of that century, sold cotton to the Dutch, and then to the French, from the 1720s onward, and used the profits to finance his military and political ambitions.

Second, there was a numerically small (about 4000 persons) yet socially significant demographic shift among Syrian Christians. Moving to the coastal cities of Syria and Egypt, they found a role as middlemen between Europe and the region during the eighteenth century, following in the footsteps of their counterparts among other minorities such as Jews and Armenians. Syrian Christians had captured the coastal trade between Egypt and Syria by the end of the century. That trade, however, was carried almost entirely on European vessels, an ominous portent. So great was Syrians' success that they wrested control of the Egyptian customs service; the Mamluks had previously farmed out this service to members of the Jewish community. The Syrians lost that monopoly, however, after the French invasion of Egypt in 1798 and the rise of Muhammad Ali. They were to resume immigration into Egypt from the middle of the nineteenth century until the First World War.

In several respects, the nineteenth century and the period just before the First World War witnessed the continuation of changes already underway, along with those most often associated with the "impact of the West" and the regional responses to that impact, such as the reform programs of the Ottoman, Egyptian, and Tunisian rulers. Unlike Peter the Great, who had crafted a strong Russian state with a relatively pliant nobility and a single, state-dominated church, the rulers of Ottoman Afro-Asia presided over a highly complex social order with many disparate groups. They ruled primarily through persuasion, patronage, and informal networks in the provinces, respecting custom within an overarching Islamic legal and political framework. Sovereignty was maintained even as some local rulers during the later eighteenth century came to exercise greater freedom of action. Urban provincial notables, leading members of the local military, religious, and commercial establishments who served as intermediaries between state and society, also gained greater influence.

Reform in this context meant change initiated from the top, from the center of state and society, whether Istanbul, Cairo, or Tunis. It also meant an attempt to shift customary local and corporate power back to the center, to reclaim the initiative lost during the seventeenth and eighteenth centuries. By roughly the mid-nineteenth century, the state had new weapons to direct and control society: modern military organization, a new layer of bureaucracy, and modern communications, along with new ideologies and claims on the ordinary subject.

All of this occurred in an international environment that compelled rulers to pay almost as much attention to diplomatic, military, and economic pressures from Europe as to internal resistance to effective centralized government. That resistance came not only from groups and individuals unwilling to surrender their customary freedom of action; it came now as well from new quarters: from nationalist movements and new Western-style intellectuals, frequently from peasants, and, by the end of the nineteenth century, from industrial workers. The nineteenth century produced economic and political dislocations that culminated in foreign occupation in two lands considered here—Tunisia in 1881 and Egypt in 1882—and in the dismemberment of what remained of the Ottoman Empire just after the First World War. Patterns of social interdependence were transformed as well.

PATTERNS OF SETTLEMENT

Disease, famine, and war, the Malthusian, premodern limits to population growth, were not overcome until well into the nineteenth century. The lands of Ottoman Afro-Asia considered here contained some twelve million persons about 1800; they lived under diverse ecological conditions. Tunisian peasants were concentrated in a territory spanning the Mediterranean coastline, with additional concentrations around several oases to the interior. The French expeditionary forces estimated Egypt's population in 1800 at about four million, virtually all packed into the narrow confines of the Nile Valley and the Delta. Anatolia and the Fertile Crescent provided somewhat broader lands to support their populations. The Anatolian plateau, with the exception of the harsh, semiarid zone near Konya, supported perhaps as many as seven million persons in 1800.

The Fertile Crescent contained perhaps one and a half million persons in 1800. The earlier pattern of abandonment of lands rimming the Syrian Desert was not reversed until well into the twentieth century. That pattern was made more severe by nomadic pressures. During the eighteenth and most of the nineteenth centuries, the 'Anaza tribal confederation moved into the Syrian region of the Arabian Peninsula, disrupting a peasant population deeply hurt by increased soil salinity in some areas and the spread of malaria and swamps (particularly on the upper Jordan River). Further disruption in agrarian settlement patterns was to be occasioned by land legislation resulting from the Ottoman reform program.

In contrast, urban life had been sustained until the nineteenth century by the extraction of rural surpluses, profits from regional and international trade, and government policies that sought social peace, uninterrupted communications (particularly for the promotion of trade and access to the Muslim pilgrimage sites at Mecca and Medina), and sufficient fiscal resources. These policies were failing by the time the reformers began their work in the nineteenth century.

The region's population probably roughly doubled between 1830 and 1914, from 12 to 25 million. Relative civil peace (the absence of major wars) and, probably more important, the end of plague and cholera epidemics (end of plague after 1820 in Tunisia, 1843, in Syria, and 1877, in Iraq; end of cholera during the 1870s, with occasional recurrences thereafter) blunted the impact of these typical premodern limits to population growth. Public health measures, particularly quarantines introduced before 1850, were of salient importance. Food supply became better assured by the growth of modern means of communication and transportation, such as steamships from the 1840s and 1850s, the telegraph after 1861, railways and new roads from the 1850s, the telegraph after 1861, and new roads from the 1850s onward, and the internal combustion engine by 1914. High mortality and short life-expectancy rates nevertheless continued into this century. Famines, along with localized civil conflict, continued to take their toll. But it was not until World War I itself that they claimed very large numbers of victims, most tragically in Anatolia and in Greater Syria.

Significantly, it was the coastal towns such as Izmir and Beirut that grew most dramatically both in population and in surface area as they developed new neighborhoods and new zones of production and exchange. Some cities, particularly in Anatolia, came to resemble collections of villages and lacked identifiable cores; this was less true of the older Arab cities, but it was true of rapidly growing seaports like Beirut. Beirut was a small walled town of 6,000 in 1800; by 1914, it had grown into a large agglomeration of neighborhoods surrounding the old town with a population of 150,000. Interior cities such as Damascus and Aleppo grew much more slowly in part because their traditional handicrafts were undermined by foreign competition during the nineteenth century. Thus, the overall urbanization rate showed relatively little change between 1800 and 1914.

The select population statistics for Ottoman Afro-Asia contained in Table 1, despite many gaps (especially for the period before 1800) and many rough estimates, reveal a consistent pattern: anywhere from 10 to 20 percent of the population was probably urban at the beginning of the nineteenth century, a relatively high rate for a premodern society. As noted earlier, however, that rate did not change much during the rest of the century. The lowest rates prevailed in the Fertile Crescent, the highest in Egypt and Anatolia, with Tunisia falling somewhere in between. The Egyptian censuses of 1882 and 1897 showed a slight increase in the percentage of the total population living in towns of more than 20,000 inhabitants (from 11.5 to 13.6 percent). In Anatolia, a large number of towns had populations over 20,000 by about 1830. This pattern shows a fairly high urbanization rate for the time, some 17 percent of the total (this percentage includes Edirne, Salonica, and Istanbul in addition to Anatolia); by 1912, it was 22 percent. Tunisia presents probably the least satisfactory data. By rough estimate, during the nineteenth century anywhere from 12 to 20 percent of the population lived in towns over 5,000; the overwhelming majority was sedentary, and the nomadic population was 25 percent at most.

Another significant pattern was that formed by migration, both internal and external, and it profoundly affected the ethnoreligious composition of Ottoman society as a whole. Some parts of Ottoman Afro-Asia, like Egypt and Tunisia, received fewer immigrants than other parts. As the Ottoman frontiers contracted, particularly to the benefit of imperial Russia, large numbers of Muslims from the Balkans, the Crimea, and the Caucasus (estimated at about 4 million) migrated to Anatolia and Greater Syria. There was a similar though numerically much smaller movement of Greeks from the Aegean Islands to the western part of Anatolia (where there was already a substantial Greek population); most were to leave during the 1920s under an agreement between Greece and the new Turkish republic.

From Syria, less spectacular but still significant emigration to Egypt (mentioned earlier) resumed in the 1850s, followed in the 1880s by emigration to the Americas and West Africa, for a total loss of perhaps 200,000 persons before 1914. Other migrants to the new world included Greeks, Armenians, and Jews. This emigration was interrupted by the war of 1914–1918, then resumed again in the 1920s.

Immigration into Ottoman Afro-Asia was represented by Jews from Eastern Europe and Russia going to Palestine and by French and Italian settlers to Tunisia and Egypt. Although numerically these were relatively small groups (in the case of Palestine, some 50,000 Jews) nonetheless they were socially and politically significant. European immigration into Egypt (up to 90,000 foreigners as early as 1864) was perhaps the most spectacular, as Alexandria, the cities around the new Suez Canal, and newer parts of Cairo gained significant proportions of foreigners (25 percent at Alexandria and 28 percent at Port Said by the end of the century).

The implications of the new patterns of settlement were profound. First, the proportion of Muslims in the total Ottoman population increased significantly, with important consequences for political organization and for the remaining non-Muslims of Anatolia and parts of the Fertile Crescent, the latter developing a variety of nationalist ideologies. However, localized shifts in religious-communal proportions were stronger in Anatolia and the Fertile Crescent, and less significant in Egypt and Tunisia.

Second, the growth of cities, particularly of seaports involved in trade with the West, perforce caused the various ethnoreligious groups to mingle more than they had in the past. City life thereafter aggravated existing social and political tensions, perhaps best illustrated by the persistent, if small-scale, sectarian violence in Beirut during the last half of the nineteenth century. Similar tensions arose between Tunisians and Europeans in Tunis. Changed organizational contexts also added to the brew.

ORGANIZATIONAL CONTEXTS, REDISTRIBUTIVE PROCESSES, AND PERSONAL RELATIONSHIPS

The social structure of Ottoman Afro-Asia underwent significant changes in the seventeenth and eighteenth centuries, but indigenous conceptions of state and society did not change appreciably until the reforms of the nineteenth century. Socioeconomic evolution undercut the foundations of the social order and contributed directly to the breakup of the Ottoman state. In Tunisia, similar processes weakened the country and exposed it to European influence and French occupation. As organizational contexts changed, so did redistributive processes and personal relationships. These entities will be treated as part of the same phenomenon.

Islamic precepts of order and community had been articulated by medieval Muslim philosophers in the Turco-Iranian tradition to produce an organic theory of state and society. The Ottomans adopted this theory in their early centuries. The just ruler, the Ottoman sultan, presided over state and society but was separate from them. It was his duty to maintain harmony and balance over the four social estates: the men of the sword, of the pen, of husbandry, and of commerce. In other words, the ruling elite—the military and bureaucracy—was distinct from the producers of wealth, who were to be protected and taxed in the ruler's name. A disorder, a lack of harmony, in any one estate would threaten the health of the whole. Therefore, the just ruler had to restrain the elite's rapacity, protect agriculture and trade, and ensure that members of one estate did not intrude upon another. Change was regarded as threatening to the whole social order. For much of its history the Ottoman state was able to survive by effectively balancing the interests and obligations of the estates and by adapting to the unwelcome changes of the seventeenth and eighteenth centuries.

Despite a tradition of urban and rural revolt, Muslim subjects, whose sentiments were articulated by the religious establishment of ulama, by and large supported the Ottoman state. The state was committed to the preservation of Islamic law, to which the rulers adhered at least outwardly. The tensions implicit in trying to make the world conform to a revealed and accepted truth were to be intensified when the rulers turned to reform in the nineteenth century. Non-Muslim subjects, in conformity with past practice, had been organized along religious-communal lines into the Ottoman *millet* system. By the sixteenth century, the Ottoman state had recognized three non-Muslim communities, the Orthodox Christian, Armenian, and Jewish, whose leadership exercised authority over their respective peoples in most social and personal-status matters. Egyptian Copts and Egyptian Jews, along with Tunisian Jews, were likewise organized.

The millets thus retained considerable autonomy from government interference. The average non-Muslim Ottoman subject dealt with government only if haled into court or in connection with commerce, trade, and taxation, and here only through intermediaries such as market inspectors, judges, and tax-farmers. Some historians have argued that Muslim subjects were also in effect organized as a millet, with the same result. The Muslim structure of communal authority was thus parallel to the non-Muslim ones: the *ilmiye*, the religious-learned hierarchy of scholars and judges, evolved from simple beginnings in the fifteenth century and came to serve essentially the same functions as its non-Muslim counterparts. Again, the intent was organic unity of the population, ironically through its separation along these lines. The divisions represented by the millets cut across ethnic, linguistic, occupational, and status boundaries.

In earlier times, the millet system had worked reasonably well for a diverse population on three continents in a premodern economy. Even the late sixteenth-century crises, the ensuing decentralization, and the gradual shrinking of Ottoman frontiers did not totally undermine it. Religious-communal identification was to prove very resistant to change, as the nineteenth-century reformers were to discover. Its legacy is still tragically evident in contemporary societies in the region. The reformers were dependent to an extraordinary degree on effective government of a modern type, one that attempted to control organizational contexts, redistributive processes, and personal relationships. Society, however, came to resist the state.

The emergence of nationalism among two of the millets, indeed the rise during the nineteenth century of new millets with a distinct self-consciousness, the subordination of much of the economy to European control, the rise of new professions and occupations, educational and ideological change, and diplomatic pressures from Europe—all prevented the process of state-controlled modernization from going forward in the direction the reformers desired.

By the nineteenth century, the old social order was bursting its bounds. Social classes in the modern sense may be discerned, except among the nomadic population. This new stratification cut across the religious-communal millet organization; but it affected Muslims and non-Muslims alike in very different ways even as it pitted state against society. The state, namely the political elites—the sultan, his bureaucratic and military groups, and the heads of the millets—tended to promote the reforms. Some elements, most notably the Janissaries, resisted the early reformers until their massacre in 1826 (in Egypt, Muhammad Ali had suppressed the Mamluks in 1811.

Muslims and Non-Muslims

A broad collection of middling groups betrayed a very sharp distinction between Muslims and non-Muslims primarily because European economic penetration tended to favor the latter. Muslim notables (the a'yan in Syria, Iraq, and Anatolia; the great landlord class in Egypt and Tunisia) derived their wealth primarily from the land and their social and political power from state service. The comparable ranks among Christians and Jews, in contrast, derived their wealth from international trade with Europe and often enjoyed the benefits of extraterritorial rights (favorable customs rates and consular protection) through the Capitulations previously granted to Europeans resident in the Ottoman Empire and extended gradually to non-Muslim Ottoman subjects. A similar pattern favored non-Muslim and foreigners resident in Tunisia and Egypt during the nineteenth century. (In Egypt, a system of mixed courts that was a part of the whole package of the Capitulations persisted until 1949.)

Further down the social scale, still within the middle ranks, Muslim artisans and small retailers, who had previously been significant elements in urban and town life, suffered because their goods generally failed to compete with European imports and because they lacked access to the international trading network and the sources of capital that went with it. Among the non-Muslims in these ranks were owners of small-scale industries (particularly textiles and metals) who were able to sell their goods in rural areas or to coreligionist merchants.

In the lower ranks of the middle group, another distinct pattern emerges. Here, lesser ulama (scholars and teachers), small landlords, and lesser merchants among Muslims tended to identify with the central government until fairly late in the nineteenth century. In contrast, the non-Muslim clergy in this rank was especially active in communal education (financed by wealthy merchants) and rural leadership; this participation was especially significant where national movements were concerned, for example, among the Anatolian Armenians. As for the Maronites of Mount Lebanon, they responded to their clergy, rebelled against their own feudal lords, and fought against their Druze fellow-peasants between 1840 and 1860.

Others especially receptive to nationalist and secularist ideas were members of the modern professions—journalism, law, medicine, teaching. Christians strongly articulated a wide variety of ideologies, from Lebanese nationalism to Arab to Greater Greece; some even supported the Young

Ottoman idea, briefly popular in the 1860s and 1870s, of an overarching Ottoman identity for all Ottoman subjects. Muslims came late to these professions, not much earlier than the turn of the century; and when they did so, they could be just as subversive of the old order, calling for Turkism and Arabism.

Finally, at the bottom of the social scale were Muslim peasants and the humblest laborers and poorest craftsmen, whose numbers appear to have been swelled by the immigration of Muslims from Ottoman territories lost during the nineteenth century. Their non-Muslim, mainly Christian, counterparts tended to be better off, owning their own land, or farming for landlords, or working for relatively low wages in new enterprises in commerce or industry. From this lower rank of society (including both Muslims and non-Muslims) came the first industrial working class in the region. It began to protest actively as early as the 1870s, but more extensively after the turn of the century.

The Rise of the Social Classes

The dissolution of the old order and the rise of identifiable social classes during the nineteenth century may now be examined more closely in organizational contexts, redistributive processes, and personal relationships. From the family to the state, organizational contexts were affected by change in different ways, with the result that many observers have spoken of social disintegration as the main pattern of the period under review here. That characterization, however, simply reaffirms an overall picture of rapid change in the social order as a whole. It does not mean that change was as rapid or even as far-reaching in some contexts as in others. For example, it would seem that extended kinship ties remained very much in evidence, weathering the storms of urbanization and rural unrest.

The extended family, whether urban or rural, continued at least in theory to be one of the fundamental units of society. In particular among the nomadic populations, kinship remained supreme and was reinforced by nomadic traditions of political authority that largely escaped governmental control. Perhaps the best example of this phenomenon may be found in Iraq, where Ottoman control did not go much beyond the towns and cities into the rural hinterland, the swamps of the south, or the mountains to the north and east, dominated by Kurds and Turkmans. Until well into the British mandate, the tribal shaykhs kept up strong resistance to central authority. To a somewhat lesser degree, the same phenomenon existed in Syria and the southern part of Tunisia; in the latter region, tribal resistance to Tunisian reformers exploded in a revolt in 1864 that spread to the settled areas.

As in many other parts of the world, the status of women changed very slowly. Small numbers of women of the urban literate elite among Muslims in Egypt, Greater Syria, and Anatolia, and somewhat more broadly among Christians and Jews, began to acquire an education and to question their customary roles. A recent, pioneering study found that between 1800 and 1914, nonelite Egyptian women struggled to preserve their rights of access to property under Islamic law. Peasant women lost ground when rural handicrafts declined; urban women held their own as textile producers or petty traders. Social attitudes, particularly those of the family—the fundamental unit of production—resisted change in women's status. Although few actual changes in women's status occurred, consciousness of their situation became a part of social thought, particularly after the turn of the century, when an Egyptian journalist, Qasim Amin, published a sensational call for women's liberation even as he secluded his own wife from public view. Some women's groups—for example, the silk spinners of Mount Lebanon—were already participating in the nonagricultural work force.

If work was one context in which there was a slight change for women in some parts of Ottoman Afro-Asia, the changes were far greater for many men. The integration of the region into the capitalist world economy, particularly after the 1838 Anglo-Ottoman Commercial Convention, reduced barriers to international trade and put severe pressure on traditional handicrafts. The old handicrafts and trades did not die all at once; some prospered with new tools and techniques (particularly the production of raw silk in Bursa and Mount Lebanon), while new types of work made their appearance. An early twentieth-century dictionary of Damascene trades and crafts includes predictable entries for greengrocers and shoemakers, but reflects the changed world of work in the entry *kamyunji* (wagoneer or trucker, from the French *camion*).

A recent study of Anatolia has shown that smugglers tried to resist the French-controlled tobacco monopoly; that coal miners working for another French monopoly resisted full-time work by falling back on their farm production and, particularly after the 1908 revolution, by going on strike; that port workers in Istanbul continued to resist the Istanbul Quay Company by keeping their guilds active; and that Anatolian railway workers were able to win important concessions during and after the 1908 revolution.

In Egypt, Muhammad Ali had created state monopolies and the nucleus of an industrial base before his protectionist policies were reversed after his retreat from Syria in 1839 and 1840. Thereafter, Egyptian manufactures were at a competitive disadvantage and virtually disappeared as European imports increased dramatically.

Low per capita income, shortage of capital, a taste and demand for foreign goods, and a lack of skilled management (which had to be imported) delayed significant industrialization until after the First World War. Unrest in the world of work—both in rural areas, where Ottoman, Egyptian, and Tunisian agriculture were heavily commercialized, and in towns—had wide sociopolitical consequences. A recent study has suggested that the 1860 massacres of Christians and Jews in Damascus, long believed to be a manifestation of primarily religious hatreds, left virtually untouched the poorer non-Muslim parts of suburban Maydan, populated by craftsmen and tradesmen, but targeted inner-city quarters with conspicuous wealth gained through links to the European economy.

Sufism

If resistance was often the hallmark of workers, the same may be said with respect to some parts of another organizational context, the Muslim Sufi orders. These organizations, of immense variety and of crucial importance to the daily life and spiritual nurture of the faithful, had broad appeal but differing rituals, disciplines, and social outlooks. Within the same order, such as the Naqshbandiyya, there could be enormous variation. The Circassian leader Shamil found the order a useful means for organizing his ultimately futile resistance to imperial Russia. The Kurd Mawlana Khalid led the order in Syria during the 1820s and took an activist stance against economic and political injustice; other leaders and members concentrated on the silent ritual and self-discipline that had marked the order from its earliest beginnings.

By the First World War, however, Sufism had serious rivals as an agent of protest. On the one hand, some famous Muslim leaders, such as the Syrian Rashid Rida (d. 1936), became Sufis in their youth, only to be repulsed by what they saw as obscurantism and passivity; instead, they turned to journalism and politics to infuse Islam with social thought and action. On the other hand, a long tradition of association between certain Sufi orders and professions (such as crafts and the military) broke down under economic and political pressures. The spectacular massacre of the Janissaries, devotees of the Bektashi order, by Sultan Mahmud II in 1826, virtually brought that order to an end as a vital organizational context.

Yet it would be wrong to say that the period between 1800 and 1914 brought an end to Sufism; many orders survive to this day. But their wider social import has been much reduced by other avenues of social action, most notably education and the modern professions. A most poignant example of this change may be noted in the memoirs of the Egyptian scholar Ahmad Amin (d.1954), who remarks that one of his school teachers at the beginning of the century, though a Naqshbandi Sufi, was a person who detested superstitions and was open-minded.

Town and Province

Two relatively new organizational contexts, both products of the Tanzimat reforms, gave further evidence of the new possibilities for mobility, conflict, and social action. One of the earliest municipal governments in the region, the municipal council of Tunis (founded in 1858), involved the city's bourgeois elite (the *baladis*) in providing services such as sanitation, traffic control, and police protection.

The origins of municipal government in both Alexandria and the European quarters of Istanbul may be dated to the 1860s, at the instigation of European consuls who tried to keep these new entities under their influence. By 1871, a new Ottoman vilayet law outlined the establishment and functions of provincial councils, the second new context. Ottoman law created municipal councils as well for other parts of the empire, making provision for budgets and sources of revenue; in Egypt, a long tradition of centralization delayed the introduction of formal municipalities: Alexandria in 1890, Cairo not until the 1930s.

The result in Alexandria was that, because of consular interference, Europeans dominated the municipal council and engendered much Egyptian resentment. In other Ottoman lands, in contrast, the municipal councils allowed members of new, upstart families to seek political and social power at the expense of established families. The same development may be discerned in the Ottoman provincial councils, which had been launched with the 1839 decree marking the start of the Tanzimat and which were reorganized by the 1871 law. The councils were designed initially to build a popular consensus in support of the Sultan's government. Rather than a response to popular demand, the institution of councils was a gift from the sovereign.

The most striking of the consequences of this reform may be seen in the establishment in 1845 of two twelve-member councils in the two parts of Mount Lebanon; until 1842, this area had been a single autonomous entity in the Ottoman Empire. Members of the councils were named and salaried for life by the government and were expected to assist in administration and taxation. Of interest here in this examination of organizational contexts is that none of the twenty-four men who served in these short-lived institutions was from the traditional Lebanese "feudal" hierarchy. Several were landowners of lesser rank, others were ulama or clergymen.

Varying interpretations are offered as to who emerged as the beneficiaries: the lords (who continued to have politico-military authority in their regions) or members of lesser social groups who now began to have roles in government. The result of the attempt to apply the Tanzimat to Mount Lebanon was the rise of sectarianism in politics, indeed its taking center-stage, with tragic results in the 1860 massacres and beyond. Once again, an organizational context became a means for mobility for new actors and the occasion of conflict and dissension, all under the auspices of reform.

The State

The final organizational context to be considered here is the state. Its expanded and ambitious role during the nineteenth century and beyond brought it into conflict with much of the population. Reform from the top not only exacerbated differences among the religious-communal groups, it tore the whole fabric of social interdependence by its interference in what had been a relatively autonomous system of social relationships. Most studies overemphasize the religious dimension, either as a dyad of Islam and modernity, or Muslims and non-Muslims.

In truth, changed socioeconomic conditions certainly exacerbated prejudices and encouraged ideologies along these lines. But the state's active pursuit of reform in the service of survival pitted it against both the established groups, still organized along premodern socioeconomic lines (the higher clergy, ulama, large landowners, higher military), and the newer groups, which resented interference in pursuit of their own destiny (the non-Muslim laity, merchants tied to Europe, Westernizing intellectuals and nationalists).

By the early 1870s, the empire's rulers tried to introduce a new organizational context—Ottoman citizenship—which was to imbue individuals with a broadly defined patriotism. Based on a perceived analogy between the Muslim notion of community—the *umma*—and European-style love of country, Ottomanism tried to develop a new common identity for all subjects. The 1876 constitution, the short-lived parliament of 1877, and the emergence of Sultan Abdul Hamid's despotism marked the rapid failure of this experiment.

Faced with burgeoning nationalist movements and shrinking frontiers, the sultan exercised the new centralizing power of the reformers for the purpose of suppressing threats to the Ottoman idea. His weapons were new technologies of power and control—the telegraph, secret police, and censorship—and the ideology of Pan-Islamism and the revived caliphate. The latter was as much a response to the reality that the empire's population was increasingly Muslim (because of the loss of European territory with Christian inhabitants and the immigration of Muslim refugees) as to resistance by nationalist movements and continued European pressure.

With the overthrow of Abdul Hamid in 1909, preceded by the restoration of the Constitution in 1908, a fresh attempt was made at a pluralistic Ottomanism; it failed when the Young Turks took power. Their policies of repression and their increased reliance on the ideology of Turkism only served to alienate the Arab Muslims who had identified with Pan-Islamism. By 1914, a strong Ottoman state could not count on the loyalty of a large part of its population. The First World War hastened its disintegration.

Compared to the relatively fast pace of change in the fortunes of the state and of some of the other organizational contexts, redistributive processes were transformed more slowly. International trade, the land regime, taxation, and social mobility were the most important of these processes. The 1838 Anglo-Ottoman Commercial Convention, which lowered barriers to the importation of foreign goods and their distribution within the empire, strengthened trends already long underway. Similar agreements at approximately the same time affected Egypt and Tunisia.

The changing balance of international trade accelerated the decline of urban crafts, which had formed the economic base of the Muslim middling ranks. It further advantaged those Ottoman subjects, overwhelmingly non-Muslim, who had commercial and cultural ties to Europe and thus had become part of a capitalist economy. And it encouraged the export of agricultural products and raw materials to the detriment of industrialization. By 1914, the overwhelming part of the region's foreign trade was in foreign hands. Moreover, European debt commissioners had been in place since the 1870s to ensure that fiscal policies in Tunisia,

Egypt, and the Ottoman central lands addressed the repayment of foreign loans.

The reorganization of the land regime, which was intended in part to undercut the power of the great landlords, substituted modern notions of private property for the customary conception of land—particularly state lands—as belonging to the sultan and being leased for usufruct. The preponderant part of land had been state land; urban freehold (*milk*) and mortmain charitable endowments (*waqf, habous*) had been significant means of capital formation and preservation for only a small portion of the population during the premodern period. Land reform also sought to remove the tax-farmer as intermediary between state and peasant.

The increasing value of agricultural products encouraged the expansion of land brought under cultivation (although apparently not in most of Syria, which was affected by nomadic pressures and soil problems well into this century) and stimulated the concentration of land ownership in the hands of landlords (some of whom had been tax-farmers, others newcomers to the elite). This produced an increased tax and rent burden amounting to anywhere from one-third to two-thirds of gross product on those peasants who still farmed small plots.

The 1858 Ottoman land law and similar measures taken in Egypt and Tunisia resulted in new attempts to devise modern land registration and taxation. But it resulted in legal disputes over title and further strengthened the power of absentee landlords. Peasants lost many of their customary rights under this system, which encouraged cash crops for export and yielded huge tax revenues for the government. Another landmark change in taxation was the ending of the poll tax on non-Muslims and the introduction of new taxes and fees that caused great fear and resentment.

Social mobility was most clearly evident in the enhanced wealth and standing of the non-Muslim population, which benefited from its ties to Europe, its early start in education, and its modern methods of work, finance, and marketing. This growing differentiation in the economic sphere between Muslims and non-Muslims exacerbated religious-communal tensions and encouraged the growth of nationalism.

These many changes in the patterns of social interdependence cut across the whole social scale, both among classes and millets. Communal and ethnic-national ties were increasingly stressed as economic and political relationships changed. Whereas individualism is thought to be an essential component of the modern social order, society in Ottoman Afro-Asia continued to cling to strong kinship and communal ties. Ironically, it was the state that insisted on the legal and social equality of individuals under the banner of Ottomanism. Society ignored that insistence. Indeed, the one relationship that broke down most completely was that between state and subject. The Ottoman successor states have had to live with their predecessor's failure.

INTERNATIONAL COMPARISONS

The complex set of forces of social interdependence in Ottoman Afro-Asia between 1800 and 1914 laid the groundwork for the very rapid changes in that region thereafter. Geographically and culturally so close to the West, the region did not achieve the levels of wealth and organization of Japan and Russia. The conclusion here seeks not to explain the absence of those levels as much as to point to some important features of Ottoman Afro-Asian social interdependence. First is the relatively slow demographic growth before 1800, despite the relatively high proportion of urban dwellers. Second, the social order, with its complex organizational contexts of family, millet, and occupations, remained self-contained even as it was challenged by the changes arising after 1800. That self-containment facilitated the process of European penetration, undermined defensive modernization by the state, and created severe social and religious-communal conflicts. Third, the state formation, which had survived the relative decline (relative to the West) of the seventeenth and eighteenth centuries, was not able to exercise control over society when it most needed to do so; and its efforts at reform, based on an accurate assessment of what was needed, had unexpected and undesired results, due to internal resistance and external pressures.

The complexities and ambiguities of social interdependence in Ottoman Afro-Asia present a picture of half-achieved reformers' dreams, new problems and dislocations for ordinary subjects, the constant threat of foreign intervention (or, as in Tunisia and Egypt, the reality of occupation), and the prospect of political and social disintegration, realized in the central Ottoman lands after World War I. A partly reformed and greatly strengthened state formation, and a disturbed and realigned social order, became the victims of war and of the dramatic changes the postwar world was to bring.

CHAPTER SEVEN

Knowledge and Education

A SURVEY OF the state of knowledge and education in the Ottoman world at the opening of the nineteenth century discloses a few factors with positive connotations for future growth, but with many obstacles. On the positive side, there had been notable signs of intellectual change among the Ottoman elites of the eighteenth century. Among these were the decline of Persian influence in literature, the launching of a translation program (which included some Western books), the founding of an Ottoman printing press (in operation from 1727 to 1742), the founding in 1734 of a military engineering school, revival of the military education effort in 1773, and the attempts of Selim III, prior to his accession (1789), to gain French assistance for his intended reforms. Another positive factor was the intellectual revival going on among eighteenth-century Islamic religious scholars.

Unfortunately, the obstacles to cultural reinvigoration outweighed the positive factors. At the end of the eighteenth century, the most basic problem was the insularity of the normal Islamic worldview. In principle, nothing inhibited borrowing from non-Muslims in matters that did not contradict Islamic values. The great Islamic scientific tradition began with the ninth-century Arabic translation movement, and the Ottomans had once been keen borrowers in such field as military technology. Yet, the possibility of keeping up with the West by borrowing on the customary scale had declined sharply by the eighteenth century. The Christian subjects of the Ottomans were, meanwhile, quicker to learn from the West. One result was the opening of a cultural gap, and thereby the worsening of intercommunal tensions, as the age of nationalism began.

In addition, the elitism of the Ottoman imperial culture, and of the Islamic literary cultures in general, proved increasingly costly in the nineteenth century. Ottoman intellectuals who did take an interest in new ideas from the West refrained from trying to propagate their ideas widely. The tardy introduction of printing, and conventional ideas about literary language, hindered their doing so in any case. In both Arabic and Turkish, learned writers preferred ornate styles that were not readily understood by the masses. The problem was especially acute in Ottoman Turkish.

Ottoman, especially at its "higher" stylistic levels, was an artificial language, with Arabic and Persian combined in a basically Turkish syntactical framework. It was a poor means for communicating with a large audience. There was a folk literature in simpler language, but its range of subjects was limited. In combination with the empire's long-term economic decline, cultural elitism produced its most serious effect: restricted literacy. The overall literacy rate for the Ottoman Empire in 1800 probably did not exceed 5 percent in any part of the Ottoman Empire, and the overall rate may well have been as low as 1 percent.

THE ISLAMIC WORLD OF KNOWLEDGE

Significant problems troubled all four realms of knowledge traditionally combined to form the learned culture of Islam: religious studies (*'ilm*), mysticism (*tasawwuf*), worldly belles-lettres (*adab*), and philosophy (*falsafah*, which included science and mathematics). At the medreses (higher schools of religious studies), for example, the curriculum had reached the point where, as at al-Azhar in Cairo, students spent their time on commentaries, essentially to the exclusion of the seminal works of Islamic religious thought.

The Istanbul government maintained an elaborate ranking scheme, at least for the upper, "official" ulama. And there was a system of examinations for appointment to a medrese teaching position. The system of ranks and examinations had been undermined, however, by moral and intellectual laxity. Nepotism had reached the point where high-ranking Istanbul ulama secured examination diplomas for sons still in the cradle; and the entire examination system had become a mockery.

Mysticism, too, had been long dominated by what has been called the "tangled magic garden" mentality of the sufi miracle-workers and ecstatics. This outlook was at odds, in principle, with the formal rationality of the religio-legal studies, and even with the shariah-mindedness of strict sufis like the Naqshbandis. Still, occultist sufism influenced the whole Ottoman world of knowledge. Not only the mystic's spiritual wisdom, but the crafts in the bazaar, even the government scribe's professional skills, tended to be regarded as secrets acquired, not by a rationally ordered teaching program, but by prolonged association with an adept. The preference for obscure literary styles expresses the same taste for the esoteric.

The belletristic *adab* culture, in turn, was to be of supreme importance in the state-building efforts of nineteenth-century reformers. While the greatest exponents of this culture had historically been writers, working under the patronage of rulers, the less talented *adibs* had generally sought employment as scribes in government offices. Including a range of worldly forms of expression, from love poetry to history, geography, and official epistolography, adab culture had practical applications in statecraft. When changing conditions forced Islamic governments to deal more extensively with the West, the scribal adibs took over this function. As they did so, they began to add new dimensions to their worldy learning, becoming the vanguard of cultural change.

Indeed, adab culture was destined for explosive growth in the nineteenth century, and this fact was to have serious consequences. The adibs gained enormous influence, as they turned from scribes into new-model civil officials and literary innovators. As this happened, however, the adib's hstoric emphasis on stylistic proficiency assumed a new form. An exaggerated esteem of linguistic skills still prevailed, with the difference that the emphasis was no longer on the classical languages of the Islamic world, but on French. Moreover, the introduction, chiefly via adab culture, of a vast body of Western ideas created a sense of cultural dualism, which became perhaps the greatest source of conflict in the cultural life of late Ottoman Muslims.

As for the philosophical-scientific tradition, it had essentially lost its vitalityand continuity. A difficult transition would ensue, as scholars from the Islamic world attempted to assimilate the rapidly burgeoning scientific and technical knowledge of the modern West.

TRADITIONAL EDUCATIONAL INSTITUTIONS

The traditional educational institutions fall into three categories. Two were under control of the ulama. The Quranic elementary schools (*sibyan mektepleri* in Turkish; *kuttab* in Arabic) and the higher religious schools, the medreses (*madrasah* in Arabic). The third embraced a variety of facilities, none of them schools, but all supporting intellectual life in some way: libraries, meeting halls of dervish orders with important literary or musical traditions, courts and government offices, and homes of prominent intellectuals. These were places for meeting, discussion, and, in some cases, teaching or research.

These institutions, together with the pious foundations that supported many of them, represented a considerable investment in learning. Yet, there were problems with all of them. Elementary schools were often poorly staffed. Disciplinary and instructional methods were not well tailored for children. Curricula, supposedly including elements of writing and arithmetic, normally focused almost entirely on memorization of the Quran, without prior instruction in the Arabic language. Even in the Arab world, this method had been under criticism since the Middle Ages. For children whose native language was not Arabic, the method could be disastrous. Those who received only a primary education might well face life as functional illiterates. For all, the main mental habit formed at the kuttab was learning by rote.

As for the medreses, with nothing but the Quranic elementary schools below them, it is obvious that most were not really institutions of higher learning. At the highest levels, while the medreses of the nineteenth century continued to produce important scholars, those who contributed most to Islamic religious thought had to go beyond the bounds of medrese scholarship to launch the Islamic reformist movement. Islamic reformism was, in any case, more associated with the Arab, than the Turkish, parts of the empire. In Istanbul, the political center, reformist energies went more toward revitalization of the state.

The libraries, dervish meeting halls, government office, and so forth had historically played a great role in perpetuating branches of learning not fostered in the medreses, such as the adab culture. While they continued to serve these purposes in the nineteenth century, and gave rise to some of the learned societies of that period, these old facilities were not well organized for efficient use in a time of growing needs. Among the Ottoman elites, for example, the gradual realization that apprenticeship was an inefficient way to train scribes became a primary motive for the founding of the first secular civil schools.

Reform of the traditional schools implied a confrontation with their teachers, the ulama. In Istanbul and the Turkish-speaking areas, however, no frontal attack on religious schools occurred for a long time. There, the idea of reforming the elementary Quranic schools was officially broached during the 1840s. Yet until the Young Turk Period, Ottoman statesmen, otherwise so willing to redirect policy in a secularlizing direction, never felt strong enough to eliminate the vested interest of the ulama in education. The reformers did gradually divert control of the pious foundations used to support the religious schools to a newly founded Ministry of Pious Foundations. They also created secular schools at supposedly higher curricular levels. But only gradually did the Ottoman government introduce its authority into primary education. There was no general measure on the Quranic elementary schools until the education law of 1869, which required the religious communities of each locality to found and finance primary schools, if such were not already in existence. By the last decades of the nineteenth century, Ottoman Muslims, acting singly or in small associations, had also begun to found private primary schools. It was in these that real reform of primary education for Muslims began. Not until 1916 did the government shift responsibility for elementary education to the Ministry of Education.

Meanwhile, Ottoman reformers took little interest in the medreses. In Istanbul, except for scattered efforts, medrese reform scarcely occurred before 1908.

In Arab lands, the development of religious schools was ultimately rather different from that of their Turkish counterparts. In the Egypt of Muhammad Ali, an exceptional phase of government interference occurred. The ulama, influential with the populace but lacking the official standing of their Istanbul colleagues, were less able to resist the will of their governor. Through 1840, Egypt witnessed a more effective assault on the position of the ulama than Ottoman Istanbul ever saw. Muhammad Ali confiscated all landed property, including that of the foundations that supported al-Azhar and the other mosques and religious schools. Thereafter, religious schools were supposed to depend on payments from the state. These were inadequate; the schools fared so badly that Muhammad Ali was forced to found new kuttabs in the 1830s. Al-Azhar was then on the verge of ruin.

After the death of Muhammad Ali, historic patterns reasserted themselves, although there were, in time, significant reforms. The foundation of Quranic schools and pious foundations resumed; and, by 1875, there were almost 5,000 kuttabs in Egypt, with 120,000 students. An important attempt at systematization occurred with the Egyptian law of 1867 on education. The law attempted to improve Quranic schools by such means as adding arithmetic to the curriculum and by requiring parents to contribute, under certain circumstances, to the schools.

In addition, an improved form of "primary" school was to be founded in the provincial capitals with even broader curricula, including foreign languages, and with special support from the Department of Pious Foundations. The 1870s brought the first attempts to found government schools for girls and a teacher training college, the *Dar al-'Ulum*. After 1882, the British tried to bring the village kuttabs under government control, by providing grants-in-aid in return for government inspection and the meeting of minimum standards. By 1906, there were almost 4,500 schools, with 156,000 students, under such control; normal schools had been set up for both men and women teachers. Most elementary schools remained outside the system, however, and the real effect on educational standards was limited.

Steps taken beginning in the 1870s regularized the curriculum at al-Azhar and provided a system of examinations. Later measures sought to provide a more truly national system of religious education, with a hierarchy from the modest provincial kuttab to al-Azhar at the top.

In Tunisia, almost the only educational institutions for most of the nineteenth century were the kuttabs, of which there were about 1,100, teaching roughly 17,000 students as of the beginning of the French protectorate (1881), and the Zaytunah mosque-university, with a prestige comparable to that of al-Azhar. Under the protectorate, the French avoided interfering with the kuttabs or Zaytunah. Demands for reform and modernization of Zaytunah did appear, however, among a group of Tunisians who formed a learned society called the Khalduniyyah in 1896, the very year that modern subjects were introduced into the curriculum of al-Azhar. This group, most of whom later joined the Young Tunisia movement, had the same goal for the Zaytunah. Later, in 1907, a leading member of the reformist Young Tunisian movement founded the first modern Quran school intended to combine French instructional method with an emphasis on Arabic and Islamic subjects. These modern Quran schools had virtually replaced the old kuttab by the end of the protectorate period.

By the eve of World War I, efforts at reforming traditional education had been made everywhere. The development of new types of education had breached the former near-monopoly of the religious institutions; yet, it was a rare individual—even among such modernists as Saʿd Zaghlul or Ziya Gökalp, leaders of nationalist thought and action among Egyptians and Turks, respectively—whose education did not include a substantial traditional component. Traditional institutions fared worst at the hands of the Istanbul government, thanks to the statist-secularist drift of Ottoman reform. In the Arab world, in contrast, madrasah reform began earlier and produced greater results, as the reforms of al-Azhar and Zaytunah attest.

GOVERNMENT SCHOOLS

The Ottoman government proceeded to develop new schools, usually by founding, first, military and, then, civil institutions. Both types of schools were intended to form new elites to serve reforming rulers.

The new types of schools began in Istanbul. The military engineering school, opened in 1734, proved short-lived but was later revived on a modest scale. The real beginning of modern military education followed, under the impact of the Ottoman-Russian wars of the late eighteenth century, with the opening of a Naval Engineering Academy (1773) and an Army Engineering Academy (1793). The abolition of the Janissaries in 1826 led to other efforts in military education, particularly the founding of medical schools (1826), intended mainly to serve the new troops, and the Military Academy (1834), which still exists.

In the 1830s, Sultan Mahmud II began to send military student missions to Europe. From 1857 to 1874, there was an Ottoman School in Paris, primarily for military students. He also founded special military preparatory schools. With the extension of the higher government schools into the provinces under Abdul Hamid II (1876–1909), the number of military academies grew to six, spread from Baghdad to Monastir. Ultimately, there were specialized military schools for everything from musicians to general staff officers.

The first important institution for training civil officials was the Translation Office of the Sublime Porte, founded in 1821 to replace the old Greek dragomanate and, incidentally, to train translators. The foundation of the first secular civil schools occurred during the years from 1838 to 1839 with the opening of two small schools intended to train boys from the Quranic elementary schools for service in government offices, so that the old practice of scribal apprenticeship could be abandoned. Gradually, more institutions of this type emerged. Among these was the School of Civil Administration (*Mülkiye Mektebi*, 1859); the school grew in size and importance after 1876 and is the ancestor of the present Faculty of Political Science at Ankara. The most important mid-century innovation in civil-elite education was the Galatasaray Lycée, opened with French help in 1868. This and, after 1876, the School of Civil Administration did most to shape the civil elite of the late empire.

All the civil and military schools were founded as higher schools. Since there were no schools offering suitable preparation, however, these schools had to start with preparatory instruction. The earliest of the new schools never got beyond that. A gradual curricular upgrading, together with the creation of schools of genuinely higher level, became possible only as real preparatory institutions emerged. This happened when the government began to extend its new schools into a generalized system.

Beginnings of an Ottoman School System

The first step toward this generalization occurred in 1845, with the formation of a council that developed what looked like a comprehensive educational plan. This called for a three-tiered system: the Quranic elementary schools, which were to be reformed; an intermediate level known as the *rüşdiye*; and a university (*darülfünun*). In the years immediately following adoption of the plan, only the rüşdiye schools became a reality, and they soon settled into being nothing more than upper elementary schools. The first rüşdiyes for girls were opened in 1858. Special military rüşdiyes began to be founded to train boys for the higher military schools in 1875. A report of the early 1880s indicates roughly 120 rüşdiyes in the provinces and 20 in Istanbul. At the end of World War I, Istanbul had almost 90 such schools, with over 10,000 students. Despite their small numbers and limited curricula, the rüşdiyes were the most important of the modern schools in that most educated Ottomans never went beyond them.

The next important effort was the Ottoman education law of 1869. This provided for a five-tiered hierarchy, with a Quranic elementary school in every village or quarter; an upper elementary (rüşdiye) in every town of five hundred households; a middle school (*idadi*) in every town of a thousand households; a lycée (*sultaniye*) in every provincial capital; and a category of higher schools (*mekatib-i aliye*), consisting of teachers' colleges for men and women, the other higher specialized schools, and, once again, a university.

Implementation of the educational plan was slow, but perceptible. Higher-level schools began to come into existence in greater numbers, and schools of all types began to extend into the provinces to a much greater degree than in the past. Under the law, rüşdiye schools continued to be developed. Idadi schools languished until the 1880s, when Grand Vezir Said Paşa hit on the expedient of a supplement to the tithe tax on agricultural produce to be earmarked for these schools. By 1890, the number of idadis had grown to 34, some of them boarding schools. As late as 1908, there were only two Ottoman lycées, both in Istanbul. After the revolution of 1908, however, the idadis of some provincial capitals were expanded into lycées. The first idadi for girls also opened after the revolution and shortly expanded into a girls' lycée. A source of 1918 mentions eleven Ottoman lycées in all. A training college for male rüşdiye teachers opened in 1848; one for women opened in 1870. Several attempts to open a university produced no lasting success until the inauguration, on a very small scale, of Istanbul University in 1900.

Overall measures of the growth of the Ottoman government school system are difficult to come by. In geographical Syria and Iraq, there were in the early twentieth century perhaps 570 Ottoman government schools, with 28,400 pupils in the elementary and 2,100 in secondary and higher grades; many from these had also gone on to Istanbul, to study at the school of civil administration or the military academy. What had been accomplished was modest in relation to need. Yet, the impact was great, partly in the ironic sense that Ottoman insistence on Turkish as the language of instruction—an insistence attributable at first to lack of qualified instructors, but later to policy—played a primary role in alienating the Arabs from the Istanbul government. Egypt, and to a degree Tunisia, also developed analogous institutions. During the career of Muhammad Ali it was often Egypt that pioneered the new developments.

Educational Reform in Egypt (before 1882)

Muhammad Ali intended his educational reforms, like essentially all his reforms, to support his military ambitions. His efforts to form new elites began accordingly with the dispatch of student missions to Europe. The first mission went to Italy in 1809 to study military science and related subjects. More than twenty years would pass before the Ottoman government sent such a mission; Muhammad Ali himself did not send a large student mission until 1826, and then to France. For a time in the 1840s, there was even an Egyptian military school in Paris. In this, too, Egypt preceded the Istanbul government.

Muhammad Ali had also begun in 1816 to open schools in Cairo to train military and administrative personnel. As his efforts to create a modern army progressed, the military schools were upgraded, and others were created. Thus emerged the Military Academy (*Madrasah al-Jihadiyyah*, 1825) and the General Staff College (*Madrasat Arkan al-Harb*). A medical school was established in 1827. In this case, the Ottomans had acted a year earlier. As in Istanbul, a variety of specialized schools followed, to train pharmacists, cavalry officers, naval officers, military engineers, and so on. A commission to supervise the military schools was first formed in 1826. In 1837, a Board of Schools (*Diwan al-Madaris*) was formed to supervise schools. Throughout these educational endeavors, Muhammad Ali made heavy use of foreigners, especially Frenchmen.

As in Istanbul, Muhammad Ali began to found schools for civil officials to improve the quality of administration and tighten his control. The first of these was the School of Civil Administration (*Darskhanah al-Mulkiyyah*, 1829). In 1836, a School of Languages (*Madrasat al-Alsun*) was formed. This survived through a number of reorganizations, becoming the School of Languages and Accountancy in 1841, the School of Languages, Administration, and Accountancy in 1868, and the School of Law and Administration in 1875. The Egyptian schools of civil administration and languages are clearly counterparts to the translation office formed in Istanbul in 1821, and to the civil schools that began to be created there in 1838.

Whereas the more highly institutionalized governmental system of the imperial center displayed greater long-term continuity in education and other fields, Egypt's educational development faltered after Muhammad Ali's last years. His educational experiments flourished, together with his military fortunes, through the 1830s. But after Europe frustrated his expansionist ambitions in Syria and forced the reduction of the Egyptian army, schools began to close. By the time of his death in 1849, only fifteen of the new schools were left in Egypt.

Under Muhammad Ali's successors, down to 1882, policy shifts continued. Under Abbas (1849–54), the schools were reduced in number even more. Educational missions to Europe were scaled back drastically, and those sent no longer went only to France. Said (1854–63) followed no consistent policy. Where his reign was most decisive for Egyptian education was in his permissive, laissez-faire attitude toward the development of foreign schools, and foreign interests in general. Under Ismail (1863–1879), the higher schools of Muhammad Ali were revived. Priority went to military, then to civil, schools. It was under Ismail, for example, that what had begun as the School of Languages reemerged as the School of Law and Administration. Ismail also reestablished the Board of Schools (*Diwan al-Madaris*). Yet, the benefits were again short-lived. Ismail's fiscal improvidence, and the collapse of the cotton boom after the end of the American Civil War led to the consolidation (or suppression) of some of the higher schools during his later years. The trend continued in the early years of Tawfiq (1879–92), and after the British occupation (1882).

Changes in Egypt Under the British Occupation

The establishment of British control over Egypt had important implications for Egyptian education at all levels. By the early 1890s, the only higher schools that remained were those for teachers, military, and police, and the schools of law, medicine, and engineering. British policy limited the development of Egyptian education in a way without counterpart earlier in the century. Government schools were intended to produce lower-level governmental employees. As a means of limiting enrollments in the government schools to what the administrative system could absorb, the British introduced tuition charges, which had never existed before in those schools.

Improvements in the higher Egyptian schools before World War I were few, but there were efforts to reform the schools of medicine and law. A university was founded in 1908 on an extremely small scale—with only ten courses and few students. This was done by private subscription and in response to pressure from Egyptian nationalists and intellectuals. Student missions to Europe had also resumed by then, with most of those sent at government expense now studying subjects in the humanities. Wealthy families sent sons to Europe at their own expense.

What had the nineteenth century, with all these shifts of leadership and policy, produced in the way of a general educational system for Egyptians? Initially, the new schools of the Cairo government, like those in Istanbul, were almost all supposed to be higher schools. Government schools therefore had to rely on the traditional schools for preparatory instruction and manpower. Having greatly weakened these schools through his depredations on the pious foundations, Muhammad Ali found himself forced to found Quranic elementary schools in his later years. These were supposed to be different from the kuttabs, but, largely for want of good teachers, were not. Muhammad Ali also forced the traditional institutions to serve his goals in a more general sense. Many former students, even those from al-Azhar, were drawn in spite of themselves into the pasha's translating and publishing ventures, into his provincial schools as teachers, and into his technical schools as students, especially of medicine.

Since Muhammad Ali's primary schools had not assumed a form clearly differentiated from the old Quranic elementary schools, and since governmental initiatives in education faltered under his immediate successors (to the extent that a general system of government schools emerged), they continued to be based on the Quranic elementary schools. The most important attempt at general systematization, the education law of 1867, was essentially an effort to upgrade Quranic elementary schools and to transform those in provincial capitals into improved primary schools.

Given the extremely limited development of Egyptian public education, even the narrow educational goals of the British enhanced the existing system. In addition to the foregoing changes in religious and higher government schools, the British increased the total number of government schools. The schools of this period continued to be buffeted by major disputes, e.g., over British attempts to promote study of English at the expense of Arabic, or over the quality and motivation of the British personnel who began to appear at all levels of the educational system. Still, the number of students in government primary schools rose from roughly 5,800 in 1890 to 8,600 in 1910, whereas those in secondary schools underwent a proportionately greater increase, from about 700 to 2,200 over the same period.

Tunisia

In Tunisia, too, the history of modern education began with the founding of a new school for the military elite. The palace of the bey at Bardo had long included a primary school and a madrasah for the training of Mamluks—slaves of the bey destined to occupy high military and administrative positions. In 1840, as part of his efforts at military reform, Ahmad Bey created a new Bardo military academy. This was followed in 1875 with the founding of Sadiqi College, which became the main training center for the governing elite and still exists. Sadiqi College became the prototype of the Franco-Arab schools created later during the period of the French Protectorate.

The French initially intended to make only limited changes in educational institutions. But the arrival of European settlers in large numbers forced a change. The *Direction de l'Instruction publique* soon found itself in charge of a full set of French primary and secondary schools, with all instruction in French. Classes were open in principle to all, although the attendance of Tunisian Muslims remained disproportionately low, almost nonexistent in the case of females, even at the primary level.

By the turn of the century, the prejudice of the *colons*, and the desire of the Muslim population for a greater degree of instruction in Arabic, had also led to the creation of a system of Franco-Arab schools, in which one-third of the instruction was to be in Arabic. Schools of both types were good, approaching metropolitan French standards; the government schools of French Tunisia were probably better than the modern schools of either Egypt or the Ottoman government. The total number of Tunisians who received this education was, however, small—only 2,800 Muslims in either the French or Franco-Arab schools in 1904, as against 22,000 in the kuttabs—and the instruction in Arabic language and Islamic culture was weak. What was perhaps most remarkable about Tunisian education was how quickly and thoroughly French pedagogy and curricula spread, and how responsive Tunisians, even future nationalist leaders, were to them.

Similarities in Educational Systems

In general, the educational initiatives of the Ottoman, Egyptian, and Tunisian governments reveal a common sequence in which elite schools emerged, first military, then civil, followed by the beginnings of a generalized educational system. In addition, while there were variations in terms of which center led with a given innovation, the degree of contemporaneity of major innovations is striking. The first of the Ottoman and Egyptian military schools were founded over a long period of time, in the late eighteenth and early nineteenth centuries; but the first new-style training facilities for civil officials appeared in the two capitals in a shorter time span in the 1820s and 1830s. The first major laws generalizing modern education appeared in Egypt in 1867, in Istanbul in 1869. In Tunisia, the founding of Sadiqi College in 1875 is virtually contemporaneous with Abdul Hamid's upgrading of the Ottoman School of Civil Administration in 1876. Istanbul University opened in 1900; the Egyptian University, in 1908. The Ottoman-Islamic lands were beginning to break up politically, but still displayed common developmental rhythms in many respects.

The new schools also faced common problems. The characteristic desire to begin educational reform with schools for elite formation, and only later to direct attention to lower levels, was one such problem. The low literacy levels from which educational reform began, and the concepts of pedagogy inherited from mekteb and medrese, obviously compounded this problem everywhere. The lag in development of girls' schools was an obvious deficiency. The lack of books and teachers was of staggering proportions at the beginning of the century, and still serious at its end.

As these educational institutions began to develop, a constant problem was an overemphasis on language study. The modern-educated Ottoman, for example, needed to study not only the Turkish, Arabic, and Persian required for proper use of Ottoman Turkish, but also the French that his contemporaries regarded as both vehicle and substance of modern knowledge. Finally, most people attending these schools assumed that they were a ticket to government jobs. In the late nineteenth century, diplomas of the Ottoman School of Civil Administration carried on them articles from the school regulations that listed the types of appointments for which graduates were eligible. This kind of bureaucratic vocationalism was equally strong in Egypt and Tunisia. Some of the characteristic problems of twentieth-century Middle Eastern education were thus clearly present from the beginnings of the educational reform.

MINORITY AND MISSIONARY SCHOOLS

Non-Muslim schools were an important part of the total educational picture, not only for members of non-Muslim communities, but for Muslims as well. Not only did Muslims gradually begin to attend schools of these types, especially foreign schools, but the fact was that non-Muslim schools were better developed in parts of the empire and sometimes educated more students, especially girls, than did government schools. Whether this fact prompted Muslims to attend non-Muslim Schools, or more typically, to demand a greater development of their own institutions, it served to stimulate educational reform.

Of the three non-Muslim peoples most prominent in the Turkish heart of the empire, the Greeks certainly led in education, both quantitatively and qualitatively. By 1878, the Greek community of Istanbul reportedly had 105 schools of all levels in that city alone, with 12,000 students, 3,000 of them girls. They included lycée-level schools as well as commercial and theological schools. Greeks were widespread in Ottoman territories, both European and Asian, and their network of schools was correspondingly far-flung. In Egypt, too, there were by the time of the British occupation numbers of Greek schools for both sexes in Cairo, Alexandria, and elsewhere.

Among Armenians, the growth of education began later. The founding in Ottoman territory of schools giving more than religious instruction appears to have been an eighteenth-century phenomenon associated with intellectual revival and the Mekhitarist uniate movement. Within the fold of the Apostolic church, modern parochial schools were founded in Istanbul in the last quarter of the eighteenth century. A major expansion of facilities began in 1844. By 1866, there were reportedly 32 Armenian boys' schools in Istanbul, with 4,700 students, and 14 girls' schools, with 1,472. Private cultural societies, libraries, adult education courses, and newspapers proliferated. By 1900, an Armenian source indicates that there were over 800 Armenian primary schools in Anatolia, including some lycées. In Syria and Palestine, the patriarchate of Jerusalem maintained a network of schools for the apostolic community. There were also a few Armenian schools in Egypt.

In last place, among non-Muslim communities prominent in Turkey proper were the Ottoman Jews. Initially they suffered from a lack of support from coreligionists in the West. The first modern school for Jews in Istanbul did not open until 1854. It and others like it were subject to attacks from conservative Jews that resembled those heard in the Muslim, but not the other non-Muslim, communities, over "infidel practices" such as using benches and desks or teaching French. The positive side of the situtation, from the Ottoman point of view, was that the Jews took the teaching of Turkish more seriously than did other non-Muslim communities, especially the Greeks, who had their own agenda of using their schools to hellenize Orthodox non-Greeks. In Egypt, the founding of Jewish schools began in 1840 in a small way, thanks to the philanthropy of individual Jews from Europe. The major work of upgrading education for Ottoman Jewry remained for the Alliance Israélite Universelle, which opened its first schools in the Ottoman Empire at Edirne in 1867, in Istanbul in 1875, and thereafter in many other places.

In Cairo, the Copts showed what a religious community that had no support from outside could accomplish. The Copts traditionally maintained communal primary schools, for boys though usually not for girls. These schools taught reading and writing in Arabic, arithmetic and geometry, and enough Coptic for ritual use. There were no higher schools, not even for monks; and the curriculum, particularly the arithmetic and geometry, was a practical adaptation to the occupational specialization of the Copts as secretaries, accountants, surveyors, and tax collectors. Educational reforms among Copts began with the work of Patriarch Cyril IV, who began in the 1850s to found modern schools, including the first school for girls established by Egyptians. These schools enabled Copts almost to monopolize service in some government agencies during the second half of the nineteenth century. A second wave of school founding occurred among the Copts in the period from 1873 to 1878. These schools provided further support for the administrative role of the Copts, and for their movement into business and finance following the British occupation.

One region that was isolated from the major political centers of the empire instituted impressive educational reforms. This was geographical Syria, especially Lebanon, where there were strong ties between the non-Muslim communities and the West. At the beginning of the nineteenth century, most of the religious communities there had their own communal schools. Among non-Muslims, the Maronites, uniates who had for centuries sent the best of their clergy to Rome for education, stood out as the first to acquire any significant educational institutions beyond the primary level. These included Ayn Tura (1728) and Ayn Waraqa (1787), plus others founded in the nineteenth century. The Greek Catholics, also stimulated by union with Rome, founded their first higher school at Ayn Traz in the 1780s. The Greek Orthodox, in contrast, made a tardy entry on the scene, founding their first school in Lebanon in 1833.

Missionary Schooling

The Catholics had temporal priority, but it was American Protestant missionaries, arriving in Lebanon in 1820, who touched off the competitive expansion of missionary education. In Lebanon, the first American missionary school was founded in 1834, a school for girls, probably the first in the Ottoman Empire. By 1867, there were Protestant schools in twenty villages. For the first time, an effective system of elementary schools brought education within reach of the ordinary layperson. Secondary boarding schools were founded for girls beginning in 1858, and for boys, in 1881. The American missionary system received its capstone with the opening of the Syrian Protestant College, later the American University in Beirut, in 1866.

In the meantime, Catholic religious orders had created a system of their own, starting in 1834; other communities soon followed suit. Gradually, Maronite and Greek Catholic schools appeared all over Lebanon. To crown the network, the Jesuits established their seminary in Beirut in 1875, where it evolved into the Université de Saint-Joseph. Eventually, the Russian Church also launched an educational effort aimed at the Greek Orthodox Arabs, and most of the other indigenous religious communities undertook school-building efforts of their own. The development of Ottoman government schools in geographical Syria, following the education law of 1869, was yet another form of competition with the missionaries. By the end of the nineteenth century, then, Lebanon probably led all Ottoman provinces in education.

A similar pattern of missionary educational efforts existed elsewhere. In Istanbul, Latin Catholic churches and schools existed from the time of the Ottoman conquest; such schools became quite numerous by the nineteenth century. American Protestant missionaries launched their educational efforts in Istanbul in the 1820s and 1830s, opened their first secondary school in 1840, and founded what later became known as Robert College in 1863. A higher school for women, known initially as Constantinople Woman's College, followed in 1871.

Over the next thirty years, seven other colleges, usually comparable in American terms to a combination of high school and junior college, followed in various parts of Anatolia. By 1914, there were 2,500 students in colleges, 4,500 in high schools, and 20,000 in elementary schools run by American missionaries in the northern part of the Ottoman Empire, plus 6,000 more in American missionary schools in Ottoman Syria. As will be recalled, the Ottoman government itself did not create a university until 1900.

In Egypt, too, Catholic missionaries were first on the scene. Before 1840, their educational efforts had been modest. Protestant missionaries, German and English, entered the country in the 1820s and began to work mostly among the Copts. The real opening for the growth of foreign schools came after 1840, when both the traditional Muslim schools and the new government schools that Muhammad Ali had created were in disarray.

By 1863, there were 3 British schools in Egypt, 8 American, and 19 Catholic schools run by different orders. By 1878, Catholic religious orders had opened 28 more schools, and Protestants had opened another 37, all but one of them American. Following the British occupation, the largest private school systems in the country continued to be those of the American and French missionaries. Foreign schools altogether taught more students than did government schools. Above all, this was true of education for women. As late as 1914, even after Egypt had a women's emancipation movement, Egyptian government schools still had only 786 women, whereas American mission schools had 5,517.

Minority and missionary schools, impressive as they were in comparison with governmental schools, heightened the complexity of an already confusing educational environment. Catering to minorities who often had their own distinctive languages, these schools emphasized language skills even more than government schools. The result was often no more than that Levantine hallmark, glibness in many tongues. Since missionary schools were bastions of foreign cultures, they also tended to exacerbate existing nationalist cleavages. In addition, the coexistence of several types of schools tended to compound the westernist-Islamic cultural conflict.

Biographical sources on the better-educated segments of the population, such as the official elites, suggest that many moved back and forth during their educational careers among schools of different types. Muslim officials normally began their studies in Quranic elementary schools, following those, in variable order, with medrese study (or perhaps private instruction in subjects from the medrese curriculum) and study in government schools. After that, a few went on to study in Europe. Among non-Muslim officials it was not uncommon to find individuals who began in non-Muslim schools, then went on to Ottoman governmental schools or missionary institutions, and then, more commonly than among Muslims, completed their studies in Europe.

The cultural cleavage was not as pronounced for non-Muslims as for Muslims, but the need to pursue a career in a predominantly Islamic environment required them, too, to study such traditional subjects as the majority language, a necessity that prompted those in the Turkish-speaking part of the empire to spend at least some time on Arabic and Persian as well as Turkish. If there was anything more complicated than pursuing an education in a cultural environment torn by conflict between westernizers and Islamizers, it was wending one's way through the multiple educational systems of the period.

LITERACY AND PUBLISHING

If the overall literacy rate at the end of the eighteenth century was on the order of 1 percent, by 1914 the figure was probably between 5 and 10 percent. In Turkey, the literacy rate had barely passed 10 percent as late as 1927. In Egypt, it stood at about 7 percent in 1907. The highest rates were reported for Lebanon, with about 50 percent literate at that time; the rate for the rest of Syria stood at about 25 percent. These figures define the limits within which the educational history of the nineteenth century has to be evaluated. It is a history of remarkable growth, but from a strikingly low starting level.

The gains that had been realized reflected not only the growth and diversification of educational institutions but also a media revolution. For it was only in the nineteenth century that the Gutenberg age, bringing with it the cultural baggage of nineteenth-century Europe, fully opened for the Islamic Middle East. The first printing presses in the Ottoman Empire had belonged to non-Muslim communities. Ottoman Jewry had a press as early as 1493. The Greeks and Armenians founded theirs over the next two centuries. Arabic presses printing books for Christian use appeared in Italy as early as 1517, at Aleppo in 1702, in Lebanon in 1733. The first press for Ottoman Turkish, however, opened in Istanbul in 1727, on the express provision that it not print books on Islamic religious studies. Under this restriction, the press produced books only on lexicography, mathematics, medicine, astronomy, physics, geography, and history. The press ceased operation in 1742 after publishing only seventeen titles, and Ottoman printing did not resume until 1783.

Following the French Revolution, French presses were opened in the

Middle East, first in Istanbul, then, following the Napoleonic invasion, in Egypt. The presses were short-lived, and the bulk of their output was in French rather than the local languages. American Protestant missionaries founded an Arabic press at Malta in 1822 to print in Arabic religious literature and textbooks for the mission schools. In 1834, the press was moved to Beirut. Catholic missionaries in Lebanon founded their press in 1847. The first Arabic press under Muslim control was opened by Muhammad Ali Pasha at Bulaq in 1822. The Bulaq press ultimately produced many works in Turkish and Arabic; these books circulated widely throughout the Middle East.

The Translation Movement

In both Cairo and Istanbul, the output of the government presses at first consisted almost entirely of translations from Western languages, mostly works of military interest. Aside from technical translations, the most noteworthy modern literature produced by Middle Eastern writers through the first half of the nineteenth century consisted of travel accounts about Europe. In Ottoman Turkish, this genre developed out of the traditional ambassadorial narrative. The first such account to provide a significant amount of information about a Western society appeared between 1720 and 1721.

Works of comparable character did not become numerous until Selim III attempted to inaugurate a system of permanent diplomatic representation in the 1790s. The genre reappeared with Mahmud II's revival of the embassies in the 1830s. Virtually the first such work to appear in Arabic was that of the Egyptian Tahtawi about Paris, first published in 1834 and translated into Turkish in 1840. In both Istanbul and Cairo, the translations produced in the first half of the nineteenth century were largely products of government efforts to train translators. The main centers of these efforts were the Ottoman Translation Office, founded at the Sublime Porte in 1821, and the Egyptian School of Translation, or School of Languages, which was under the direction of Tahtawi himself from 1837 to 1849.

About mid-century, the translation movements of both Turks and Arabs began to overflow the confines of the official translation programs. This broadening of subject matter appears to have begun with Tahtawi, who, while in France (1826–31), began to read works of Voltaire, Rousseau, Montesquieu, and Racine. Even within the official translation movement in Egypt, a half-dozen works of such writers were published between

1841 and 1850. One of these, translated by Tahtawi himself, was Fénelon's *Les aventures de Télémaque* (1699), an attack on royal despotism that nineteenth-century Middle Eastern audiences, reacting to the rapid reforms and centralizing tendencies of their rulers, responded to strongly. After 1850, the Arabic translation movement entered a new phase. The Egyptian School of Languages was closed for a time and, while Tahtawi and others who had worked in it remained active as translators, writers, teachers, or officials, Syro-Lebanese writers such as Faris al-Shidyaq (1805–87), Butrus al-Bustani (1819–83), and the Taqla brothers, who founded the newspaper *al-Ahram*, in 1875, began to assume greater prominence. No longer merely translators, these were professional literary men, innovators in style and genre, and especially influential through their work in journalism and the popularization of Western ideas. In Istanbul, a similar broadening of literary horizons began in the 1850s and 1860s. The range of translations began to widen in 1859 with publication of selections from the *philosophes*. As in Arab lands, Fénelon's *Télémaque* was one of the first such works translated. The introduction of Western literary genres, the massive popularization of Western ideas, and the rise of the Young Ottoman ideological movement, inspired by European political thought, got under way in the 1860s, in tandem with the growth of a reading public.

Changes in Communications

The Ottoman ruling class sensed that the old official style was inadequate to project reformist concepts clearly and consistently across a vast empire. A new concern for mass communication began to manifest itself, in ways ranging from simpler language in documents intended for wide circulation to publication, from 1862 on, of volumes containing newly enacted laws and regulations.

The translation movements simplified communications in various ways. Most of the works translated were written in relatively straightforward language. Even the efforts of American missionaries to translate the Bible and write textbooks in Arabic played a part; their attempts— with gifted Arab collaborators—to achieve a style close to the classical but intelligible to contemporaries helped launch a new literary style. The rise of ideological controversy, beginning in Istanbul and spreading to other political centers, furthered the communications revolution. Political activists searched for forms of expression that would not merely titillate the learned, but stir the hearts of the many. Venerable terms in Arabic or Turkish were given new meaning to express such ideas as "fatherland," "liberty," and "reform."

Of the many changes in communications, none was more influential than the rise of journalism. The first newspapers in the Middle East were ephemeral, published by the French at their presses in Istanbul and Egypt. By the 1820s, non-Muslim minorities and resident foreigners began publishing European-language newspapers. Journalism in Arabic and Turkish did not become a permanent feature of the literary scene until the founding of the official gazettes, starting in Egypt in 1827 and in Istanbul in 1831. The first non-official Ottoman-language newspaper, the *Ceride-i Havadis*, appeared in 1840; it was run by an Englishman. In Egypt, there were no privately controlled Arabic newspapers until the time of Ismail Pasha (1863–79). By 1860, however, privately owned newspapers and reviews began to appear elsewhere.

In 1858, Khalil al-Khuri began publication in Beirut of his *Hadiqat al-Akhbar*, "a civil, scientific, commercial, and historical journal." The first private newspaper owned by Turks was the short-lived *Tercüman-i Ahval* of 1860, launched by Yusuf Agâh and Ibrahim Şinasi, followed by the latter's *Tasvir-i Efkar*, started in 1862. Also in 1860, Ahmad Faris al-Shidyaq began publication in Istanbul of *Al-Jawa'ib*, which enjoyed the widest circulation of any Arabic newspaper for the next twenty years. By the 1860s, there were many presses producing a wide variety of books, newspapers, and even journals, in both Turkish and Arabic. In Ottoman territories, the growth continued, despite the censorship of Abdul Hamid (1876–1909). After the British occupation of Egypt, the freer atmosphere there attracted writers and journalists from other Arab countries, especially Syria and Lebanon, and thus consolidated the reputation of Cairo as the intellectual metropolis of the Arab world.

Nothing better illustrates the extent of the media revolution than the careers of its leaders. The Maronite writer Butrus al-Bustani (1819–83) stands out as a lexicographer, encyclopedic popularizer, educator, and advocate of the revival of Syria. His greatest monuments are his Arabic dictionary, *Al-Muhit*, and the unfinished eleven-volume encyclopedia, *Da'irat al-Ma'arif*. Together, these helped to revitalize Arabic as a means for the expression of new ideas; also, these two works popularized the scientific, technical, and political ideas of the contemporary West. The spread of literacy produced influential modernist men of letters from very modest backgrounds in the 1860s and 1870s. Two of these were the Egyptian writer Abdullah al-Nadim (1845–96) and the Ottoman Ahmed Midhat (1844–12).

Abdullah al-Nadim became one of the leading literary spokesman for Egyptian nationalism and an advocate of national self-strengthening through borrowing from the West and popular education. He was the author of one of the first modern plays in Arabic, *Al-Watan*, "The Fatherland." The son of a poor craftsman, Ahmed Midhat made an even greater impact as printer-publisher, journalist, novelist, encyclopedic popularizer, and propagator in Turkish of the activist "self-help" philosophy of Samuel Smiles. The weaving together of educational reform, cultural change, and social mobilization themes that is so pronounced in Ahmed Midhat and Abdullah al-Nadim was to become more evident in later generations, as the growth of literacy and the media revolution continued.

CULTURAL DUALISM
AND
CHANGING INTELLECTUAL VISTAS

Educational reform, the media revolution, and the literary exertions of innovators like those just described brought cultural dualism home to Ottoman Muslims in ways that were hard to ignore. It seemed as if two worlds were colliding; the alien one—attractive for its richness, fearsome for its power—would destroy the other, unless some specifically Islamic mode of accommodation or resistance could be found. The discomfort of the situation was heightened by the readiness of non-Muslim minorities to assimilate Western ideas. Among Muslims, the widening cultural cleavage created a division into traditionalists and modernist-westernists, each camp suffering from its divisions and its conflicts with the other.

This cultural dualism, fraught with dangers for the individual and society, provides the psychosocial context within which to assess changes in the intellectual vistas of nineteenth-century Ottomans. To anchor the discussion in an Islamic perspective, we may return to the quadripartite concept of the traditional Islamic learned culture. In concluding our survey of these four domains of endeavor, it will be worthwhile to comment on two types of cultural institutions—libraries and learned societies—that have received little comment so far and that could, with fuller development, have done much to encourage the technical fields, where the nineteenth century, in fact, produced the least progress.

Religious Studies

To begin with the domain of religious studies, we have already noted that the nineteenth century witnessed a differentiation between Turkish and Arabic cultures in terms of the extent to which reformist thought became oriented toward the state, rather than religion. Many religious scholars from the Istanbul elite became alienated from the reform movement after the 1830s. A few, however, shifted into the civil service. The outstanding example of this type is Ahmed Cevdet Paşa (1822–95). Trained as a religious scholar, he changed careers in 1866, becoming a leading scholar-statesman, holder of such ministerial portfolios as justice and education, author of a monumental history, and leading figure in the compilation of the *Mecelle*, an attempt to codify the section of shariah law dealing with "transactions" (*muamelat*).

There were other important thinkers and activists among the Turkish ulama. Such were Hoca Tahsin Efendi (1813–1881), enthusiast for modern science and Pan-Islam, and Mehmed Akif Ersoy (1870–1936), leading Islamicist poet and spokesman for the Young Turk Period. The Pan-Islamist movement under Abdul Hamid, or the Islamicist movement of the Young Turks, proves that there was a popular response to such figures. As long as there was an Ottoman state to save, however, the Turks' best reformist efforts went to that goal.

For Arabs, the emphasis was different. A state-building reform movement had emerged in Egypt under Muhammad Ali Pasha, but faltered under his successors. The nationalist movement that had emerged by the 1870s perforce assumed the form of an anticolonial independence movement when it resurfaced after the British occupation. What remained more conspicuous in the long run, certainly as compared to the Ottoman center, was an orientation to reform and revitalize Islam. Cairo, especially, became the center for a succession of religious thinkers or, at times, publicists expressing themselves in an Islamic idiom. The most important of these are Jamal al-Din al-Afghani (1838/1839–1897), from Iran but active in Cairo in the 1870s, followed by his major Egyptian disciple, Muhammad Abduh (1849–1905), and then by the Syrian-born Rashid Rida (1865–1935).

In the effort of men like these to formulate a specifically Islamic response to the challenge of the modern West, there was a danger that a lapse of rigor concerning Islam would lead simply to permissive westernization. In fact, some students of al-Afghani and Abduh did become leading secularists. Yet, the ideal of returning to the fundamentals of Islamic faith and thought in order to seek a response to the demands of the modern world persisted. In the progression from the political expediency of al-Afghani to the fundamentalist rigor of Rashid Rida, there is a growth in Islamic strictness that recalls earlier revivalist movements, especially the Wahhabis of Arabia, and anticipates the Islamic resurgence of the twentieth century.

Mysticism

In the realm of mysticism, the situation in the different parts of the Ottoman-Islamic world appears to have been more uniform. The evidence indicates that many Muslims still espoused the mystical outlook of the "tangled magic garden." Yet, this mentality was coming under attack everywhere, both from westernizers and from the increasingly vocal shariah-minded Muslims, the latter found not only among revivalists like the Wahhabis but also in shariah-oriented sufi orders like the Naqshbandiyyah. By the late nineteenth century, the stage was set for sufism to lose its centuries-old standing as a prevalent Muslim style of religious expression, whether at the hands of secularists like Atatürk or at the hands of Muslim revivalists like Rashid Rida. The orders, and their influence on other milieux, did not cease to exist; yet, their loss of prominence is unmistakable.

The Literary Culture

As concerns the wordly dimension of literary culture, the adab tradition, we have already mentioned its historic links with government service, especially with the scribal class, and commented on the extent to which nineteenth-century westernization began as an expansion of adab culture into a new dimension. The consequences, by the end of the nineteenth century, included not only an infusion into the Islamic thought-world of vast quantities of new ideas, but the emergence of a class of professional *littérateurs* independent for the first time from government patronage, thanks to the growth of journalism and of the reading public. Also, adab culture, perhaps even more than religious thought, became a major medium for the articulation of protest against rapid change. This occurred with the rise of political journalism and political-ideological movements expressing their views primarily in terms not of traditional religious vocabulary but of imported ideas of patriotism, state, and society.

The Young Ottoman movement of the 1860s and 1870s, the first movement of its kind, displayed an interest in traditional Islamic jurisprudence that was more typical of Islamic revivalists than of later political-ideological movements. It was followed by other nationalist movements around the region, such as the Egyptian nationalists of the 1870s and after. The Young Turks of 1889 and later, as successors to the Young Ottomans, have the distinction of being the first such movement to succeed in staging a revolution. By that time (1908), the belletristic adab tradition had burgeoned into a whole new world of thought and action.

Philosophy and Science

Less impressive were the changes that had occurred in the philosophical-scientific (*falsafah*) component of the old learned culture. At the beginning of the nineteenth century, exponents of both this and adab culture were back where their predecessors of a thousand years earlier had been in the sense of being dependent on translations to form, or reform, a tradition for themselves. For the belletrists, interested in a general mastery of Western concepts, this could be done relatively rapidly. For would-be specialists in scientific and technical fields, progress was painful, particularly given the rapid development of these fields in the West at the time. By the end of the nineteenth century, Turks and Arabs had made some progress in technical and applied fields, such as telegraphy, military science, agriculture, veterinary medicine, and medicine. Beyond this, some of the best minds were beginning to complete scientific and technical studies in the West; in the twentieth century, they would become participants in the *modern* community of science, still centered largely in the West, but made up increasingly of men and women from all parts of the world.

Learned Societies

Hand-in-hand with this weakness in science and technology went a limited development of learned societies and other facilities to support scientific or other intellectual endeavor. Such institutions as existed tended to be short-lived, ill-equipped, and directed, of necessity, toward modest goals. Virtually none rivaled the scholarly academies, or other learned institutions, that could be found even in Russia. In Istanbul, there was briefly, as early as the 1820s, a "scientific society" that met in the homes of learned individuals in or near Beşiktaş. In 1850, a "learned society" (*Encümen-i Danis*) was inaugurated, with Ottoman and foreign members, to promote science and letters. This society came to an end in 1862, with only three of the books it sponsored having been printed.

The Ottoman Scientific Society of 1861 had a greater impact, particularly through its *Journal of Sciences* (*Mecmua-i Fünun*), which was published on and off until 1882 and played a major role in popularizing encyclopedic knowledge of Western achievements. Particularly in the Hamidian and Young Turk periods, a large number of private or official societies were formed to foster religious and educational goals. As for libraries, there were reportedly 49 in Istanbul in 1908; but the largest still had under 10,000 books.

In the Arab world, the development of modern amenities of this kind began more grandly with the founding by the French of the *Institut d'Egypte*. This produced a tremendous outpouring of scholarship about Egypt, all in French; but it functioned in Egypt only for a few years after the Napoleonic invasion (1798). Its direct impact on Egyptians hardly went beyond confronting a few scholars with a world of knowledge of which they had no prior idea. The *Institut* was, however, reopened in 1859 and continued to operate and publish its research during the reign of Ismail. The Society of Knowledge (*Jam'iyyat al-Ma'arif*, 1868), by publishing original and translated works, had a larger impact. This society was especially active in editing classical Arabic texts.

Ismail Pasha founded what became the National Library and the Geographical Society (1875), which had an international membership and produced major research. By that time, private individuals in the Arab world, too, were actively founding societies for cultural goals. Such was the Islamic Philanthropical Society (*Al-Jam'iyyah al-Khayriyyah al-Islamiyyah*, 1878), founded in Egypt under the leadership of Abdullah al-Nadim to create private schools for boys and girls. There were also private associations for the sponsorship of education in geographical Syria.

The nineteenth century had clearly produced substantial changes in the intellectual life of the sultan's Muslim subjects, creating a sharply felt rift in the learned culture as historically known. In this sense, change had been too great. In another sense, it was not great enough. For the limited growth in the scientific and technical fields, and the minimal development of facilities to encourage work in those fields, showed how far Middle Easterners still had to go to acquire mastery of some of the intellectual resources that had done most to create the dynamism behind the Western challenge.

INTERNATIONAL COMPARISONS

Whereas the Ottoman Middle East displayed a notable degree of ethnic and cultural diversity, its intellectual life developed largely with a common rhythm.

Within the region, such development did not exclude a certain range of variation. At times Egypt moved ahead of the Ottoman central government in reform, whereas the latter at other times took the lead. Tunisia displays a somewhat exceptional pattern as a result of being a "late starter" that quickly passed under foreign control. The most important variation, visible at almost all times, reflects the contrast between the statist orientation of Ottoman reformers and the Islamic orientation of most of those in the Arab world.

Nonetheless, what is impressive in the long run is the extent to which major developments in education and cultural life occurred in similar sequence, and nearly contemporaneously, for Turks and Arabs. In the development of modern governmental schools, there were many such parallelisms between Istanbul and Cairo. As for the higher religious institutions, while the Ottoman government neglected these, the reforms of 1896 at al-Azhar produced immediate demand for similar measures at the Zaytunah Mosque in Tunis. Among missionary schools, there was a similar parallelism in the development of Protestant and Catholic schools.

A number of faults were shared by these schools: the neglect of education for women, reliance on rote learning, overemphasis on languages, bureaucratic vocationalism, and the confusion of multiple school systems. Parallelisms are also strong in other phases of intellectual life. "Modern" literary productivity, Turkish and Arabic, began with translation and travel works. About mid-century, major works of the Enlightenment began to be translated. Official gazettes appeared in Cairo in 1827 and in Istanbul in 1831, and locally owned private newspapers emerged in Beirut and Istanbul in the period from 1858 to 1860. Encyclopedic popularizers like Butrus al-Bustani and Ahmed Midhat were active by the 1860s. The emergence of an active opposition in the form of an intelligentsia occurred soon after, with the Young Ottomans of the 1860s and the Egyptian nationalists of the 1870s. Clearly, an important degree of unity coexisted with the heterogeneity of the Ottoman-Islamic Middle East of the nineteenth century.

At the same time, important contrasts appear between the Ottoman-Islamic environment and other regions of the world. For example, a major contrast between Ottoman Afro-Asia, on the one hand, and both Japan and Russia, on the other, lies in the phenomenon of cultural dualism. In both Japan and Russia, traditional religious interests had ceased to dominate general education before the nineteenth century, although a form of

cultural dualism continued to characterize Russia. The educational reformers of both these countries were thus able to proceed more efficiently
than their Ottoman counterparts. In only a few decades after the Meiji
Restoration (1868), for example, the Japanese created a modern, unified
national school system that included everything from compulsory coedu-
cational elementary schools to a number of universities. After more than
a century of trying, the Ottomans had not matched this accomplishment.

Comparison with China suggests that here the crux of the problem
had to do, not so much with the power of traditional vested interests as
with the costs of dualism per se. In the Chinese imperial center, the
Confucian scholar gentry—counterparts of the Islamic religious scholars
as custodians of the dominant value-system—remained in power virtually
throughout the ninteenth century. There were revolts and protest movements on the periphery, but little counterpart at the center to the western-
ism of the Ottoman reformers.

In China, the first institution for training interpreters and experts
in foreign affairs did not open until the 1860s; student missions to the
West did not become a regular practice until the 1890s. No reform program
as radical as the Ottoman *Tanzimat* (1839) occurred until the "Hundred
Days" of 1898. The collapse of China's traditional institutions was cata-
strophic when it came. It would be difficult to argue, however, that having
suffered through a century of cultural bifurcation, coupled with radical
reform efforts, made the transition to the postimperial era any less difficult
for most parts of the Middle East. The successor state for which such an
argument would be most plausible is the Turkish Republic, as heir to
the imperial center.

In the Ottoman-Islamic intellectual environment the modernists
were unable to proceed as freely as in Japan, and the traditionalists were
unable to control the terms of debate as fully as in China. What made
matters worse was that, while there was a history of borrowing from other
cultures in certain respects, the dominant worldview emphasized the
superiority and self-sufficiency of Islamic culture. Islamic religious-legal
thought, too, posed exacting demands for cultural integrity in Islamic
terms. For concerned Muslims, there could be no easy syncretism, no
unreflective borrowing from another culture, in any matter that the
shariah addressed. Here, again, was an important difference with Japan,
where there was a historic memory of having borrowed from other cultures
before borrowing from the West.

Here, in religious terms, was an important difference with Hindu
India, too, where the same degree of doctrinal closure did not exist. This
difference arguably has much to do with the relatively positive reaction

of Hindus to British ideas, as contrasted to the more mixed reaction of Muslims to the Western cultures with which they came into contact. For Muslims, the need to test the compatibility of each intended borrowing from another culture with Islamic values was keenly felt, a fact obvious in Young Ottoman thought, and in that of Jamal al-Din al-Afghani and his followers. That some Muslims opted not to apply this test and willingly assumed the stance of secularists does not change the significance of their action in Islamic terms.

Less insulated than the Chinese from Western encroachment, and more bound by their religious-legal tradition than Hindus or Japanese in responding to alien ideas, Ottoman Muslims also found their situation complicated by certain features of their social environment that did not have counterparts in other major centers, at least not in the same combination. The most important points are the ethnic and religious complexity of the Middle East and the Ottoman tradition of an elite-mass culture dichotomy.

Both of these problems had counterparts in nineteenth-century Russia, although the first, at least, was not then perceived as much of a political problem. In India, such problems were perhaps smothered under the weight of the British Raj. In contrast, China had a phenomenal degree of cultural integrity; Japan was exceptional for both ethnic and cultural homogeneity. Ethnic and religious diversity was more of a political problem in the Ottoman Empire than in Russia precisely because the politically dominant Muslims were not the most advanced segment of the population in assimilating the leading ideas of the period, including nationalism. The access of the subject minorities, under the capitulations, to foreign protection assured that the Ottomans would not be able to ignore this problem, and inflamed cultural antagonisms all the more.

Meanwhile, the elite-mass dichotomy, while rooted in the traditional culture, was modernized into a more acute form, where Frenchified ruling elites, ensconced in an administrative apparatus of much-increased power and effectiveness, lorded it over a mass still much closer to its own tradition. The cultural alienation was at least as profound as that of lord and peasant in Russia. What is more, Muslim traditionalists, and non-Muslim activists, were vocal in expressing their resentment.

Under the circumstances, it is little wonder that Middle Eastern Muslims of the twentieth century have sought, first, to reorganize their collective life along national lines—a process not without ambiguities— and then, once again, to return to the question of accommodating the modern world of knowledge within the framework of Islamic beliefs and values.

CHAPTER EIGHT

Conclusion

THE OTTOMAN EMPIRE, a political system that had endured for centuries, finally came to an end following the First World War. The balance sheet of assets and liabilities relevant to modernization then facing the successor states can be summarized as follows.

INTERNATIONAL CONTEXT

Assets: The longstanding and close, even if usually hostile, Ottoman connection with Europe did provide a source of modernizing institutions and ideas throughout the nineteenth century and, indeed, earlier. The governing elite was able to see at a relatively early time the need to "catch up" with a threatening Europe. Moreover, the manifest nature of the threat (defeat in war) served to mute traditionalist reactions; in short, the nature of the challenge was perceived in good time. A consistent pattern of response along lines of defensive modernization had begun even before the end of the eighteenth century among the governing elite in Istanbul, only a few years later in Cairo, and then last but still in the early nineteenth century in Tunis. The appreciable Christian and Jewish minorities throughout Ottoman Afro-Asia were a potentially significant conduit of westernizing and thus modernizing impulses in economic as well as cultural matters. Tunisia was a partial exception, with no native Christians and a Jewish community exposed to significant westernizing influences later than their coreligionists to the East.

Liabilities: These were almost the obverse of the foregoing. Europe was contiguous but was the infidel enemy. The Ottoman tradition was of borrowing from within the larger Islamic world, adapting both material and ideological culture from Persian, Arabic, and indeed (especially in matters of government) central Asian and Turkic sources, not from Christian Europe. That Christian and Jewish subjects of the Ottoman Empire often served as the westernizing vanguard made it psychologically even more repugnant for Muslim rulers and the Muslim majority to mimic the despised and now threatening European enemy.

International Comparisons: In terms of geographical proximity and foreign access, the Ottoman Empire was more open to modernizing Western influences than either Japan or China, but less open than Russia.

In timing as well, defensive modernization in response to the challenge coming from Europe began earlier in the Ottoman Empire than in Japan or China but somewhat later than in Russia. The comparable Japanese response was more intense but started roughly a half century later, whereas that of China did not become significant until the twentieth century and was even then further delayed by domestic disorder and strife.

The dialectic pattern throughout the nineteenth century of Westernizing borrowers pitted against traditionalist nativists was similar in Russia and the Ottoman Empire. In Japan the Westernizing forces came to power later, but thereafter they tended to remain dominant. They were thus able to impose modernizing change rapidly and thoroughly without effective challenge from traditionalists.

The Ottomans had forged a state system and a civilization by synthesizing many institutions and ideas, all however from within the Afro-Asian Islamic world. There was virtually no tradition of borrowing from neighboring Europe similar to that of Japan borrowing from China or Russia from Europe to the West. There was, however, in the Ottoman Empire greater cultural diversity and less resistance to outside influences than in China.

Like Russia and unlike Japan or China, the Ottoman Empire became a part of the European state system (officially with the 1856 Treaty of Paris terminating the Crimean War) but in a way that merely legitimized constant European abuse of Ottoman weakness. The Ottoman Empire in this regard was least favored of all four—unlike Russia not strong enough to resist pressure from the rest of Europe (even less to impose pressure itself as Russia could) but not geographically remote enough as were China and Japan to obtain some security.

POLITICAL STRUCTURE

Assets: The Ottoman Empire had a centuries-old heritage of a relatively effective central government. The ruling class had as well considerable experience in controlling the parts of the extensive empire, with all their ecological and cultural differences, and of doing this in a low-cost fashion that would enable government to maintain at least minimal public order even in times of crisis or of extended penury. The rulers were few in number in proportion to the total population, and they accordingly restricted access to their ranks, leaving the great majority of subjects both outside government and with slight prospect of joining government. At the same time, however, government demanded little of the governed. That plus the careful balancing of potentially antagonistic groups within society made government, by premodern standards, reasonably efficient and not excessively onerous. To most of society, the existing government was better than any conceivable alternative.

The ruling class had both the organizational capacity and the clear group interest (it being a matter of its survival as an organized body) to undertake defensive modernization. They had ready access to European models. The European military advisers who came could be assimilated in accordance with the venerable Ottoman practice of co-opting outsiders (as Janissaries or Mamluks, renegades or Turks by profession in European terms). Diplomatic missions to Europe were readily accomplished. Much was to be learned in combat with the European enemy.

Liabilities: The attempted westernizing reforms increased the cost of government and placed considerable burdens (from increased taxation to conscription) on the governed. The implicit social contract between governors and governed (or despotism mitigated by a limited intrusion of government in the daily lives of the governed) was thus broken, but without the governed being able to see any improvements commensurate with the increased burdens. Government expenditures far outpaced economic development. The possibility of increased governmental activity without increased tax burdens was thus ruled out. The fateful decision to cover part of the shortfall by foreign borrowing led to state bankruptcy in all three cases—Tunisia, Egypt, and the Ottoman Empire.

Efforts on the part of the governors to instill among the governed a sense of participatory citizenship, replacing the venerable preference on the part of the governed to have as little contact with government as possible, failed in the short run. Instead, the European concept of nationalism, the very antithesis of the Ottoman ideal of a multireligious, multilingual, and multinational political community, undermined the Ottoman political synthesis.

International Comparisons: Along with Russia, Japan, and China, the Ottoman Empire was one of the few late-modernizing societies with a heritage of effective political administration capable of being converted to modern functions.

The Ottoman political structure throughout the nineteenth century more closely resembled that of China in being unable to parry intrusive interference from Europe, whereas both Japanese and Russian governing elites maintained greater cohesion and autonomy.

Both Japan and China had the linguistic and cultural potential to embrace nationalism and adapt it to prevailing political norms. Even Russia, while increasingly absorbing non-Russian areas, remained essentially uniform in religion (Orthodox Christian) and language and culture (Russian).

The political elite in the Ottoman Empire could not preside over an effective "nationalization" of existing political structure. Their plight was more like that of the Austrian Hapsburgs.

ECONOMIC STRUCTURE AND GROWTH

Assests: Agriculture, by far the largest economic sector, was partly commercialized and had much slack. This made it possible to increase output severalfold, and the marketed surplus even more, by extending cultivation and also (especially in Egypt) by intensification and shifting to more valuable cash crops. Development of minerals was also significant.

World market conditions were favorable. Except during the Great Depression of the 1870s and 1880s, foreign demand for the region's products rose rapidly, and the terms of trade improved. The policies imposed by European powers on Middle Eastern governments also greatly facilitated the expansion of both imports and exports. European initiative and capital helped set up the commercial and financial networks required for international trade and provided much of the transport system—shipping, ports, and railways.

Government policies promoted economic growth by ensuring a much greater degree of law and order; adopting commercial, penal, and land codes that facilitated the penetration of foreign enterprise and the establishment of capitalistic relations; providing the infrastructure (telegraphs, ports, railways, and roads) either directly or through financial subsidies; building irrigation works and supplying improved roads; and opening a small number of schools and training tiny but significant technical cadres.

Liabilities: The surplus produced was mainly spent on public and private consumption, not used to raise the savings rate, build up industry, or develop the region's resource.

The frequent and prolonged wars waged by the Ottoman Empire, and to a lesser extent Egypt, drained vast sums and largely contributed to the accumulation of a huge foreign debt.

Commercial treaties with Europe prevented the raising of import duties, thus depriving local industry of needed protection. This plus the lack of venture capital, the paucity of fuels, the shortage of skilled labor, and high internal transport costs prevented the development of a modern manufacturing industry.

Low import duties, together with the capitulations, which made it impossible to tax foreigners, deprived the governments of a large potential source of revenue.

International Comparisons: Ottoman Afro-Asia's pattern of economic development was closer to that of Russia and Japan than to that of China. A large segment of the economy was drawn into close contact with the world market through improved transport, financial links, and commercial networks. Indeed, Middle Eastern involvement in the world market was even closer, as is shown by the region's higher figures for foreign trade per capita and foreign trade as a proportion of GNP.

Yet, in certain even more important respects the Ottoman pattern resembled the Chinese. There was the incapacity of governments to cushion their countries from the European impact and to guide the developmental process in the direction long-term interests demanded. Like China, the Ottoman Middle East was engaged in unsuccessful wars that increased governmental debt and added costly indemnities. Like China, their hands were tied by the capitulations, which in the Middle East went back several hundred years. And like China in the period under review, the region failed to industrialize, developing only a small fraction of its human resources.

SOCIAL INTERDEPENDENCE

Assests: To the extent that the cosmopolitanism and functional specialization associated with urbanism favor modernization, the Middle East started modern times in a good position. The region had a very old and developed urban culture and began the modern period with a high percentage of the total population living in cities and towns. The commercialization of agriculture and the region's entry into the world market thereafter enhanced urbanization, especially along the Mediterranean littoral. As early as 1800, the empire had three cities with over 100,000 inhabitants.

Although marked by considerable religious, ethnic, and even linguistic diversity, the Ottoman lands did offer considerable social and geographical mobility. There was a single unifying language of government— Ottoman Turkish—and a single unifying language of religion and, to a large extent, culture—Arabic. The network of cities and towns with their caravansarais, not to mention lodges of Sufi orders, facilitated the movement of men, goods, and ideas. So, too, did seasonal Muslim pilgrimages to the Arabian holy cities of Mecca and Madina.

The millet system gave religious minorities the minimal security of state-protected status, but at the same time the pattern of non-Muslim upper mobility via conversion was accepted (e.g., the earlier devshirme and the Mamluk system). The resulting social system offered assurances to the overwhelming majority of the inhabitants who did not want to change location or religion or status while leaving an accessible if small window of opportunity for those few who did.

Liabilities: The potential advantage of a high percentage of urban population was largely vitiated by relatively weak ties binding together cities and the countryside. The overwhelming majority of the population consisted of peasants caught in the pincers of aloof and oppressive governments in the cities on the one hand and potentially predatory tribal nomads on the other. Generally speaking, the peasantry lacked the leadership capable of bargaining with government that was found among notables in the cities and towns or tribal shaykhs among nomads and pastoralists.

Middle Eastern ecology, with its patchwork of cities and towns, land suitable for extensive dry farming, arboculture, intensive irrigated farming, deserts and mountains, enabled the tiny number of individuals constituting government to "divide and rule" vast areas and appreciable populations. This same ecological system, however, imposed a series of barriers to the centralization and social integration needed for effective modernization. Mountaineers and nomads were not easily brought to order, and the vulnerable peasantry reacted with flight or passive resistance.

International Comparisons: Ottoman Afro-Asia offers greater geographical and cultural diversity than Japan, China, or Russia. As a cosmopolitan urban and urbane culture, the region ranks with China and would seemingly have had an advantage over Russia in this regard. The compact size of Japan serves to put it in a category apart.

In terms of social group differentiation, the Ottoman system comes closest to that of China. In both cases, distinction for the scholar was based on learning, for the governing elite on mastery of an elaborate cultural code, whether that of mandarinized Confucianism or the "Ottoman way." Ever since the dying out of the timariot system, there had been nothing quite similar to the sociopolitical class distinctions found in Russia that ranged from noble to serf or in the Japanese variant of feudalism.

The millet system institutionalized separation according to religious affiliation and the devolution to the religious community of many activities normally the responsibility of government; such system had no parallel in China, Japan, or Russia.

KNOWLEDGE AND EDUCATION

Assets: The concept of rigorous education and training for the governing class was effectively institutionalized. Indeed, since the early days of the Ottoman Empire, such education and training had been recognized as the appropriate way to enter the governing class.

Literacy and learning were highly valued, and education was the avenue for advancement in the religious as well as the governmental elite.

Models for modernizing educational institutions and disseminating knowledge (e.g., books, newspaper with the concomitant idea of research and writing as a profession from which one can earn a livelihood and not be beholden to a governmental or private patron) were readily at hand in neighboring Europe. Moreover, both the governmental elite and limited numbers of those governed (especially the Christian and Jewish minorities) had access to these new models and often championed them.

The schooling brought by European Catholic, Protestant, and Orthodox missionaries (plus the work among Jews of such groups as the Alliance Israélite) provided, on balance, good education, preparing its students in European languages and in foreign techniques and mores that could be adapted to Middle Eastern society. Among the results of this European education within the Ottoman Empire were translations of European books, the rise of Middle Eastern journalism, the movement toward modernizing the Arabic and Turkish languages (i.e., language simplification, efforts to bridge the gap between the popular language and the cultural language of government or religion), and the growth among the population of the notion that social mobility can be achieved by means of a modern education.

Liabilities: There was no tradition of a statewide (or national) educational system. Instead, except for the special education and training of those destined to be numbered among the governors, education was deemed the responsibility of the different religious communities.

Efforts by early modernizers from within the governing class to create a centrally controlled educational system faced multiple obstacles, including lack of teaching personnel, the sharply increased financial burden of bringing into existence a new school system, resistance from the religious leadership challenged in its hitherto near-monopoly control of education, and finally traditional resistance of both Muslim and non-Muslim subjects suspicious of governmental initiative.

The advantages brought by European missionary education were offset by important disadvantages. Such education attracted mainly non-Muslim minorities and served to increase their identity within their own religious community rather than develop a needed sense of identification with the modernizing state—Ottoman, Egyptian, or Tunisian. The education being given in different languages (mainly English and French but also Russian and others) added to the linguistic and cultural diversity at the very time when a trend toward linguistic and cultural unity was needed. Moreover, foreign schools often siphoned off children of the Muslim governmental and nongovernmental elite. To this extent, it was not a priority for the existing elite to improve the still fragile but growing governmental school system.

For all the value given literacy and education, the Middle East began modern times with a very low literacy rate. Moreover, the prejudice against the education of women further held back change.

Aside from the reasonably practical education and training provided those entering the governing elite, the prevailing educational philosophy emphasized rote learning of the religiously sanctioned cultural tradition. The idea of technical education or of pragmatic on-the-job training was virtually absent except among the craft guilds, but these were dying out as a result of imports of cheap European manufactures.

International Comparisons: The Ottoman Empire began modern times with far greater linguistic and cultural diversity than Japan, Russia, or China. The multiform pattern of European influences (especially in education) served to increase linguistic and cultural diversity throughout the nineteenth century somewhat in the manner of the European missionary impact on China. But the more solid linguistic and cultural cohesion of China survived this challenge. Yet, the European missionary educational impact was minimal when compared with the intrusive educational philosophy brought by the British to the Indian subcontinent. The result, in contrast with all these other countries, was an increase in linguistic and cultural diversity.

Although members of the ruling elite began educational Westernization and modernization before China and even before Japan, and not all that long after Russia, the rulers of Ottoman Afro-Asia were not able to maintain and control the educational reform as in the other three countries. The religious establishments (both Muslim and non-Muslim) resisted government's efforts to reduce their control over education; it only succeeded in delaying change.

The ensuing Kulturkampf between a religiously sanctioned indigenous tradition and alien Westernizing influences bears comparison with the struggle pitting Slavophiles versus Westernizers in nineteenth century Russia. Both are in contrast to the dynamic, reform-from-the-top unity characterizing Japan or the sluggish but coherent cultural unity of China.

In holding on to a venerable but nontechnical and even impractical educational system, the Ottoman Empire is to be compared with China. Its cultural tradition was intellectually sophisticated but not atuned to worldly problem-solving. This made its replacement even more difficult.

The disinclination in Ottoman society to educate women or involve them in active work outside the home (aside from the peasantry and the lower urban classes) was probably, on balance, no stronger than in China or Japan.

Yet another significant fissiparous factor contrasting the Ottoman Empire with the experience in China, Japan, and Russia was the imposition of outright Western colonial rule on parts of Ottoman Afro-Asia, beginning with the French Protectorate in Tunisia and the British occupation of Egypt, in 1881 and 1882, respectively. This western colonial rule (begun earlier in parts of the Ottoman world not considered here, such as in Algeria, 1830) was to be followed after the First World War by the division of the Fertile Crescent into four different mandates under British and French control. The nature and the timing of Western colonialism thus greatly strengthened the forces making for cultural and linguistic diversity.

SUMMARY

It may be useful now to restate the findings presented in the foregoing balance sheet of assets and liabilities in a more narrative style.

A major characteristic of this first modernizing period ending in 1914–24 was the great amount of time and effort expended in determining the boundaries, nature, and purposes of the political community. To the extent that modernization requires the creation of strong, effective centralized political units, the early modernization process in Ottoman Afro-Asia offered nothing like the almost linear progress achieved in Japan or Russia among the late modernizers.

Sustained efforts at political centralization and at adapting Western interventions and institutions to the Middle East were not lacking. Indeed, the leitmotif of Middle Eastern political history during roughly the century before 1914 was that of modernizing efforts by established political elites ruling in Istanbul, Cairo, and Tunis. Even the small area of Mount

Lebanon achieved a measure of political centralization after 1860. This period, however, produced no clear consensus concerning the political legitimacy of the existing de facto political units. "Egypt for the Egyptians" became a nationalist slogan during the latter years of the nineteenth century, but many Egyptians still pinned their political hopes on some form of Ottoman unity. The same held for Tunisia. And although the Young Turks can now be seen as the penultimate link in the historical chain leading to the establishment of the Turkish Republic, it would be anachronistic to argue that the Young Turk leadership after 1909 was prepared to do what Atatürk did 14 years later—abolish the empire and establish a Turkish nation-state.

As for the Fertile Crescent, the extreme case of religious diversity within Ottoman Afro-Asia, there was neither experience in political centralization (with the partial exception of Lebanon) nor any consistent move toward accepting any single political unit as the goal.

The modernizing efforts of all late modernizers have necessarily been carried out under pressure from the early modernizers of the West, but only in the Ottoman Empire among Third World societies was there an appreciable minority of people who, as Christians, could more readily identify with the intrusive West. This fact, added to the earlier sense of superiority and self-sufficiency that had long characterized Ottoman Muslims, set up strong psychological barriers to imitating the West among the Muslim majority.

Given these circumstances, the amount of conscious cultural borrowing and the explicit appeals for such borrowing by Ottoman Muslims were remarkable, and should serve to call into question Western prejudices concerning Muslim resistance to non-Muslim influences. What really needs careful explanation by the historians is why, given this operating reality, Pan-Islam was not more successful and why movements such as the Sudanese Mahdiyya did not have even greater resonance throughout the region.

Even viewed from this perspective, the resistance to change and massive borrowing from outside were here clearly stronger by far than in Latin America, culturally a part of the dominant West, and probably stronger than in the colonized Indian subcontinent, where Western pressure in the form of the British Raj was politically, economically, and culturally unifying. Only the indigenous and alien factors in early modernizing China added up to a stonger predisposition against acceptance of outside influences.

This political divisiveness and cultural ambivalence was exacerbated by Western colonial rule. Colonial rule began in Tunisia and Egypt in 1881 and 1882, respectively, and was followed after the First World War by the colonial partition of the Fertile Crescent. Different colonizing powers, different forms of colonial rule, and different periods of colonialism combined to deny the Middle East any possibility of an alien-imposed unity as in India.

The many economic changes taking place in the century before the First World War were also to a considerable extent reduced in their modernizing impact by the same continued confusion over the boundaries, nature, and purposes of the political community. In addition, much of the progress in developing a modernized infrastructure (e.g., roads, railroads, maximizing indigenous economic advantage in expanding world trade) was keyed to the needs of outsiders.

In the same way, the economic impact of Western imperialism on the region could not be the same as, say, that of the British Raj on the Indian subcontinent. There a single imperial overlord was able to impose what amounted to a single large free trade area. Europe's economic and commercial competition in the Middle East not only predated the advent of European imperial rule, it continued thereafter as well. A region that had once enjoyed imperial and thus economic unity lost both in the wake of the many political divisions marking the nineteenth century.

In terms of social integration, considerable progress had been achieved against imposing odds. A study of the region's ecological characteristics (with the juxtaposition of desert, mountains, precarious dry farming, and irrigated agriculture with its need for central control) plus the historically shaped political culture (a centralized bureaucratic empire exercising only limited control over its disparate subjects) suggests the model of a society strong in its ability to survive sundry disasters because of the neatly balanced autonomous disjointedness of its many component parts. This very strength, however, created a powerful inertia against change, whether from a centrally controlled government or elsewhere.

Modernizing rulers in Istanbul, Cairo, and Tunis had imposed a certain degree of political and social integration. The nomads were less able to resist governmental control. Land ownership, generally speaking, became more nearly under central government control as well as more in the hands of those (whether urban notables or tribal shaykhs obtaining personal ownership of what had been communal land) disposed to commercialized exploitation of the land. The many injustices of this process are undeniable, but somewhat like the enclosures in England centuries earlier, this process enhanced the potential for intensive agricultural development.

Yet, once again the political disjunctures impeded the otherwise impressive movement toward greater social integration. The ill-fated Urabi Pasha revolt in Egypt, which set the stage for the British occupation in 1882, may be seen as an abortive effort by a rising Egyptian middle class to secure greater control from the centuries-old system of authoritarian politics controlled by an alien elite (the Turko-Circassians). In a less dramatic way, the widening of the circle of wealth and power was frustrated in Tunisia, as well, with the establishment of the French Protectorate in 1881.

Of course, in these two countries (as later in the Fertile Crescent), the age of Western imperialism thereafter served to foster modernizing social integration by championing capitalistic control of economic resources over surviving patterns of communal control. Such a system provided security, created appropriate credit facilities, and facilitated social and economic mobility through education and governmental employment. From another perspective, however, the break between the modernizing efforts imposed by indigenous political elites before the imposition of Western imperialistic rule and subsequent modernizing efforts under Western imperial control offer one more example of the fits and starts characterizing early modernization in Ottoman Afro-Asia.

Yet another major example of disjuncture was the move toward one form or another of linguistic or ethnic or religious nationalism. One can hardly deny that the creation of a strong sense of political community among a specific group enhances the modernizing possibilities open to that group. To this extent, nationalism and modernization have often marched together. When, however, as in Ottoman Afro-Asia, the question remains unresolved concerning the boundaries, demographic and geographic, of that would-be nation state, precious time and resources may be squandered on this essential point to the exclusion of any incremental advances in development.

Nor can it be overlooked that most of Ottoman Afro-Asia, and especially the Fertile Crescent, is poorly adapted to the creation of a single large nation-state based on the presumed unity of language or religion or ethnicity. Indeed, the splitting up of this region into political units according to any of these criteria risks substituting a stunting parochialism for the earlier cosmopolitanism characterizing the Ottoman Empire.

In the abstract, a case can be made for a political-economic-cultural unit more or less following the lines of Ottoman Afro-Asia. A case can be made for some variety of Arab nationalism. A case can be made for ethnolinguistic nationalism or for religious nationalism. A case can even be made that the political boundaries emerging in the period following the First World War are workable. Whatever might be said about any of these, however, it is clear that considerable modernizing momentum was lost in the necessarily disruptive and time-consuming competition of these many different integrative options.

The progress in education during this period was impressive. Again, however, many of the advantages of a steady incremental development were lost in the welter of confused political and even cultural developments. That rulers from political units of such different size and complexity as Egypt, Tunisia, and the central Ottoman Empire embarked on separate state educational programs was not, in itself, especially disruptive. The efforts in all three political units were similar (all, grosso modo, intent on creating westernized educated cadres), and the resulting devolution of central control (three state educational institutions instead of one) may well have been an advantage.

More troublesome were the rivalries between state and private school systems. What could have been a healthy pluralism of public and private schooling (as in the Anglo-Saxon world) became instead a divisive battleground for political loyalties, for most of the private school programs were advanced by the different Western (including Russia) Christian missionary groups with the tacit support of one or another of the rival European powers.

Even when the missionary educational effort supported, at least implicitly, the concept of a multiconfessional political community, the linguistic factor was divisive. A region needing a new, modernizing foundation for social and cultural integration (to replace the impressive but nonmodernizing cultural unity for which the traditional Ottoman Empire had provided a powerful matrix) was clearly hampered by the intrusion of foreign languages seeking to serve as vehicles of modernizing communication (English and French).

The formidable linguistic problem can be posed differently. It is not so much the case that the educated elites of the region were being challenged to move from monolingualism to bilingualism or even multilingualism. Among the educated, multilingualism had long existed, with knowledge of both Arabic and Ottoman Turkish, perhaps even Persian as well, the mark of the intellectual. Now, however, at least two different languages, English and French, coming from an alien culture, seemed to provide the keys to progress and development. Whereas previously the individual with some claim to learning (whether religious leader, bureaucrat, or merchant) literally spoke the same language(s) as other educated persons, thenceforth there were two different learned worlds—the indigenous traditional and the intrusive westernized. And the latter, in turn, was further divided among those whose cultural and educational formation had been influenced by English or French, not to mention Russian, German, or other.

This first period of modernization brought considerable intellectual and cultural activity, breaking down to some extent the previous isolationist cultural self-sufficiency of Ottoman Afro-Asia. Nevertheless, receptivity to needed outside influences was hampered by habits, forged over the previous centuries, of disdain for foreigners and their culture. Moreover, resistance to such outside influences could easily take the explosive form of religious nativism, for foreign influences appeared also to threaten religion as well.

Add to this the political and economic disjunctures already mentioned, and the psychic strains of such cultural borrowing were extreme. On balance, Ottoman Afro-Asia in this period proved more adaptively than might have been expected. Even so, the result was at best only a highly tentative move toward a new, modernizing cultural synthesis.

It was in this period that an increasingly arrogant Western world began to refer to certain Middle Eastern individuals precariously balanced between the two cultural worlds as "Levantines." Extending the usage, one might well sum up the confrontation of traditional Ottoman Afro-Asia with hectoring Europe as having "Levantinized" the former. Many notable efforts at modernization had been made, first by native political leaders and then later by religious and intellectual leaders as well. Much progress had been achieved. Yet, the emerging picture after the First World War revealed too many different, and often contradictory, impulses and institutions struggling in an untidy confrontation.

Part Two

The Modernizing Transformation

CHAPTER NINE

Introduction

FOLLOWING THE PATTERN set in the two earlier books, *The Modernization of Japan and Russia* and *The Modernization of China*, Part One sought to describe how the premodern heritage of Ottoman Afro-Asia affected the early modernization process in the Middle East. Part Two deals more directly with the modernizing transformation. We have chosen the First World War as the chronological dividing line. While all efforts at periodization are imprecise, this date seems much less so than any other that might be advanced.

With the demise of the Ottoman Empire following the First World War, the Middle Eastern political map took a shape that still essentially holds today. Moreover, the question of whether to seek some restoration of the area-wide unity that the Ottoman Empire had represented for centuries was made irrelevant by Kemal Atatürk's creation of the Turkish Republic. Subsequent pan-Arab developments illustrate the nostalgic hope for the larger political unity that the Ottoman Empire once represented, but the feeble results of these Arab unity efforts underscore how much easier it is to maintain an existing imperial system, however creaky, than to create one where none exists.

The period after 1918 also completed Western imperial division of the Middle East, with all of the area under study here save Turkey coming under one form or another of control by a single European power. Equally, as we can now see more clearly, this period immediately following the First World War marked the high point of Western colonialism in the Middle East. Soon, the decolonizing impulses of indigenous nationalism were to become increasingly prominent. Economically, the Middle East had by this time reached a high point of integration into a Western-dominated international economy.

If the First World War appears to be the most important date dividing the two phases of Middle Eastern modernization, it is not for lack of other plausible turning points. To mention only a few such examples, the major losses of European territory suffered by the Ottomans in their 1877–78 war with Russia constituted a giant step in the direction of creating the Middle East as it is perceived today. Europe had by that date wrested most of the European territories from Ottoman control. In the process, the Ottoman Empire had lost a large proportion of its non-Muslim subjects, and this served to undermine any lingering notion among members of the political elite that Ottomanism (the idea of a multinational, multilanguage, multireligious political community) was a viable option. The door was thereafter even more widely open to other ideological possibilities such as Pan-Islam or Turkism or Arabism.

Another date that could be advanced as marking a turning point was the year from 1881 to 1882. In that one-year period, first Tunisia and then Egypt fell under direct European control. This foreign domination sharply reduced indigenous elite control. Instead, a major shift toward alien-controlled societal change ensued.

Yet another turning point might be the early 1860s in Lebanon, when religious conflicts triggered European intervention and resulted in a form of European-monitored self-government.

Or one might opt for a somewhat longer period of time marking the change to a more accelerated phase of modernization and choose the years from 1869 to 1876. In that time, all three of the states exercising at least some degree of institutionalized political independence—the central Ottoman Empire, Egypt, and Tunisia—fell into state bankruptcy. Tunisia came first in 1869, followed by the Ottoman Empire and Egypt in 1876. This fiscal failure essentially brought to a close the first phase of reform-from-the-top as implemented by the indigenous political elite and left the way open for a more direct imposition of alien control.

On balance, however, the First World War period offers the sharpest break in the process of a modernizing transformation. The decade from 1914 to 1924 imposed rough-and-ready answers to political questions that had seized the people of this area since the beginnings of modern times. The belief in Ottoman imperial unity had, admittedly, long been an ideal woefully out of line with fissiparous political reality, but thenceforth that ideal died with the death of the Ottoman Empire.

Pan-Islam, another effort to construct a larger political and cultural unity, also was discredited by events. Acting in his capacity as caliph, the Ottoman sultan in 1914 had declared a jihad against the states at war with the Ottoman Empire. But the political-military impact of this call for jihad was negligible. A decade later, Kemal Atatürk abruptly declared the abolition of the caliphate. Many Muslims in the Middle East and elsewhere were shocked, but the incapacity of ulama or political leaders to come up with an agreed-upon new caliphate brutally exposed the unreality of Pan-Islam or the caliphate as political forces.

The nation-state principle that Atatürk explicitly championed seemingly loomed thereafter as the only option available to others as well, whether they liked it or not. Even the unrealized Arabism of the Fertile Crescent was essentially a nationalist movement, not a Pan-Islamic effort, as the almost universal scorn greeting Sharif Husayn's bid for the caliphate demonstrated.

The ups and downs of Pan-Arabism since the 1920s are best explained in terms of frustrated nationalism, and so, too, the Islamic resurgence that became a force a half century later. Witness that no one today seriously poses the matter of the caliphate.

This pattern of interpretation does, however, tend to place considerable emphasis on political boundaries as the principal, almost as the preemptive, explanatory model. From this perspective, our study of the Middle East in Part One was subdivided into four political units: the central Ottoman Empire, Egypt, Tunisia, all of which had their own independent or autonomous governing institutions, and the area of the Fertile Crescent that formed simply a number of provinces ruled from Istanbul. The period following the First World War eventually leads to an exact doubling of that number, with today's eight states—Egypt, Iraq, Israel, Jordan, Lebanon, Syria, Tunisia, and Turkey.

Certainly, it is a useful organizing principle. Following the fate of peoples institutionally yoked together by political instruments of persuasion and coercion is a plausible way to trace modernizing transformation. Even so, we must be cautious not to assume too much. First, labelling all eight units by the same name—"state"—risks positing a uniformity or a comparability that should, instead, be very much a matter for examination. It must be remembered that these political units both before and after 1914 have varied in size, potential or actual power, legitimacy, and efficacy of their governing institutions.

Moreover, Part One demonstrated the existence of a cluster of mores, institutions, and historical developments that characterized the entire region. Ottoman Afro-Asia constituted a single cultural area, and many of the more basic attitudes and actions of its peoples were not only shaped and sustained by societal forces beyond the purview of any existing state but even continued to influence the attitudes and actions of different statesmen. The basically similar pattern of political developments in the three autonomous and distinctive state systems existing before 1914—the central Ottoman Empire, Egypt, and Tunisia—suffices to put us on guard against assuming that the major modernizing stimuli always came from those exercising an accepted monopoly over the legitimate use of coercion.

Indeed, this venerable Austinian-Weberian definition of the state must, itself, be carefully questioned as we turn to tracing the next phase of modernization in the Middle East.

In other words, to accomplish our task we must abstain from prejudging the issue of whether events since 1914 are best interpreted in terms of a single cultural area or of a discrete number of sovereign units (eight at this time, but perhaps more or less in the future: e.g., Egypt and Syria briefly combined to form a single state; tomorrow may bring an independent Palestinian state).

This complicating factor does, however, offer the heuristic prospect of testing the role of the state in the process of modernization. Such a possibility, adumbrated in the Introduction to this book, becomes especially pronounced in our examination of the modernization process since 1914. All the more reason, acccordingly, to follow strictly the pattern of previous books in this series as well as the pattern set out in Part One and treat seriatim the international context, political structure, economic growth and development, social interdependence, and knowledge and education.

These chapters will be followed by a concluding chapter offering a summary and interpretation of the entire book.

CHAPTER TEN

International Context

THE PEACE SETTLEMENTS that followed the First World War changed the political map of the Middle East. The Ottoman Empire, whose leaders generation after generation had struggled against European ambitions, finally went out of existence. No single state or empire took its place. Instead, both the reality and the operative ideal of the Ottoman Middle East as a political and cultural system embracing the entire region disappeared. In its place came different realities and different operative ideals. Most clear-cut was the creation of Turkey.

Under the leadership of Mustafa Kemal, who later assumed the name Kemal Atatürk (Father of the Turks), Turkey turned its back on the idea of an empire bringing together peoples of different races, languages, and religions. The new Turkey chose instead ethnolinguistic nationalism. Seldom in history has the revolutionary substitution of an alien political ideal been more dramatically demonstrated than in Republican Turkey's rejection of its Ottoman past for a political system "made in Europe."

A protonationalist choice was also available to two other Afro-Asian political communities emerging from the Ottoman past—Egypt and Tunisia. Geography had endowed both with a nation-state potential. No people in the world have been more clearly influenced by their environment to be a single nation than the Egyptians. Egypt—the "Gift of the Nile"—has nurtured a population distinct from all its neighbors since the dawn of history.

Rather more like other parts of formerly Ottoman Afro-Asia, Tunisia has a mix of mountaineers and plainsmen, nomads and sedentaries, remote oases and central cities. Yet, if the striking ecological homogeneity of Egypt is put aside as a special case, Tunisia offers perhaps more geographical advantages predisposing its people toward a political community than any other region of Ottoman Afro-Asia. Tunisia has an inner core of territory radiating out from the capital city of Tunis easily accessible to central control. Unlike the situation in Syria, Algeria, Morocco, or Iraq, the nomads and mountaineers (always most resistant both to central government and to homogenizing cultural impulses) tend to be located on the fringes of Tunisia, where they are less apt to divide the country into so many pockets of particularism.

Both Egypt and Tunisia, moreover, had possessed autonomous governments for centuries. After falling under Western imperial control (the French Protectorate in Tunisia beginning in 1881 and the British occupation of Egypt of the following year), both were ruled by imperial powers bent on maintaining the juridical distinctiveness of each.

Accordingly, Turkey, Egypt, and Tunisia began the post-Ottoman period as distinct political entities whose peoples either explicitly accepted that political identity or at least did not tend to challenge it. To this extent, the imposing problems of modernization in these three states could be addressed without excessive concern over what was—or what ought to be—the political matrix.

No such beginning advantage accrued to the Fertile Crescent. There the only area that might be seen as sheltering a protonation was historic Mount Lebanon, long a refuge for two religious communities—the Maronites and the Druze—who from their inhospitable mountain fastness had resisted the control and cultural influences of the urban-based Muslim empires. The nineteenth century brought brutal civil war between Maronites and Druzes; this led to European intervention. In 1860, Napoleon III had sent French troops to Lebanon to quell the disorder; soon thereafter, the European state system agreed to the establishment of a special autonomous province in Mount Lebanon with a legislative council and a Christian, but non-Lebanese, governor. Nominally still a part of the Ottoman Empire, Mount Lebanon experienced about a half-century of quasi-independence before the system was abolished by Istanbul during the First World War.

The distinctive autonomy of Mount Lebanon was not, however, restored during the period of the French Mandate. Instead, in 1920, France created "Greater Lebanon" (the borders of the present Lebanese state). The new boundaries brought into existence a more realistic economic unit, but they compounded the political problem by adding great numbers of Sunni Muslims. They resisted becoming a minority community in a Maronite-dominated polity. Added as well were many Shi'a Muslims and a number of non-Maronite Christians.

Moreover, the political leadership of what was to emerge as Syria viewed those lands added to Mount Lebanon to create Greater Lebanon as "irredenta." Yet, to speak of Syrian irredenta is inaccurate. After the First World War, there was no sense of "Syrianness." Neither past history nor future aspirations predisposed the people of Syria to think in such terms. The same can be said for Iraq, Palestine, and Transjordan. In 1919, it had been almost exactly four centuries since the entire Fertile Crescent had come under Ottoman rule. Thereafter, the area had been divided into different provinces, the lines of which had changed from time to time over the centuries; such lines did not in any case accord closely with the boundaries that emerged in the period of British and French mandates. Political loyalties had been directed, according to different social contexts, to family, tribe, religious community, locality, and, in a vague, passive fashion, to the Ottoman Empire.

Beginnings of Arab Nationalism

The stirrings of what became Arab nationalism—always strongest in the Fertile Crescent—can be traced back to the early years of the nineteenth century, just as was the case with the origins of Turkish nationalism. One can, however, easily exaggerate the extent of a fully articulated Arab nationalism in the Fertile Crescent during the second decade of this century. The celebrated Arab revolt against Ottoman rule during the First World War in alliance with Britain (made famous in the West by the exploits and mystique of T. E. Lawrence) is more accurately to be seen not as a mass movement of political liberation but as an awkward coalition among a few—an ambitious family (the Hashimites) whose leader, Sharif Husayn, was actually an Ottoman-appointed official in the Holy City of Mecca; a bedouin following in the Hijaz (Western Arabian Peninsula); a number of disaffected Arab officers in the Ottoman army; and a handful of Fertile Crescent Arab intellectuals who, having taken note of Western dominance and Ottoman decline, were developing the idea of Arabism.

Not a few of the notables living in the Fertile Crescent regarded Sharif Husayn's alliance with infidel Britain and revolt against the Ottoman sultan/caliph as treasonous. And the great majority took the prudent position of avoiding being identified with either the established Ottoman government or the Arab revolt. Just as their ancestors during the previous four centuries of Ottoman rule, they viewed the political battles of soldiers and statesmen as best left to those rash few (usually in any case not well-established natives of the Fertile Crescent) who chose to play the dangerous games of imperial politics.

This is not to deny that Arabism was destined to become a major political ideology not just in the Fertile Crescent but eventually throughout the entire Arab world. Nor is there any doubt that with the total disappearance of the Ottoman Empire after the First World War, and with Atatürk's championing of Turkish nationalism, Arabism was no longer associated with contributing to the destruction of the last great Muslim empire. The coup de grace had finally been delivered not by Arabs but by the most successful Ottoman general during the First World War, Kemal Atatürk.

Ataturkism

Ataturkism told Turks to seek their political salvation as Turks. In so doing, they were to turn their backs on Arabs, on ideas of a reconstituted Arabo-Turkish Ottoman Empire, and on notions of a Muslim political solidarity. All this served to enhance the still-emerging idea that the vulnerable peoples of the Fertile Crescent should seek their political salvation according to their own appropriate nationalism, that of Arabism. This necessarily meant, however, that the peoples of the Fertile Crescent faced the task of seeking independence from outside control and also of reaching agreement on the appropriate boundaries of a hoped-for state that did not then exist. All this, moreover, had to be sought in the virtual absence of an existing political or administrative structure.

Zionism

To this challenge facing the Fertile Crescent could be added yet another—that of the confrontation between Zionism and a still-rudimentary Arab nationalism. The struggle between Zionist settlers and Palestinians—in addition to all the usual problems that arise from two different groups at different levels of development disputing control over the same small territory (mandate Palestine being the size of New Jersey)—can be understood as a collision of two diametrically opposed political ideologies—Arabism aspiring to a new overarching political identity that would make possible a large political community binding together peoples of different religions and ways of life who shared a common Arab culture as opposed to the Zionist ideal of nationalism based on a common religious heritage. The former, if successful, would have realized a political cosmopolitanism replacing the imperial ideal and reality associated with the centuries of Ottoman rule. The latter would be a harbinger of a quite different political solution—smaller and more cohesive nation-states—a Jewish state in Palestine, a Maronite state in Lebanon, and then perhaps states for Druze, Kurds, Alawites, Shi'a Muslims, with the majority Sunni Muslims piecing together in political community what remained. On the one hand, the prospect of larger integration reached by some combination of consensus and force. On the other, the prospect of countless partitions and a Balkanization of the Fertile Crescent.

Breakdown of the Ottoman Empire

Following the First World War, the single political world for which the Ottoman Empire had served as armature, even in its decades of weakness, was gone. One important new political entity—Turkey—explicitly rejected any effort to put it back together. Two states—Egypt and Tunisia—could realistically pursue the most immediately pressing political goals within the framework of existing territorial boundaries. In the Fertile Crescent, even this first step of defining the appropriate political unit or units remained to be accomplished.

Egypt and Tunisia, while similar to Turkey in being coherent territorial political units, were more like the Fertile Crescent in having succumbed to outright Western imperial rule. Only Turkey escaped that fate. The difference between the two situations—independence in the context of facing several larger and potentially threatening outside states on the one hand and direct, preemptive control by a single outside imperial power—can create substantially different approaches to international relations. In the former case, the country's political leadership deals with a multipolar world and attempts to achieve security by carefully balancing off the several outside powers. In the latter case, the colonized political leadeship acts within a bilateral colonizer/colonized framework.

The former more nearly characterized the situation prevailing in Ottoman Afro-Asia from the late eighteenth century onward, when the European state system became clearly capable of dominating the Ottoman world and also disposed to intervene—a thoroughly kaleidoscopic international relations system characterized by a number of different political "players," both within the Middle East and among the outside powers. The distinction between political vulnerability in a multipolar international relations system and bilateral colonized/colonizer vulnerability is, however, clearer in theory than in modern Middle Eastern political reality.

The British in Egypt

Britain in Egypt, for example, never really attained the preemptive dominance to be found in British India or for that matter in most other parts of the vast British Empire. For reasons of intra-European international politics, the British position in Egypt from 1882 until 1914 remained simply a military occupation. Only when the Ottoman Empire (still nominally the sovereign over Egypt) joined the Central Powers during the First World War did Britain establish a protectorate over Egypt. This, in turn, lasted only eight years, until 1922, when Britain unilaterally declared Egyptian independence subject to major reservations (all part of British efforts to cut back on expensive imperial commitments and accommodate Egyptian nationalism while assuring minimal strategic needs). The 1936 Anglo-Egyptian treaty, negotiated in the shadow of Italy's invasion of Ethiopia (revealing to Britain and Egypt at least a temporary common interest), loosened somewhat more the British hold over Egypt.

During the entire period of British presence in Egypt, until the British evacuation of the Suez Canal base (negotiated in 1954 and completed in 1956), the reality of ultimate British dominance was, of course, clear to all concerned, however veiled that power might be at times. The British action in imposing a Wafdist government on King Faruq in 1942, in the darkest days of World War II, when Rommel's Afrika Korps threatened to overwhelm the British position in the Middle East, revealed the real locus of political power in Egypt.

The disguised, indirect British rule of Egypt created a distinctive political environment in Egypt. The fiction of Egyptian independence coupled with the reality of Britain's ability to make and break cabinets at will reinforced the already deep-seated pessimistic attitude toward politics and government that had always characterized the Egyptian polity. At a time when the demands of modernization required widening the circle of political participation and increasing the capacity of all to adjust to more complex forms of group activities directed toward shared societal goals, Egypt's evolving political institutionalization offered a limited parliamentary constitutionalism in form but a sham in fact. The political reality was that of two clusterings of Egyptian forces, one organized around the monarchy and the other around the popular Wafd Party, with each attempting to challenge or neutralize or even at times openly accommodate the British, who ultimately made all important decisions. Such a situation fostered political cynicism as well as the wild swings of political extremism usually associated with group frustration and a pervasive sense of political impotence.

The resulting politics of court and cabal concentrated the attention of the political leadership on the handful of political players in Cairo (king, British ambassador, and a few score establishment politicians) and frustrated efforts to "nationalize" the Egyptian body politic. In a manner reminiscent of Louis XIV's taming of the French nobility, Egyptian politics, especially in the interwar period, became increasingly centralized, while links to the periphery, historically always weak, failed to grow. The poignant story told in Tawfiq al-Hakim's novel *Yawmiyyat Na'ib Fi al-Aryaf* (translated as *The Maze of Justice*) of the impact of national elections on village life demonstrates the tendency. Following an election and change of government, the old ritual was reenacted. The one telephone in the village was removed from the house of the defeated headman, to the wails and lamentations of the womenfolk, and installed in the house of the new headman representing the winning party, accompanied by shouts of triumph and exultation. Thereafter village life continued as before.

Egypt was, however, given enough apparent independence to stimulate efforts in international, and, even more, in regional affairs. Following the 1936 treaty, Britain sponsored Egyptian membership in the League of Nations. Throughout the entire period, Egypt remained in competition with Britain over the Sudan. Britain worked to make the vast Sudan (one-third the area of continental United States) independent of Egypt, whereas Egyptian politicians of all persuasions sought "unity of the Nile Valley." The interwar period also witnessed the slow development of Arabism in Egypt, stimulated by several factors—use of emotional foreign policy issues (as the problem of Palestine) to upstage domestic political rivals, attempts to blunt British hegemony in the region, the Egyptian aspirations as the largest and most advanced Arab state to play a predominant role in the region. The same tendencies toward pessimism, cynicism, and "court politics" also characterized Egyptian ventures in the regional and international arenas.

Colonialism in Tunisia

Colonial rule took quite a different form in Tunisia. Legally, Tunisia was a French protectorate. France ruled through the bey of Tunis, who continued to have his own official staff of ministers and bureaucrats. The provincial governors, or qaids, were "advised" by French *controleurs civils*. At the same time, the French penchant for bureaucratic centralization and the experience in neighboring French Algeria induced a more direct control. Moreover, Tunisia—like neighboring Algeria—was exposed to colonization by European settlers. These settlers dominated commercial, export-oriented agriculture, but also were present in quite small-scale family farming (especially Italian settlers from Sicily and southern Italy). Europeans held virtually all of the high posts in the protectorate bureaucracy (as is common in all colonial situations) and most of the middle level posts as well (which in nonsettler colonies are available to natives using the bureaucracy as an avenue of upward mobility). Europeans dominated in the professions, in business, and in the media. Demands that their children receive a European standard of education brought about the creation of many good schools, but only a trickle of native Tunisians were able to find places there.

Most of all, the great numbers of colons (who in the last decades of the protectorate averaged between 6 and 8 percent of the total population) formed effective pressure groups intent on forcing the French protectorate administration to attend to their interests, not to those of the native population. The existence of a Franco-Italian rivalry during the interwar years, matched by an Italian settler community in Tunisia that outnumbered the French until the early thirties, even further diverted French eyes away from native Tunisian problems.

The result was a tightly controlled polity and economy in Tunisia. The idea that France was rightly in charge of politics and the economy, the notion that the major threat to that rightful position came not yet from native Tunisians but from Italy and Italian settlers in Tunisia, ruled out anything more than the most pro forma native Tunisian representation. Yes, the bey and his entourage existed. Legislative assemblies of quite limited jurisdiction had been created (but under the control of European settlers). The result was not nearly so brutally harsh as what pertained in neighboring Algeria, which since 1848 had been juridically integrated into France. It was, however, a far cry from nonsettler colonization in Egypt and the Fertile Crescent.

Paradoxical as it might seem, the less liberal regime in Tunisia may well have facilitated native Tunisian modernization much better than did the British behind-the-scenes rule in Egypt. Not so much Tunisian political thought and action were consumed in the game of politics at the top. Instead, faced with a clear challenge, Tunisian political forces moved in steady stages toward the creation of a widely participatory nationalist movement with a modernizing program.

The equivalent to this party (the Neo-Destour, formed in 1934) in Egypt was the Wafd, which came into existence at the end of the First World War. The Wafd remained from that time until the overthrow of the entire regime with the Free Officers Revolt in 1952 an impressive mass party. It did, however, lose much of that modernizing single-mindedness that can properly be attributed to both Ataturkism and the Neo-Destour led by Habib Bourguiba. Many reasons for this difference can be adduced, not the least important of which was surely the tantalizing form of British behind-the-scenes control in Egypt as contrasted with the challenge of an independence that remained to be consolidated in Turkey or a dangerous dependence that only a mass political organization seemed capable of upsetting in Tunisia.

Another impressive mass organization that did thrive in Egypt beginning in the late twenties can be explained in these terms. The fundamentalist, neotraditionalist Muslim Brethren, founded in 1928 and attaining a peak membership estimated at about 500,000, within the next few years, was to a large extent symptomatic of the failure of Egypt's political system to increase political participation and channel the combined frustrations and confusions of worldwide economic depression and limited, disjunctive modernization. Neither Turkey nor Tunisia in the thirties and forties witnessed an equivalent to the Muslim Brethren, largely because acceptable organizational structures and political ideologies were being created.

Europe and the Fertile Crescent

The period of outright Western imperial rule in the Fertile Crescent reveals yet another pattern. There colonial rule came late, lasted only a few years, and was of limited extent. The mandate system and the role of the League of Nations in supervising each mandatory, although largely a concession in form but not substance to the new ideas of Wilsonism, still augured a new age in which Europe was no longer "imperialist in good conscience." The idea that the mandatory had only a transitional role of guardian leading the mandated society to independence gave all concerned—colonized and colonizers—a sense that the existing system was impermanent.

Britain in the Fertile Crescent combined its traditional preference for indirect control in the Middle East with the postwar needs of an overstretched Empire and remained in Iraq scarcely more than a decade. By 1932, Britain had managed to establish an Iraqi monarchy, place Faisal, the son of Sharif Husayn, on the throne, end the mandate, negotiate an Anglo-Iraqi treaty providing Britain base rights, and sponsor Iraqi membership in the League of Nations. In neighboring Transjordan (soon separated from mandated Palestine), de facto autonomy under Faisal's brother, Amir Abdullah, was arranged, with Britain remaining in control of defense and diplomacy. Only in the very special circumstances of Palestine did Britain fail to disengage from daily problems of administration while maintaining ultimate control.

France in Syria was handicapped by the lack of any local "clients" (as the Hashimites in their relations with Britain) willing to accommodate French interests. The strong French position among the Maronites of Lebanon served to intensify the opposition of Muslims and many others to France. Moreover, the British example elsewhere in the Fertile Crescent added further pressure. France never quite recovered from a shaky start in Syria. Bested in wartime and postwar jousting for regional influence by Britain, France was obliged in 1920 to enter Damascus by force of arms after routing a hastily assembled Syrian citizen army on the way. Thereafter, the short-lived Syrian Republic was overthrown, and France attempted to buttress a weak position with crude divide-and-rule policies. A revolt among the Druze (who, ironically, had received from the French special consideration) spread throughout the country in the mid-twenties; in response, French forces twice bombarded Damascus.

Franco-Syrian efforts to achieve a settlement similar to that between Britain and Iraq failed in the thirties when the French Parliament refused to ratify the treaty that had been negotiated. Then, between 1936 and 1939, France—busy as it was preparing for the expected military confrontation with Nazi Germany—permitted Turkey, stage by stage, to annex the Syrian province of Alexandretta (renamed Hatay).

The defeat of France in 1940, the subsequent intra-French struggle between supporters of the Vichy Regime (inclined to adjust as best it could to the Nazi victory) and the Free French, the Allied and Free French military defeat of the Vichyites in Syria (1941), and the ensuing Allied control of the Middle East undermined what chance remained for a postwar France to establish even an indirect, British-style position of strength in the Fertile Crescent. The new realities of power were symbolized by an alliance in Lebanon between Maronites and Muslims (1943) to achieve independence. This was the so-called national pact, according to which the Maronites abandoned the old policy of relying on France and accepted the idea of belonging to the Arab world while the Muslims agreed to the independence and territorial integrity of Lebanon within that Arab world.

By 1946, both Syria and Lebanon were independent. The next year brought the United Nations General Assembly resolution for the partition of Palestine into separate Arab and Jewish states. With no agreement between the two parties, there followed the creation of Israel and the first

Arab-Israeli war in 1948. Jordan thereafter acted to absorb the West Bank of Palestine (1950). Egypt administered the tiny southwest portion of mandate Palestine known as the Gaza Strip. Israel existed but was not accepted by any of its neighbors. Palestinian refugees remained scattered in temporary housing throughout the area.

In sum, the age of direct European imperial rule in the Fertile Crescent came to an end roughly three decades after it had begun. Given the vicissitudes of that short era, one can hardly speak of major institution-building. Five independent states (Syria, Lebanon, Iraq, Jordan, and Israel) emerged in this brief period out of a region that before had experienced four centuries within a single imperial system, the Ottoman Empire. Only in perhaps two of the states—Israel and Lebanon—was there a reasonably clear consensus making possible the emergence of a nation-state from the existing territorial state.

Israelis agreed on the need for a sovereign state to insure the appropriate development of a Jewish National Home, but they faced the problem of an appreciable Arab minority. Lebanon, after the 1943 "national pact," faced the challenge of attempting to become the Switzerland of the Middle East, a state and society to be based not on a single religious, linguistic, or ethnic group, but rather on a delicately balanced combination of different peoples. As for the other three states—Syria, Iraq, and Jordan— neither rulers nor opposition groups laid any claims to nationhood.

What little political institutionalization had taken place during the short period of Western imperial rule could not readily serve as a base for continuing development given the limited legitimacy of the existing states.

Legacy of Western Imperial Rule

To speak then of Western imperial rule in the Middle East as if to describe a uniform process taking place throughout the area is misleading. Only Tunisia approached what might be called "classical" imperial rule. Its colonial experience lasted for several generations and was also intensive during that period. British paramountcy in Egypt was as long, but it was more indirect and more tantalizing in its impact on the Egyptian political elites. Imperialism in the Fertile Crescent was brief and disjunctive, contributing to the destruction of old patterns and institutions rather than to the creation of something new and destined to survive.

From this perspective, the age of direct Western imperialism in the Middle East or—an overlapping but different periodization—the years between the First World War and the 1950s (by which time those colonized states had attained independence) must appear as an interlude. The international context of the post-Ottoman Middle East is best explained as a continuation of the old Eastern Question pattern that began to develop fully three quarters of a century before the establishment of the French Protectorate in Tunisia.

The bilateral colonizer/colonized relationship characteristic of pure colonialism never prevailed in the entire area of former Ottoman Afro-Asia and, except for Tunisia (plus Algeria and Aden), never existed for long in any part thereof. Even in Tunisia, rivalries between France and Italy, which had predated the establishment of the French Protectorate, intensified after the First World War, especially during the period of Mussolini's rule in Italy.

The kaleidoscopic pattern of multiplayer diplomacy (many outside powers vying for influence and many regional parties serving at times as pawns but also as clients capable of manipulating their patrons) that had distinguished nineteenth-century Eastern Question diplomacy was necessarily modified by Western colonial rule as it developed here and there throughout the region. Even so, colonial rule did not cause a systemic change. If the venerable term for international relations in the Middle East from the late eighteenth century to the demise of the Ottoman Empire after the First World War—the Eastern Question—is used to describe a system of international relations rather than a period of time, then it can be said that the Eastern Question never went out of existence. It exists to this day as the dominant pattern of Middle Eastern international relations.

Western imperial rule failed to achieve the one goal that can normally be expected of imperial ventures, that of creating larger and more centralized political entities. In the Fertile Crescent, the division of territories between Britain and France plus the special circumstances created by Zionism fostered the emergence of five successor states. In Egypt, the British presence largely explains the emergence of a separate, independent Sudan instead of a "unity of the Nile valley." And, in Tunisia, the quite different colonial experience, while leaving a legacy of strong state institutions, tended to separate that country from the former Ottoman world of which it had been for so long a part.

Interpreting the period of Western imperial rule as a brief interlude that further divided the area and continued the disintegrative forces at work since the beginning of the Eastern Question serves also to illuminate the otherwise confusing international politics of the region since the 1950s.

Arabism can then be seen as a major expression of the idea that only a large and strong political entity can enable the region to hold its own against pressures pouring in from the outside. What a Western journal dismissed years ago as the Arab "urge to merge" appears as an understandable effort to overcome internal weakness and to confront the West, regarded to this day as both tormentor and tempter.

The recent and continuing wave of Muslim religiopolitical fundamentalism can be similarly studied. The crisis of ideology and political legitimacy continues. Arabism reached its heights in the 1950s and 1960s under Egypt's Gamal Abdel Nasser. But it seemed not to provide the needed answers following, first, the breakup of the union between Egypt and Syria (which lasted only three years, from 1958 to 1961) and then the major Arab defeat at the hands of Israel in June 1967.

The subsequent period marked by extremes of political and ideological alliances with outsiders has seemed to offer no better answers (e.g., Sadat's Egypt and Saudi Arabia's ties to the United States at one extreme and governments in Syria, Iraq, and South Yemen, plus most antiestablishment radical movements elsewhere seeking salvation in cooperation with the Communist world at the other extreme). Muslim fundamentalism stands out as one more phase in the search for a satisfactory ideology and a sense of political legitimacy.

Political Transformations

Before the Nasser years, political leadership in much of the Arab world sought to achieve its goals in cooperation with the dominant, outside West. Politically, Hashimite rule in Jordan and Iraq (until the 1958 revolution) offers the best example, but similar tendencies existed elsewhere. Ideologically, this was the age of secularizing and Westernizing elites, and the roots of this ideological predisposition go back even further to the beginnings of Eastern Question diplomacy. During this time, there emerged the belief, at times consciously expressed but more often unconsciously assumed, that the region had only to graft a limited number of Western institutions and ideas (especially technology, usually beginning with the military side) onto its cultural system in order to succeed in the modern world, or, in a word, to modernize. As regards the Arab world, these ideological developments have been well summarized in Albert Hourani's classic study significantly titled *Arabic Thought in the Liberal Age.* Equally significant are the dates for Hourani's "Liberal Age" (1789–1939). At the end of this period, so Hourani argues, Middle Eastern optimism about the effectiveness of massive cultural borrowing from the West had faded. Equally in decline by this time was the attraction of liberalism and secularism.

Other ideological responses have always been present, of course, even in the "Liberal Age." For example, cycles of religiously expressed nativism, puritanism, and xenophobia can readily be set alongside accommodationist and adaptive phases. Present-day fundamentalism has its antecedents in the Egyptian Muslim Brethren beginning in 1928, in Pan-Islam, in the messianic Sudanese mahdiyya, and in the rise of Wahhabism in the Arabian Peninsula.

All such movements—from unabashed Westernization to inflexible nativism—have shared two critical characteristics. First, they represent efforts to achieve a new societal synthesis to replace the values of a passing Ottoman world. Second, they all take place in the context of persistent outside pressures. It is in this sense that neither the age of outright Western imperial rule nor the First World War and the subsequent disappearance of the Ottoman Empire provides a clear-cut turning point in the international context. Political elites in the Middle East both before and after these two overlapping periods have been obliged to wrestle with problems of political legitimacy. And both before and after, they have done this while looking over their shoulders at an intrusive Western state system that never absorbs their region into a new imperium but also never leaves them alone. For these reasons—general lack of a consensus concerning the political legitimacy of existing states or of existing governmental systems and an omnipresent cluster of outside powers choosing the Middle East as an arena in which to compete—the usual distinctions between politics at the local, national, regional, and international levels continue to be blurred.

Coming closest to escaping what can be called the Eastern Question pattern of international relations are those societies that have reached a consensus concerning the legitimacy and the territorial boundaries of the political community. This is not to assume that only a Western-style nation-state can become modern—although that form has offered thus far the most successful model. Rather, lack of agreement concerning the nature and extent of the political community dissipates the human resources that could otherwise be yoked for a common purpose. And when the ensuing political confusion is compounded by a consistently high level of intervention into the region by foreign powers, a tenaciously long-lived system of international relations results. The system itself then becomes a major barrier to the efforts of individuals or groups to effect major institutional changes.

Atatürk's Turkey

The relative success of certain successor states to Ottoman Afro-Asia supports the foregoing interpretation. Atatürk obliged the newly created Republic of Turkey to abandon all hope of keeping alive an Arabo-Turkish Ottoman Empire. He insisted on secularizing the state, and, in 1924, he defied traditional religious circles in Turkey and flouted Muslim sentiments throughout the world by abolishing the caliphate. The nation-building impetus of these dramatic changes has long been understood. Equally important, however, was the virtual revolution in international relations achieved by Atatürk's actions. What if instead of Atatürk's policies following the First World War the Istanbul political elite had sought to preserve as much as possible of the Ottoman Empire?

Or what if the idea of an Arabo-Turkish political community had been pursued? Such a policy had historical roots. It could build on strong religious ties, the overwhelming majority of both Arabs and Turks being Muslim, largely Sunni Muslim. In the confused situation existing after the First World War such a policy might have achieved territorial gains, especially in the Fertile Crescent. An Arabo-Turkish strategy would have given Turkey (or whatever entity instead of Turkey might have emerged in the Anatolian Peninsula) the regional leadership to which Nasser's Egypt later aspired.

Yet, the later experience throughout the Arab world suggests that such policies, seemingly with prospects of a larger state and greater international influence, would have produced only a post-World War variant of the old Ottoman Empire—that is, Turkey as preeminent power in the Middle East but one almost completely at the mercy of regional political squabbles and intrusive foreign politics.

Atatürk's rejection of Pan-Turanism (the political union of all Turkic-speaking peoples) was consistent with his nation-building plans, but equally an ideological wrench for those who, like Atatürk, grew up in the days of the Young Turk movement. The same logic held, however. One could not achieve progress with a certain people while being equally concerned with the fate of Turkic peoples to the east or, for that matter, with fellow Muslims to the south and west.

The new Turkish policy was realistically modest but by no means defeatist. Turkey succeeded in its vulnerable early years by defeating the Greeks militarily and by defying British diplomatic pressure. Atatürk succeeded also because he was willing to strike a bargain with the equally vulnerable new Soviet Union just as he settled for British and French control of the Fertile Crescent, sharing Turkey's longest land border (the

Turkish border with Syria and Iraq extends 1171 kilometers, that with Iran 472, whereas the border with the Soviet Union is 593), as long as the British and French did not trifle with Turkey in traditional Eastern Question fashion.

This is not to suggest that Turkey became a model of nonintervention. The Turkish wresting of Hatay (formerly Alexandretta) from French-mandated Syria can best be described as a power grab, and later Turkish pressures against Syria in the 1950s (in cooperation with the United States) were crudely intimidating. These moves also got dangerously close to reengaging Turkey in Eastern Question politics, for the Cold War in the Middle East has been a replay of older nineteenth-century games. The continuing dispute with Greece over Cyprus since the 1950s can also quite fairly be labelled petty politics rather than statesmanship (on the part of both parties, Greek and Turk).

On balance, however, the international politics of Turkey have largely succeeded where those of the earlier Ottoman Empire failed. The major reason for this success is that Turkey was able to break out of the Ottoman mold, to create a Turkish national community of manageable—and defensible—size, and to resist ambitions to create a regional hegemony.

The Armenian massacres and ensuing emigration during the last years of the Ottoman Empire and the massive population exchange between Greece and Turkey in the early twenties, tragic as both events surely were, did produce a more cohesive population—linguistically and religiously—in Anatolia, thus approximating a demographic reality in accord with Atatürk's nationalist goals. Indeed, except for the Kurds, no numerically significant non-Turkish population remains in the Republic of Turkey. Even the Kurds, as Muslims, share a common religion and culture with the Turkish majority.

Yet, Turkey has not become totally free of Great Powers politics. Since 1951, Turkey has been in NATO because this has seemed the best response to the danger posed by the Soviet Union. Geography will not enable Turkey to become a Switzerland or a Sweden. Turkey must continue to play the Great Powers game as long as the Middle East remains an arena of Great Powers competition. From the time of Atatürk, however, Turkey has chosen to play a limited wager game. A Turkey maintaining its neutrality until the last days of the Second World War is to be contrasted to the rash entry of the Ottoman Empire into World War I. Turkey has shown a wilingness to consider regional security arrangements, such as the Sa'dbad Pact of 1937, joining Turkey, Iran, and

Afghanistan, or the Baghdad Pact of the 1950s, joining Turkey with, Iran, Iraq, Pakistan, and Great Britain. But neither regional pact excessively consumed Turkish energies.

Tunisia

Turkey has never experienced even a brief period of Western imperial rule. Tunisia, by contrast, was subjected to a long and intensive form of settler colonization from 1881 to 1956. Yet, these two quite different experiences were especially important in enabling the two states to escape the old Eastern Question pattern of international politics. Obliged to concentrate on the formidable challenge of escaping French colonialism, the Tunisian political elite was spared the temptation to engage in multilateral international politics.

At times, Tunisian nationalist leaders tested the possibility of using outside pressures against the French presence. But always disappointed in the results achieved, they returned to a bilateral colonized/colonizer confrontation with France. The Tunisians who would soon thereafter form the Old Destour political party petitioned President Wilson at the time of the Paris Peace Conference to no avail.

Tunisian nationalist leaders also perceived the folly of attempting to use Italy as a counterweight to France, for the prospects of a continued and massive Italian colonization were even more disturbing. Moreover, Mussolini's harsh policies in neighboring Libya were well known in Tunisia. For the same reason, most Tunisians were not eager to cooperate with the Axis Powers after the defeat of France. Later efforts to use Anglo-American pressures against the Free French government were of limited use. Then toward the end of the Second World War, at the time the Arab League was being created, Habib Bourguiba, the founder of the Neo-Destour party, journeyed to Egypt. He sought help from Arabism in the independence struggle; but, this, too proved disappointing.

The special international context facing Tunisia in the period of French colonial rule fostered the diplomatic style that Tunisia's leader himself immodestly dubbed "Bourguibism." Bourguibism involved a strategy for a weaker power to deal directly with a stronger one by (1) emphasizing common interests; (2) demonstrating a willingness to compromise and proceed in stages; (3) alternating shows of strength—boycotts, demonstrations, and the like—with periods of accommodation, depending on the response of the adversary; (4) providing a realistic review of tactics and goals to one's own constituency; and (5) always using the same language in addressing one's following as well as one's adversary.

Other factors contributed to the negotiating style of Tunisia's Neo-Destour, but the clear need to face the single most important international challenge, that of French colonial rule, helped dictate the tactics chosen. A small state surrounded by larger states, Tunisia could hardly aspire to a regional hegemony. Spared the tantalizing, indirect rule that Britain adopted in Egypt, Tunisian leaders were diverted from sterile politics-at-the-top to, instead, organizing the countryside. Finding no solid support from abroad, they were obliged to rely on themselves. This enhanced the already well advanced Tunisian sense of nationhood.

Israel

Israel's historical experience would predispose that country's leadership to take an intensive and multilateral diplomatic posture. From the earliest beginnings, Zionists were obliged to think in global and Middle Eastern terms simultaneously. The Jews they sought to bring to Palestine were scattered throughout the world, and, to succeed, Zionism had to be equally world-wide in scope. The search for legal standing in Palestine involved negotiations with the Ottoman Empire and with a number of European powers until the Balfour Declaration—later incorporated in the League of Nations Mandate for Palestine—gave Zionism its opportunity. Zionist historians have labelled the effort involved in gaining the support of the European state system "political Zionism." Theodor Herzl, the cosmopolitan Viennese Jew who founded the World Zionist Organization in 1897, had been obsessively concerned with obtaining for Zionism its European "charter." The tradition of seeking to line up support from the Great Powers for the Zionist cause has continued to this day.

Yet, from the earliest days the so-called practical Zionists believed that not all the assurances in the world from the Great Powers would avail unless great numbers of Jews were resettled and self-sufficient on the land in Palestine. These Zionists focused their attention on the immediate situation in Palestine and the Middle East.

Because of this dialectic between political and practical Zionism, the movement that created the state of Israel, although born in Europe, tended to blend together local, regional, and international issues in a manner quite similar to that of native Middle Eastern political elites. The prevailing diplomatic style might well have remained like that of Egypt and the rest of the Fertile Crescent but for two major developments giving Zionism, and later Israel, a distinctive history. The first was the Holocaust, which in its horrors and in the outside world's ineffective response convinced Israelis that they must always rely first and foremost on themselves. They must never assume that security can be trusted in the hands of an outside patron or outside forces. Second was the Arab tactic of boycotting Zionism and of taking the public posture that Zionism, not having been accepted by the Arabs, did not exist. This not only increased Israel's tendency to rely solely on itself, but it also impeded all but the most fugitive Arab-Jewish contact.

If the horrors and struggles of modern Jewish history increased Israel's sense of nationhood (which is certainly the case), this experience has not totally separated Israel from the Eastern Question. Instead, Israel, while developing a strong self-identity as a nation and an almost defiant self-reliance vis-à-vis the rest of the world, remains in other respects the extreme example of a Middle Eastern polity that is a prisoner of international politics. Until the 1979 Egyptian-Israeli peace treaty, Israel had not been recognized as a state by any Arab neighbor. As a result, Israel has adopted a defensive policy of retaliation against hostile neighbors. It has pushed that position to such extremes that, over the years, Israeli governments have with clocklike consistency supported groups hostile to her enemy neighbors. Examples include, at different times, clandestine support for the Sudan against Nasser's Egypt; the Southern Sudan rebels against the Sudanese government; the Kurds against the Iraqi government; Iran of the Shah against Iraq; Maronites against others in Lebanon; and even limited secret support for the Islamic Government of the Ayatollah Khomeini against Iraq.

At the same time, Israel, for all its self-reliance, has worked diligently to maintain a position of strength among the Great Powers. The Suez War of 1956 involved a secret collaboration among Israel, France, and Great Britain against Egypt. Even earlier, a France bedevilled by nationalist movements in North Africa had sought a "tacit alliance" with Israel as a reliable partner in anti-Arab activities. Earlier Israeli efforts to achieve a strategic relationship with the United States were not very successful, but, from the mid-sixties on, what might be called a very strong, if unwritten, alliance binds this small Middle Eastern state with one of the two superpowers, insuring thereby the continuity of the Eastern Question system in the Middle East.

The tactical successes of Israeli military and diplomatic actions since 1948 have perhaps obscured Israel's strategic weaknesses. Israel keeps winning wars but losing opportunities for peace. Having bristled during the years of Arab boycott and nonrecognition, Israelis have seemingly relied too much on a single tactical weapon—that of retaliation, often massive. Even the major breakthrough of a United States-mediated peace with Egypt was jeopardized by the 1982 Israeli invasion of Lebanon.

Israel thus offers yet another Middle Eastern variant, a state with an acute sense of self-identity and self-reliance but thus far an inability to scale down its military-diplomatic activities. The ensuing picture is grotesque and not easily compared to that of other countries, whether in the region or beyond. By most indicators, Israel is clearly the most modern society in the Middle East. Yet, Israel spends almost one-third of its gross national product on defense, the highest percentage in the world. This expenditure would be impossible without massive infusions of governmental and private financial aid, amounting from the United States alone since 1949 to more than $70 billion (calculated in mid-1980s dollar value). For a country with a population of 4.5 million, this is the largest per capita figure in the world. Israel has less than one-tenth the population of either Egypt or Turkey and roughly half that of Tunisia; yet, it consistently ranks among the world's top ten arms exporters.

This raises important questions for Israel and for modernizing countries in general. Are Israeli modernizing successes attributable in large part to the special elan and defiant self-reliance that the horrible history of modern Jewry has imposed on them? Is there a correlation between modernization and military proficiency? Can a state that has grown and developed in adversity live in normality? Can Israel, since 1967 an occupying power ruling over 1,615,000 Arabs (1,115,000 in the West Bank and Gaza plus 500,000 Israeli Arabs), maintain an esprit de corps coming from the sense of being a plucky David fighting Goliath now that the roles are reversed? Could an Israel at peace with its neighbors manage to scale down its military expenditures and move toward economic self-sufficiency?

Even to pose these questions illuminates the extent to which an activist Israeli foreign policy dictates the rhythm of Israel's daily life and the life of its neighbors as well. Imposed on that country over the decades by outside circumstances, this diplomatic activism is now seemingly embraced by and perhaps on the way to being institutionalized into the Israeli body politic.

Tiny Israel today comes close to assuming the role of the nineteenth-century Ottoman Empire. It seeks to intervene and orchestrate the international politics of the entire Middle East. The Ottoman leadership, admittedly, would have been hard put to do otherwise, for the territories in dispute had long been part of the empire ruling from Istanbul. No such juridical constraint binds Israel. But can that state break its diplomatic habits now as old as the state itself?

Other States

The other states of the Fertile Crescent are, by contrast, all afflicted with limited political legitimacy in their existing territorial and constitutional form. Lebanon came closest to achieving a Swiss-like political consensus because the balance of so many different groups—after the creation of Greater Lebanon—make this an eminently realistic policy. This working compromise was tested during the first civil war of 1958 and then, seemingly, destroyed following the second civil war that began in 1975.

Since 1975, analysts of Lebanon's turmoil have tended to be divided into two diametrically opposed camps: (1) those who attribute the breakdown of public order to Lebanon's inability to create a genuine Lebanese identity, a Lebanese (as opposed to Maronite or Druze or Muslim) civic spirit; and (2) those who insist that Lebanon, the weakest of the Arab states bordering Israel, became the hapless arena of the still unresolved Arab-Israeli confrontation.

Both factors are important, but the second is the more persuasive. It is unrealistic to expect peoples who for centuries have been organized on lines of religious communalism to become within a generation or two secularist patriots of a nation-state called Lebanon. The Lebanese, over the past half-century, were making impressive modernizing advances, learning in the process the utility of compromising communal differences. The continued presence of a sizeable Palestinian refugee population who could not be granted citizenship without upsetting the Christian-Muslim balance, the rallying, especially after 1967, of that Palestinian community into an activist Palestine Liberation Organization, the continued intervention of other Arab states and of Israel put too many strains on the still fragile sense of Lebanese-ness that was slowly developing.

Syria, where the ideology of Arab nationalism has always been strongest, served in the post-World War Two years as the cockpit of an inter-Arab struggle pitting the Hashimites ruling in Jordan and Iraq against an alliance of convenience linking Egypt with Saudi Arabia. In addition, Britain usually leaned toward its old clients, the Hashimites; whereas France, struggling to regain lost positions, and the United States, coming forward as a new outside power with Middle Eastern interests, were involved as well. The Soviet Union—having been foiled in its postwar advances against the "Northern Tier" states of Greece, Turkey, and Iran—achieved a compensatory diplomatic breakthrough with the Soviet-European arms deal of 1955. From that date, the Soviets remained heavily involved in Arab politics, relying in the Nasser years on increasing ties with Egypt, until that was reversed by Nasser's successor, Sadat, who turned to the United States. The Soviet Union had looked to Syria as a potential regional client from the mid-fifties onward. Even though the Soviet Union now appears to be entering an inactive phase in the Middle East (rather like the years immediately following the Bolshevik Revolution), the long-term prospects are for an active Soviet (or Russian?) role in the diplomacy of its Middle Eastern neighbors.

The 1958 Iraqi revolution that overthrew the Hashimite regime demonstrated the danger in those years to any Arab government holding out against Arabism. Yet, later Iraqi developments demonstrated just as clearly the difficulties of creating a new, larger political entity in accord with the vague, but strongly felt, sentiments of Arabism. The successors to the Hashimites in Iraq, although espousing Nasserist Arabism, neutralism, and anti-Westernism, were soon at odds with Nasser's Egypt. The many changes of government since the late fifties in both Syria and Iraq have not come closer to either political unity or accommodation within the framework of existing states. For several years, both Syria and Iraq have been ruled by governments claiming to represent the Ba'th political party, a revolutionary socialist nationalist movement. But the presumed common ideology has in no way mitigated the strong rivalry between Damascus and Baghdad.

Adding to the irony, the Syrian Ba'thist government—which presumably speaks for Arab unity—now relies almost exclusively for its support on the minority 'Alawite community in Syria. The 'Alawites, a heretical Muslim sect, account for only about 11 percent of Syria's multicommunal population.

As for Jordan—an even more artificial entity created by the British to mollify the disappointed family of Sharif Husayn following the First World War—a possible accommodation of the sort that has eluded Lebanon remains open. Jordan's King Husayn, the last of the ruling Hashimites, has maintained an essentially low-profile, unobtrusively pro-Western diplomatic stance as a means of binding together his population of sedentary Palestinians and of Transjordanians largely of bedouin roots. In regional and international diplomacy, he has tried, not always successfully, to keep Jordan's Arabist credentials in good order without provoking the powerful Israeli neighbor to the West. Most of all, King Husayn and the Jordanian regime stand out as clearly etched examples of dogged survivors, of the weak living uneasily among the strong.

Interestingly, even after losing the most productive part of the kingdom (the West Bank) to Israeli occupation during the June 1967 War, Jordan—lacking oil and other economic assets and starting existence after the First World War with virtually no modernizing infrastructure (whether in education or economy or government)—continued until recently to achieve a healthy rate of economic growth.

If the states or would-be states (such as the Palestinians') of the Fertile Crescent could hardly have avoided being caught up in the web of interregional politics, Egypt had, even more than Turkey, the opportunity to soft-pedal its regional diplomacy. Exactly the opposite occurred during the Nasser years. Even before, during the interwar years, Egypt was excessively concerned with foreign policy. The focus of attention then was different, revolving around relations with Britain and the fate of the Sudan to the south, but Egypt's shift from domestic to international concerns was already appreciable.

The diplomatic revolution achieved by Sadat—moving from a pro-Soviet to a pro-American position and signing a peace treaty with Israel—and the ousting of Egypt from the Arab League as a result gave Egypt another opportunity to adopt a less activist diplomacy. It might be argued, however, that for all his political virtuosity, Sadat realized only half of the reforms needed. His actions in breaking away from Egypt's reliance on the Soviet Union (which had neither the capability nor the motivation to advance Egypt's goals) were highly successful. Sadat assumed that the answer lay simply in changing superpower patrons (from the Soviet Union to the United States). But the optimal answer for Egypt may be to rely as little as possible on outside powers and thereby break out of the now two-centuries old Eastern Question system.

The same in substance can be said for the other successor states in Ottoman Afro-Asia. Equally important to finding an acceptable political community in the post-Ottoman world is the goal of developing an approach to international relations in which domestic and developmental concerns are not always hostage to regional and international issues. Indeed, the two problems are bound together. The temptation to engage in excessive foreign adventurism is, of course, present in all political communities. But the problem is especially acute in the Middle East, where history and geography have conspired to create a pattern of politics in which all participants—Middle Easterners and outsiders—solicit regional and international intervention even while deploring such interference. The result is a persistent international relations system that any single player to the game has difficulty in changing.

International Comparisons: The steady dismemberment of a major imperial system, the Ottoman Empire, and the continued difficulty in realizing throughout much of the region a sense of political community possessing political legitimacy offers a major contrast not only to the first modernizers in Western Europe and North America but also to such states as China, Japan, and Russia. Even British India, which did not emerge from imperialism as a single unit, presents today only three states—India, Pakistan, and Bangladesh. All are large in territory and population. Border disputes exist (as between India and Pakistan over Kashmir), but since the creation of Bangladesh out of former East Pakistan (separated over 1,610 kilometers from West Pakistan), an acceptable concordance between political and cultural boundaries has been reached.

The Western colonial experience in the Middle East is somewhat like that of Western colonialism in Black Africa, where several European powers divided up territories in a crazy-quilt pattern. Even here, the contrasts are greater than the similarities. No single Black African imperial system was then in place to suffer the fate of the Ottoman Empire, persistently picked to pieces by the Western state system. European imperialism in Africa usually contributed to the creation of centralizing political and economic systems that might eventually replace subsistence economies and tribalized societies. In general terms, Black African nationalists could accept without reservation the political armature brought by European colonialism. Even the continent-wide ideology of Negritude (which had never existed in Africa's past) is an implicit acknowledgement of imperialism's role in widening Black African horizons.

The Middle East, by contrast, has been haunted by the loss of an earlier political unity (the Ottoman Empire) and a religiocultural self-sufficiency (the Islamic umma). In one sense, the post-Ottoman Middle East is much less cosmopolitan than it was centuries earlier, when a Muslim religious scholar or merchant or soldier could feel as much at home anywhere from the Maghrib to the Indies, as a late Victorian would have in any part of the British Empire.

The legacy of two major European languages used by elites to communicate throughout Black Africa (English and French) has also been to some extent unifying, for neither English nor French replaced an indigenous language serving as the vehicle of a high cultural tradition. The Ottoman Middle East, by contrast, possessed two indigenous languages (Ottoman Turkish and Arabic), written in a single Arabic script. Those two languages contained all that an individual of whatever profession or occupation needed to communicate religious, social, economic, political, or aesthetic ideas. One of the two, Arabic, was deemed a sacred language by Muslims, but unlike the Latin of European Christendom or Hebrew among Jews (until Zionism and the creation of Israel), Arabic had the distinction of being a sacred language and a living language, a language learned by the elite but also (in its many dialects) the mother tongue of the majority in Ottoman Afro-Asia.

The modern period has dealt harshly with this cultural and linguistic cosmopolitanism. Modern Turkish is written in the Latin script (one of Atatürk's more revolutionary acts, beginning in 1928). Moreover, modern Turkish has dropped many of its words of Arabic or Persian origin in favor of those having impeccable Turkish roots, a development begun under the impulse of Atatürk's Turkish nationalism. As a result, today Ottoman Turkish, the language of imperial rule for over six centuries and surely the most highly developed court language of any Muslim empire, is an instrument of daily communication for no one and is studied by only a few scholars.

The linguistic division between the Arabic- and Turkish-speaking world is especially dramatic to anyone who has bothered to study the Middle East's Ottoman past. In today's Arab world, only a handful of Arabs speak Turkish, usually the few remaining greybeards belonging to the sociopolitical elite that reached maturity before the end of the Ottoman Empire. Only a tiny number of Arab scholars—perhaps on balance fewer than are to be found in the West—know Ottoman Turkish and can thus use the rich historical sources to be found in Ottoman literature, its chronicles and most of all the still largely unexploited official Ottoman archives. The number of Turks who know either written or spoken Arabic is not appreciably higher.

That many members of Middle Eastern elites (especially those in the Arab world) know either English or French and often both does bring to bear a new cosmopolitanism. But it is a cosmopolitanism of cultural dependence linked to a cosmopolitanism of political and military dependence. Or, at least, it is often so perceived within the Middle East. The sense of linguistic alienation is an often overlooked aspect of the fundamentalist religiopolitical nativism now sweeping the Middle East. Africa and other parts of the colonial world have also been seized with the problem of whether—or to what extent—to continue the use of the colonizer's language after independence. In Africa, however, and for that matter in India as well, the issue does not raise the same religiopolitical nostalgia does in the Middle East.

The sundering of the Austrian Empire into successor nation-states more nearly approaches the post-Ottoman experience. Still for all the untidy irredentas throughout southeastern Europe, there is little hankering for a recreated imperial or religious or linguistic unity as is to be found in the Middle East, especially in the Arab world and most of all in the Fertile Crescent. The neutrality of Austria, one of the few post-World War II diplomatic successes emerging from Soviet-Western negotiations, offers no parallel in the post-Ottoman Middle East. It could well serve as a model solving such problems as that of Lebanon or of Israel and Palestine. Equally, the neutrality of Austria and the restrained regional diplomacy of Turkey both suggest the wisdom of setting aside any longing for the imperial past that once radiated from Vienna and Istanbul.

Yet another possible broad comparison is with Latin America—a region, which, like the Middle East, is made up of an overwhelming majority belonging to a single religious faith (Catholic) with two languages rich in cultural tradition (Spanish and Portuguese), having long been part of an imperial system (Spain and, for Brazil, Portugal), who emerged from that imperial experience into a number of successor states that live uneasily with each other all the while claiming a strong sense of cultural identity. Even the extent to which so much of Latin America has been economically dependent on the United States and, to a lesser extent, Western Europe, offers a point of comparison with the modern economic history of the Middle East.

On the other hand, Latin America, like North America, is an immigrant culture whose religion, languages, and ruling institutions were imported by peoples coming from Europe and Africa over the last four centuries. There has been no such massive importation of outside peoples and cultures into the Middle East since the time of the Arabo-Muslim conquest that began in the seventh century. Yet, even on this score, certain resemblances emerge. The native Indian populations of Latin America are generally to be found at the bottom rungs of the economic ladder; their success lies in seeking upward social or economic mobility and adopting the mores of the ruling elite. They are somewhat like the Druze, Kurds, Alawites, Berbers, and other Middle Eastern minorities. Equally, Latin America's old nobility, priding themselves on a lineage that traces them back to Spain or Portugal, are roughly equivalent to the

Turko-Circassians or Andalusian or Sharifian (descendents of the Prophet Muhammad) notables in the former Ottoman Middle East.

Perhaps, on balance, the most important variable in considering the international context is that of a distinctive cultural entity that was long brought together in a single imperium. That imperial political unity has now been lost. Many of the successor states have been unable to establish their political legitimacy. A sense of impermanence and instability pervades the region. Moreover, the resulting political struggles and ideological groupings take place in a region that for two full centuries has served— more than any other region in the world—as an arena where the Great Powers compete.

CHAPTER ELEVEN

Political Structure

SUCCESSOR STATES TO the Ottoman Empire share two important aspects of common heritage with implications for their contemporary political cultures.

One is Islam. With the exception of Israel, all countries in the region have Muslim majorities. Non-Muslim minorities amount to 10 percent or less of the total population of these countries, except for Lebanon, in which non-Muslims now may constitute roughly 40 percent. The other shared heritage is an Ottoman past common to all.

Characteristics of the Ottoman Heritage

A major characteristic of the Ottoman Empire was that it had a status-oriented rather than a market-oriented culture, essentially the reverse of Western Europe. Instead of economic power (i.e., ownership of the means of production) leading to political power, political power (i.e., position in the state bureaucracy) gave access to material wealth. The wealth thus accumulated, however, could not be converted into permanent economic assets, because it was liable, both in theory and practice, to confiscation by the state. The Ottoman state, unlike its Western European counterparts, did not pursue mercantilist policies and did not favor the emergence of a powerful merchant class.

The ethnic or, more precisely, the religious division of labor was another factor that hindered the growth of a politically influential merchant class. Non-Muslim minorities, both because they were excluded from the ruling class and because their linguistic skills and contacts with Europe gave them an advantage over Muslim merchants, took the lead in commercial activities, especially international trade. The minorities, however, were barred from the opportunity of converting such economic power into a significant political role.

As for land, another potential source of economic power, the state in theory retained the ownership of all cultivable land and, until the decline of central authority, also controlled it. Fief holders (*sipahi*) were not a land-based aristocracy, but a military-service gentry who were paid by the state in taxes they collected from peasants. Their titles could always be revoked by the central authority. After the decline of this land-tenure system (*timar*), and its replacement by tax-farming (*iltizam*), the tax-farmers were more interested in maintaining their government connections and squeezing resources from the peasants than in moderniz-ing agriculture and producing for the market.

To a limited extent, the commercialization of agriculture took place only in the nineteenth century. The rise of a class of local notables (*ayan*) in the eighteenth century, who often combined local social and military power with government connections and tax-farming privileges, did not fundamentally alter this state of affairs. In any case, the effective centrali-zation drive under Sultan Mahmud (1808–39) deprived the ayan of much of their political influence. A similar development took place in the Egypt of Muhammad Ali and, to a lesser extent, Tunisia under Ahmad Bey.

In short, the power of the state bureaucracy was seriously threatened neither by commercial nor agricultural interests. Neither the mercantile bourgeoisie nor the landowners developed into a class that could effectively control and limit the authority of the state. There was, on the one hand, the ruling "military" (*askari*) class, which actually included the military, the civil bureaucracy, and the ulama. On the other hand, there were the ruled (*reaya*), a broad category embracing all Muslims as well as non-Mus-lims; they paid taxes and were excluded from any role in government or the military.

The second characteristic derived from the Ottoman heritage can be labelled the absence of a "civil society." This absence can be attributed to a weakness or lack of corporate, autonomous, intermediary social struc-tures operating independent of government and playing a cushioning role between the state and the individual. In Europe, the church was the foremost of these corporate structures, and may have served as a model for other corporate structures such as the guilds, autonomous cities, and the like. These had no parallels in the Islamic Middle East. Islamic law does not, as a rule, recognize corporate entities. Nor does the Muslim religious class have a corporate identity (for all the theoretical supremacy of the sharia). This class depends on the state for its appointments, promotions, and salaries.

Similarly, neither the cities nor the artisan guilds played an autono-mous role in the Ottoman Empire comparable to their counterparts in Western Europe. The *ahi* guilds (artisan organizations with a strong religious coloring) played some role in the formative years of the empire, but were later deprived of their corporate privileges and put under strict government controls. Thus, no autonomous structures stood between political authority and the ruled.

Despite some recent vitality on the part of professional associations, such as bar associations, the relative ease with which authoritarian regimes have been able to abolish parties (e.g., Egypt in 1953; Turkey in 1980), tame or suppress labor unions, co-opt or neutralize professional associations, curtail or abolish the autonomy of universities testifies to the weakness of corporate structures in the Middle East.

There is a strong sense of individualism in the Middle East, but it is fundamentally different from its Western counterpart. It refers to equality of status within the religious community (*umma*) and individual freedom in matters of religion (the state in the Islamic Middle East having—contrary to Western experience—seldom attempted to impose religious orthodoxy). It does not mean political equality and participatory rights in the conduct of governmental affairs. Such individualism and egalitarianism in the absence of mediating voluntary associations even encourages a strong state.

A related political and cultural characteristic that can be traced to the Islamic-Ottoman heritage is the blurring of lines between political opposition and treason. The concept of a loyal opposition is extremely rare in the Middle East. The stakes of politics are consequently high. Politics becomes a zero-sum game often involving conspiracy and violence. This feature is more marked in the Arab world, but certainly not absent in Turkish politics; here the competitive political process has been interrupted thrice by military intervention in the last quarter century, one prime minister (Adnan Menderes) executed and another (Suleyman Demirel) twice forcibly driven from office. Pressures toward conformity are strong in all parts of formerly Ottoman Afro-Asia, and deviance in politics or in other spheres of life is viewed with suspicion. The Ottoman Empire and its successor states have never gone through a genuine "liberal" phase.

It would be wrong, however, to explain these differences between Western Europe and Ottoman Afro-Asia solely in religious terms. In fact, the Ottoman Empire shared many important characteristics with premodern Russia and Japan. In neither of these two successful latecomers to modernization did "civil society" develop in conformity to the West European pattern. All three shared the following characteristics—strong state, absence or weakness of independent corporate groups, and a state service class dependent on the state for status and well-being. In all three, religion was effectively fused with the authority of the state, and institutional religion wielded little independent political power. Nor did the state in Japan, Russia, or the Ottoman Empire allow commercial interests to develop into a strong, independent bourgeoisie.

The implication of state autonomy for political modernization is that an autonomous state, unhampered by established class interests, has a greater capacity to accumulate and expand political power and to use it for the economic and social modernization of the society. Reformist regimes in the nineteenth century (beginning with Sultan Mahmud in the Ottoman Empire; Muhammad Ali in Egypt; Ahmad Bey in Tunisia) did so with considerable success. Their twentieth-century counterparts have been Kemalism, Nasserism, Bourguibism, and Baathism.

Thus, in terms of accumulation and expansion of political power, the Ottoman Empire and its successor states resemble Russia and Japan, but without the same success in modernization. Seemingly, the Ottoman successor states, while developing powerful political control mechanisms vis-à-vis society, were not as successful as Japan or Russia in using state power to shape society according to its views.

The Ottoman path to modernization did not facilitate the rise of democratic political institutions. The two Ottoman attempts to establish constitutional and representative government (the 1876 constitution and the 1908 restored constitution after the Young Turk revolution) were precarious and short-lived. The same fate greeted efforts in Egypt during the 1870s and Tunisia a decade earlier. Among successor states, only three (Turkey, Israel, and Lebanon) have been able to maintain a competitive democratic system for any considerable length of time. Furthermore, Lebanese democracy (as well as the Lebanese state itself) broke down beginning in 1975, and Turkey has experienced three military coups in the last 20 years. The instability in Syria and Iraq after independence from Western colonial rule has been even more marked, relieved seemingly for a time by the Ba'thist authoritarian regimes.

The so-called liberal experiment in interwar Egypt was neither truly liberal nor truly democratic, since effective political power remained in the hands of the king and the British authorities, and during much of the time it was exercised in a heavily authoritarian manner.

A third political-cultural characteristic of the Ottoman Empire was the sharp division between the culture of the center and that of the periphery. The center and the periphery represented two very distinct ways of life, with different operational codes; different symbols (state and religion versus village and tribe); different languages (highly literary and stylistic Ottoman versus colloquial Turkish in Anatolia; the even sharper division of two distinct languages, Ottoman Turkish versus Arabic in the Arab provinces); different occupations (military and statecraft versus farming and artisanship); different types of settlement (urban versus rural); different literary and artistic traditions (court music and diwan literature versus folk music and folk literature); and even different versions of Islam (highly legalistic orthodox Islam versus often heterodox folk Islam). The Westernization movement of the nineteenth century did not eliminate this cultural dualism, but probably exacerbated the split by making the culture of the elites even more alien and inaccessible to the masses. Linguistic differences even among the Muslim subjects of the empire (e.g., Turks, Arabs, Kurds, Circassians) further contributed to this cultural fragmentation.

Finally, the millet system—which gave the ecclesiastical authorities of non-Muslim communities substantial control over their communal affairs without granting them participatory rights at the state level— meant that these communities maintained and developed their own cultures autonomously from that of the state. All this resulted in the low level of social and cultural integration in Ottoman society. This was perhaps one of the fundamental differences between the Ottoman Empire and the other two late modernizers, Japan and Russia—for the homogeneity of Japanese culture and the numerical and cultural dominance of the Great Russians in the Russian Empire gave these two societies a greater cultural unity and a sense of national identity.

At the same time, major political and cultural differences distinguish Turkey from the Arab states. The state is given a central and salient role in both Turkish political thought and in the minds of the Turks themselves. The state is valued in its own right, is relatively autonomous from society, and plays a tutelary and paternalistic role. This paternalistic role is reflected in the popular expression "father state" (*devlet baba*). Regard for the state is expressed in yet another popular expression: "May God preserve the State" (*Allah Devlete zeval vermesin*). This view of the state has been consistently fostered for centuries, chiefly through the educational system and the military. Indeed, the military and (at least until quite recently) the civilian bureaucracy have traditionally seen themselves as guardians of the state and protectors of public interest. Consequently, they have viewed with suspicion all particularistic interests and political parties.

The state does not occupy as lofty a place in Arab political thought. Arabs do not see themselves as heirs to the Ottoman legacy. Some political writings have even depicted the Arabs as wrestling to escape the domination of, first, the Ottoman Empire and then Western imperialism. Although such interpretations are historically unsound as regards Muslim Arab sentiments toward the Ottomans, it is nevertheless true that Arabs do not see themselves as carrying on the Ottoman Empire imperial tradition. Only the Turks do.

Even though states such as Egypt and Tunisia have a long history of distinctive territorial and national cohesiveness (with a concomitant sense of Egyptianness and Tunisianness), this has not sufficed to overcome a feeling of alienation from government.

Moreover, countervailing claims to political allegiance (e.g., Pan-Arabism, Pan-Islam, Greater Syria, unity of the Nile Valley, Maghrib unity) have divided the Arabs in this century. The result has been—unlike the Turkish experience—a lack of political and ideological continuity such as might foster identification with the state.

THE EROSION OF TRADITIONAL AUTHORITY

In general, modernization involves an erosion of traditional authority based on ascription, religion, and heredity and the rise of new legitimacy formulae based on secular assumptions. Although this is a universal phenomenon, by no means limited to the Middle East, it has acquired particular salience there. The most common change in the region has been from a traditional monarchy to a republic as the result of a revolutionary break—Turkey in the early 1920s, Egypt in the early 1950s, Iraq in 1958, and Tunisia in 1957, when it abolished the beylicate one year after independence. Only the Hashimite Kingdom of Jordan has continued as a monarchy. Israel, Lebanon, and Syria are in a different category, for they all started as republics.

In nature and depth, the legitimacy of these republican regimes varies widely. Electoral legitimacy is important only in three of the successor states—Turkey, Israel, and Lebanon—but with certain reservations. The Lebanese democracy, even the very existence of the state, has been under extreme threat since the beginning of the civil war in 1975. Perhaps one moderately comforting fact is that for years no group or leader during this long struggle has demanded the overthrow of the democratic system but instead has sought to change the power balance within the system. Even this, however, is now being challenged with the extremist Shiite Hizbullah demands of an Islamic state—whatever that could mean in a country composed exclusively of religious minorities.

In Turkey, the principle of electoral legitimacy is questioned in theory only by extreme left and right fringe groups; but the reality is that the military sees itself as the guardian of the nationalist and revolutionary (Kemalist) principles. The military thus refuses from time to time to accept a particular electoral result when it appears to be incompatible with these principles. The Turkish military has, however, never repudiated electoral legitimacy in principle and has restored competitive electoral processes relatively soon after each intervention.

In Israel, free elections are more securely established, but the avowedly Jewish character of the state coexists with an important Arab minority having a distinct identity of its own and of doubtful loyalty to this state. This creates a bifurcated polity wherein the minority is unlikely to become reconciled to the existing state or be accepted as full citizens (even if possessing such rights formally) by the majority.

Noncompetitive, one-party rule has been more nearly the norm in Syria, Iraq, Tunisia, Nasser's Egypt, and Kemalist Turkey, with semi-competitive elections appearing fleetingly in post-Nasser Egypt, recently in Tunisia, and generally in Jordan. All states show a need to maintain elections in some form for purposes of legitimization. Yet, most of these regimes tend to view entirely free and open elections as inimical to other goals. Revolutionary regimes express the fear—in justifying limiting electoral freedom—that free elections may bring reactionaries and counterrevolutionaries back to power.

Such arguments were often heard in Turkey during the Kemalist Era and especially during the transition to competitive politics in the period from 1945 to 1950. Thus, the official explanation for dissolving the short-lived opposition Free Republican Party in 1930 was that the party, despite the impeccable Kemalist credentials of its top leadership, had become a haven for reactionaries. A similar argument was heard in the 1940s and at the time of the later military interventions in Turkey.

Similar sentiments were consistently expressed in Egypt during the Nasser Period. Even Sadat, after Nasser, in spite of his "opening" to the West, which—just as in Turkey after 1945—could have justified Western liberal policies, never overcame his suspicion of free elections.

In addition to these appeals to revolutionary legitimacy, nationalism has been advanced as an important source of legitimacy, for the revolutionary republics of Ottoman Afro-Asia were either born out of nationalist struggles against colonial domination (as in the case of the Arab successor states) or in a struggle to resist Western efforts to bring about such domination (as in the case of Turkey). Nationalist legitimacy, however, presents other contradictions. Secular nationalism conflicts with traditional Islamic legitimacy as well as with different parochial, ethnic, linguistic, or sectarian loyalties.

There is also the conflict between a territorial nationalism in the Arab states and an overarching Pan-Arabism. It might be added that

Pan-Turanism once offered a similar tension of conflicting ideologies in Turkey.

Similar, but on a smaller territorial scale, is the Israeli ideological conflict between the concept of a small but overwhelmingly Jewish state as opposed to a Greater Israel obliged to absorb (or expel?) a huge Arab minority? Expressed differently, in all three cases—the Arabs, Turkey, and Israel—there looms the challenge between reality-challenging "impossible dreams" and pragmatic politics of pushing for the best possible within recognized constraints.

CHANGING SOCIAL BASES OF POLITICS

A major social change affecting politics throughout the region has been the sharp increase in the numbers and power of government functionaries (civilian and military) with a concomitant decline in the power of the landowning elite. This is in one sense a new elite—the product of modern (essentially Western) educational curricula but in another representing more nearly an impressive increase in the number of those representing and conforming to the venerable Ottoman pattern of an officialdom completely beholden to the state. The *kullar* (slaves of the sultan) of yesteryear have now become kullar of a state system that presumes to control the economy and society in a totalistic manner undreamed of by earlier Ottomans.

Yet, these new ruling classes—these "Neomamluks"—neither possess the esprit de corps nor enjoy the traditional political legitimacy that girded the Ottoman system. The increased power of the state coupled with the decreased legitimacy of the rulers makes for an exacerbated form of "winner take all" politics at the top.

Accordingly, those vying for state authority show greater cohesion prior to seizing power, but soon thereafter policy differences become visible. Examples abound: factionalism among the Young Turks after the constitutionalist revolution of 1908, among Kemalists after the victory in the War of Independence, among the Free Officers in Egypt; the Bourguiba-Salah bin Youssef confrontation at the time of independence in Tunisia; factionalism within the Syrian Ba'th reflected in the coups of 1966 and 1970; and the showdown between David Ben Gurion and Menahem Begin's Irgun on the eve of Israel's statehood.

An important characteristic common to the revolutionary republics created by this modernizing ruling elite is the autonomy of the state. In addition to the Ottoman heritage of state autonomy, other developments in class structure favored such autonomy. Capitalist development within the Ottoman Empire remained very limited during the nineteenth century. Moreover, most of the existing enterprises were owned by foreign companies or by members of non-Muslim minorities. Despite efforts from Young Turks and Kemalists to promote the growth of a Turkish business class, results were extremely meager. Only after the end of World War II, and particularly with the encouragement received from the Democrat Party governments, did capitalist development accelerate in Turkey.

Even so, an uneasy balance prevailed for another 30 years between the state bureaucracy and private entrepreneurs, with the latter depending heavily on the former (tariff protection, import quotas, credits, various subsidies, and tax relief). The coming to power of Turgat Ozal and his Motherland Party in November 1983 may now represent a decisive shift in favor of policies promoting capitalist development.

Similarly, the economic and political power of the Egyptian capitalist bourgeoisie remained vulnerably weak against the combined forces of the state and foreign capitalist interests. Tunisia presented a difference in intensity (not nearly so enticing a country for foreign capital as Egypt) but not in kind. There, too, the state and foreign interests held any significant indigenous private capitalist enterprise in check.

Lebanon experienced considerably more indigenous private commercial activity, and it is not surprising that the Lebanese state stands out as an exception to the Middle Eastern rule of increasing state power and autonomy vis-à-vis society.

Syria also had similar private commercial activity, but, with much of it being in the hands of non-Muslim minorities, this did not limit state power. Indeed, the existence of a non-Muslim minority commercial sector probably made the growth of state power more acceptable to the majority.

The combination of these two factors—the tradition of state autonomy and the greatly increased size and power of the state-oriented salaried ruling elites—has facilitated what can be called "command politics" (as opposed to consensus politics). As a result, most of the post-Ottoman successor states share many of the following characteristics: (1) extralegal seizure of power; (2) an alliance of the military and the civilian technocrats; (3) limited mass participation largely organized and controlled by the rulers; (4) a governmental program heavily statist and extremist in ideology but pragmatic and flexible in implementation; and

(5) a marked expansion of the ruling elite, with many of the older, more nearly ascriptive elite members replaced by parvenus having attained power by means of a technological education or a military career.

Differences of style, substance, and timing among the several successor states do, of course, exist. The transition from the Ottoman state to the Republic of Turkey involved violence and resistance against a foreign invasion (Greece supported by the Allies) and later quelling a revolt in Eastern Turkey in the mid-twenties. By contrast, the July 1952 Free Officers coup in Egypt dispatched the old regime in a stroke as did the 1958 Iraqi coup. Bourguiba in Tunisia faced a short challenge from his former comrade Salah bin Yusif, but this was controlled within a few months following independence.

Syria offers a more fluctuating picture. Military coups began as early as 1949 and were followed in the fifties by a civilian government and a temporary union with Egypt (1958–61); then long-lived Ba'thist governments based on an alliance of party and army were put in place during the sixties. Iraqi history since the overthrow of the Hashimite regime in 1958 provided similar violent fluctuations throughout most of the 1960s but then settled into a durable Ba'thist regime which, as in Syria, relied on an alliance of party and the military. In both Syria and Iraq, as well, the regime durability of the last generation has been based on the increasingly autocratic rule of a single, would-be charismatic leader—Hafiz al-Asad in Syria; Saddam Husayn in Iraq.

In implementing dramatic steps against established groups and institutional patterns, Kemalist Turkey stands out as the boldest. Among the more electrifying moves were the abolition of the caliphate, complete secularization of the legal system, banning Sufi brotherhoods, and replacing the Arabic script with Latin while at the same time "de-Arabizing" and "Turkifying" the language. In striking out against the Muslim religious establishment, only Bourguiba's Tunisia came close to Kemalist daring (especially with the 1957 Tunisian Personal Status code).

Nasserist Egypt, after the Suez War in 1956 and even more after the breakup of the United Arab Republic (union of Egypt and Syria) in 1961, essentially crippled the economic (and political) power of the private sector while greatly increasing that of the state bureaucracy. The earlier agricultural reform law of 1952, expanded in 1961, had also realized significant structural change in landownership; the share of the largest landowners (fifty feddans or more) declined from 33 percent of the cultivated area to 15 percent, whereas the share of the poorest sector (five feddans or less) rose from 35 to 52 percent.

In Kemalist Turkey, by contrast, no such bold moves were needed to curtail the power of the private sector. Much of the economic power until the end of the Ottoman Empire had been in the hands of minorities and foreigners, few of whom remained in the Turkish Republic. Furthermore, most of the politically important groups had been statist or bureaucratic in orientation for generations, consistent with the Ottoman ethos of a state-service class. To this extent, the Kemalists are in the tradition of the Young Turks, who for all their revolutionary opposition, were also in the tradition of Ottoman state service.

These many differences—important as they are in other contexts— pale before the prevailing pattern of state autonomy. Even those states not to be described as revolutionary republics have been influenced by the pattern. The Hashimite Kingdom of Jordan relies on the military as both arbiter and defender of regime legitimacy somewhat as in Turkey. Moreover, although based on different legacy and circumstances, the mystique of the army and the state is very powerful in Israel.

The one exception is Lebanon, with a fragile state whose bureaucrats neither have nor seek expanded power and an army too weak and divided to defend against outside intervention or domestic disorder. The existence of such a polity in a region surrounded by strong states possessing in most cases quite weak legitimacy helps explain Lebanon's vulnerability.

POLITICAL INSTITUTIONALIZATION

Everywhere in formerly Ottoman Afro-Asia, politics has ceased to be exclusively the domain of elites, and the common man has increased relevance for national governments. Yet, since institutional channels for political participation are not, in general, well-developed, political participation often takes on a sporadic, violent character. It is worth noting that the two most important events in recent Egyptian history were precipitated by two major urban riots in Cairo: the burning of Cairo in January 1952 (which led to the July Revolution) and the January 1977 riots (which convinced Sadat of the need for peace with Israel).

The failure to develop working institutional channels for political participation is one of the more conspicuous weaknesses of the Ottoman successor states. Parties and institutionalized elections do exist in Lebanon, but the unresolved questions of identity and legitimacy have limited their effectiveness. Tunisia, with a better resolution of these two questions, was—even as a single-party state—able to achieve a rather impressive degree of institutionalized participation. But regime reluctance or inability to foster steadily increasing participation later produced a severe legitimacy problem.

Egypt, although possessing more identity and legitimacy than others, failed to develop an effective mobilization single-party despite three attempts by Nasser (the Liberation Rally, the National Union, and the Arab Socialist Union). These single-parties were unimpressive even as recruitment agencies for the bureaucratic elite. Studies show that all but a few of the top ministerial positions during the Nasser years went to those with no party background until coming to office.

The Syrian and Iraqi Ba'ath parties have perhaps proven to be more effective instruments of control but largely by relying on coercion.

The balance sheet is decidedly more positive in the development of administrative institutions. In response to growing popular demands, which themselves were generated by social mobilization, governments have been working to increase their capabilities, to introduce or expand public services, and to take a more direct role in economic development. Although the Ottoman Empire had already achieved a degree of governmental penetration into society not commonly found in other parts of the Third World, the decisive wave of penetration came with postindependence economic modernization, social mobilization, and military build-up.

The extent to which central government dominates the economy and society may be gauged by a few representative statistics:

CENTRAL GOVERNMENT EXPENDITURES AS A PERCENTAGE OF GNP

	1972	1987
Egypt	26.7*	45.5
Israel	43.9	63.8
Jordan	52.3	44.6
Syria	28.8	37.1

(*The 1972 figure for Egypt is an estimate extrapolated from the late 1960s.)

The significance of these figures can best be appreciated by comparison with the following:

CENTRAL GOVERNMENT EXPENDITURES AS A PERCENTAGE OF GNP
(*averages for all countries*)

	1972	1987
Low-Income Economies	14.7	21.6
Middle-Income Economies	20.5	25.5
High-Income Economies	22.6	28.7

The preponderant position of these Middle Eastern governments within their societies is thus shown to be vastly above the average of all other Third World economies (whether low-income or middle-income) and well above that of the developed world as well.

Admittedly, it is the excessively large military expenditures that serve to account for these figures, so sharply out of line with what prevails elsewhere. More in line with world norms are the same figures for Tunisia and Turkey, two countries with considerably smaller central-government expenditures devoted to defense:

	1972	1987
Tunisia	23.1	36.8*
Turkey	22.7	22.7

(*an average of five years in the 1980s; the figure for 1987 was not available)

Total central-government revenues shows a similar dominance of government:

CENTRAL GOVERNMENT REVENUES AS A PERCENTAGE OF GNP

	1972	1987
Egypt	n.a.	39.0
Israel	31.3	55.2
Jordan	26.6	30.7
Syria	28.8	37.1
Low-Income Economies	n.a.	17.8
Middle-Income Economies	19.6	20.4
High-Income Economies	21.9	24.4

Interestingly, again Tunisia (for the 1970s) and Turkey are the only two successor states with percentages more nearly in line with the world norm:

	1972	1987
Tunisia	23.6	34.2*
Turkey	20.6	18.5

(*an average of five years in the 1980s; the figure for 1987 was not available)

These comparative figures can, of course, be interpreted to suggest that but for exorbitant military expenditures in most of the successor states, central-government expenditures and revenues are in line with world norms. That, however, would be to overlook the reality of this principal governmental activity in the region as a whole and especially in that part—the Fertile Crescent—in which the tradition of government penetration was less than in Anatolia, Egypt, or Tunisia. The major point to be emphasized at the region-wide level of analysis is the consistently high level of governmental penetration.

The increase in percentage of the work force in public employment conforms to the same pattern. About one-third of the Egyptian work force is currently on the public payroll (i.e., 3.2 out of 10 million persons, excluding the armed forces and teachers). The civil service alone reached 2.1 million in 1980, having sextupled in less than 30 years. In Iraq, the following figures demonstrate the tremendous rate of growth in public-sector employment:

1938	9,740
1958	20,031
1968	224,253
1972	385,978
1977	580,132

Between 1976 and 1980, some 88 percent of all allocated investments were public.

Government capabilities have increased not only in the economic and welfare sectors but also in the military, public security, and intelligence; by increasing coercive capabilities, the latter may have increased regime stability. The ability of the formerly unstable Ba'thist regimes in Syria and Iraq to weather several political storms in recent years is noteworthy, although the example of neighboring Iran evokes quite different possible outcomes. There the shah's seemingly solid grip based on considerable coersive power and a strong state apparatus was quickly brought to naught.

SEQUENCES IN POLITICAL MODERNIZATION

In the Ottoman Empire the emergence of an elaborate system of administration, which penetrated more deeply into the society than was the case in most of Asia, Africa, and Latin America, preceded the development of a sense of collective identity. The Ottoman elite culture provided a unity among the members of the ruling class, and this was instrumental in the expansion and, thereafter, the preservation of the empire. This culture, however, was not shared by the masses (reaya).

Even the theoretical unity of Muslims in a common umma was belied by countless village, town, and tribal communities very loosely connected with each other and often separated by linguistic and cultural differences.

Moreover, substantial non-Muslim minorities had no part in the umma and maintained, through the millet system, their own religious, linguistic, and cultural identities. In the nineteenth century, these were transformed into national identities, as a result of which the predominantly Christian peoples of the Balkan regions gained their independence, one after the other.

The Tanzimat reformers attempted to stem this tide by fostering the concept of Ottomanism; this concept stressed loyalty to a common dynasty and fatherland with equality before the law for all subjects regardless of religion. This effort, however, bore little fruit. Virtually all of Ottoman Europe (including Muslim Albania) had been lost by the outbreak of World War I, and even the Asian heartland of the empire witnessed Armenian separatism and then the Arab revolt during the First World War.

Thus by the turn of the century, the Ottoman rulers faced three possible options: They could continue the increasingly discredited Ottomanism, or pursue a policy of state-supported Pan-Islam, or promote Turkish nationalism (with or without Pan-Turanist overtones).

Pan-Islam, carefully nurtured by Sultan Abdulhamid II, could at best help the Ottoman state retain the loyalty of its Muslim Arab population. In time, the empire could perhaps have evolved into a federal, binational Turko-Arab state (rather like the Austro-Hungarian Empire).

The third alternative of building a new collective identity around Turkish nationalism was energetically followed by the Young Turks (1908–18). It was this choice that was adopted and refined by the Kemalist revolution. Turkish nationalism, rather than a more diffuse Ottoman or Islamic identity, was to provide the necessary group political loyalty.

No such neat resolution of the identity problem developed for the Arab successor states. Contrary to Allied commitments and Arab expectations, neither an independent nor a unified Arab state emerged in the Fertile Crescent. Instead, these former Ottoman lands were divided into five mandated territories: Iraq, Transjordan, and Palestine under the British, with Syria and Lebanon under France.

The borders imposed from outside had scant relationship with historical political entities or even with earlier Ottoman provincial borders. There was accordingly little group loyalty to the particular territorial units established. Moreover, the Fertile Crescent had always been the part of Ottoman Asia most segmented by the millet system. The same fissiparous tendencies that had dismantled the Ottoman Empire in the

Balkans throughout the nineteenth century were still at work in the Fertile Crescent. Indeed, with Zionism and the acceptance of the Jewish National Home idea in the mandate for Palestine yet another milletlike nationalism was added.

Even so, the territorial lines fixed by the mandates survived into independence (with Israel becoming the successor state to the Palestine Mandate less the West Bank and Gaza, these latter two territories later coming under Israeli occupation following the June 1967 War).

Except for Israel, with its powerful integration of territorial patriotism (*eretz Israel*, the "Land of Israel") and religious nationalism (the Jews as the people of Israel), territorial nationalism remains weak in the Fertile Crescent. Furthermore, it is challenged on two fronts. There is, first, the continued existence of primordial ethnic, religious, or sectarian "subnational" identities—as Maronites, Druze, Shi'i Muslims, Kurds, and Alawites. Then, at the other end of the spectrum is the powerful force of Arabism, namely a sense of "supranational" Arab identity. The Fertile Crescent (particularly Syria) was the region in which modern Arab nationalism began. Schemes for Arab (or at least Fertile Crescent) unity have continued to hold sway throughout our entire century.

Even so, the remarkable fact is that, despite these imposed, seemingly artificial borders, the states of the Fertile Crescent display considerable staying power. Not a single Arab state has been fragmented or fused into a larger territorial unit, the short-lived United Arab Republic (1958–61) linking Egypt and Syria being the exception that tests the rule. The regional (and world) reaction to the August 1990 Iraqi invasion of Kuwait reveals, inter alia, the strong pressure to maintain existing territorial units. So, too, does the reluctance of all neighboring states to consider dismembering a defeated Iraq.

Given this persistence, it is possible that in time a distinctive Syrian, Iraqi, Lebanese, or Jordanian identity may develop. At present, after some two generations of independence, such territorial identities are weak compared to the more established European states and to Turkey, Egypt, Tunisia, and Israel. Identification with and loyalty to the state are made more difficult in Syria and Iraq because these states are presently ruled by small minorities, sectarian moreover in the case of Syria. In Jordan, the tension between Palestinians and Jordanians (or those tracing their origins from the west or east bank of the Jordan River respectively) remains unresolved. Lebanon's civil war has raged since 1975 and stems in large measure from the political need to readjust what had long been

Maronite politicoeconomic domination to meet new demographic realities.

One Fertile Crescent Arab group that has developed a strong group identity are the Palestinians, both those living under Israeli occupation and those in the diaspora. If the Palestinians could manage to overcome the many complex obstacles to achieving statehood (either independent or merged with an existing state such as Jordan), there is good reason to believe that they could become a political community with a strong sense of group identity. The parallels of Palestinian experience with that of Zionism and Israel are, in many ways, striking. This is a phenomenon accepted by many Palestinian leaders themselves, who wryly observe that they are "the Jews of the Middle East."

Another possible cohesive state (strained as such an interpretation might now appear) is Lebanon, for each of the religious communities in Lebanon—except the Sunni Muslims—is a minority in the larger Fertile Crescent or Middle Eastern context. A sense of Lebanon as the homeland and refuge for regional minorities could possibly provide the needed sociopolitical cement. Recent Lebanese history indicates, moreover, that Lebanese Sunnis would also accept such an arrangement. In principle, Lebanon as the Switzerland of the Middle East (once a proud boast) is still feasible.

A satisfactory resolution to the identity problem may not be a prerequisite for, nor will it guarantee, a government's successful handling of problems in other areas. Still, a strong sense of common identity enhances a government's legitimacy; it is seen as emanating from that society and not as an alien force.

High levels of legitimacy, in turn, increase the penetrative capabilities of governments. Conversely, demands for participation and distribution in societies with little sense of common identity may well be seen by the ruling elite as disruptive of state integrity and hence less acceptable. It is not surprising, therefore, that the four successor states with apparently the strongest legitimacy also possess the strongest sense of national identity—Turkey, Egypt, Tunisia, and Israel.

In Turkey national identity is bolstered by linguistic and religious unity, the sense of continuity with the Ottoman heritage and the strongly nationalistic but territorially realistic policies of Kemalism. Turkey under Atatürk disclaimed any interest in either the Arab lands or the Turkic-speaking populations of the Soviet Union and other neighboring countires.

In Egypt, the ecological homogeneity of the Nile Valley produced a socially homogeneous population with a strong sense of Egyptianness and a historical continuity extending over millennia. Even though Egypt was ruled from the end of Pharaonic times until this century by non-Egyptian elites (some 2,500 years), this sense of identity persisted, the ruling elites in time becoming Egyptianized. The only significant minority in Egypt today are the Christian Copts (about 10 percent of the population); but as the oldest community in Egypt, there can be no question about their Egyptianness. Although Egypt under Nasser became the champion of Arab unity, this never resulted in the loss of Egyptian identity. Moreover, the post-Nasser years have demonstrated the limitations of Egypt's Pan-Arabism.

Tunisia's relatively small size, a homogeneous population and the dominant position of the capital city of Tunis, combined with a historical continuity as a distinctive political community second only to Egypt, has produced a strong group identity. Egyptian and Tunisian identities were also reinforced by these countries having been ruled for centuries by autonomous governments. While both were juridically part of the Ottoman Empire, each had its own local (if not native) ruling dynasty, its own bureaucracy and army.

In conclusion, several points stand out concerning the sequences of crises or challenges facing the Ottoman successor states and the effect all this had on their political modernization. First, with few exceptions, problems of identity, legitimacy, penetration, participation, and distribution have tended to arise simultaneously, thus greatly increasing the "load" on the political system.

Second, no doubt partly due to the Ottoman heritage of an elaborate administrative structure, the successor states have done rather well in "penetration" in comparison with similar states (except Lebanon, the only institutionally weak state in the area).

Third, the unresolved nature of the identity problem in many of the successor states, particularly those of the Fertile Crescent, complicates the quest for legitimacy. This remains the central problem of the Arab world.

Fourth, weak group identity and legitimacy at the state level obstruct the development of effective participatory institutions of either the competitive, pluralistic variety or the single-party, mobilization variety.

Fifth, although much has been done in the revolutionary republics in the field of distribution, there have also been significant setbacks such as in Sadat's Egypt. More generally, a wide gap still persists between the proclaimed egalitarian ideals of these regimes and their actual practice.

International Comparisons

The Ottoman legacy of strong, centralized states manned by powerful bureaucracies that the successor states have built on and expanded would suggest comparison with the first modernizers of Europe or with Japan and Russia. On the other hand, the legacy of European domination and, in the case of all save Turkey, of European domination including a period of outright Western colonial rule, places the region squarely within the larger Third World, as a region obliged in modern times to adapt to the intrusive and dominant West.

This distinctive combination of political characteristics can be epitomized as follows: Greater achievement in state building, less in nation building. Here then is the basic scale for international comparisons in terms of political structures.

The successor states generally rank higher than most states of Africa in the centralized strength of governments as measured in terms of capacity to control the populace. To the extent that ability to make its writ (in terms of sheer physical control) extend throughout the entire territory these states rank higher than most states of Africa or, for that matter, most of Afro-Asia.

The successor states are in the very top echelon of world rankings in size of military and security organizations and in the proportion of GNP devoted to military and security expenditure. When measured in terms of armies and police size, access to technologically sophisticated weaponry (most, but not all, imported) and capacity to mobilize state resources for internal or interstate warfare the states approach the levels of the early modernizers.

In resisting the notion that multipartyism and organized pressure groups can produce political stability most of the successor states are more in line with the many one party states of Afro-Asia.

The peoples of the successor states are more inclined than in many parts of Afro-Asia to accept the notion of a strong state as a political reality and, indeed, potentially as an ideal. The concept of a just ruler setting things right even if acting arbitrarily runs deep in Middle Eastern political thought. This evokes comparison with Imperial Russia where the dream of the oppressed held that "if only the Tsar knew" he would root out the rascals and let justice prevail. A major current in Middle Eastern political thought, moreover, is an aversion to, if not indeed fear of, anarchy. This is to be compared with the passion for order found in

Japan or Germany. The historical circumstances sustaining this political thought are, however, quite different. In the Middle East it is more nearly the concern of the urban-based "haves" to keep the peasantry, nomads, and mountaineers in check. The more recent fear of urban riots has been integrated into this old pattern of political thought so well summarized in the classic maxim from earlier Islamic times: "Better 60 years of tyranny than one hour of anarchy." Yet, while government is accepted in principle and the strong leader idealized, most of the governments existing in this period since roughly the First World War have had limited political legitimacy.

The relatively weak development of a dynamic bourgeoisie or of other significant private sector activity creating a degree of autonomy vis-à-vis government is another region-wide characteristic. Here the comparison might well be with the states of the Soviet bloc or China.

An interesting contrast with much of Latin America, the Middle Eastern military has offered an avenue of upward social mobility, and the military leadership tend to come from quite modest socioeconomic families. On the other hand, rather more like the caudillo syndrome in Latin America (and elsewhere), the tendency for military intervention in politics has become marked.

There are many exceptions to the above very general comparisons. Neither Israel nor Lebanon fits well into the categories suggested. Their problems and prospects are generally of a different nature. Even so, as a broad generalization this image of strong state building and weak nation building highlights both the prospects and perils (and portions of both have already appeared. States and their leaders have the mobilizational capacity to move quickly by imposing their will on the populace and, thereby, assuming the achievement of goals valued by the people, increasing their legitimacy and enhancing civil society. They also have the capacity to put in place and sustain patterns of political control approaching the oppressiveness of earlier European fascism.

CHAPTER TWELVE

Economic Growth and Development

GROWTH PHASES

THE DECADE PRECEDING the First World War was one of economic growth and promise. The war was a setback for the whole region. Tunisia and Egypt were spared the hostilities, but both suffered from the disruption of shipping and from severe inflation, and both sent large numbers of men to serve abroad. Syria and Iraq saw large-scale fighting throughout the war. Syria and, in particular, Lebanon experienced famine and some 500,000 people may have died. However, it was Anatolia (soon to be the Republic of Turkey) that suffered most, for after a short respite the war of independence followed the World War. Loss of life due to fighting and massacres and countermassacres exceeded 1,000,000. Many of the most flourishing branches of the economy, such as the tobacco and silk industries and carpetmaking, were crippled; mineral output was drastically reduced. The infrastructure was severely damaged. Inflation ran wild, and the currency lost most of its value. Moreover, the loss of the Armenian and Greek minorities, who had played a leading part in many sectors of the economy, left a large gap.

In the 1920s, the upswing in world demand and favorable prices for agricultural produce led to a revival of exports from the region, and the prevalence of peace and order made it possible to restore or expand agricultural production; by 1928, the quantum of exports had generally regained the prewar figure.

The world depression, however, struck the region a heavy blow. As in other areas of the world exporting primary products, prices fell sharply, exports were drastically reduced, the terms of trade greatly deteriorated, and the burden of international debt became much heavier. The quantum of exports in the 1930s was only a fraction of what it had been in 1913, and its purchasing power in terms of imports was far smaller. In view of the growth in population (see Chapter 11), this decline was even more serious. It therefore forced the governments to reassess their basic economic strategy and to reduce their hitherto almost complete reliance on the export of primary goods as the engine of growth.

Fortunately, the commercial treaties of 1838 and 1861, that had severely restricted the fiscal autonomy of the governments, lapsed in the years between 1928 and 1930. This meant that tariffs could be used for both revenue and protection. The abolition of the Capitulations in Egypt in 1937 (in Turkey, this had taken place in 1923; in Syria, Iraq, Lebanon, and Palestine, with the award of the League of Nations mandates; and, in Tunisia, before the First World War) meant that the governments now had full fiscal autonomy. They used their powers to increase their revenues, foster industry, and transfer control of certain activities to their nationals.

The Second World War spared the region, except for Tunisia, which was badly damaged. Military actions in Syria and Iraq were small-scale. Once again, there were shortages due to the disruption of production and the sharp reduction of imports, loss of output due to mobilization in Turkey, and severe inflation. At their peak, in 1944 or 1945, the official cost of living indexes (1939 = 100), which understate the extent of inflation, stood at: Egypt, 293; Iraq, about 600; Lebanon, 607; Palestine, 253; Tunisia (foodstuffs only), 512; and Turkey, 350.

The presence of thousands of Allied troops and the shortage of capital equipment also put a heavy strain on the infrastructure. However, there were three offsetting advantages. First, thanks to massive Allied expenditures, the region built up huge foreign exchange balances. Secondly, thousands acquired mechanical and other skills in Allied workshops and bases. Lastly, the diminution of foreign competition and the increased military and civilian demand encouraged industries that had developed before the war and enabled them to expand output and accumulate capital.

In the postwar period, the region has grown more rapidly than ever before, and its economy has developed and become more diversified. The end of the war and the resumption of normal relations with the rest of the world put industries under great pressure and caused other dislocations, such as the discharge of people working for the Allies. But this was more than offset by the revival of trade and the favorable prices received for exports. The Korean War caused a sharp boom in raw materials prices, from which the cotton exporters particularly benefitted. But the boom was over by 1952, and, on the whole, the 1950s was a decade of moderate growth. The period from 1960 to 1973, on the other hand, saw a sharp acceleration of growth as well as a profound transformation in the economic structure.

The high growth rates shown by the national account statistics are confirmed by two sets of physical indices showing, respectively, various aspects of physical activity and levels of mass and luxury consumption. Among the favorable factors were a vast inflow of foreign aid from a variety of sources; the impact of the rapid expansion of oil production and revenues; and the sustained rise in world demand. All this made it possible to raise the investment ratio (and to a smaller extent the savings rates) to unprecedentedly high levels and obtain rather rapid growth. At the same time, in Egypt, Iraq, Syria, and—to a lesser extent— Tunisia, the government took over large sectors of the economy that had previously been controlled by foreign or local private capital, and introduced various forms of planning.

Since 1973, the economy of the region, like that of other parts of the world, has been buffetted by two powerful forces: the explosion of oil prices and world-wide inflation and recession. The first of these has hurt the oil importers—Israel, Jordan, Lebanon, and Turkey—and benefitted the exporters: Iraq, Egypt, Syria, and Tunisia. However, except for Iraq, none of the countries covered in this study is a major oil producer. The second has had its usual adverse consequences. Other unfavorable factors have been the numerous wars since the 1970s: the 1973 Arab-Israeli War following the 1969–70 "War of Attrition"; the Turkish occupation of parts of Cyprus since 1974; the Lebanese civil war that has raged since 1975, with Syrian and Israeli interventions and occupation of parts of Lebanon; the Iraq-Iran War (1980–88); and the short but devastating coalition military action (Operation Desert Storm) in January-February 1991 forcing Iraq to surrender its conquest of Kuwait. All of this has caused vast destruction, diverted large sums from investment to military purposes, and undone some of the progress achieved in the previous decade. And even in peacetime, the military has absorbed resources and manpower to a far greater extent than in other parts of the world (see Conclusion, p. 313).

GROWTH MECHANISMS

Although in the past the region had often had a "command economy," in the nineteenth century the role of government had shrunk. Only recently has government begun again to intervene actively in economic affairs. For one thing, except for Turkey, all the countries remained, for part of the period under consideration, under direct or indirect foreign rule, and economic policy was formulated and implemented in the metropolis. Even after that, the fiscal, financial, and tariff autonomy of the national governments remained restricted. Partly as a consequence, the interest, energy, and efforts of both people and rulers were overwhelmingly channelled into political, not economic, activities. Lastly, the large number and small size of the sovereign states in the region made it impossible to pursue programs based on a large degree of self-sufficiency, as in Russia, China, Japan, India, and other bigger and more populous countries.

Direct Role of Governments

Traditionally, Middle Eastern governments had felt some responsibility for two economic sectors, irrigation and transport (more specifically the maintenance of roads and caravansarais), and for quite a long time their attention remained confined mainly to those two. In Egypt, in the interwar years, the Aswan Dam was heightened once more, and the Gabal al-Awliya Dam was built in the Sudan to increase Egypt's water supply. The Nag Hamadi Barrage was built to raise the water level of feeder canals, and pumping stations were installed in the Delta for the same purpose. Some attention was also paid to drainage, since the accumulation of water and salt in the soil was reducing crop yields. In Iraq, the Habbaniya Escape was built on the Euphrates and the Kut Dam on the Tigris. In addition, a large area was brought under pump irrigation by private capital. In Syria, a small dam was built on Lake Homs, and minor works were carried out in the other countries.

Egypt's main railways had been built by the government, and those of Iraq, Palestine, and Transjordan (including the stretches built by the British during the war) were handed over to the mandatory authorities and run and extended by each of the governments. Turkey soon took over the railways built by foreign capital and, in the interwar period, doubled the network by new construction. Road-building was extensive, especially in Lebanon, Palestine, Syria, and Tunisia; and in practically all the countries, there was considerable port improvement, almost always by the government.

Only in Turkey did the government go substantially beyond those two fields. Here, public utilities and most mines were taken over, by expropriation or purchase. In addition, as part of the Five Year Plan launched in 1933, the Eti and Sümer banks were founded to finance and promote mining and manufacturing, respectively. A total of about $75 million were invested, and several factories and mines were opened. The Second Plan (1938–43) was designed to invest about $90 million, with the help of a British loan, but was interrupted by the outbreak of war.

During the years between 1939 and 1945, governments gained considerable powers. They imposed exchange controls and restricted currency movements. Hitherto, except in Turkey, the local currencies had been on a sterling or franc exchange standard, with free movement between the local currency and sterling or the franc. This meant that local financial conditions were determined by balance of payments and external factors, and no independent monetary policy was possible. Exchange control, which has continued in almost all these countries, and the postwar severance from sterling and the franc, marked the beginning of an independent monetary policy.

The sharp inflation and shortage of goods and materials during the war necessitated some system of price control, rationing, and allocation, and most of the measures taken in these fields have remained in one form or another. All these, and other factors, helped greatly to swell the size of the bureaucracy, and the imposition of income and other taxes increased somewhat the resources government had at its disposal. The sequestration of enemy property (German and Italian), particularly in Egypt, where it was significant, whetted the appetite for further, similar measures. It was followed, in 1956 after the Suez War, by the sequestration of British, French, and much Jewish property in Egypt. In the meantime, following independence, Lebanon, Syria, and Tunisia had taken over most of the French-owned railways and public utilities.

The 1960s saw a vast extension of state ownership. In 1961, the Egyptian government nationalized most branches of the economy: banks, insurance companies, large-scale transport of all kinds, manufacturing, and mining, and, in addition, sequestrated the holdings of the richer classes. A similar measure was applied to Syria (then joined to Egypt in the United Arab Republic), repealed after the break-up of the union and then gradually reimposed. Iraq passed similar legislation in 1964. Tunisia also took over a considerable amount of French property during these years.

Turkey and Jordan have not carried out similar measures, but in both the public sector is large, and government-owned enterprises account for a significant share of transport, manufacturing, mining, and banking. Only in Lebanon has the private sector remained predominant, whereas in Israel the private and cooperative (Histadrut) sector account for the bulk of production.

As in the past but on a larger scale, governments have continued to build and manage irrigation works. Major projects have been built in the last thirty years, including the High Dam in Egypt, a series of dams in Iraq (which have at last succeeded in controlling the twin rivers), the

Thawra Dam in Syria, the Keban and Atatürk dams in Turkey, the Litani Dam in Lebanon, the Mejerda Project in Tunisia, and a vast network in Israel bringing water from the north of the country to the drier south.

Government share in both consumption and investment is large; for both combined, it stood in 1976 at an estimated 40 percent in Iraq and Israel; 38 percent in Egypt; 29 percent in Tunisia; and 24 percent in Turkey. It was also high in Jordan and Syria, but low in Lebanon. (In investment alone, the government's share was about 80 percent in Egypt, Iraq, Jordan, and Syria, from 1978 to 1980; and 60 percent in Tunisia and Turkey.)

Practically all the countries have drawn up fairly comprehensive four or five year development plans; these plans have been implemented with various degrees of success. They have helped to promote growth by focussing both government and public attention on economic questions, by imposing the need to select priorities among competing objectives, and by pointing out inconsistencies between and within projects submitted by government agencies.

The nationalization of large segments of the economy was also designed to promote growth by nationalizing enterprises, reducing luxury consumption, and raising the investment rate. In some cases, these objectives may have been achieved, but more often nationalization has decreased efficiency. This has arisen partly because the officials who took over the enterprises have proved less able and dedicated than the former owners and managers, but mainly because government ownership has resulted in bureaucratization, routine, and the replacement of economic and financial criteria and incentives by administrative directives. Many examples could be cited, including the deterioration in numerous Egyptian, Syrian, and Iraqi enterprises following nationalization and the poorer performance, overall, of the public sector, compared to the private, in Turkey.

To make matters worse, the governments have, for political reasons, put pressure on private enterprises to take on many additional workers—with a corresponding decline in productivity—and have made it almost impossible to dismiss employees for inadequate performance. Those handicaps are particularly severe for industries that aspire to export and compete in world markets. Hence, in the last ten years, measures have been taken in Egypt, Turkey, Iraq, and Syria to relax government control and encourage the private sector.

Indirect Role of Government

From the early 1920s on, these countries' governments have fostered development in a variety of ways. First, the imposition of a greater degree of order than had prevailed berfore the First World War constituted a very favorable factor in Iraq, Lebanon, Palestine, Syria, and Transjordan. So did the marked improvement in administrative organization and the rise in administrative efficiency all over the region. The great expansion of general education achieved also had favorable effects as did the foundation, or enlargement and improvement, of schools of engineering, agriculture, and commerce, notably in Egypt and Turkey. More students were sent abroad to study, particularly for technical subjects; this expanded the small available stock of scientific, technical, and administrative personnel.

The tax system was, to a small but increasing extent, streamlined and reformed, so as to increase its elasticity and equity, and in recent years tax concessions have been granted to foreign investors. Some relief was given to farmers, particularly in Turkey and Egypt. Light but progressive taxes were gradually introduced on most categories of income and on inheritances. This process accelerated during, and especially after, the Second World War. But, in sharp contrast to the generally large share of government *expenditure* in Gross Domestic Product, the percentage of GDP absorbed by taxation (some 15 to 20 percent) is little above the average for developing countries. The difference is, of course, made up by nontax revenues, including foreign aid. It is still generally true that the incidence of taxation is not sufficiently progressive and that certain incomes (e.g., earnings of professionals and profits of unincorporated commercial and financial firms) are greatly undertaxed.

Another government-sponsored valuable service was the introduction of a uniform and generally stable currency. In Egypt and Tunisia, this had been achieved before the First World War, but not in the Ottoman Empire, particularly its Arab provinces, in which conditions had been chaotic, with a wide variety of currencies (European, Indian, Persian, etc.) circulating. Instead, national currencies now circulated, all except the Turkish lira being linked to either the pound sterling or the franc. This greatly facilitated transactions, but it had two disadvantages. First, depreciation of the metropolitan currency (franc in the early 1920s and the late 1930s; pound in the early 1930s) led to a corresponding depreciation of the local one, and shook confidence in paper money. And secondly, as pointed out earlier, such a system precluded the pursuit of an independent monetary policy, a not totally disadvantageous fact since it subjected the local authorities to some external accounting.

Credit facilities improved, with the increase and expansion of commercial banks, most of which continued to be foreign-owned. Almost no control was exercised over them, and indeed, until the Second World War, only Turkey had a full-fledged central bank. But these governments tried to fill some of the larger gaps in the banking systems by setting up agricultural banks or providing funds designed to meet the needs of small farmers. The Egyptian government also took over part of the farmers' debts, which had become intolerably heavy because of the fall in agricultural prices. Governments also provided industrial credit, either by founding special institutions such as the Bank for Industry and Mining in Turkey in 1925, or the Iraqi Agricultural and Industrial Bank of 1936, or through existing institutions such as Bank Misr in Egypt. Farmers were also helped by tariff protection and by support prices. This reflected the great political power of landowners (in Egypt, Syria, and Iraq until the 1950s; in Turkey, in the 1950s) and put a heavy burden on urban consumers. Conversely, in the last two decades, these governments have reverted to their traditional urban bias. Delivery prices for farmers have generally been set well below world prices, and this has resulted in a large transfer of funds from the rural to the urban sector.

Other Institutions

As in the past, foreign capital continued until recently to play an important, though diminishing, role. In the interwar period, the only countries that received a large influx were Palestine, which during the years from 1919 to 1944 got over $600 million in transfers by Zionist agencies, and Iraq, where a small oil industry was developed. Until the end of the Second World War, the governments themselves were careful not to float any foreign loans, except for a few small loans contracted by Turkey; some, notably Egypt, reduced their outstanding debt by redemption, whereas Turkey succeeded in cutting down its indebtedness by negotiation.

A significant amount of foreign capital was invested in manufacturing, especially in Egypt, and usually in partnership with local interests. Starting in the 1950s, most governments contracted huge foreign debts: a substantial amount of foreign capital has also gone into the oil industry (Iraq, Egypt, Tunisia, Syria) and manufacturing (Israel, Turkey, Egypt,

Tunisia, and Lebanon), here again usually in partnership with either the state or private local capital.

The main agency of growth was, however, for several decades, local private enterprise. In the 1920s, and more particularly in the 1930s, the Egyptian bourgeoisie, led by Bank Misr (founded in 1920), played the leading part in the country's industrialization. In Turkey, the loss of Greeks and Armenians, who had constituted the mainstay of the bourgeoisie, was gradually made up by the emergence of Turkish entrepreneurs, some of whom were helped by the private Iş Bank founded in 1924; in the last two or three decades, Turkish entrepreneurs have shown much vigor.

The immigration of European Jews with business and technical skills and some capital gave a great impetus to the economy of Palestine and Israel. The predominantly Christian Lebanese bourgeoisie continued to show much enterprise, first in such services as trade, finance, and tourism and later in industry and, to a certain extent, agriculture. In Syria in the 1940s and 1950s some landowners greatly extended the cultivated area and revived the planting of cotton, making it the leading export, and a group of merchants started the country's industrialization. In Jordan, Palestinian refugees, with government help, have been largely responsible for the country's rapid rate of growth. In Tunisia, local entrepreneurs took advantage of the facilities offered by the government and often worked in close partnership with foreign capital attracted by the country's tax and other incentives and by its cheap labor.

OVERALL GROWTH, SECTORAL COMPOSITION OF GNP, EMPLOYMENT, AND INVESTMENT

Accurate figures are available only for the last three decades. In the interwar period, there was, almost certainly, no significant per capita growth in output and income. During the Second World War, GNP seems almost everywhere to have declined. In the late 1940s and 1950s, the growth rate picked up and, in most countries, accelerated until the early 1970s. Thereafter, various factors, including wars, high oil prices, and world inflation and recession, once more slowed it down.

In the interwar period, agriculture accounted for a third to a half of GNP and was the most important single factor affecting total income; it was also by far the largest element in the balance of payments. Almost everywhere there was an appreciable increase in physical output, but this was more than offset by the sharp fall in agricultural prices starting in the late 1920s and by the deterioration in the terms of trade. In the 1930s, output in manufacturing and mining (including oil in Iraq and Egypt) grew quite rapidly but, in view of the small size of the industrial sector (10 percent or less of GNP), this fell short of offsetting the decline in agricultural income. The growth in population (about 1 percent per annum) further depressed per capita income. A series for Egypt shows a decline in real per capita income (1913 prices) from £E 12.4 (1919) to £E 12.2 (1921–28), and £E 8.2 (1930–33), followed by a recovery to £ E 9.6 (1935–39). In Turkey, per capita GDP (in 1948 prices) rose from the very depressed level of £T 254 (1923–25) to 330 (1926–30), 370 (1931–34), and 474 (1936–40). Only in Palestine, where the Jewish sector advanced rapidly, and possibly in Lebanon, where services were expanding, was there significant overall growth.

From 1939 to 1945, industrial output increased significantly, but agricultural production was severely disrupted by hostilities, mobilization, and shortage of fertilizers. As a result, GNP declined almost everywhere. In Egypt, available estimates put per capita real income in 1945 somewhat below the 1938 level. In Turkey, because of a 30 percent decline in agriculture, per capita income is estimated to have fallen by a quarter. In Palestine, per capita income rose in both the Arab and Jewish sectors, and it may also have done so in Lebanon and Syria.

In the immediate postwar years, agriculture continued to be the main engine of growth. Output recovered and soon surpassed its prewar level. Prices of agricultural exports rose rapidly, especially during the Korean War. By the mid 1950s, the rate of increase in output had greatly slowed down, and agricultural prices levelled off or tended to decline. At this point, however, growth in industrial output (including oil) accelerated appreciably, and began to exert a larger pull on overall production.

The Service Sector

More important was the large expansion in services, both public and private, which by now account for nearly a half, or more, of GNP in all these countries except Iraq, which has a large oil sector. This expansion was due to several causes. The huge upsurge in oil production in the Gulf greatly increased the revenues earned by the countries through which oil passed in transit: Egypt, with its Suez Canal and Suez-Mediterranean pipeline; Syria, Lebanon, and Jordan, with the pipelines carrying Iraqi and Saudi oil to the Mediterranean; and, for a while, Israel, with its

Table I
Composition of Gross Domestic Product (percent)

	1950				1985			
	A	I	O	S	A	I	O	S
Egypt (1953, 1985)	35	13		52	23	35	(15)	42
Iraq (1953, 1980)	22	50	(40)	28	7	74	(62)	19
Israel (1953, 1984)	11	30		59	5	27		68
Jordan (1960, 1985)	16	14		70	8	28		64
Lebanon (1950, 1971)	20	18		62	8	21		71
Syria (1953, 1985)	44	15		41	22	21	(3)	57
Tunisia (1960, 1985)	25	25		50	17	34	(15)	49
Turkey (1950, 1985)	49	16		35	23	30		47
Brazil (1950–60, 1985)	18	34		48	13	35		52
Greece (1950–60, 1985)	27	26		47	17	29		54
India (1950–60, 1985)	49	22		29	31	27		41
South Korea (1965, 1985)	39	26		35	14	41		45

A — Agriculture, forestry, fishing
I — Industry
O — Oil, partly estimated; included in Industry
S — Services

(Sources: World Bank, *World Tables*; idem, *World Development, 1986*.)

Table II
Economic and Social Indicators[a]
GNP

Country	Population (millions) 1985	GNP Growth 1980–85 (%)	GNP per capita 1985 $	Growth per capita 965–85 (%)	Adult Literacy Rate 1985 (%)	Life Expectancy at Birth 1985 (years)	Urban Population % 1980
Egypt	49	2.8	610	3.1	40	61	45
Turkey	50	2.5	1,080	2.6	70	64	47
Tunisia	7	2.3	1,190	4.0	62	63	52
Jordan	4	3.7	1,560	5.8	70	65	56
Syria	11	3.6	1,570	4.0	50	64	50
Lebanon	3	–	–	–	75	66	76
Iraq[b]	13	3.6	3,020	5.3	50	56	72
Israel	4	1.8	4,990	3.6	85	68	89
India	765	2.2	270	1.7	36	56	22
Brazil	136	2.3	1,640	4.3	74	65	68
South Korea	41	1.5	2,150	6.6	95	69	55
Greece	10	0.6	3,550	3.6	95	68	62

[a] Countries ranked according to GNP per capita
[b] 1980

(Sources: World Bank, *World Development, 1986*; Central Intelligence Agency, *The World Factbook*, 1985.)

Elat-Mediterranean pipeline. Very recently, Tunisia has also begun to benefit from the pipeline carrying Algerian gas to Italy and beyond. The enormous rise in oil revenues created a great demand by tourists, students, and other nationals of the producing countries for services provided in the non-oil countries, particularly Egypt and Lebanon. The vast foreign aid received by the region accrued to the governments and helped to swell the bureaucracy, which was also growing for other reasons, including the great increase in education, health, and other social services. And the unprecedented expansion in the armed forces was an important factor in both the overall increase in GNP and in the sharp rise in the share of the service sector.

The result of all these factors was a marked shift in sectoral shares. At present, the share of the service sector is much higher in the region than in countries with comparable incomes, and the share of agriculture much lower. In developing countries, the share of the service sector is usually twice as high as that of the manufacturing sector, but in this region the gap is far higher.

As regards the rate of growth in the 1950s, the following approximate estimates may be given:

Egypt	2 percent per capita per annum
Iraq	5 to 6
Israel	5
Lebanon	2.5
Syria	3
Tunisia	1
Turkey	2.5

These represent a distinct improvement over the prewar situation. Rates of growth for the period from 1965 to 1985 are shown in Table II.

The marked rise in GNP resulted from the great increase in the input of the factors of production: labor, capital, land, and technology. The increase in labor was primarily the result of population growth, through natural increase or, as in Israel and to a very small extent Turkey, immigration.

Population Increase

In the interwar period, the natural increase ran at about 1 percent, accelerating to about 2 in the 1940s and between 2 and 3.3 after that. As in other parts of the world, this was caused by a sharp decline in death rates, particularly infant mortality. In the 1920s, death rates in the region stood at around 25 to 30 per thousand, today at around 10. Life expectancy at birth has risen from about 30 years to 60 to 65. For a long time, birth rates remained unchanged, at about 45 to 50 per thousand, but in the last ten to fifteen years, they have declined to 30 to 35 in Egypt, Lebanon, Tunisia, and Turkey. This is largely due to the fact that birth control, until very recently confined to the middle class, has begun to spread to lower social strata; in most countries this has been helped by government policy. There is reason to believe that this trend will persist, and the birth rate will decline further.

Nevertheless, present indications are that population will double in twenty-five to thirty years. This is a grave prospect, for even today the region is overpopulated in the sense that, in almost all countries, smaller numbers would probably result in higher per capita incomes. In addition, the high rate of growth means that, in several countries, the greater part of investment is absorbed by population increase and is not available for raising per capita income. Moreover, the combination of high birth and death rates results in a high dependency ratio (i.e., the number of persons under 15 or over 65 who are supported by the population between those ages). In the region, the ratio is around 1.0, as compared with under 0.6 in developed countries, including Japan and the Soviet Union.

Growth of Labor Force

Broadly speaking, the labor force has grown in the same proportion as population. For although the proportion in the lower groups has risen, this has been offset by the large expansion in the school population. Labor force statistics are confusing, since some countries (e.g., Turkey) include women working on family farms, whereas most countries exclude them. Excluding such women, the labor participation rate is very low—little over 30 percent of the total population—compared to 45 in developed countries; this is due partly to the age structure and partly to the very low rate of female participation in urban activities, compared not only to advanced countries but to other cultural areas such as Africa and Southeast Asia, and is only very slightly offset by the lower proportion of children attending school. The increase in population has meant that, except in a few spots at certain times, shortage of unskilled labor has not been an impediment to growth. Indeed, the informal urban sector and the public sector both have large surpluses of underemployed. Some of this has been relieved by the large outflow of workers from Turkey and

Tunisia to Europe and from these and the Arab countries to the oil producers of the Gulf and Libya.

As regards the distribution of the labor force, the proportion engaged in agriculture has fallen sharply from the 70 percent or more prevailing a few decades ago. In Egypt and Turkey, it is about 50 percent; in Iraq, Syria, and Tunisia, 33 to 40 percent; and in Israel, Jordan, and Lebanon, 7 to 20 percent. A quarter to a third work in industry, and the rest are in services.

Education

The quality of the labor force has also risen appreciably. In all the countries the overall adult literacy rate is close to, or over, 50 percent (compared to under 20 percent in the 1930s), and almost all male industrial workers can now read and write. In other words, the region has reached the level of primary education which some economists regard as the most important single factor in the absorption of technology and, consequently, in economic development—the level attained by Western Europe and the United States in the first half of the nineteenth century, by Japan before the close of that century, by the Soviet Union and the larger Latin American countries in the 1920s or 1930s, and by China in the 1960s.

As regards technical education, two rough indicators of the advance registered may be given. First, the number of students in higher education in the Arab countries (the vast majority of whom are included in the countries covered in this book) rose from 20,000 in 1945 to 400,000 in 1971 and to 1,000,000 in 1979; however, only a small proportion of these students was in the scientific or technical fields. For Turkey, the corresponding figures were 80,000, 170,000, and 270,000; and for Israel, 9,000, 52,000, and 89,000. Secondly, whereas there were only five engineering colleges in the Arab countries before 1973, there are now about thirty-four. Moreover, the region has continued to supplement its stock of skills by sending larger numbers of students abroad than ever before—in the 1980s, there were nearly 100,000 Arab students in the United States alone—and by hiring large numbers of foreign experts. However, the latter have gone mainly to the oil countries not covered in this study, which have also drawn a significant proportion of both technicians and skilled workers from Egypt, Lebanon, Jordan, Turkey, and Tunisia.

It should be immediately added that all these facts and figures give a greatly exaggerated notion of the region's capacity to absorb and develop technology, as distinct from that of using the technological products imported from abroad. Moreover, the development of vocational education, and the training of skilled workmen and foremen, lags even further behind that of engineers and scientists.

Saving, Investment, and Distribution of Income

The second main input, capital, has risen very rapidly. In the interwar period, gross investment everywhere seems to have been distinctly higher in the 1930s than it had been in the 1920s. It reached a level of around 5 percent of national income in Egypt, somewhat higher in Iraq (which had begun to receive oil revenues) and in Syria, and distinctly higher in Turkey, where the government was investing heavily in transport and industry. In all these countries, the inflow of foreign funds was very small, and the savings rate must have been close to the investment rate. In Palestine, gross investment has been put at 30 percent of national income, but this was almost wholly due to the vast inflow of Jewish funds; the Jewish saving rate was negative, but the Arab rate seems to have been higher than in neighboring countries.

During the Second World War, vast Allied Army expenditures (well over $2,500 million from 1935 to 1945), inflation, and the shortage of goods led to a great increase in savings; this took the form of official foreign exchange reserves. By 1946, these stood at $1,427 million for Egypt, $180 million for Iraq, and $307 million for Turkey. Gross investment, on the other hand, probably declined everywhere owing to shortages of machinery and materials, and the extra wear and tear on roads, railways, and machinery together with the failure to carry out their maintenance probably resulted in a negative net investment.

In the postwar period, these trends were reversed. Investment rates rose to unprecedentedly high levels, but, except in Iraq, which received large oil revenues, savings failed to increase correspondingly. The gap was filled first by drawing down the foreign exchange balances accumulated during the war and then by foreign aid of various kinds. In Egypt, gross investment in 1950 amounted to 12 percent of GNP and savings to 11, and, in 1954 to 14 and 13 percent. In Iraq, in 1949, gross investment stood at 10 to 15 percent of GNP, the savings rate being somewhat lower; with the increase in oil revenues in 1956, they rose to 27 and 30, respectively. In Israel, in 1950, gross investment equaled 31 percent of GNP, but the savings rate was only 5 percent; in 1954, the figures were 30 and 5 percent, respectively. In Syria, from 1953 to 1957, gross investment averaged about 14 percent and savings 11 percent of GNP. In Turkey, in 1950, gross investment and savings were about equal, at 9 percent of GNP, and by 1954 had risen to 14 and 11 percent. More recently, savings rates have risen in a few countries, but they are still everywhere well below investment rates (Table III).

Table III

Gross Investment (I) and Savings (S) Ratios

(as percentages of Gross Domestic Product)

	1957 or 1958[a]		1960–2		1966–8		1973		1980		1985	
	I	S	I	S	I	S	I	S	I	S	I	S
Egypt	14	12	17	13	19	18	12	7	31	16	25	16
Iraq	23	27	19	18	16	22	11	29	33	59		
Israel	29	13	26	12	19	5	31	7	22	8	16	9
Jordan	13	0	17	9	16	4	27	8	48	−27	31	−13
Lebanon	16	15	22	15	23	8	22	12				
Syria	20	20	17	11	17	17	20	18	25	10	24	14
Tunisia			19	8	22	11	23	18	28	25	27	20
Turkey	13	13	15	11	17	16	20	19	27	18	20	16

[a] Percent of GNP

(Source: United Nations, *World Economic Survey, 1969–70*; World Bank, *World Development*, 1986).

A comparison of these investment rates with the growth rates in output in Table I suggests that incremental capital-output ratios were generally between 2.5 and 3.5. Given the fact that inputs of labor were increasing rapidly as we have seen, these figures seem relatively high and may indicate that capital was not being used efficiently. However, they do not compare badly with those of most developing countries.

As regards the distribution of income, in the Middle East, as everywhere else, data are scarce and must be interpreted with caution. Judging from such indices as Gini coefficients (Israel 0.3346, Iraq 0.3615, Egypt 0.4043, Tunisia 0.4436, Turkey 0.5100, Lebanon 0.5370), which measure concentration of income, or the percentage of national income received by the top 5 and bottom 20 percent of the population, the region seems to have a more equalitarian income distribution than Latin America (e.g., Brazil, 0.5244 and Colombia, 0.5615) and one roughly comparable with that of India (0.4475), though of course it is less equalitarian than advanced countries, whether capitalist or socialist.

There is also much social mobility, and a large proportion of the administrators and professionals are sons of workers or peasants. These facts reflect the expansion of education and the displacement, through land reforms, nationalizations, and expropriations, of former privileged groups consisting of the upper class and foreigners and members of minorities.

In recent years, however, there seems to have been a tendency for income inequality to increase, a trend by no means confined to the region and powerfully helped by world-wide inflation. There is also much inequality between regions in most countries (e.g., western and eastern Turkey or coastal and inland Tunisia), and the gap between the rural and urban sectors seems to be widening, partly because of world-wide factors and partly because of the governments' policy of fixing low prices for farm products and subsidizing prices of consumer goods in the cities.

Agriculture

Important changes have taken place in agriculture during the last sixty years or so, but, except in a few areas and for a few crops, the basic pattern of cultivation has not yet been transformed. There has, however, been significant development in the structure of land tenure.

In the interwar period, there was an appreciable increase in the area under crops, except in Egypt and Lebanon, which had already reached the limits of cultivation. From 1939 to 1945, there was no significant change, except for a slight extension of cultivation in Syria. After the war, the sown area was considerably increased in Turkey, Iraq, Syria, and, on a smaller scale, Israel and Jordan. After the early 1960s, there was little change, except for a sharp decline in Iraq due to the disruption caused by the 1958 revolution and land reform.

As in the past, some 80 to 90 percent of the cultivated area continues to be planted to cereals, more specifically wheat and barley; the only exceptions are Egypt, Israel, and Lebanon, where their share is close to 50 percent. Until recently, cereals accounted for half, or over, of the total value of crop production; even today their share is at least one-third and in some countries (e.g., Iraq, Jordan) more.

Yields have continued to be very low; until very recently, wheat yields were below 1 tonne per hectare, except in Egypt, where they stood at 2 tonnes, and in several countries—e.g., Iraq, Lebanon, Palestine, and Tunisia—they fell below 0.5 of a tonne. This compared very unfavorably with the prewar West European average of 2 to 3 tonnes, and even the

Eastern European average of about 1.5, and was comparable to India's 0.7. Starting in the 1960s, however, an effort was made to diffuse improved varieties ("miracle wheat"); as late as 1973, only in Egypt, Israel, and Lebanon were over 30 percent of the planted areas given to such varieties, compared to over 50 percent in India and Pakistan. Since then, Turkey and Syria have made notable strides, raising their yield to 1.9 and 1.5 tonnes, respectively, and the other countries, notably Lebanon, have registered significant progress. Present-day yields in Western Europe are about 4.5 to 5 tonnes, in the United States, 2.6, in the former Soviet Union, 1.5, and in India, 1.8.

The shift to cash crops that started in the nineteenth century has continued. Cotton in particular is the largest single crop (measured in value) not only in Egypt but also in Syria, where it was successfully developed during the Korean War boom; it is also significant in Israel and Turkey. In all these countries, yields have risen appreciably. Fruits and vegetables, notably citrus, form the leading crop in Israel, Lebanon, and Jordan and are exported to both Europe and the Gulf; Egypt, Tunisia, and Turkey are also significant producers. One can expect this trend to continue much further, since the region has some obvious advantages in concentrating on early ripening and labor-intensive crops for Europe and cool climate products for the nearby Gulf. The shift to cash crops has greatly increased the monetization of agriculture. By now, the bulk of output is marketed, and only grain is consumed, in significant proportions, on the farm.

As regards techniques, overall there has been little improvement. By far the greater part of the land is still cultivated by light ploughs, used since time immemorial, drawn by oxen. Until the Second World War, there were very few tractors or other agricultural machines. In the 1950s, mechanization was introduced to Turkey under the Marshall Plan, and then spread to other countries; in the 1970s the rate of increase in the use of tractors was about 5 percent per annum. However, the regional average of tractors per acre of sown land is only about half the world average. Irrigation works have been built by every government in the region. The percentage of total cultivated area under irrigation varies widely, in 1984, from 100 percent in Egypt to 4 in Tunisia; for the other countries it was: Israel 50, Iraq 32, Lebanon 29, Syria 11, Jordan 9, and Turkey 8. Irrigation not only gives much higher yields but makes it possible to grow valuable cash crops that could not be otherwise culti-vated. It also assures regularity of yield, in sharp contrast to the wild fluctuations caused by the region's erratic rainfall.

Another input that has markedly increased is that of chemical fertilizers. Until the 1950s, these were practically confined to Egypt, Lebanon, and Israel, whose use per hectare is very high: 287 kilograms, 115, and 67 respectively, in 1984, compared to 388 in Japan, 140 in the United Kingdom, and 46 in the United States. Since then, there has been a large increase in their use in Jordan and Turkey (to 32 and 47 kilograms), and the regional average is now distinctly above that of the developing world. A favorable factor has been the great increase in the output of chemical fertilizers, usually from a gas base, in most countries. Experiments have shown that the value-cost ratio of fertilizers is high, and, for some crops, very high. Pesticides are also now being employed on a fairly large scale in most countries.

Overall, the rate of growth of total agricultural production has been low. In the interwar period, physical output generally outstripped population growth, but during the war it declined appreciably. Since then, output has been sluggish, with a few exceptions. Overall, agricultural output is only just keeping pace with population growth; in several countries, it is failing to do even that (Table IV). Its contribution to total growth has been small. And since consumption of food is rising rapidly, imports have increased enormously.

Levels of productivity vary widely. Perhaps the best basis for comparison is output in wheat units for 1960. Output per hectare was high in Egypt (6.9), moderate in Israel (1.6) and Lebanon, and low in the other countries—Turkey, 0.6, Syria, 0.4, and similar or lower figures in Iraq, Jordan, and Tunisia. The latter compared with 10.2 in Taiwan, 7.5 in Japan, 1.11 in India, 0.8 in Colombia, 0.6 in Brazil, and 0.3 in Mexico. Output per male worker was high in Israel (28.9) and low in the other countries: Syria, 9.4 (which seems an overstatement), 7.1 in Turkey, 4.4 in Egypt, and roughly similar figures for Iraq, Jordan, Lebanon, and Tunisia. These compared with 10.7 in Japan, 10.3 in Colombia, 9.4 in Brazil, 8.1 in Taiwan, 5.2 in Mexico, and 2.1 in India.

As regards the growth rate of productivity, a recent study gives data for some Arab countries for the period between 1961 and 1976. Output per hectare of arable land rose by 1.4 percent per annum in Egypt, 1.7 in Iraq, 3.0 in Syria, and 3.3 in Lebanon; in Jordan it declined by 4.8 because of the disruption of the 1967 War. Output per farm worker declined by 0.2 percent in Egypt, 1.9 in Syria, and 4.2 in Jordan, and rose by 0.8 in Iraq and 8.5 in Lebanon; there was a large exodus from the countryside to the towns in the latter two countries. In Turkey, in

Table IV

Index of Agricultural Production

(1961–65 = 100)

	Prewar	1948–52	1976–78	1979–81	1983–85	1987–89
Egypt	67	76	104	111	123	139
Iraq	90[a]	93	105	118	133	137
Israel		47	143	148	170	163
Jordan			71	75	92	106
Lebanon			129	167	179	
Syria	40[a]	72	171	209	236	244
Tunisia	95	92	146	161	179	181
Turkey	62	75	119	128	137	145

[a] estimate

Source— FAO *Production Yearbooks*; indexes linked

the same period, output per hectare of sown land rose at 2.5 percent per annum; per farm worker it rose at 3.6 percent.

Until the 1950s, the agrarian structure of the region—except in Israel, Jordan, and Lebanon, where small-scale or cooperative farming prevailed—had grave defects, which not only resulted in a highly inequitable distribution of agricultural income but also seriously impeded its progress. Large estates accounted for anything from a quarter of the cultivated area (Turkey) to four-fifths (Iraq). A few of these were centrally operated, but the vast majority were let to sharecroppers. Rents were high, absorbing one to two thirds of gross output, and leases were short and precarious, discouraging improvements. Rural debt was large and, in the absence of institutional credit, interest rates were very high. The population increase, which generally exceeded the extension of cultivation, was producing a growing class of landless peasants. Lastly, in Tunisia and Palestine, and to a smaller extent in Egypt, a large part of the land was owned by foreign immigrants.

Corrective measures were taken by these governments in the 1950s. The Turkish land reform law of 1945, enforced after 1950, distributed 1.8 million hectares of unowned or unused state or community land to 360,000 families, with good results. Further measures imposing a ceiling on estates are under consideration. A 1952 Egyptian law imposed an 80-hectare limit—subsequently lowered to 40 and then to 20—on estates and distributed some 400,000 hectares (or one-sixth of Egypt's cultivated area) to 400,000 families, or nearly 10 percent of the rural population. The beneficiaries were obliged to join cooperatives, where they were provided with various services and technical assistance. Rents were also reduced, and an unsuccessful attempt was made to raise agricultural wages. It is generally agreed that the economic as well as the social results of the reforms were beneficial.

The Iraqi and Syrian land reforms of 1958, closely modelled on the Egyptian, have been much less successful. In Iraq, implementation was held up by political instability, defective records, and the lack of trained personnel. Much higher ceilings were imposed initially than in Egypt (250 hectares of irrigated and 500 of rain-fed land), but they were drastically lowered in 1970. By 1975, some 2.3 million hectares had been expropriated, but only 1.6 million distributed, and the balance suffered from uncertain ownership. Moreover, Iraq's fragile ecology was more easily disrupted than Egypt's. Irrigation works were neglected, land was salted over, and agricultural output declined, in spite of large government investments. By the end of 1984, 2.4 million hectares had been distributed to 262,000 families, and output began to recover.

In Syria, the 1958 ceilings were 80 hectares for irrigated and 300 for rain-fed lands, but these were lowered in 1963. By 1970, over 1.5 million hectares had been expropriated, and half of these distributed to individuals or collectives. As in Iraq, the initial impact was disruptive, particularly since landlords had played a more active part in rural life and provided more services than in Egypt or Iraq. But in recent years, government attempts to increase agricultural output through irrigation schemes and other measures seem to have been quite successful.

In Tunisia, Europeans owned about one-fifth of the cultivated area. After independence, the government bought back some of this land and took about half of it under the nationalization law of 1964. Service cooperatives were developed, to provide various kinds of help to farmers, and in 1969 an attempt was made to extend production cooperatives to the bulk of farmers. This proved disruptive and was soon abandoned.

In addition to land reforms, these governments have helped agriculture by various organizational improvements. Rural roads have been laid, linking the villages with the main highways for the first time in history. Grain elevators have reduced crop losses through spoilage, but losses are still very high. Agricultural research is being pursued, but extension services are still very weak, and the diffusion of improvements continues to be very slow. Service cooperatives have been set up, under government sponsorship, and although they are deficient in many aspects, and seldom enjoy self-government or show initiative, they have served as a means of chanelling to the farmers both cheap credit and such resources as seeds and fertilizers, as well as providing a certain amount of technical advice. But government investment in agriculture is still very small, and the low prices set for many crops discourage production.

Industry

In the 1920s, industrialization proceeded rather slowly and received from the governments of both the independent countries and mandates tax exemptions and other forms of help. In the 1930s, when these governments recovered their tariff and fiscal autonomy, protection was granted to industry and credit was extended, and the rate of industrial growth accelerated. In Turkey, from 1929 to 1938, net manufacturing output rose at a compound rate of 7.5 a year; in the Jewish sector of Palestine, growth was somewhat more rapid, in Egypt, rather slower, and in the other countries very much slower. Import substitution was pushed quite far in the "first-stage" industries (i.e., textiles, food-processing, building materials, and some chemicals). At the outbreak of the Second World War, there was a wide range of light industries in Egypt, Turkey, Palestine, Iraq, and Lebanon and the beginnings of heavy industry (coal, iron, steel) in Turkey; in Iraq, oil production became significant with the opening of the pipelines to the Mediterranean in 1934.

Nevertheless, industry continued to play a minor part in the economy. In 1939, employment in manufacturing and mining was everywhere well under 10 percent of the total, and in most countries was nearer to 5 percent. Industry's contribution to Net Domestic Product was put at 20 percent in the Jewish sector of Palestine, 12 in Turkey, and 8 in Egypt; it was much less in the other countries. However, this nucleus served the region well during the Second World War; when imports were cut off, local demand (both civilian and military) increased, and technical assistance and spare parts were provided by the Anglo-American Middle East Supply Centre, anxious to reduce the strain on Allied shipping.

By 1946, industrial output had risen by some 50 percent, and it doubled again during the years from 1946 to 1953 (at an annual compound rate of about 10 percent). In the 1960s, manufacturing increased at about 6 percent a year. From 1970 to 1979, the following rates of growth were registered in value added in manufacturing: Egypt, 8 percent; Iraq, 12; Syria, 8; Tunisia, 12; and Turkey, 6. For the years from 1980 to 1985, the figures were: Jordan, 6; Tunisia, 7; and Turkey, 8.

These rates are distinctly higher than those of most other regions of the world, developed or underdeveloped, capitalist or socialist. They reflect the high priority assigned to industrialization by government for the usual reasons: to speed up overall growth, absorb technology, provide employment, reduce imports, decrease dependence on external forces, and supply arms and munitions. As a result, the share of manufacturing, mining, and energy (including oil) in total investment in the late 1970s stood at: Syria, 46 percent, Egypt and Iraq, 42, and Turkey, 23.

By now, industry is fairly diversified and includes a large chemical component and assembly sector as well as some basic metals, metal products, and machinery and equipment. A wide range of durable consumer goods is being made or assembled. Israel, and to a much lesser degree Egypt, has a substantial armament industry, and it also produces and exports precision tools. Nevertheless, except in Israel, food-processing and textiles and clothing continue to account for a half to three-quarters of total value added in manufacturing. As regards mining, oil is by far the leading product. The only other significant minerals are: phosphates in Tunisia, Jordan, Egypt, and Syria; potash in Israel and Jordan; and chromium in Turkey. Coal and lignite are produced in Turkey and iron ore in Turkey and Egypt.

The relative position of the region's industrialization is indicated by the amount of gross manufacturing output per head of total population in 1978: Egypt, $208 (in 1970); Iraq, $124 (in 1970); Jordan, $120; Tunisia, $330; and Turkey, $401. These may be compared with: India, $113, South Korea, $621, Brazil, $410 (in 1970), Colombia, $261, and Greece, $1,346.

Another comparison is provided by Table V, which gives per capita figures for production in industries representing the following groups: energy, food-processing, textiles, building materials, chemicals, and basic metals. Judging by these criteria, the region stands far below southern Europe and distinctly below Latin America but well above Asia (except for Korea) and far above Africa. However, in more advanced industries such as those of machinery, machine tools, and electronics, it compares unfavorably with such countries as China and India, and even more unfavorably with Latin America and southern Europe.

At present, industry (including mining and power but excluding petroleum) generally accounts for 20 to 25 percent of GNP and employs 15 percent or more of the labor force. But these percentages tend to exaggerate its contribution, since the very high protection it receives inflates its "value added." Indeed, there is little doubt that certain indus-

Table V
Per Capita Industrial Production, 1980[a]
(kilograms per annum, except electricity kilowatt hours)

	Electricity	Refined Sugar	Cotton Yarn	Cement	Sulphuric Acid	Nitrogenous Fertilizers	Crude Steel
Egypt	440	13	5	71	1	10	18
Iraq	615	2	1	408	–	27	27
Israel	3,132	5	5	525	82	20	26
Jordan	350	–	–	29	–	–	–
Lebanon	667	4	2	81	–	1	–
Syria	377	5	2	222	–	2	–
Tunisia	468	2	2	278	197 (sic)	7	28
Turkey	517	27	4	329	15	10	38
Spain	2,978	29	3	777	80	26	339
Brazil	1,116	71	–	210	–	3	83
Colombia	765	45	2	161	2	–	10
Mexico	893	37	2	228	35	10	97
China	302	3	3	80	8	10	37
India	175	9	2	27	3	3	14
Indonesia	–	48	8	1	36	–	7
South Korea	1,052	–	11	411	44	18	152
Nigeria	68	1	–	23	–	–	–

[a] Or last available year
(Source: *United Nations Statistical Yearbook, 1981*; United Nations, *Yearbook of Industrial Statistics, 1980*).

tries have a negative value added (i.e., the value of their output is smaller than that of their inputs, both reckoned at world prices). Good examples are the airplane, motor car, and steel industries in almost all countries.

Very few industries are capable of competing on world markets, and, except for textiles in a few countries, the percentage of their output that is exported is still very small. Output per worker is low, whether reflected in measures of physical productivity (e.g., output of cement or sugar or number of spindles or looms per worker) or in value added per employee. Around 1972, the latter stood at $1,400 per annum for Egypt, $2,500 for Jordan, $2,600 for Iraq, $7,200 for Israel, $3,000 for Tunisia, and $6,500 for Turkey. The Turkish figure was inflated by an artificially high exchange rate; comparable figures were: India, $900, Colombia, $5,000, and Italy, $10,400.

Among the many handicaps under which industry operates are the small size of the local markets; the scarcity and poor quality of raw materials; the weak link between industries; the inadequate skills and poor health of workers; bad planning and organization; high transport costs; continued high dependence on imported inputs; scarcity of good managers; and, not least, the stultifying effects of bureaucratic control.

None of this applies to the oil industry, which is one of the most efficient and productive in the world. Iraq is the only major producer among the countries covered in this study. But in recent years, Egypt has greatly expanded its output and so have Syria and Tunisia. In 1980, Iraq produced 130 million tons, Egypt, 29 million, Syria, 8.5 million, Tunisia, 5.5 million, and Turkey, 2.5 million. Revenues received by the government from oil production in 1979 amounted to $22.2 billion in Iraq and $2.4 billion in Egypt and were also large in Syria and Tunisia. The oil industry employs only a tiny fraction of the labor force, but it makes an incommensurately large contribution to GNP and overall growth.

Balance of Payments

There has been little fundamental change in the region's foreign trade. As in the past, most of its transactions continue to be with Western Europe, with which its economy is complementary. But trade with the United States and Japan is far bigger than it was before the Second World War. There is little trade with the former Soviet bloc or the developing countries. Intraregional trade is still small, but increasing.

As in the past, almost all the region's exports consist of raw materials, but in recent years oil has accounted for the bulk, with cotton constituting a small fraction. Exports of manufactures, principally textiles, have risen appreciably in the last decade and now form a significant share of the total in Israel, Lebanon, Tunisia, and, more recently, Turkey.

On the import side, the main change has been the sharp reduction of fuel imports and the great decline in the share of simple consumer goods, which are now mainly manufactured locally. As for imports, the main changes have been the sharp reduction of fuel imports and the great decline in the share of simple consumer goods, which are now mainly supplied locally. Luxury goods and consumer durables have, however, increased, as have capital goods, spare parts, and raw materials, to supply the growing local industry. In most countries, imports of machinery account for nearly half the total imports; however, a large part of this consists of equipment for transport and other infrastructure rather than for manufacturing. And whereas until the Second World War, and beyond, the region was a net exporter of cereals and certain other foodstuffs, today such imports are greater, per capita, than in any other region in the world. In 1980, imports of cereals constituted the following proportion of the 1978 crops (by weight):

Syria	40 percent
Egypt	73 percent
Tunisia	83 percent
Iraq	138 percent
Jordan	544 percent
Israel	819 percent
Lebanon	942 percent

Today Turkey is the only net exporter of food in the region, after having been a fairly heavy importer in the 1960s and early 1970s.

Generally speaking, the countries of the region have pursued an inward-directed policy of import substitution, marked by very high protection, administrative regulation of trade, and exchange rates that greatly overvalue the currency, though there are exceptions, notably those of Lebanon, Israel, Turkey since 1980, and, very recently, Egypt. However, partly because of the very small size of most countries, partly because the high price of oil has greatly raised the value of exports of several among them, and partly because of the large amount of invisible income and foreign aid received allowing high import levels, the ratio of foreign trade to GNP is generally high. For 1980, the ratio of imports to GNP ranged from 12 percent in Turkey and 21 in Egypt to 45 in Israel, 53 in Jordan, and 85 in Lebanon; that of exports, from 4 in Turkey and 13 in Egypt and Jordan to 30 in Israel and 67 in Iraq.

The balance of payments shows one uniform feature, an enormous excess of merchandise imports over exports. This was not true of Iraq before the outbreak of war with Iran in 1980, since oil exports more than covered all imports. But it has become so now. Part of the deficit is (or was) covered by transit and tourist services: Suez Canal tolls in Egypt; pipeline tolls in Syria, Lebanon, Jordan, and Tunisia; and tourist expenditures in all the countries except Iraq. A still larger item, which in the aggregate amounts to several billion dollars, is remittances by workers from the Gulf countries and Libya, and, for Turkey and Tunisia, from Europe as well. Jewish remittances to Israel have been consistently large. In spite of these receipts, however, the current account everywhere shows shows a deficit.

This has been covered—and sometimes more than covered—by the enormous amount of foreign aid received. Four main donors may be distinguished. First, the United States, which, from 1945 to 1985, extended $60.4 billion in economic grants and credits to the region covered in this study. Except for Iraq, all countries received a very large amount of American government aid: Israel ($30.1 billion); Egypt ($14.9 billion); Turkey ($10.8 billion); and Jordan ($2.5 billion). In addition, many billion dollars of military aid were given.

Secondly, from 1954 to 1984, the Soviet Union and Eastern Europe gave a total of about $11 billion in economic aid (grants and credits) to the region. Military aid was several times as high. The main beneficiaries were at first Egypt ($3.1 billion) and then Turkey ($2 billion), Syria ($2.9 billion), and Iraq ($2.7 billion).

Thirdly, Western Europe and Japan have contributed their share of aid. Noteworthy in this category are German reparations and other payments to Israel, French aid to Tunisia, and, for a while, British aid to Jordan.

Lastly, and by now far the largest, is aid from the Arab oil states of the Gulf. A large part of their aid is extended through the various national or multilateral funds, such as the Kuwait Fund founded in 1961, and the Saudi and other funds established in 1970s. From 1974 to 1976 alone, they disbursed some $7.8 billion to four Arab states (Egypt, Syria, Jordan, and Lebanon) covered in this study. In addition, many billions were extended in bilateral aid to Egypt, Syria, Jordan, and, in recent years, Lebanon and Iraq. Iraq is estimated to have received some $80 billion since the outbreak of war with Iran.

Altogether, in relation to their population, the countries covered in this study have received more aid than any comparable region of the world. Shortage of capital has not been a major constraint on growth, compared to lack of skills or organization.

Since much of this aid was in the form of loans, the region is heavily indebted. In 1985, external public debt amounted to:

Country	Debt	Debt Service as Percentage of Exports of Goods and Services
Turkey	$17.8 billion	32
Egypt	$17.8 billion	34
Israel	$15.9 billion	29
Tunisia	$4.4 billion	24
Syria	$2.8 billion	15
Jordan	$2.7 billion	22
Lebanon	$0.2 billion	?

For Lebanon the figure was negligible and for Iraq very high but unascertainable. This remains true for both Lebanon and Iraq. For the other countries World Bank estimates for 1990 are as follows:

Turkey	28.2
Syria	26.90
Tunisia	25.8
Egypt	25.7
Jordan	23.0

The figure for Israel, not calculated, may be estimated at about 30 percent.

INTERNATIONAL COMPARISONS

From the economic point of view, the region stands today somewhat above the world's median, though well below the mean. On a per capita basis, it compares well with India, China, and Africa, but poorly not only with Japan and Russia but also with Southeastern Europe, Latin America, and the Asian fringe (see also Tables II and V). As regards the last group, the region stands much lower than several countries that in 1914 were only a little ahead of it; the region has been overtaken by several others that were distinctly behind it. The statistical explanation of this lag is clear. Until the 1950s, growth in the region was slow; in addition, the high rate of population increase absorbed, for several decades, the bulk of the increment in GNP.

The Middle East has experienced both growth and development. GNP has risen, in some countries rather fast. In marked contrast to the situation in 1914, when only Egypt and Tunisia had adequate facilities, the region has a good infrastructure of railways, roads, pipelines, ports, airports, and other public utilities. As regards power, total output of electricity has risen from 820 million kilowatt hours in 1938 to 9.6 billion in 1960 and 71.4 billion in 1980. In agriculture, there has been a shift to more valuable cash crops and increased monetization, irrigation has been extended, mechanization has increased, and fertilizers and pesticides are used on a rather large scale. Perhaps more important, the agrarian structure has been deeply transformed, usually with good results.

Although only Iraq ranks among the major oil producers, petroleum output in Egypt, Syria, and Tunisia is significant, and these and other countries have benefitted from the huge expansion of wealth in the neighboring oil-producing countries. Industry has greatly increased in scale and diversified; it now accounts for nearly a quarter of GNP, employs about a sixth of the labor force, and is growing very fast. Other sectors of the economy, which either hardly existed in 1914 or were in foreign hands, have developed and are run by nationals: banks, insurance houses, shipping, airlines etc. Lastly, there has been an increase in the stock and annual output of managers, administrators, engineers, scientists, technicians, and skilled workers. Whereas before the First World War—and for many years after—most skilled jobs were held by foreigners (and a large proportion of the rest by members of minority groups), today such persons stand out as conspicuous exceptions.

If the region's achievements are impressive, its shortcomings loom no less large. Its agricultural productivity is, with few exceptions, still rather low, and the rate of growth of its agricultural output is also very low. This has created major difficulties and constitutes a heavy drag on the whole economy. In this respect, the region finds itself in a very large company, including several countries that are much more advanced.

Another source of weakness is industry, which suffers from overstaffing and overprotection, poor planning and management, and low productivity. Industry is also still very heavily dependent on imported raw materials and chemicals, as well as machinery and spare parts, and overall has achieved only a small part of its anticipated contribution to reducing the import dependence of the region. As regards exports of industrial products, the performance of most countries has been extremely disappointing.

A more general weakness, which has affected all branches of the economy, is excessive state control and management. This goes far beyond what is common in nonsocialist states. By now, in most countries, the government owns and operates transport, banking, insurance, and the bulk of industry and has considerable control over agriculture. At the same time, Middle Eastern bureaucracy is far from being up to the huge task laid upon its shoulders. This heavy handicap can be, and is being, borne, but it certainly slows down the rate of advance. At a still more general level, the progress achieved in the last few decades has been in great part due to the inflow of external funds, in the form of foreign aid or oil revenues, and has resulted in a huge foreign debt.

The region has not reached the point where it can generate on its own the capital needed for sustained growth or develop its human resources so that they can make the contribution required of them. Savings rates are still low, though they have risen somewhat in the last few years. The gap between investment and savings, which is far larger than in most developing countries and is reflected in the heavy deficit on current account, has been filled by outside resources. This raises doubts as to whether the progress recently achieved can be sustained.

Human resources constitute a more serious weakness. It is noteworthy that, judging from the various attempts to construct a physical quality of life index, the region stands much lower in the international social scale than in the international economic scale; for example, it is far below poorer countries like Thailand, Philippines, Sri Lanka, or Burma. This is largely because birth rates have shown little, or no, tendency to decline from their very high level. And of all available indices, birth rates are perhaps the best in showing the degree of a country's modernization. The region also scores poorly on other indicators of social advance, such as death rates, infant mortality, and literacy (see Table II). In recent years, however, all these have shown considerable improvement.

A large part of this region's human resources still lies untapped, notably its women, and this fact is shown by the small percentage of people engaged in the labor force. In other words, both its recent economic performance and the economic level it has presently attained tend to give an unduly favorable picture of its degree of modernization; they suggest rather better prospects than may, in fact, be lying ahead.

CHAPTER THIRTEEN

Social Interdependence

DESPITE THEIR DIVERSITY, the Afro-Asian successor states of the Ottoman Empire arose out of common historical circumstances. The region was overwhelmingly Muslim. And these states were linked together by two major languages (Arabic and Turkish) and were subjected to the same forces of political centralization that were a hallmark of the Ottoman Empire. They were also exposed, at different interludes, to nearly the same set of technological, economic, and ideological changes.

It is instructive within such a context to ascertain how the experiences of these successor states, both collectively and individually, comply with or diverge from patterns observed elsewhere. The focus is on selected attributes of social interdependence, the distinctive demographic features, patterns of human settlement, and processes of social mobilization and redistribution.

HUMAN RESOURCES

Taken together, the demographic experiences of the successor states stand in sharp contrast to world trends and to other comparable regions of the Third World. There are also marked differences within the states themselves.

The most striking demographic feature is the generally high fertility rates that have long characterized the countries under study.

For the world as a whole, the rate of population growth rose gradually from the nearly stationary level that had prevailed prior to the mid-seventeenth century to an all-time high of 2 percent a year during the late 1950s and 1960s. During the years since then, however, it has declined slightly, if gradually, to a level of 1.7 percent annually in the early 1980s. In other words, except for a brief period during the mid 1950s, the overall pattern of the world's rates of growth has never exceeded the 2 percent level.

As can be seen in Table 1, the industrialized and developed countries maintained a rather stationary rate of growth that ranged from 1 to 1.3 throughout the first half of this century. By the mid or late 1960s, it started dipping to the relatively modest rate of 0.6 percent a year, with several countries in this group already moving close to the zero population growth.

Among the less developed countries (LDCs), however, rates of annual growth exceeded the 2 percent level during the 1950s, but rather than declining, they continued to increase during the 1960s and 1970s. It is only during the past few years that the rate began to go below the 2.5 level.

Growth trends among the Ottoman successor states differ from the rest of the world's in at least two significant respects. First, growth trends appeared earlier (early 1930s) and sustained their accelerated pattern until they peaked at 3.0 in the late 1970s. Second, particularly in Syria,

Table 1
Average Annual Rate of Population Growth
(percent)

	1900	1925	1935	1945	1955	1965	1975	1987
Syria					3.4	3.5	3.8	
Iraq	1.8	1.7	1.5	2.4	3.1	3.5	3.3	3.6
Jordan					3.2	3.0	3.9	
Egypt	1.6	1.2	1.2	1.9	2.3	3.1	2.6	2.7
Tunisia		0.7	2.2	2.2	2.0	2.1	2.0	2.1
Turkey				1.7	2.9	2.6	2.5	1.9
Palestine/Israel		3.5		3.5	3.1	2.8	1.7	
Lebanon					2.6	2.5	2.5	0.3
Average		1.2	2.1	2.0	2.8	2.9	2.8	2.5

Comparative Trend in Rates
of Annual Growth

	1925	1935	1945	1955	1965	1975	1987
Successor States	1.2	2.1	2.0	2.8	2.9	2.8	2.5
Developing Countries	1.2	1.0	1.3	2.3	2.4	2.5	2.2
Industrialized Countries	1.3	1.0	1.1	1.3	1.1	0.7	0.6
World	1.0	1.0	0.9	2.0	1.9	1.8	1.7

(Sources: League of Nations, *Statistical Yearbooks*; UN *Demographic Yearbooks*; World Bank, *World Development Reports*; Cairo Demographic Center, *Demographic Measures and Population Growth in Arab Countries* [1970]; Cairo Demographic Center, *Fertility Trends and Differentials in Arab Countries* [1971].)

Iraq, and Jordan, rates of growth have not as yet begun to taper off. In all three, rates of annual increase have been in excess of 3 percent for over three decades. By 1987, they continued to average 3.8, some of the highest rates of growth in the world. Syria's population has almost doubled in less than two decades. It leaped from about 5.2 million in 1965 to 11 million in 1987. This doubling time of 18 years is substantially higher than the rates observed in countries like Lebanon, Israel, and Turkey. (The net decrease of − 0.3 noted for Lebanon is an anomalous and transient situation generated by the high casualty and exodus rates incident to the protracted civil strife.)

If one excludes Lebanon's unique experience, the successor states could fall into two distinct groups: Syria, Iraq, and Jordan, characterized by extremely high growth rates (above 3.8 percent annually), sustained over three decades, and having a population doubling time of about 20 years. The rest—Tunisia, Egypt, Turkey, and Israel—have all witnessed their decline during the past two decades and converge on rates of growth of 1.9 to 2.7, with a doubling time of about 30 years.

The comparative trends in crude death rates (CDR) reveal that there is little differentiation in the incidence of mortality today among the different regions of the world. They all converge, based on 1987 estimates, at around 10 deaths per year, per 1,000 people. The difference, naturally, is in the timing and sequence of such declining mortality. Such reduction began in the industrialized and more developed countries at least 30 to 40 years earlier. Shortly after World War II, evidence of such decline began to appear, and, by the early 1950s, the CDR started to fall below the 10-level. By contrast, the successor states, as elsewhere in the Third World, did not commence their effective control over mortality (particularly infant mortality) until relatively recently. As seen in Table 2, Tunisia, Jordan, and Syria dropped below the 10-level only during the past few years, whereas Egypt, Turkey, and Iraq continue to retain relatively high (about 9), if declining, death rates. The Israeli and Lebanese CDR declined earlier.

Although infant mortality has been substantially reduced, the change is clearly not even. Egypt has not yet managed to reduce its rate considerably. An infant mortality of 85 is almost twice the world's average and is still higher than the average of developing countries (76). Tunisia and Turkey went below the 100 threshold during the 1980s; Iraq, Jordan, and Syria during the late 1970s; Lebanon and Israel, two and three decades earlier, respectively. This sequence, as with other demographic features, is associated with such factors as levels of literacy, urban, resi-

Table 2
Trend in Crude Death Rates (CDR)
(Number of deaths in a year per 1000 people)

	1925	1935	1945	1955	1965	1975	1987
Egypt	29	27	27	23	15	13	10
Iraq					18	15	8
Turkey		30	33	22	17	16	9
Tunisia					14	13	7
Jordan				21	18	14	7
Syria					15	14	7
Lebanon					12	9	
Palestine/Israel			18	6	6	7	7
Average		28	26	24	14	13	8

Comparative Trend in CDR

	1925	1935	1945	1955	1965	1975	1987
Successor States		28	26	24	14	13	8
Developing	31	29	28	22	18	15	11
Industrialized	16	14	15	10	9	9	8
World		24	22	18	16	13	9

dence, status of women, and, of course, access to medical and public health facilities.

The substantial decline in infant mortality is reflected in the appreciable increase in life expectancy, particularly during the last three decades. On the whole, the average person today in the Arab world is expected to live almost 30 years longer than in 1945. The magnitude of this change is significantly larger than increases in life expectancy registered elsewhere. During the same interval, for example, life expectancy in the developing countries increased by about 20 years, compared to 12 in the more industrialized countries and about 10 in the rest of the world.

Changes within the successor states have not been uniform. In general, three coterminous groups may be identified. First, Egypt and Iraq have not, despite advances made in standards of health, literacy, and nutrition, achieved a life expectancy of 64. Egypt, in particular, because of its high infant mortality, continues to suffer from relatively low life expectancy (seven years lower than its counterparts among the successor states). Second, Syria, Turkey, Jordan, and Tunisia have all just broken into the 60 barrier during the early 1980s. By 1987, they managed to add, on the average, another 5 or 6 years to their life expectancy. Finally, Lebanon and Israel have had, once again, a headstart over other countries. At 74, Israel has a life expectancy equal to if not slightly higher than many more developed countries.

The overwhelming demographic feature, one which has far-reaching implications for social mobilization, is the persisting high fertility rate. Although the overall crude birth rate (CBR) of the successor states displayed a slight decrease in the 1980s, and dropped for the first time below 40, it is still comparatively very high. It is more than twice as high as the fertility rates observed among the more developed countries. It is even higher than those of the less developed regions of the world. A CBR of 36 in 1987 is exactly what the rest of the world had attained in the early 1920s. This is a lag of more than half a century.

Table 3
Trend in Crude Birth Rates (CBR)
(Number of live births per 1000 people)

	1910	1925	1935	1945	1955	1965	1975	1987
Syria						49	46	45
Iraq						49	47	43
Jordan					45	46	48	43
Egypt	42	49	46	47		45	39	36
Tunisia					40	46	34	30
Turkey			45	43	48	38	34	30
Lebanon					39	36	34	
Israel		46	44	42	28	27	26	22
Average		47	45	44	40	42	39	36

Comparative Trend in CBR

	1925	1935	1945	1955	1965	1975	1987
Successor States	47	45	44	40	41	39	36
Developing States	41	41	40	41	40	37	31
Industrialized States	28	22	20	23	20	19	14
World	36	34	33	35	34	31	27

Differences in fertility patterns within the successor states are striking. As shown in Table 3, once again Syria, Iraq, and Jordan stand out. They have sustained their high fertility at CBR levels that continue to be in excess of 40. Egypt, Tunisia, and Turkey have just managed during the past decade to dip below that level. Lebanon and Israel, on the other hand, as early as the mid-1950s, had reduced their fertility below the 40-level, and are today the two countries with a CBR of less than 30.

A striking demographic feature is the overwhelming youthfulness of the population. The successor states, with an overall average of 43 percent below 15 years of age, rank markedly higher than patterns and trends observed elsewhere. More significant, whereas the proportion of those below 15 either remained the same or decreased slightly in both the more and less developed regions of the world, this proportion has been increasing in the successor states during the past three decades. This is particularly so in Jordan, Syria, and Iraq, whose youthfulness today is almost twice the rates observed in some of the advanced industrial societies. Differences within the successor states are equally striking: ranging from as high as 51 percent in Jordan to only one-third in Israel.

Such a population profile means that nearly half the population are dependents, outside the labor force, and overloading the capacities to cope with the growing demand for basic amenities and public services.

Early female pubescence accompanied by an early marriage age correlate with high birth rates due to the prolonged child-bearing period. For example, with 44 percent of females of child-bearing age, the Egyptian population continues to be characterized by high fecundity. Although there has been a recent decline in early marriage—mostly due to growing female literacy and urbanization—the proportion of married women continues to be comparatively very high. Over the past 30 years or so, the average age at first marriage has risen by about 3 years (Egyptian Fertility Survey, 1980: 119), hardly enough to reduce the overall high fertility of the Egyptian population.

Excluding West Africa, there may not be any other region in the world with as high a level of fertility. The difference, as shown in Table 3, is in the order of 9 births per 1000 when compared with the rest of the world, and as high as 22 births per 1000 when compared with the industrialized countries.

Differences within these countries are equally striking. Crude birth rates continue to be extremely high (i.e., 45 to 43 per 1000) in Syria, Iraq, and Jordan; moderate in Egypt, Tunisia, and Turkey (36 to 30); and comparatively low in Lebanon and Israel (29 to 22).

Marriage and Culture

These demographic problems reflect a cognitive dissonance between secular forces associated with the reduction of mortality, on the one hand, and normative expectations encouraging high fertility on the other. Fertility reflects a culture's attitude toward the value of children, the role of sexuality, early marriage, the status of women, and religion. It is only when such natalist norms change that significant reductions in fertility can occur.

The survival of such norms is visible in the feelings of pity tinged with social stigma that unmarried adults, widows, orphans, fatherless children, and childless marriages continue to evoke in many of the societies discussed here. Most of the conventional economic justifications associated with pronatalist values are also present. In rural areas, both wives and children are perceived as economic assets, as extra hands in domestic chores, or as sources of extra cash at harvest time or at other times when their help is needed. Boys assist their fathers in the field, and girls help their mothers around the house and attend to younger siblings. As in other rural communities, children assume such responsibilities at a relatively early age.

Children working in the fields, particularly since the nature of agriculture employment is conducive for child labor, continues to be a familiar sight in rural areas. Consequently, the proportion of children of school age who are not attending school is correspondingly higher in such areas.

A large family, particularly in rural communities, is more than a source of welfare and a hedge against social isolation and economic insecurity. In a fundamentally gregarious and leisure-oriented culture—in the absence of institutionalized outlets of recreation—a large family is also an important source of entertainment. Much social interaction and everyday life occur within small and closely-knit family circles. Expecting an additional child—pregnancy, childbirth, child-rearing, socialization, and all the rituals and ceremonies associated with the early stages of a life cycle—take on added meaning in an otherwise drab and uneventful existence. Children live up to the Quranic saying and truly become "the adornment of life." An added child is not only an added source of entertainment. Members of an extended family often share the responsibility of looking after younger children, and as such reduce the burdens of child-rearing.

As in other patrilineal, patrilocal, and patriarchal societies, a strong preference for male children has also survived. The birth of a boy is greeted with joy; it is an occasion for lavish festivities. The birth of a girl, on the other hand, is generally hushed and muted. A male child perpetuates the family name, reinforces the continuity of the family, and, perhaps more important, preserves the family's inherited land and wealth. Inheritance laws among Sunni Muslims—since a boy inherits twice as much as a girl—continue to place a premium on male descendants. As a result of the foregoing, female infant mortality continues to be disproportionately high in certain parts of the Middle East.

On moral and ethical grounds a son is also perceived more favorably than a girl. He is a source of security for his sisters and parents in old age, a provider in times of need, and a protector and defender of his sister's virtue and family honor. This is increasingly so since the relaxation of sexual standards is already threatening conventional morality and weakening the family as a source of moral and social restraint. The preference for early marriage, as a means for protecting a girl's chastity, is no doubt an expression of this ethical concern. Despite the relaxation of sexual standards, a premium continues to be placed on a girl's virginity. Early marriage frees parents from such anxiety.

There are enormous pressures on the young bride to have her first baby as promptly as possible. The social stigma she suffers when she fails to do so is also quite menacing. Indeed, the woman, her husband, her parents, and her in-laws—plus her extended circle of close relatives and acquaintances—are all anxious for proof of fertility and fretful about its delay.

There is a definite relationship between the participation of women in the labor force and fertility. It is in areas where such participation is low that fertility is the highest. Where women have little access to employment opportunities outside the house, the wife derives much of her self-esteem and recognition from her traditional role as wife and mother.

Given such persisting pronatalist sentiments, family-planning efforts—whether explicit population policies or indirect programs—have faltered either for lack of vigorous official support or because of general reluctance on the part of potential users.

Contraception

Knowledge and use of contraception are a major factor in recent declines in fertility in developing countries. Available data indicate that in the successor states, with the exception of Israel and Lebanon, a gap exists between a knowledge of contraceptive methods and their use by married women. This gap is very high in Iraq, Syria, Egypt, Jordan, and Tunisia. Whereas virtually everyone has heard of such methods, less than one-fourth of the married women actually use them.

High fertility rates may also reflect persisting attitudes (official or otherwise) towards family planning in general. For example, in Turkey, the official attitude since the establishment of the republic has favored rapid population growth. Legislation was enacted in 1930 empowering the Ministry of Health with promoting necessary measures in order to increase and facilitate births. Likewise, the import, manufacture, advertisement, and sale of contraceptives were made illegal, and tax exemptions were granted for each new child.

It was not until the 1960s, as population pressure began to mount (rates of annual growth were beginning to approach 3.0 in the late 1950s), that earlier, pronatalist attitudes gave way. The Turkish Family Planning Law of 1965, among other things, removed the ban on the sales of contraceptives. More important, a nationwide system of birth-control clinics, including mobile units, were introduced into rural areas.

Overpopulation had been a public issue in Egypt as far back as the 1930s, but it became a prominent issue only after the 1952 revolution. President Nasser hesitated, however, to arouse religious opposition over birth control. He also harbored hopes that economic reforms would bring fertility down. A full decade lapsed before Nasser was forced to conclude, in May of 1962, that family-planning services were needed, and it was not until 1966 that the Supreme Council on Family Planning was established.

Nasser's reluctance was not due to any lack of conviction. He understood national opinion. While Islamic leaders in Cairo issued government-inspired statements supporting contraception, *imams* in villages were proclaiming its immorality. Medical authorities in the capital preached the virtues of child spacing, but local midwives spread rumors about the adverse effects of pills on users.

President Sadat, like Nasser also sympathetic to family planning, was equally handicapped by a lack of public enthusiasm. By then, also, the wars with Israel occupied government's attention and resources. To this day, family planning, including programs introduced in the late 1970s, has faltered for lack of public support.

Tunisia has undergone similar family-planning experiences. Pronatalist sentiments continued to survive and were largely uninfluenced by the European presence. It was not until the early 1960s that such sentiments began to be modified. The government became increasingly aware that economic development was being impeded by population growth. Successive decrees (between 1960 and 1965) were passed limiting family allowances to four children, sanctioning the import and sales of contraceptives, and legalizing abortion for women over 30 with five or more children. Tunisia became in 1964 the first Arab and African country to undertake a national family-planning program.

More remarkable in Tunisia were some of the social transformations, again the result of special legislation, antedating family planning. In 1956, a pathbreaking "personal status code" modified Quranic law. Polygamy was prohibited, divorce modified, and the minimum age of marriage raised to 17 for women and 20 for men. Women were given the vote, and the veil was decried as a "dust rag." Increased educational and employment opportunities for women also advanced social mobilization. Despite all this, the family-planning program has had limited success: a large number of women refused to experiment with contraception. There was even a rise in the annual rates of growth during the 1970s and 1980s.

Regional Variations

Regional variations in the rural-urban fertility spectrum are noteworthy. For example, whereas regional differences have begun to disappear in Jordan largely because of substantial migration from rural to urban areas (as well as to the survival of pronatalist norms in both areas), they are still pronounced in others. In Egypt, the CBR in the mid-1940s was almost the same in Cairo and Alexandria as in the rest of Egypt. By the mid-1970s, however, the CBR ranged from about 32 in Cairo and Alexandria to about 45 in rural upper Egypt. In Iraq and Syria, likewise, rural-urban variations remain pronounced.

Israel is characterized by variations in fertility and mortality rarely observed elsewhere. Much of this variety is associated with the ethnic and religious heterogeneity of the population. There has always been a sharp differential between the Jewish and Arab population. By the early 1940s, the CBR of the Arab population was almost twice that of the Jewish; 49.2 for the former compared to 20.7 for the latter. In the postwar years, fertility rose in the Jewish population of Israel, largely due to the influx of Eastern and Sefardic Jews. The same thing happened within the Arab population. By 1946, while the CBR of the Jewish population registered 29.1, that of their Arab counterpart had risen to 54.2. The contrast grew sharper during the 1960s. By the early 1970s, gross reproduction rates among Jews had declined to the level of 1.65, while, among non-Jews, the figure rose to more than 4.0.

Variations in mortality are even more striking. In the mid-1930s, while the Jewish population had reduced its CDR to 9.2, that of the Arabs was almost three times higher and remained at 26.3. The same was true of infant mortality. By the mid-1940s, the death rate for Jewish infants four years of age or younger in Palestine continued to be about four times lower than that of the Arabs (i.e., 64 compared to 251).

All this has meant a much higher rate of natural increase for non-Jews. More important, whereas rates of the Jewish population continue to decline, those of the non-Jewish population have been increasing considerably. The political implications of such demographic realities, with mounting pressures in the territories occupied by Israel in 1967—the West Bank, the Gaza Strip, and the Golan Heights—are becoming increasingly evident.

In Lebanon, demographic variables have always been associated with the multireligious composition of its society. The relative ranking of the fertility rate of each of the religious groups (from high to low) is as follows: Shi'as, Sunnis, Druzes, Catholics, and other Christians.

The Shi'a are the fastest-growing community but the least developed socioeconomically. During the latter years of Ottoman rule, the Shi'as constituted only about 5 percent of the population of Mount Lebanon. By 1920, when the French incorporated Jabal 'Amil and the Beqa along with Mount Lebanon and the coastal cities to create Greater Lebanon, the proportion of Shi'as in the new entity had increased to 17 percent. Whereas the proportion of other sects remained essentially the same, or even declined, the Sh'ia increased to almost 20 percent by the early 1940s. Today, it is estimated that they make up at least 35 percent of Lebanon's population.

What is perhaps most significant about Lebanon as a pluralistic entity is that basic demographic attributes—such as fertility, family size, and birth-control practices—correlate with the indexes of social mobilization. In all religious groups socioeconomic mobility, family income, husband's occupational status, wife's education, degree of urbanization, and the like are positively related to fertility control.

HUMAN SETTLEMENT

For centuries, a free and often massive movement of tribes, families, and individuals has been a distinctive feature of Middle Eastern civilization. Long before migration assumed its current dimensions and patterns, the premodern Islamic world sustained a fairly free flow of movement across national borders.

Population Shifts and Migration

Because of persisting myths about Arab unity, no Arab regime—divisive ideologies notwithstanding—has dared to challenge this professed national self-identification with the Arab *umma*. Hence, many of the Arab states, until very recently, made no distinctions between their fellow countrymen and Arabs on the other side of the national border. In several of these countries a legal tradition exists whereby Arab immigrants are able to enter without a visa. Iraq and Syria, for example, extend this right to the nationals of all Arab countries.

Even so, with the introduction of the modern state, this free flow of migrants has become more selective. Growing numbers travel as tourists, students, and, with the discovery of oil in the Arabian Peninsula, as migrant labor. Disruptive of this flow have been the two world wars, successive Arab-Israeli military confrontations, and other local and regional conflicts. Some countries suffered more than others. For example, whereas Egypt and Tunisia were spared some of the damaging consequences of World War I, Syria, Iraq, and particularly Lebanon and Turkey, suffered immensely. In Lebanon alone some 300,000 perished as a result of fighting and famine. Casualties in Turkey exceeded a million. The war also generated a massive exodus of minority groups (particularly Armenians, Greeks, Kurds) from Turkey. As many as 2 million people left Turkey, whereas only 400,000 Muslim Turks came from Greece to Turkey.

Migration to and from Palestine has also been a source of population dislocation and relocation. Since the outbreak of Arab-Israeli hostilities (beginning with the expulsion of more than 700,000 Palestinians from areas occupied by Israel in 1948 and in the subsequent wars of 1967 and 1973), altogether more than 3 million Palestinians have been uprooted from their homes and subjected to all the hardships of dispersal and banishment.

This dislocation of Palestinians has been aggravated by the fact that they have not been integrated into the Arab states or repatriated to Palestine. Only Jordan has extended to them the rights of citizenship. Their number has also swelled, often at much higher rates than those found in their respective host countries.

Lebanese experience with migration is a unique historic phenomenon—more Lebanese live abroad than in Lebanon. Since the 1860s, an outflow (peaking during World War I to about 9,000 to 10,000 annually) of both lower socioeconomic groups and highly skilled professionals has produced socioeconomic mobility. Foreign remittances have helped Lebanon to enjoy higher per capita income than most countries of the Middle East and North Africa. The Lebanese have traveled almost everywhere (initially to North and Latin America, then to Australia, Egypt, Canada, West Africa, and, more recently, to Europe and the Gulf states), and this has fostered their openness and receptivity to new ideas and life-styles.

Israel's experience with migration is also unique. In fact, the political history of the state of Israel is bound up with the displacement of indigenous populations. In 1948, shortly before its proclamation of independence (which declared the state to be "open to the ingathering of the exiles"), less than 6 percent of the world Jewish population lived in Israel. In the initial period (1948–1951), immigration was intensive. Almost 700,000 came in during the first four years. In 1949 alone, nearly 250,000 entered Israel. Rates at times rose to as high as 5,000 a week, averaging close to 700 per day. By the end of 1967, altogether 1,247,000 had reached Israel. Between 1919 and 1948, about 90 percent came from Europe or other Western countries. Since 1948, the proportion of Middle Eastern and North African Jews increased. By 1981, 25 percent of the world Jewish population was located in Israel, as compared to just 6 percent in 1946. Of these immigrants, 44 percent came from Asia and Africa and 54 percent from European and American countries.

The early Zionists laid the foundations for an essentially European culture in Palestine. Many of the early immigrants, by virtue of their Western background, had reinforced such tendencies toward Westernization. *Yishuv* structures and their supporting ideologies found expression in the development of land settlement, labor unions, political parties, and a Western-oriented educational system. The influx of Oriental Jews, with strikingly different value systems and lower socioeconomic standards, exacerbated problems of integration. On virtually all the indices of socioeconomic mobilization—i.e., literacy, living conditions, public health, and economic and political participation—they continue to be visibly disadvantaged. More recently, waves of Soviet Jewish immigrants with their own particular problems have rendered assimilation even more problematic.

Added to all this are the problems of the Arabs of Israel as a distinct minority (those 600,000 or more who have lived in Israel since independence as distinct from those in areas occupied during the June War of 1967). Although formally they are accepted as full-fledged citizens—with voting privileges, the right to sit in the Knesset and serve in government bureaucracies—they are far from being integrated into the society. They live in isolated quarters, attend separate schools, speak Arabic, and cannot serve in the army. More damaging, they continue to suffer many of the discriminatory intimidations, unofficial or otherwise, of second-class citizens. Many are becoming politicized, particularly with the escalation of tension on the West Bank and in the Gaza Strip, both administered by Israel since the June 1967 War.

But problems of ethnic imbalance, associated with massive population shifts, are not unique to Israel. Successive ideological and revolutionary changes in Egypt, Syria, Jordan, Iraq, along with the protracted civil disturbances in Lebanon, have exacerbated the problems of political management inherent in the factional tension of pluralistic societies.

More consequential has been the discovery and exploitation of oil in the Arabian Peninsula, generating during the 1950s and 1960s an inter-Arab labor migration of large proportions. Since all the capital-rich Arab states are underpopulated, they had to rely on expatriate manpower to meet the heavy demand for labor at all levels of the skill hierarchy. Many of the successor states—particularly Egypt, Jordan-Palestine, Syria, Lebanon, and Tunisia—became the reservoirs from which this large supply of itinerant labor was drawn. Since much of this movement is often illegal and undocumented, estimates vary. By the mid 1970s, at least one million were being drawn from the foregoing five countries alone. To this must be added about 70,000 West Bank and Gaza Arabs who cross the border every day in order to work in Israel. They are engaged mostly in unskilled tasks, on construction sites, in hotels and restaurants, in the fields and orange groves, and in assembly lines.

Such a movement has had far-reaching implications for the internal composition of all the successor states. "Replacement migration" (i.e., the filling of vacancies created by the outflow of migrant labor by the immigration of other nationals), has been one such major consequence. For example in Jordan, as a result of the departure of workers to the Arabian Peninsula, the less attractive jobs were left vacant. Egyptians, Pakistanis, and Filipinos replaced the Jordanian migrants. Lebanon has attracted migrant workers from other countries of the region for many years. Syrians in Lebanon, for example, who numbered over 100,000 in 1970, were integrated into most of the economic sectors. In contrast with the relatively settled Syrian community, other migrant workers, estimated at over 300,000 in the early 1970s, became associated with specific sectors of the economy, particularly construction, agriculture, and domestic wage labor. With the exit of Syrians during the war, the gap has been filled by Kurds, Filipinos, Sri Lankans, and others.

Remittances sent home by the migrants have been a valuable source of foreign exchange. Egypt is a striking example. In 1970, Egyptian remittances were barely $10 million. By 1977, according to official Egyptian sources, the level had reached or exceeded $2 billion, a two-hundred fold increase. This amount equalled the combined returns of Egyptian cotton export, the Suez Canal revenues, tourism, and the value added from the Aswan High Dam.

The initial euphoria associated with labor migration has given way in Egypt to more realistic assessments. These range from critical shortages in high-talent manpower, the downgrading and demoralization of the labor force, to the "feminization" of the Egyptian family, since wives have had to assume, given the prolonged absence of their husbands, a greater share of domestic responsibility. More poignant is the feeling of bitterness, rampant now among those who are being replaced by Asian workers. This displacement, incidentally, has become more acute during the past decade. The implications of such displacement include the loss of remittances (about $3 billion in 1986–1987) direly needed by Egypt to reduce foreign debt, and the betrayal of Arab sentiments of unity and solidarity and consequent disillusionment and radicalization of growing segments of the population. Many of the embittered returnees have become recruits for the growing pool of Muslim militants and fundamentalists.

Urbanization and Urbanism

It was not until the 1920s that the proportion of people living in urban areas began to increase appreciably, accelerating even further after World War II. War-generated conditions, such as the earlier availability of supplies in towns, industrial development, and the requirements of Allied forces, increased employment opportunities and stepped up the urban-bound movement.

Large cities, however, were comparatively rare until the late 1950s. This swift urbanization (the consequence of both internal migration and natural population growth rates) was sustained by a host of the familiar "push" and "pull" factors common to other developing regions.

As late as the 1950s, the majority of villages had no motorable road connections with even the nearest urban centers. Newspapers, radios, and telephones were also comparatively rare (though radios were increasing). With the exception of Lebanon and Israel, most newspapers and radios were largely confined to urban centers and large towns. Village isolation was most extreme in the hinterland and border regions of Iraq and Turkey. Many villages, often only a few kilometers from major cities, were still (early 1950s) without the benefit of secular education, medical facilities, and the burgeoning technology available in the cities themselves.

The "pull" into urban areas is easily explained. City life has always been regarded by villagers as the embodiment of many of their hopes and aspirations. In the postmandate period, cities experienced, because of the exodus of foreigners and minority groups, gaps that were readily filled by village youth harboring dreams of better lives awaiting them in the cities. Newly established regimes, eager to assert their independence and autonomy, launched developmental programs that increased sedentarization. This is particularly true of Iraq, Turkey, Egypt, and Jordan. For example, the Jezirah district between the Tigris and Euphrates in northeastern Syria was, up to World War I, inhabited almost exclusively by nomads and seminomads. By the early 1950s, it contained more than 1,600 villages and towns with a majority of the population consisting of settled farmers and townspeople. Similar processes have taken place elsewhere.

As shown in Table 4, the proportion of people living in urban areas has been sharply increasing since the 1950s. By the early 1980s, virtually all the eight successor states, with the exception of Syria and Turkey, had exceeded the 50 percent level. Even in Turkey, with a comparatively moderate level of urbanization, the scale of rural-urban migration has been such that since 1970 large parts of the country have shown a net decline in population. Two-thirds of the inhabitants of Ankara are recent migrants; most of whom are living in squatter settlements.

The case of Israel is unique. The almost 75 percent level of urbanization Israel reached as early as 1950 was more the result of historical imperatives than ideological choices or urban planning. The rate of immigration into Israel during the first years of the state's existence (a composite of European Jews who survived the Holocaust and those fleeing en masse from Arab countries), generated a massive urbanization in a short span of time.

Lebanon's experience is equally phenomenal. Its urban population has more than tripled and attained an 80 percent level of urbanization in the short span of 30 years. While in the other states, the pattern and magnitude of the increasing scale of urbanization has been relatively steady, Lebanon experienced sharp and sudden leaps, particularly during the 1950s and 1960s. In those two decades alone, the proportion of urban residents more than doubled.

On the whole, then, the annual growth rates of urbanization in the

Table 4
Proportion of Urban Population
(in percentages)

	1950	1960	1970	1975	1980	1985	2000
Israel	74.4	77.6	81.8	83.6	85.1	86.5	90.6
Lebanon	24.5	34.8	53.4	49.8	65.3	78.1	79.6
Iraq	36.4	42.6	57.4	61.9	66.1	69.8	78.5
Jordan	34.6	42.6	52.2	51.1	60.1	63.7	73.1
Tunisia	25.9	32.3	42.6	46.9	51.0	55.0	65.5
Egypt	31.9	37.5	44.4	47.7	51.1	54.4	64.3
Turkey	21.3	29.7	38.5	43.1	47.5	51.7	62.7
Syria	34.8	26.9	42.9	45.5	48.2	51.0	60.5

(Source: UN, Department of Economic and Social Affairs, *Selected World Demographic Indicators*, May 1975.)

successor states continue to be comparatively higher than those observed elsewhere. It is almost four times higher than the more developed regions of the world. While the less developed regions have been able to reduce their rates below 4 percent during the past decade, Iraq, Jordan, Syria, Tunisia, and Turkey have not as yet been able to pass this threshold. Once again, the experience of Israel and Lebanon stands out. Their average annual urban growth rate in 1950 was already 8.5 and 8.1, respectively, almost twice as high as the rest of the successor states, with the possible exception of Turkey. Shortly after, however, Israel's magnitude of increase declined sharply, whereas Lebanon's continued to be fairly high.

A few distinctive features of urbanization influence the character and magnitude of socioeconomic mobilization and cultural change.

1. Today, more than 80 million, compared to about 16 million in 1950, live in towns and cities of 20,000 or more. This is about 64 percent of the total population of this region. While the population in the successor states has been increasing at about 2.5 percent annually, urban settlements are growing almost twice as fast. At current rates of urban growth, Iraq, Jordan, and Syria will attain a 70 percent degree of urbanization before the year 2000. Israel reached that level in the 1960s and Lebanon in the late 1970s.

This means that the major dislocations resulting from increased urbanization that Western Europe experienced over roughly two centuries have been compressed in the Middle East into a roughly fifty-year period.

Table 5
Selected Indexes of Urbanization
(1987)

	Total Population (millions) mid-1988	Urban Population in totals (1000)	%	Average Annual Growth Rates	% of Urban Population in Largest City 1960	% of Urban Population in Largest City 1980	Density Inh/km²
Israel	4.4	3,897	86.7	2.7	46	35	211
Lebanon	–	2,146	80.4	–	64	–	323
Iraq	17.6	11,071	69.8	5.5	35	55	36
Jordan	3.9	2,259	63.7	4.7	31	37	38
Tunisia	7.8	4,916	55.0	3.8	40	30	46
Egypt	50.2	25,726	54.4	3.0	38	39	47
Turkey	53.8	24,042	51.7	4.0	18	24	66
Syria	11.6	6,628	51.0	4.3	35	33	54
Totals		80,685	64.0	4.0	–	–	–

(Sources: *World Development Report*, 1986; UN, *World Population Prospects*, New York, 1988.)

2.   As shown in Table 5, in all the successor states, with the exception of Turkey, more than one-third of the urban population are now concentrated in one major city. In Lebanon, Iraq, and Tunisia, the principal city is many times larger than the second largest city, whereas in Egypt and Syria the first two cities have a dominant position over the rest. By the early 1960s, Beirut had already absorbed more than 64 percent of the entire urban population of Lebanon.

Sometimes, one urban district within a metropolitan region assumes such urban dominance. Ras Beirut, prior to the devastations of Lebanon's civil war, was a prototype of such disjunctive dominance. With roughly 2 percent of the country's population, Ras Beirut had a disproportionate number of Lebanon's professionals, hospitals, government ministries, embassies, travel agencies, hotels, cinemas, and other forms of public entertainment. One of the rare auspicious, albeit unintended, consequences of the war has been the inevitable decentralization of such amenities and public utilities.

3.   A two-step pattern of rural-urban migration is giving way to a one-step pattern. Earlier, the typical rural migrant would go to the nearest town and middle-sized city before he moved to the big city. Much of the

recent migration is taking the form of a sudden and direct leap from village to city. This compounds the problems of adjustments and adaptation to urban expectations and life-styles.

4. One of the outstanding features of urbanization in the successor states is the disjunction between *urbanization* as a purely physical phenomenon (as measured by urban densities, overconcentration in primate cities, migration, etc.) and urbanism as a qualitative and sociocultural phenomenon (as measured by the so-called urban ethos of adaptability, rational interests, and impersonal social networks). Changes in the former, impressive and far-reaching as they are, have not been accompanied by any significant change in urbanism as a way of life. Perhaps because of the scale and rapid pace of urbanization, along with the one-directional pattern of migration, the process has been more a function of "push" from rural areas than a "pull" from urban centers. As such, people might be *in* but not *of* the city and not committed to urban life styles. The city is sought largely for employment opportunities, secular facilities, seasonal flights of adventure—but one's roots are back in the village. More often than not, it is there that one seeks a spouse, keeps one's savings, votes, celebrates kinship and communal festivities, and ultimately retires and is buried.

The survival of communal and nonurban ties can be a viable source of social support and psychic reinforcement, protecting the recent migrant from alienation and providing social needs. Such ties, however, obstruct the development of a truly urban culture.

5. While in some respects contributing to improved living conditions, urbanization has happened too quickly, clearly outstripping whatever institutional agencies of social control emerged to impose some order.

6. While the survival of communal networks and family ties might have been sheltering rural migrants from the alienation, anomie, and rootlessness often associated with urban life, they have not, however, deflected their political mobilization. Swift and unguided urbanization has aggravated the level of grievances while expediting the mobilization and articulation of protest in ways conducive to political unrest. Under the rubric of Islamic militancy, or other forms of collective protest, communal solidarities are being reasserted and reactivated. In other words, it may not be so much the erosion or destruction of such mediating groups that is generating political unrest. Just the contrary, it might well be an expression of the revival of communal solidarity as manifested in the density and vitality of such relations in urban centers.

SOCIAL MOBILIZATION

Such differential patterns of transformation are also visible in changes in the labor-force distribution and other indexes of social mobilization.

Labor Mobilization

Here, the experience of the successor states, in general, falls somewhere between that of the industrialized and less developed countries. In fully developed countries, the industrial era, beginning around the mid-nineteenth century, led to a steady decline in the (primary) agricultural labor force with a concomitant rise in the (secondary) industrial and the (tertiary) commercial-services sector.

Developing countries raised their industrial productivity significantly between 1920 and 1960; as a result, industrial employment scarcely grew at all. Reductions in agricultural employment, owing to mechanization and commecialization, were taken up almost exclusively by the burgeoning service sector or by unemployment. These same long-term trends have been sustained recently.

Put simply, albeit crudely, the developing countries, at least in terms of labor mobilization, do not experience a three-stage process of modernization, from agrarian to industrial to services. Instead, their labor force shifted from mainly agricultural to mainly commercial and service-biased economies. Concomitant with these trends, indeed because of them, rapid urbanization and primate cities became characterized by a bloated or overcrowded service sector and its twin feature, high rates of underemployment.

The Middle Eastern experience follows this pattern. As shown in Table 6, the decline in agriculture has been sharpest. It absorbs now less than one-third of the labor force. The industrial sector has been fairly stable though moderately larger than that of other developing countries. The proportion of those engaged in services is even larger. Today, 42 percent of the labor force in the successor states are engaged in services and affiliated forms of employment, compared to only 26 percent in other developing regions. In this respect, the collective experience of the successor states is closer to the more industrialized and developed countries.

There are, however, striking differences among them. For example, Tunisia and Syria have a fairly well-balanced labor distribution, with nearly one-third of their manpower in each of the three main sectors.

Table 6
Labor Force Distribution
(in percentages)

	Agriculture			Industry			Services		
	1960	1970	1980	1960	1970	1980	1960	1970	1980
Turkey	78	68	54	11	12	13	11	20	33
Egypt	58	54	50	12	19	30	30	27	20
Iraq	53	50	42	18	20	26	29	30	32
Tunisia	56	50	35	18	21	33	26	29	33
Syria	54	51	33	19	21	31	27	28	36
Jordan	44	34	20	26	9	20	30	57	60
Lebanon	28	20	11	33	25	27	39	55	62
Israel	14	10	7	35	35	36	51	55	57
Average	50	42	31	20	20	27	30	38	42

Comparative Trend

	1960	1970	1980	1960	1970	1980	1960	1970	1980
Successor States	50	42	31	20	20	27	30	38	42
Developing Countries	69	65	57	12	13	17	19	22	26
Industrialized Countries	17	11	14	38	38	40	45	51	46
World	48	34	31	23	26	29	18	40	40

(Source: World Bank, *World Tables*, 3rd edition, Baltimore: Johns Hopkins University Press, 1989.)

Turkey and Egypt, however, are disproprotionately high in terms of the size of their agriculture labor force (54 and 50 percent, respectively), whereas Turkey is lowest in industry and Egypt in services. Only 13 percent of Turkey's labor force is currently engaged in industry. Egypt's service sector is not only deficient, but it has also declined from 30 to 20 percent over the past two decades. Lebanon and Israel, once again, stand out. They have the lowest agricultural labor force and an equally disproportionate service sector.

Women's Education

Undoubtedly, one of the most powerful vectors of social mobilization within the region has been the movement towards universal primary schooling and an expanded secondary and higher education. Because of the particular relevance of women's education to social mobilization, a few observations are called for.

Some of the early ventures, limited as they were, were due to missionary efforts, particularly in Lebanon, Palestine, and Turkey. At the turn of the century, feminist liberation and reform movements in Egypt spurred the active participation of women in political and public life. In Cairo, Damascus, Jerusalem, and Beirut, as early as 1928, women were already taking active part in street demonstrations and other protest movements against foreign occupation.

The relaxation of traditional family norms and the consequent undermining of some of the deeply entrenched cultural and attitudinal bias against female emancipation did not, however, promptly reflect themselves in any substantial increases in female school enrollment. For example, in Egypt, the bastion then of feminist and liberation movements, female illiteracy prior to the revolution of 1952 was as high as 91.3 percent. Female school enrollment ratios were 26 percent (primary), 19 percent (secondary), and 7 percent (third level). One of the major objectives of the post-1952 regime in Egypt was to bring about a greater measure of social justice and equality. The regime tried, through legislation and other reforms, to create new opportunities for peasants and the urban underclass for socioeconomic mobility. Likewise, it expanded benefits for women in areas of employment, suffrage, and child care. Such measures, however, along with increased government expenditure on education, did not eradicate the wide gender disparities in school enrollment. After some initial gains, Egypt experienced a negligible increase in women's primary-school enrollment, perhaps the lowest among the successor states. In fact, between 1960 and 1970, it achieved only a 4 percentage point increase, from 52 to 56 percent. Iraq and Syria did not fare much better.

The experience of Tunisia in this regard is more encouraging. The relative advances made in female education, and the consequent elevation of women's status in general, may be attributed to the direct efforts of the Tunisian government of the 1950s to transform education into an effective force of social change. Hence, legislative measures were enacted to liberate women from oppressive practices and to prepare them to assume new roles consistent with the emerging social order. For example, polygamy was outlawed, women's prior consent in marriage was stipulated, a minimum age of marriage was established, and divorce laws were rendered equal. The ministry of education was granted a stronger mandate to carry out educational reforms, to achieve the desired universal primary school enrollment, and to bridge the gender gap in literacy.

The ratio of female school enrollment nearly doubled in the short span of ten years. It increased from 43 to 80 percent between 1960 and 1970. Both Lebanon and Israel had, late in the 1950s and early 1960s, already attained universal elementary school literacy among both sexes. With the exception of Egypt, which is still very deficient, all the other successor states have only begun to approach these levels during the past few years.

This is also seen in the proportion of women enrolled in higher education. Here as well, recent improvements have been quite impressive. On the whole, however, the proportion of women enrolled in universities is at least 6 percentage points below the world's average. Egypt, Tunisia, Turkey, and Syria are still very deficient. All four suffer averages below those registered by the less developed regions.

Women's education is a source of socioeconomic mobilization. Educated women are more prone to delay their marriage, have more knowledge, and make more effective use of contraceptives. While education, per se, in several of the successor states may not be increasing the employability of women, the rate of return to investment in education is almost always high.

Female Participation in the Labor Force

Female participation in the labor force, particularly the nonagricultural, sector is limited. The interplay of both the avoidance by women of certain occupational activities because of their socially stigmatizing features, along with the prohibitions imposed by males, account, no doubt,

Table 7
Labor Force Participation
(in percentages)

	1960			1970			1975			1985		
	Total	Male	Female	Total	Male	Female	Total	Male	Female	Total	Male	Female
Egypt	30	55	3	28	51	4	27	49	4	25	47	4
Iraq	26	50	2	26	49	2	25	47	2	24	46	2
Israel	36	52	19	36	50	21	36	50	21	35	50	21
Jordan	25	48	3	25	45	3	24	44	3	24	43	3
Lebanon	28	48	8	26	43	9	26	43	10	27	44	11
Syria	28	49	4	25	43	5	24	42	5	24	42	6
Tunisia	27	50	3	23	44	3	25	45	4	26	47	4
Turkey	–	–	–	–	–	–	–	–	–	–	–	–
Successor States	28	50	6.1	27	46	6.5	27	46	7	26	45	7.1
Developing Countries	42	55	28	40	52	26	40	52	27	40	53	26
Developed Countries	43	59	27	43	57	30	43	58	30	45	60	33
World	40	55	25	39	51	25	40	51	26	40	53	26

(Source: ILO. Yearbook of Labor Statistics; World Bank, *World Tables*, Baltimore: Johns Hopkins University Press, 1989.)

for the marked absence of women from particular forms of public employment.

The magnitude of male participation in the labor force (as shown in Table 7) is consistent with patterns observed elsewhere, although slightly lower. On the whole, economic activity is about 5 percentage points below world averages and about 10 percentage points below those observed in the more developed countries. It is female participation that is consistently and strikingly lower.

Greater accessibility to educational opportunity and the apparent emancipation of women have had negligible impact on the relaxation of any of these restrictive taboos over the past three decades. Excluding Israel and Lebanon, where the magnitude of female participation is more appreciable (21 percent in the former and 11 percent in the latter), the rest vary from as low as 2 percent in Iraq to 6 percent in Syria.

The bias becomes even more pronounced when one considers the sector of women's economic participation. The bulk of female labor (Table 8) continues to be in the agricultural sector. Although the proportion has declined considerably in recent years, it remains large in Turkey, Syria, Iraq, and Tunisia. Many of those engaged in agricultural activities toil under the status of "unpaid family member." This is particularly true in Turkey, where out of the 83 percent engaged in agriculture, only 1.5 percent are wage employees. In other words, the overwhelming proportion of rural women carry on productive activities as a natural extension of their household duties, as daughters or sisters at one stage of their life cycle, and then as wives or mothers at the next. Many of the women are, in effect, being deprived of the fruits of their labor.

The employment status of rural women also helps to explain the survival of such customs as the payment of bride price by the husband's family to that of the bride. In these instances, the bride price may be regarded as a compensation to the bride's family for the loss of a free farm hand.

The experience of Israel and, to a lesser extent, Lebanon is quite distinct. The proportion of Israeli females engaged in agriculture was, at 12 percent, low to begin with. It dropped to a diminutive 3 percent during the past three decades. Conversely, those engaged in professional, technical, and related services increased from 20 to about 30 percent. Lebanon and, more recently, Jordan have also been experiencing a similar shift. Close to 20 percent of the economically active women in both countries are now engaged in professional and related activities. In Turkey and Syria, however, the proportion is as low as 3 to 4 percent.

Table 8
Percentages of Females in the Total Active
Female Population

In Agriculture

	1950s	1960s	1970s	1980s
Israel	12	10	4	3
Lebanon	–	–	23	23
Egypt	74	57	44	37
Tunisia	89	90	68	–
Turkey	96	99	90	83
Jordan	35	32	25	–
Iraq	30	21	26	65
Syria	–	84	82	81

In Professional, Technical, and Related Activities

	1950s	1960s	1970s	1980s
Israel	–	20	27	30
Lebanon	–	–	20	–
Egypt	11	14	17	–
Tunisia	–	–	10	–
Turkey	–	0.7	2	3
Jordan	–	18	–	–
Iraq	–	–	–	11
Syria	–	4	9	4

(Source: ILO, *Yearbook of Labor Statistics*, 1986; Massialas and Jarrar [1983: 242]; ECWA, *Selected Demographic Socioeconomic Indicators*, 1970.)

Public Health Standards

All the successor states, though to varying degrees, have also been making appreciable improvements in standards of public health, particularly as measured by their ability to control communicable diseases and provide greater access to medical and sanitary facilities, better hygiene and dietary habits. (Table 9.)

Such estimates can be misleading since they disguise internal disparities. Lebanon is a notorious example of such regional variations. While Beirut enjoys about 400 doctors per person, the ratio is over 5,000 in southern Lebanon. Yet, Iraq, like many of the other states, suffers from both a deficiency in the number, as well as maldistribution, of medical personnel and services. Close to 60 percent of the doctors in the early 1970s were concentrated in Baghdad, an area accessible to only 10 percent of the population. Despite increases in health expenditures in most countries of the region during the past three decades, health as a share of total expenditure has declined in Iraq, Jordan, Syria, and Lebanon.

Table 9
Health-Related Features

	Public Expenditure per Capita	Population/ Physician	Population/ Hospital bed	Calorie Supply/per Capita	Percent Population With Safe Water
Israel	157	380	285	3,045	99
Lebanon	13	520	253	2,496	92
Egypt	7	970	498	2,950	84
Turkey	12	1,690	481	2,965	69
Iraq	22	1,790	534	2,643	76
Syria	5	2,270	883	2,863	71
Jordan	27	1,820	1,175	2,397	66
Tunisia	30	3,760	464	2,751	62
Successor States	34	1,650	571	2,763	77
World	100	1,125	272	2,614	57
Industrialized	381	416	100	3,426	94
Developing	12	2,310	580	2,360	44

(Source: World Bank, *World Tables*, Johns Hopkins University Press, 1983.)

REDISTRIBUTIVE PROCESSES

The successor states have all experimented with different redistributive strategies to modify interclass relationships and insure a greater degree of equity and social justice. The revolutionary regimes, for example, initially adopted strictly socialist measures such as land reform, cooperatization, nationalization, reductions in salary differentials, subsidization and price control on popular consumption commodities, labor security laws, and broadened public employment to reduce inequality. But at one point or another more pragmatic forms of economic liberalization have been introduced. This is true of Egypt, Syria, and Iraq, where a medium-sized, private capitalist sector is allowed to exist in internal trade, housing, construction, small industry, and agriculture (although subject to state regulation in the interest of equity). Tunisia also offers instances of such dramatic shifts in basic strategies. Its extensive cooperative movement, perhaps its most distinctive socioeconomic feature during the 1960s—intended as a comprehensive social experiment in collectivized agriculture and political and cultural mobilization—was abandoned in 1969 and replaced by more liberal economic policies.

Turkey, too, has hovered, often precariously, between its Ottoman legacy of state-directed reform and intermittent interludes of economic liberalization. Centralized planning, the enduring hallmark of Turkish reform, has been tempered by greater receptivity to entrepreneurship and private enterprise. Atatürk's original vision of a single-party state has given way to a proliferation of parties, interest groups, and informal networks. The economic progress of the past two decades and the growing appeals of entrepreneurship have exacerbated the intensity of the debate over redistributive strategies. While the Turkish Labor Party, the only officially recognized Marxist party, has been the spokesman for a general redistribution of wealth, the Republican Peoples' Party continues to articulate its less radical rhetoric for social justice.

Jordan and, to a much greater extent, Lebanon continue—despite occasional muted calls for greater measures of centralized planning—to pursue their largely unfettered strategies of laissez-faire economic change. These normally range from specific programs of economic development, industrialization, sedentarization, and urban planning to free and generally unregulated trade and banking.

All the successor states, to varying degrees, had suffered from land-tenure systems that left large numbers of the rural population landless and in a state of extreme poverty. In Iraq, for example, prior to 1958, only 2 percent of the landowners owned 68 percent of the total agricultural holdings, whereas almost 90 percent of the peasants remained landless. This acute unevenness in the possession of property and wealth extended to other sectors of the economy. Fewer than two dozen families amassed up to 65 percent of the entire private corporate commercial and industrial capital.

In Egypt, on the eve of the Free Officers' takeover in 1952, more than 75 percent of the population were landless peasants. The deplorable living conditions of the peasantry and the widening disparity between them and the landowning rich were further compounded by Egypt's population problem and the perennial difficulty of keeping food production in pace with population growth.

Given this widespread rural poverty and the concentration of political power in the hands of absentee landlords and local landowners with close connections to the ruling urban elite, land reform became a major redistributive strategy. Results of such efforts have often fallen short of objectives, but, on the whole, thousands of sharecroppers and landless farmers in Egypt, Syria, Iraq, and, to some extent, Jordan have become small landowners.

In Iraq, the social power of private large-scale property has been uprooted. This is most visible in the agricultural sector, in which big landed shaikhs and merchants were gradually undermined. This process was maintained throughout the 1970s as land redistribution programs continued to cut down the size of private holdings into a small or moderate category.

In Egypt, the Agrarian Reform Law of 1952 limited individual holding to fewer than 200 feddans (roughly two hundred acres) and reduced rents paid for lands while increasing agricultural wages. Because land distribution diminished the power of major land owners, it was also intended as a political act. Fairly early, however, Nasser realized that land reform alone could not bring about such a redistribution. It was not extensive or swift enough to undermine the power of the traditional ruling elite. It was in this context that Nasser initiated the comprehensive nationalization schemes of the early 1960s. By this transformation, technocrats and army offficers became part of the new middle and upper classes.

Ba'th policies in Syria have also radically altered the socioeconomic structure there. The great latifundia that once dominated the agrarian structure have been wiped out. Land redistribution, cooperatization, and state aid have nearly halved the landless stratum and rendered the small-holding peasantry a force to be reckoned with in rural areas. An extensive state cooperative system—encompassing credit, marketing, supply and provision of technical services—has displaced most of the old landlord-merchant monopolistic privileges. Hence, rurals are now enjoying greater access to education and nonagricultural state employment. The Syrian regime, however, has not eliminated all abusive relics of the old order. Both urban landlords and rich peasants rent land to tenants or use hired labor. An assortment of middlemen and brokers, between producer and consumer, continues to persist. The penetration of state agencies particularly through cooperative structures, intended as the main institutional groups of social mobilization, has been handicapped by corruption and factional rivalry.

In more democratic and open states (Lebanon, Jordan, Israel, Turkey, and Tunisia), redistributive processes are more likely to be associated, though not exclusively, with broader and spontaneous forces of change and a larger magnitude of private initiative. They remain, however, and in varying degrees, mixed economies. The state continues to assume the decisive role in national planning and in fostering specific programs for socioeconomic development.

Turkey's redistributive capabilities, as with virtually all the present nonrevolutionary regimes in this group, are inconsistent. While there may not have been much redistribution in monetary income, there are some indications of greater prospects for social mobility. During the past two decades or so, this has been seen in the improved access lower-class children have to education. It is also apparent in the general increase in nonelite political power and the growing importance of trade unions as voluntary associations. University education, occupation, and income are gaining ground as criteria for differentiating status and determining chances for mobility. Indeed, university education is more than ever the dividing line between the elite and the rest of the population. Yet, in highly status-conscious societies, and to varying degrees all the successor states are such, ascribed attributes (particularly those based on kinship, ethnic, religious, and fealty ties) are still very important.

Characteristic of all the states has been the expansion and growing importance of the new middle class. The "traditional" middle class was mostly composed of civil servants, small merchants, and religious functionaries. They derived their livelihood and prestige from their association with three conventional and basic institutions in society: *makhzan*, bazaar, and mosque or government, marketplace, and religious establishment. The "new" middle class, on the other hand, is largely an outgrowth of modernization and professionalization. Whatever power and social prestige they have come to enjoy is derived more from their newly acquired skills and education and less from ownership of property, business, or trade. Its membership is drawn mostly from fairly contemporary occupational groups such as professionals, teachers, professors, writers, journalists, intelligentsia, and, in the case of revolutionary states, army officers.

Despite the growth it has recently witnessed, the new middle class is still relatively small, heterogeneous, diffuse, and weak in strength and collective consciousness. In part, this is a reflection of its economic weakness, being largely employed or self-employed but rarely an employing stratum. More important, however, this is doubtless due to the survival of primordial and nonclass loyalties. Even in regions that witnessed extensive urbanization and other modes of secular and ideological transformations, ethnic, tribal, communal, patronage, and kinship loyalties continue to take precedence over class allegiances. Deep fissures within each class obstruct the formation of genuine class-based collective movements. Instances of such failure are legion. The weakness of labor movements and parochialized and splintered voluntary associations and ideological platforms all tell the same story.

Membership in a given "class" does not usually provide the average person with a meaningful identity; such identity is still provided by a plethora of primordial groups and nonclass mediating structures.

Even so, while characterized by little collective consciousness, members of the middle class have been the carriers of new values, life-styles, consumption patterns, and ideologies. Because they are drawn from relatively marginal groups, they have been more innovative.

INTERNATIONAL COMPARISONS

In virtually all dimensions of social interdependence, the successor states have experienced intensive and swift processes of societal transformation, particularly during the past three decades. Naturally the pattern and direction of some of these changes display striking differences within the states themselves inasmuch as they stand in sharp contrast to world trends. One general characteristic draws the experience of the Ottoman successor states closer to other comparable regions in the world; namely, the disjunctive character of such processes. The interplay between a premodern heritage and the forces of modernization is neither consistent nor uniform in its character or direction. In some instances, deeply rooted indigenous loyalties and local traditions have retarded or obstructed processes of social transformation. In others, they have been supportive and reinforcing.

The subversive character of premodern values is apparent, for example, in the survival of pronatalist sentiments and the consequential cognitive dissonance between the secular forces (reflected in improvements in standards of public health and reductions in mortality) and the normative expectations (value of children, early marriage, subordinate status of women, and the like) that encourage high fertility. As was shown, there may not be any other region in the world, excluding perhaps West Africa, with as high a level of fertility. When compared with the industrialized countries the disparities are as high as 17 births per 1000.

Disjunctions between urbanization as physical phenomenon and as a way of life are also more striking, clearly more so than elsewhere. Swift urbanization, the result of both massive population shifts and demographic pressures, is almost four times higher than rates of urban growth observed in the more developed regions of the world. Yet, it has not been accompanied by the erosion of communal and nonurban ties. While the survival of such ties should be viable sources of psychological and social support, they have often obstructed urban planning and exacerbated communal tension and political violence.

Equally damaging has been the exclusion of women from growing opportunities in technical and higher education and from the labor force. Here, as well, the magnitude of female participation is almost negligible. For example, it is as low as 2 percent in Iraq, compared to 25 percent in the rest of the world.

The persistence of a large residue of personal and communal ties in social relations has also undermined the growth of collective consciousness and the formation of class-based mediating structures. The weakness of labor movements, deficient civility, parochialized voluntary associations, factionalized ideological groups are all manifestations of the highly personalized and primordial character of social interdependence. Virtually none of the successor states, regardless of their political leanings and ideological orientations, have been able to root out the dysfunctional consequences of such traditional loyalties.

Even in centralized and secular regimes like Syria, where state and party allegiance have managed, particularly during the past two decades, to create a sense of national identity, sectarian and communal affinities continue to be strong. Indeed, they appear to have become sharper. The once-appealing and overarching broader identities, particularly those embodied in movements of Arabism, Pan-Islam, Ba'thism, or socialism, have given way lately to factional cleavages and cloistered and exclusive forms of social bonding. Such tendencies, are similar to manifestations of local and ethnic resurgence in the Baltic states, former Soviet republics, and elsewhere in Eastern Europe.

In other instances, premodern institutions and values have been readily converted into, or have become effective vectors, of socioeconomic mobilization. Because of the survival of a large residue of kinship sentiments, the family and other informal networks continue to offer social, psychological, and economic supports, particularly in periods of rapid change and social unrest. In small-scale societies, where personal, tribal, and fealty ties have not been eroded, they have become vehicles for dispensing welfare and providing access to power and privilege. This is also true of patron-client networks. Finally, in virtually all the successor states, religion is often exploited in soliciting support for vital but controversial policy issues and reform programs.

Manifestations and consequences of this interplay, by virtue of the diversity they have assumed in the successor states, may be ambiguous. What is unambiguous, however, is that processes of modernization almost always carry with them imbalances and dislocations. Clearly, not all premodern institutions and values can be converted to modern uses. As old social forms are lost and new ones evolve, there is a particularly vulnerable phase when attitudes and patterns of behavior may be without anchor, controlled more by shifting winds of demagogy, charismatic leadership, and the frenzy of mob spirit than by established values of family and community.

In this regard, the successor states do not depart much from the experience of other developing countries in the throes of swift transformation. They all have, to varying degrees, experienced such unsettling interludes. Old institutions, values, loyalties, authority and status systems, even modes of employment, are being threatened either because they are too deeply identified with the past or because they are incongruous with the demands of urban and industrial requirements or the ethos of secularization. Some, however, are tenacious. They stubbornly resist such encroachment and are not as readily displaced. Arranged marriages by parents, the dominant role of the husband in matters of consent, family name, residence contacts with the community, and the old dynamics of male-female sexuality still prevail. Yet, the basic family unit is tending to become smaller, whereas kinship loyalty evinces some decline.

Herein, perhaps, lie some of the distinctive attributes that differentiate the successor states from other regions. The family and its supportive values and networks continue to play more pervasive roles in the private and public lives of individuals. Inevitably though, growing segments of the literate, urban, mobile groups, and those exposed to alternative lifestyles, are beginning to question the nature and direction of their society's transformation and the bases of their allegiance to it. In such times of flux and uncertainty, mere physical separation from family and community, and other conventional forms of social solidarity, can deprive the individual of social identification and of material and moral support when they are most needed.

Little wonder that religious resurgence—whether it assumes popular, reformist, or militant expressions—is gaining grounds and extending its appeal to wider segments of the population. More and more disgruntled groups are seeking shelter in religion as a deliverer from distress. The source of their discontent may vary: intolerable living conditions, crushing poverty, unemployment, urban alienation, decadence and demoralization of public life, humiliation and the military impotence of Arab armies, the failure of alternative revolutionary ideologies and the inability of political regimes to confront persistent social and economic problems. To many resurgents, Islam offers simplistic but reassuring answers. It is a promise, delusive as it may seem to outsiders, to restore their damaged identities. To throngs of believers it is a quest for greater justice, for participation and more authentic forms of communal solidarity.

CHAPTER FOURTEEN

Education and Knowledge
in the Ottoman Successor States

THE MOST SIGNIFICANT factor shaping education in any society is the character of its political system, for educational policies can be designed to maintain the status quo or to promote change, to enhance social justice and equality or to preserve existing socioeconomic and ethnic divisions. In the years following World War I, in the Middle East, as in much of the Third World, the most important political consideration was whether the state was independent or ruled by a colonial power.

THE IMPACT OF COLONIAL RULE

Since modern schools had been established for different purposes, at different times, and by different actors, the successor states inherited varied educational systems. All of these systems, however, were of limited size, and none sufficed to build new nations out of territories that had been administrative units of a defunct empire and were inhabited by a mosaic of peoples with particularistic loyalties. Accordingly, every regime confronted the need to build new systems or to expand and differentiate the limited ones that already existed.

Efforts to do so, however, were often frustrated by the policies pursued by the mandatory powers, Britain and France. Driven by parsimony and political considerations, they sought to preserve the status-quo and to introduce their language and culture. They believed that a low level of traditional schooling sufficed for the masses and that a limited public system, attended by a select few, would graduate the needed professionals. In addition, the upper classes favored foreign and private schools. Run by missionaries or foreign organizations, such schools tended to offer an education of higher quality than was the norm in the state schools and represented an important alternative for the upper classes.

With the rise of nationalism as an ever more powerful force, the role of these schools in the national system of education became increasingly controversial. The missionary schools were accused of proselytizing, and the schools run by foreigners, especially the French and Italian, were charged with damaging the well-being of the nation by propagating foreign cultures and thus enhancing existing cleavages. As a result, in one country after another, especially after independence, legislation was enacted that brought them more or less under complete state control.

Mandatory Educational Systems

The major difference between the mandatory powers lay in the type of Western education they introduced. Areas under British control received instruction in English history and culture and learned English, whereas those under French rule learned about the glories of France. The French, however, being imbued with a sense of their *mission civilisatrice*, went much further than the British in promoting their culture. In Lebanon, they imposed French syllabi and requirements upon all educational institutions and neglected the state schools—in 1944, only 10 percent of the students were attending public primary and secondary schools, but over 70 percent of all school-age children were receiving a modern education. In Syria, too, they forced the existing public schools to teach French and opened very few new ones. By the early 1940s, under 25 percent of the cohort was attending primary schools, 13 secondary schools enrolled fewer than 5,000 students, and about 1,000 more were studying law and medicine. The literacy rate was only 20 percent.

The British were equally restrictive. In Egypt, Lord Cromer pursued a highly elitist policy designed to prepare a small cadre for colonial administration. And, though the number of schools expanded under his successors, educational opportunities remained limited. At the time of World War I, fewer than 10,000 students were receiving a secondary education, 70 percent of them in private or foreign schools. Jordan's situation was similar. Its small system was also based on fees and limited to the lower levels; there was only one secondary school. In Iraq, too, the British did little to promote public education. In 1944, only 20 percent of Iraqi children were attending school, many of them private and foreign; the literacy rate had climbed to only 20 percent by 1947.

Higher Education

Higher education flourished in only two places—Lebanon, with its private institutions, and in the Jewish community of Palestine. The latter developed an integrated system (70 percent of all children were enrolled in school) that included a large number of secondary schools, several teacher-training colleges, and two full-fledged universities—the Hebrew

Table 1

	1920			1944		
	Number of Students	Percent Female	Percent in Private and Foreign Schools	Number of Students	Percent Female	Percent in Private and Foreign Schools
Egypt (1913; 1942)						
1st level	324,374	10	28	1,010,433	45	11
2nd level	9,110	16	72	62,390	15	41
Iraq						
1st level	8,001	NA	NA	117,532	NA	17
2nd level	110	NA	NA	18,127	NA	38
Israel						
1st level	8,368	NA	0	68,634		19
2nd level	992	NA		11,092		14
Jordan						
1st level	3,316	10	NA	9,364	NA	NA
2nd level	(1st & 2nd level)	NA	NA	438		
Lebanon (1924, 1944)						
1st level	67,383	NA	92	125,854	NA	83
2nd level	(1st & 2nd level)			10,776		97
Syria (1923)						
1st level	45,027	NA	50	148,428	31	43
2nd level	(1st & 2nd level)	NA	NA	11,592	27	48
Turkey						
1st level	341,941			1,357,740	36	NA
(1923)						
2nd level	7,146			347,502	42	

(Source: Matthews and Akrawri, op. cit., Tables 3, 19, 45, 46, 51, 52, 59, 66, 72; Szyliowicz, op. cit., Appendix 3, 4.)

University of Jerusalem, which was inaugurated in 1925, and a technical university, the Technion, at Haifa, which dates back to 1912. Table 1 summarizes the available data concerning enrollments, the role of private and foreign schools, and female education in the decades following World War I.

Whatever their size, all these systems suffered from severe problems of quality and relevance. A rigid examination system ostensibly designed to maintain quality and enhance national integration by ensuring that all schools, private and public, taught subjects in the same way led to an emphasis on memorizing a large amount of information with little relevance to local needs or even to the national situation. The question of standards was exacerbated by the shortage of qualified teachers. Even where adequate numbers were being trained, as in Egypt and Iraq, quality remained a major problem. In addition, the best teachers and the best facilities were always to be found in the capital. The further one went into the rural areas, the fewer the schools, and the worse their condition. As a result, all schools were afflicted with a very high drop-out rate, and usually less than 10 percent of the total student body was enrolled in the upper grades.

Clearly, Western colonial rule profoundly affected the development of modern education. Despite numerous obstacles and shortcomings, every state possessed, by the end of World War II, at least the nucleus of a modern system. Nor should the progress that was achieved be measured in these terms alone. The importance of a modern education was widely accepted, and students flocked to the new schools in ever-increasing numbers. The traditional school, the kuttab, with its emphasis on the Quran and some rudimentary mathematics and knowledge of languages, retained its importance, especially in rural areas, but Western-type schools proliferated at its expense. Furthermore, women everywhere were enrolling in modern schools at all levels, although their education was usually conducted in special schools. This new outlook stood as testimony to the extent to which educational developments had affected political affairs. Graduates of the modern schools became the intellectual leaders and political activists who spearheaded the nationalist movements in all these countries. They were remarkably successful in both their political and their educational goals. They achieved independence and, in the course of the struggle, aroused public awareness of the significance of modern education.

THE ROLE OF A MODERNIZING LEADERSHIP

The achievement of independence marks a turning point in any country's educational policy. The road that was taken by the independent successor states, however, differed markedly and depended upon the kind of political system that emerged. Unless the leadership possessed a strong commitment to modernization, the reforms have focused on nationalizing schools and expanding educational opportunities while failing, however, to transform the system into one that is consonant with the needs of modernizing society. The contrast between the policies followed by Iraq and Egypt under monarchical rule and those of Turkey under Atatürk—as well as those of postrevolutionary Egypt, Iraq, and Syria and the Tunisia of Habib Bourguiba—illustrate this point.

Both Iraq, which gained its formal independence in 1932, and Egypt, which proclaimed its constitution in 1922, were ruled by weak governments. For Iraq, relations with Great Britain continued to be troublesome, ethnic groups often challenged the rule of Baghdad, and most cabinets lasted but a few months. The case of Egypt is particularly instructive because of the faith of its secular elites in modern knowledge. Education was widely regarded as a panacea for the country's problems—largely in reaction to the heritage of British neglect. But here, too, the decades following independence were marked by political instability and immobilism. The struggle between the nationalist Wafd Party and the court, with the British holding the balance, created a political environment where no coherent, systematic policy could be implemented.

As a result, both governments pursued similar policies. First, they moved to purge schools of foreign influences, then tried to transform them into instruments for building a sense of community and nationhood among peoples who had heretofore been divided rather than united by education. In Iraq, for example, the government established firm control over all private and foreign schools, denied them financial favors, and made Arabic the primary language.

Second, both governments moved to expand and equalize educational opportunities. Iraq, for example, sought, through low fees and scholarships, to provide opportunities for education to students from the lower classes. As a result, primary enrollments in Iraq rose in the interwar years from 38,000 to 117,000; in Egypt, from 324,000 to over a million. These efforts, however, produced only quantitative gains. Teaching continued to be characterized by rigidity and formalism. Thus drop-out rates were high, and the schools of limited relevance to national needs. Moreover, gains in educational opportunities were largely offset, especially in Egypt, by rapidly growing populations.

The Egyptian government was especially concerned with higher education because of its need for skilled manpower and the role of the university as the symbol of independence and modernity. Thus, whereas only a few colleges were opened in Iraq, the Egyptians nationalized and expanded the university, hitherto a small, poor, private institution, and subsequently opened a second university, in Alexandria. Quality, however, remained a problem; the orientation remained on preparing students for examinations and for entry into a civil service that soon proved incapable of absorbing all the graduates.

Egypt thus possessed two separate educational systems, the modern and the religious, for the traditional kuttab continued to function and, indeed, was the sole educational institution available to most Egyptians. At the apex of the religious system stood the venerable al-Azhar University, which remained a bastion of orthodox Muslim education despite various efforts at reform and change. English-language instruction, for example, which was first listed in the curriculum in 1901, was not actually offered until 1958. Maintenance of the dual system and the ability of conservative religious elements to fend off innovation promoted a continuing cultural divide within the country.

Reforms in Turkey

Such a cultural divide was not tolerated in Turkey, whose contrasting policies in these decades highlight the crucial role of a modernizing political leadership. Recognizing the profound structural and ideological changes required if the new society that he envisaged were to emerge, Atatürk assigned education an important role. He not only implemented the kinds of reforms that were carried out in Egypt and Iraq, expansion and nationalization, but he moved swiftly to completely transform the limited and fragmented system inherited from the Ottoman Empire. He began by abolishing the dual system of religious and secular schools and by placing responsibility for all education in a secular ministry of education. New curricula were prepared that were consonant with modern times and provided greater relevance, flexibility, and integration. Foreign and private schools, however, were permitted to operate, as long as they did not violate the nationalist and secularist principles of the new republic.

Secularism and nationalism were ideologies to be made an integral part of the culture. Atatürk launched his transformation by enacting such dramatic legislation as replacing the Arabic alphabet, a major symbol of Islamic solidarity, with the Latin one, by introducing European law codes to Turkey, and by changing the calendar—and by the "Hat Law," which, by forcing all Turks to wear Western-style headgear, eliminated visual distinctions between Muslims and non-Muslims.

The new government also moved to expand educational opportunities at all levels for all its citizens. All fees were abolished, coeducation was initiated, and a compulsory program of adult education launched in the late 1920s that affected almost 2 million persons. Despite such efforts, however, the educational system remained limited and marked by serious qualitative problems, particularly in the rural areas. Moreover, the Darül-fünun, the university noted for its intellectual sterility, continued to function essentially as it had decades earlier.

To transform this state of affairs required a basic shift in political priorities, and that shift came as a result of Atatürk's failure to increase political participation by establishing a loyal opposition party in 1930. The experiment revealed the limited extent to which modern knowledge and attitudes had penetrated Turkish society. It convinced Atatürk of the urgent need for reform in three areas: first, to change the orientation of intellectuals, many of whom still espoused traditional views; second, to bridge the elite-mass gap; and, third to transform the position of the masses.

Accordingly, the 1930s witnessed a series of great educational reforms. Among these were the establishment of a national network of People's Houses designed to serve as centers for educational and cultural programs that stressed Turkish nationalism as well as Westernization; they helped disseminate the values of the republic as well as modern knowledge. Shortly thereafter, the Darülfünun was abolished; a new institution, Istanbul University, staffed to a significant degree by German professors, opened. A few years later, a new university was inaugurated in Ankara. Concomitantly, attention was paid to rural education through the establishment of the innovative Village Institute Program, which was designed to train teachers explicitly for service in rural areas.

Thus, by the time of his death in 1938, Atatürk had created a modern educational system that was unified, coherent, secular, and consonant with the goals of the new state. Enrollments had increased sharply, particularly at the higher levels, and the number of women receiving an education had risen dramatically. The number of primary students climbed by 280 percent, to 1,350,000, the number of vocational students rose by 600 percent, to 54,000, and the number of students enrolled in higher educational institutions rose by 475 percent, to 19,000. This growth continued during the World War II years; although many problems of quality and educational opportunities still remained, Turkey had successfully carried through a genuine revolution in knowledge and education.

Educational opportunities continued to expand when Atatürk's dream of a multiparty system was finally realized in 1950. From then on, the concern was also with numbers rather than with quality. Although many governments came to power in the following decades, the amount of resources allocated to education declined steadily as other sectors were accorded priority, even though the system expanded significantly. Between 1963 and 1970, investments in education amounted to 11.25 percent of total government expenditures; but, by 1980, the figure had fallen to 5.9 percent.

Bourguiba and Nasser

Until Tunisia, after World War II, achieved its independence and President Nasser came to power in Egypt in 1952, no other successor state (except Israel) enjoyed such leadership. Both President Bourguiba and President Nasser were, like Atatürk, dedicated to transforming their countries into modern states. President Bourguiba's 1958 blueprint for educational reform called for universal primary education and the expansion of the higher levels to meet the manpower needs created by the departure of the French. Access to secondary education was to be determined by achievement, and students were to be tracked into academic or vocational streams depending upon their ability. In 1961, the University of Tunis was established and a generous scholarship program initiated. At the same time, selectivity was maintained by enrolling only a small percentage of all the students in the higher levels. The results were dramatic. Enrollments increased sharply at both the primary and secondary levels by 400 and 550 percent, respectively, and the literacy rate climbed to about 60 percent.

President Nasser's first reforms were also designed to create an integrated and unified educational system that would serve individual and national needs. The former dual elementary system whereby only graduates of urban primary schools could continue their education was abolished. Subsequently, the elementary cycle was extended to six years, and the curriculum was modernized. In 1962, all public education was made free as the government sought to equalize educational opportunities.

Educational planning was also initiated, and new goals, such as universal primary education, the upgrading of postprimary education, especially in technical and vocational fields, and qualitative improvements in such areas as curricula, teacher-training, and administration, were proclaimed. They were reaffirmed and expanded in subsequent national plans.

Nevertheless, each leader found it no easy matter to devise and implement a coherent strategy to transform schooling. Confronted with an irresistible and ever-growing demand for educational opportunities that could not be denied because of ideological and political considerations, they often implemented policies on an ad hoc basis, with little concern for their systematic implications or for the fit between the particular policy and economic realities.

In Egypt, enrollments at all levels mushroomed (between 1950 and 1965), primary enrollments rose by over 260 percent; secondary, first and second level, by 148 percent; but quality deteriorated rapidly because financial, human, and physical resources were not increased at an equal pace. As a result, schools were subject to high wastage rates, and those students who graduated were often poorly prepared for college and university study or employment. The increase in enrollments and the drop in quality inevitably affected higher education.

By the mid-1970s, almost 100,000 students a year were enrolled in 11 universities (there were 4 in 1951) and in al-Azhar, which had been metamorphosed into a new institution. Even this growth did not satisfy the demand, which was furthered by the abolition of fees and by such arrangements as external study and by the establishment of numerous higher institutes. The result was that thousands of additional graduates, poorly prepared for fields in which a surplus already existed, entered the labor market. However, educational opportunities have been greatly equalized, and every year more students of lower class backgrounds are receiving a university education.

Tunisia confronted many similar problems. Despite President Bourguiba's commitment to education as a vehicle for modernization, and the allocation of large amounts of resources (Tunisia consistently spent a higher percentage of its budget on education than any other country in the world), the results were disappointing. The schools' output did not mesh with the needs of industry, qualitatively or quantitatively. To some degree, this was due to the difficulties caused by Arabization. Like the other North African countries, Tunisia had to face the language issue after independence, for the French had imposed their tongue upon their colonies. Seeking a middle ground, it attempted to teach both French and Arabic in the primary schools. But many students emerge with an inadequate grasp of either tongue. At the higher levels, serious steps toward Arabization began only about a quarter-century after independence had been achieved. In short, a de facto bilingual state, but of decreasing quality in French, long characterized the post-independence period.

At first, no attention was paid to the problem of placing graduates and drop-outs; it was assumed that they would all find employment. But by the mid-1960s, it became obvious that a problem existed. Various reforms were adopted, including the opening of new kinds of vocational centers that would provide youths with marketable skills. But these have proven only partially successful because, as is the case in Egypt and other countries as well, many students still do not acquire the relevant skills. Even those who have completed technical courses often find that their training did not prepare them adequately. Moreover, these graduates often have an outlook not in accord with their employment prospects.

THE CONTEMPORARY SCENE

The goals that Nasser and Bourguiba tried to achieve—greater equality of educational opportunity for all citizens and the creation of a school system that would promote national unity and increased economic growth—have been pursued by every successor state. Many common elements can be identified, especially among the Arab states, which have made considerable efforts to achieve a cultural unity. In 1957, Egypt, Syria, and Jordan agreed to establish a common educational structure (6 years of primary school, 3 in a middle school, and 3 in a secondary school) to replace what they had inherited from the colonial powers. Most Arab states have followed suit but with variations in the length of the school year (ranging from 168 days in Tunisia to a high of 240 in Iraq) and in the emphasis accorded to various subjects. (Islamic studies, for example is taught for 36 periods a week in Jordan, 30 in Tunisia, but only 21 in Iraq; Arabic for 84, 72, and 111 hours, respectively; and science and math for 107, 68, and 91 hours.)

These states, except for Lebanon (where the educational system, organized along denominational lines, helped to perpetuate societal cleavages), share another common characteristic. Education is centralized in a ministry of education although, in some countries (Egypt, Iraq, and Turkey, for example), higher education is the responsibility of a separate body. Everywhere, despite some attempts at decentralization, the ministries exercise tight control over all educational matters. Local authorities have the power to make decisions only in limited areas. Centralizaton tends to be accompanied by poor administrative practices. The Abu Dhabi Conference of Ministers of Education (1977), one of many such meetings designed to improve and integrate education in the Arab states, agreed on the need to transform educational administration.

Many states (Iraq 1946, Tunisia 1959) also initiated educational planning in these decades, but long-term plans were not drawn up until the early 1960s (Turkey, Egypt, Syria). These plans share many similarities as all sought to nationalize the existing system and to expand educational opportunities at all levels. Thus, Jordan enacted, in 1955, a law calling for free and compulsory education and placed strict controls on foreign schools, especially missionary schools. Syria, too, especially from the mid-1960s onwards, when the radical Ba'thists under President Asad came to power, established state control over all private schools; it announced its intention to eliminate illiteracy, to equalize educational opportunities, and to meet the country's manpower needs.

Although many of the educational goals may not have been realized, every state has achieved dramatic increases in the number of children enrolled in school. As a result, practically every male student of primary-school age and a large percentage of girls are now attending school. At the secondary level, too, the number of students enrolled has increased sharply (the percentage of the cohort in secondary schools has doubled over the past twenty years). In Israel and Jordan, over 75 percent of the cohort is receiving a secondary education; in Egypt, Iraq, and Syria over 50 percent; in Tunisia and Turkey, over 30 percent. The decline in Lebanon's student population is, of course, a result of the anarchy that has engulfed that country since 1975. Table 2 presents the available data on the growth of school enrollments in the past decade.

Educational Shortcomings

This impressive expansion of educational opportunities has, however, often been achieved at the expense of quality because financial, human, and physical resources did not increase at an equal pace. Yet, all governments are allocating a large percentage of their budgets to education. The latest data indicate that Tunisia ranked first, with 14.2 percent. Iraq ranked last, with 6.9 percent. In between came Egypt, 11.5 percent;

Table 2
School Enrollments

	Total Pupils (1975)	% Female	Total Pupils (1985)	% Female
Egypt				
1st level	4,181,198	38	6,002,850	43
2nd level	2,176,362	34	3,089,002	39
Iraq				
1st level	1,176,095	33	2,816,326	45
2nd level	525,255	29	1,190,833	35
Israel				
1st level	535,320	49	699,476	49
2nd level	170,168	52	251,466	51
Jordan				
1st level	386,012	46	530,906	48
2nd level	164,186	41	335,835	48
Lebanon				
1st level	388,482		329,340	47
2nd level	290,736		267,970	
Syria				
1st level	1,273,944	40	2,029,752	46
2nd level	488,409	31	875,383	40
Tunisia				
1st level	932,787	39	1,291,490	45
2nd level	201,845		457,630	
Turkey				
1st level	5,463,684		6,635,858	47
2nd level	1,746,160	31	2,927,692	35

(Source: World Bank, *World Development Report, 1986; UNESCO, Statistical Yearbook, 1986.*)

Jordan, 8.7 percent; Israel, 9.2 percent; Syria, 11.8 percent; and Turkey, 10.5 percent.

As a result, primary and secondary education is marked by serious deficiencies in curricula, facilities, and teachers. A 1980-study of primary education in Egypt, for example, revealed that almost half of the primary schools are not suitable facilities, that a large percentage of teachers need more training, and that many schools are operating on double shifts or on shortened school days. Table 3 presents data on the size of classes and on the teacher/student ratio in selected countries in the late 1970s.

Table 3

Class Size and Teacher/Student Ratio

	Egypt	Iraq	Jordan	Syria	Tunisia
Elementary Education					
a) Class size	40	33	35	24	34
b) Teacher-student ratio	NA	1/32	1/33	1/34	1/44
Intermediate Education					
a) Class size	39	39	32	40	34
Secondary Education					
a) Class size	NA	36	37	39	32
b) Teacher-student ratio*	NA	NA	1/30	1/21	1/21

(Source: Massialas and Jarrar, Tables 4.17, 4.20.)
* Includes intermediate, secondary, and technical schools.
NA = Not available

As a result, although most students who enter primary school eventually receive a primary-school certificate (the range is between 65 percent in Tunisia and 84 percent in Jordan), a large percentage (about 50 percent in Tunisia and Iraq; 35 percent in Syria; and 20 percent in Egypt and Jordan) do so only after repeating one or more classes.

This problem is aggravated by the nature of the examination system that students must generally pass in order to proceed to the next stage. Although only limited data are available, the pass rate is estimated at about 70 percent, but it varies by country and by level. In Tunisia, for example, 26 percent pass at the end of primary school, 90 percent pass the intermediate level, 74 percent, the secondary level; in Iraq, the figures are 93, 80, and 81 percent. Most experts agree that the examination system (which has endured since colonial times) suffers from serious deficiencies. It possesses low reliability and validity, tends to measure the ability to memorize, focuses on passing the examinations, fosters a rigid classroom culture, and imposes a heavy psychic toll upon students and their families.

Female Education

Female education represents another area where traditional patterns retain their influence. Despite the established relationship between women's education and such critical dimensions of development as birth rates and children's welfare, female school enrollments are, in every country except Israel, relatively low. And the higher up the educational ladder one looks, the lower is the percentage of women students. (Enormous progress, however, has been achieved in recent years.) (See Tables 2 and 5.) These figures reflect both the efforts of governments and the factors that inhibit women's education in the region, even in countries such as Egypt and Turkey, whose feminist movements date to the early 1900s. Cultural definitions of a "good woman" and of "honor" reinforce family constraints, such as a need for girls to work, and the shortcomings of the available education, which is not geared to women's needs and is dominated by men.

Egypt's experience demonstrates how difficult it is to overcome these patterns. When Nasser came to power in 1952, female illiteracy was over 90 percent; female school enrollment ratios were 26 percent in primary schools, 19 percent in secondary, and 7 percent at the third level. His regime sought to transform this situation, and women's primary-school enrollment did double to 52 percent by 1960, but increased by only 4 percent in the next decade. Today Egypt lags behind some of the other successor states (see Table 2).

President Bourguiba was more successful. Believing, like Atatürk, that functional changes in the position of women were an essential part of modernization, he not only accorded women's education priority but also initiated a wide-ranging program of legal reform that transformed traditional Islamic practices such as polygamy, divorce, and marriage and gave women equality in social and political life. The reforms achieved impressive results. Between 1960 and 1977, the percentage of the female age group enrolled in primary school rose from 43 to 81 percent, and has since reached 100 percent.

Despite the considerable gains achieved, however, female illiteracy remains significantly higher than men's, in most countries (Table 4).

Special Programs

Several governments have launched special programs to deal with the problem of illiteracy. One of the most noteworthy, Iraq's, was designed not only to increase the low literacy rate (about 26 percent in the early 1970s) but also to strengthen the government by inculcating the people with the ruling, Ba'th, party ideology. Launched in 1977, the massive

Table 4
Male Versus Female Literacy

Country	Age Group	% Male Literacy	% Female Literacy	Total Literacy
Egypt	15+	63	34	48
Iraq	15+	70	48	60
Israel	15+	95	89	92
Jordan	15+	90	70	80
Lebanon	15+	88	75	80
Syria	15+	78	51	64
Tunisia	15+	74	56	65
Turkey	15+	88	64	76

(Source: UNESCO, *Statistical Yearbook*, 1990, Table 1.3.)

five-year campaign was carefully organized with specific departments for mobilization, evaluation, technology, and teaching, and was implemented by literacy councils in each region according to particular needs. It consisted of two stages. The first provided instruction in basic literacy and numeracy; the second, in technical and vocational fields. Each contained a heavy dose of political indoctrination. The Iran-Iraq War ended the program prematurely; but the program had been very effective.

Educational innovations have been initiated in other areas as well. Hoping to increase relevance, reduce wastage, change cultural attitudes towards the schools, increase female enrollments, and improve the students' knowledge of technical subjects, Egypt, in 1972, introduced a new nine-year curriculum. It culminates in a certificate that is equivalent to the general academic one. In 1978, practical training was added to the curriculum in 450 pilot schools. In 1981, a comprehensive reorganization took place, and basic education became the norm. At the secondary level, too, new curricula were introduced that incorporate vocational training and expand the basic-education concept. Egyptian educators are also striving to improve evaluation techniques, to upgrade the quality of primary school teachers, and to improve teacher-training programs generally. By 1985, many schools were operating according to these principles, and thousands more were using special materials. Tunisia and Syria have also introduced the basic-education curriculum.

Science Education

Science education is receiving particular attention. Several regional meetings have emphasized the significance of improving the way these subjects are taught. An integrative biology curriculum has replaced separate subjects in many Arab countries, and an environmental education program is being developed. Turkey, too, has attempted to upgrade the quality of science instruction. Despite significant improvements, however, many subjects require updating, and qualified science teachers remain in short supply.

Vocational and Technical Education

Similar problems limit the development of vocational and technical education, even though all countries have sought to expand this field because shortages of midlevel manpower constitute an important bottleneck to economic development. They have done so in various ways. In Jordan, all students at the intermediate level study technical and vocational subjects. Tunisia has introduced practical courses beginning in the fifth grade, and the eighth grade includes a job-training course. Specialized vocational training is available at the elementary level and becomes more diversified in the secondary schools. Graduates are eligible to enter higher institutes that train technicians and teachers. Egypt, in 1983, increased the entrance requirements into the academic secondary schools (whose programs have also been revised) in order to achieve higher enrollments in the technical secondary schools. Turkey's vocational education stream begins at the secondary level and continues through a system of junior colleges being established with World Bank support. Since the early 1970s, Iraq has established new specialties, introduced workshops in the general intermediate schools, and opened a number of comprehensive schools combining academic and vocational training.

How these reforms will work is uncertain, for the expectations have often been frustrated. In Syria, despite attempts to change traditional values—the slogan "knowledge for the sake of work" was widely disseminated—academic training has retained its appeal. Nor have Egypt's previous attempts to channel students into technical and vocational schools proven successful. Enrollments there did increase, but serious shortages of skilled manpower in various areas remain. Moreover, existing deficiencies were aggravated because of inadequate investments, and programs for needed specialties are lacking. In Turkey, too, efforts to direct students into vocational and technical fields have yielded limited results; the percentage of students receiving a technical and vocational education remains low. The same situation prevails in all the other countries except for Tunisia, which has managed to increase vocational school enrollments.

Several factors account for this situation. First, as in many other societies, white-collar employment has always enjoyed higher prestige than manual labor. Second, the quality and relevance of vocational and technical education are quite poor because such schooling is extremely expensive, and the problem of training and retraining teachers is particularly acute in this area. Qualified persons are in great demand in industry, where they enjoy higher salaries and better working conditions. Third, educational patterns encourage able students to continue academic training. As a result, only students with the poorest scores enter vocational and technical schools; the others, quite naturally, opt for academic preparation, regardless of the difficulties in gaining admission to a university or in finding a suitable position after graduation.

To some extent, however, the military serves as an important source of vocational and technical manpower. The military represents one of the most important sectors in every state, one upon which vast resources are lavished. Recognizing the relationship between education and an effective military, all governments have taken steps to ensure that officers and men are well trained in the wide range of skills that are required in a modern army, many of which are relevant to civilian life. In some countries, the military has also been used for civilian education. In Turkey, for example, officers have served as teachers in various literacy drives.

The problems of vocational and technical training for industry have been replicated in the agricultural sector. There is a shortage of qualified extension agents and other specialists everywhere. Moreover, the bias towards the higher levels means that rural education is neglected even though the need for agricultural modernization in national development requires that peasants have a wide range of skills.

Only in Israel has rural education received the attention it deserves. Everywhere else, the education that is available to the rural mass is of poor quality and remains irrelevant to its needs. Fewer rural than urban children attend schools, rural schools tend to have poorer facilities and teachers than urban ones, and drop-out rates are high. The significance of such regional variations for educational mobility have been demonstrated empirically and raise important questions of social justice and equity. In addition, since most upper-level schools are located in urban areas, outmigration by ambitious rural youths who wish to continue their education is spurred. Thus agriculture loses many promising individuals, the phenomenon of overurbanization continues, and the development of this important sector is further hampered.

The Universities

The appeal of a traditional university education and the concomitant prejudice against technical or practical training has affected higher education in several ways. First, its appeal continues to grow and, the greater the expansion of the lower levels, the greater the pressure to enroll additional poorly prepared students in the already crowded colleges and universities. From an individual perspective, these aspirations are rational. A university diploma remains the passport to upward mobility, to a good marriage, to a successful career. Hence, the tide of applicants has become a flood, as everyone seeks admission to any niche in higher education, regardless of one's interests and capabilities. If one is forced to enroll in another type of institution, every effort is made to maneuver into a university upon graduation rather than enter into a career utilizing the skills learned. And, powerful pressures are exerted to transform all higher training institutes into new universities.

Such demands could be contained only by a government willing to accept the political and ideological costs involved. None was willing or able to do so. Thus, increased school attendance was translated into larger enrollments at the higher levels, enrollments that exacerbated the problems of quality as the available resources simply did not keep pace with the growing numbers. As a result, all faculties became more or less overcrowded; the humanities and social sciences suffered the most, since enrollments there could be expanded easily. However, the scientific and technological fields emphasized in many countries, though with varying results, have also suffered. In Egypt, despite the opening of 7 new universities between 1970 and 1979, lecture classes of 5000 students are not uncommon. In Turkey, the number of universities increased during the 1970s and exploded to 27 after the military takeover in 1980, greatly straining human and physical resources. Even this expansion, however (41,500 new students were admitted to the universities in 1980; 115,000 in 1982), could not accommodate all applicants, and new arrangements, such as an "open university," were made to absorb them. Table 5 shows the dramatic expansion which has taken place:

Table 5
Enrollment Increase

Country	1960	1975	% Female	1984	% Female
Egypt	98,000	451,187	30	838,142	32
Iraq	12,800	71,456	29	84,751	(1983) 33
Israel		52,980	44	61,155	48
Jordan	500	5,307	32	25,929	31
Lebanon		79,073	(1980) 36	70,510	39
Syria	15,200	65,348	22	131,224	30
Tunisia	5,000	20,505	26	41,594	36
Turkey	65,000	93,541	23	351,769	39

(Source: Francis Boardman, *Institutions of Higher Learning in the Middle East*, Washington, DC, MEI, 1977, p. 58; UNESCO *Statistical Yearbook*, 1987, Table 3.11.)

Government attempts to limit admission to universities through examinations have often served to introduce a strong class bias into the student body, for admission to the desirable faculties (e.g., medicine and computer sciences) is dependent upon the grade that one obtains. Students whose family backgrounds made it possible for them to study in private schools or to receive private tutoring, an activity that has become a major industry in Turkey, Egypt, and elsewhere, pass the examinations with the requisite grades. Students without such advantages end up in whatever faculty they can gain admission to, regardless of the subject and their interest in it. It is, after all, better to study philology at a university than not be a student there at all.

Thus, thousands struggle under difficult conditions to acquire diplomas in areas already crowded, a situation that contributes, at least in part, to student activism, a common phenomenon in many states, including Egypt, Tunisia, and Turkey. Student activism in Turkey during the late sixties forced the military to intervene in 1971; a wave of terrorism in the late seventies, in which students were involved, culminated in a military takeover in 1980. To reduce student unrest, many governments, especially Egypt, have attempted to find some sort of government position for every graduate. The costs of such a policy are very high; the jobs provide little satisfaction, and their sheer numbers (it has been estimated that there are about 30 percent, or 1.5 million, too many bureaucrats in the administration) reduce efficiency even further.

Governments have also moved to establish strict control over all aspects of university life. Only in a few societies, especially Turkey, Lebanon, and Israel, have universities ever enjoyed academic freedom as it is understood in the West. Even Turkish universities have not always been free of political interference. In the 1970s, they became so politicized that all aspects of university life were affected; when the military came to power in 1980, it severely restricted their autonomy, and many academics were dismissed.

Tight control over university affairs is the norm in the Arab world, where governments permit little academic freedom and try to use schools and colleges to disseminate the prevailing ideology. In Syria, for example, the Ba'th Party encourage students to act as informers. They are expected to fill out forms on the actions and attitudes of their classmates. Such an environment does little to enhance scholarship. The faculty teach in ways that will not create controversy. And, those who are interested in carrying out research, and have the opportunity and facilities to do so, slight topics that might be politically sensitive, especially in the social sciences. Even research dealing with less sensitive topics must be presented in a noncontroversial manner.

The possibility for serious scholarly work in any field is further hampered by the heterogeneity of approaches that characterizes institutions of higher learning. Because of the colonial heritage, one finds colleges and faculties modeled after, for example, the French tradition (or the British) co-existing with institutions rooted in another educational tradition. Moreover, given the active involvement of the United States and the former Soviet Union in the Middle East since the Second World War educational influences of these two superpowers were superimposed on the confused earlier legacy of indigenous and alien educational models. Often the faculties consist of persons trained in Germany, France, the United States, Britain, as well as the former Soviet Union and Eastern Europe. There is little uniformity within countries, even within universities; there is much duplication; and fields and disciplines are seldom coordinated. Integrating scholars with such diverse backgrounds into a cohesive scholarly community agreeing on such matters as curricula or even the goals of education has been no simple matter.

ISLAMIC REVIVAL

These difficulties have been compounded in recent years by the emergence of a new orientation towards knowledge—an Islamic one. The rapid dissemination of modern education and knowledge in the successor states has not been welcomed everywhere. There still remains, in all societies, a powerful undercurrent of Islamic feelings that have been nurtured by traditional religious educational systems in one form or another. Even in Turkey, for example, large numbers of religious teachers are being trained in state schools. The concern with Islam has affected all segments of society, and, increasingly, intellectuals are noting what they consider to be a destructive impact of Western institutions and methods. Thus one can identify a strong reaction against the influence of the West, a reaction that obviously played a major role in the Iranian Revolution. This reaction, which finds its expression in the rise of Islamic fundamentalist movements, has become a factor in many societies. A growing number believe that traditional Islamic values have been eroded by Western knowledge and that the basis of that knowledge is an erroneous paradigm, one that separates science and values, that disaggregates reality into separate and artificial components. What is needed is a holistic epistemology, one that is based on the humanistic values embodied in Islam. Numerous Islamic scholars have called for the creation of a new "Islamic science" or a "Muslim economics" that would enable Islamic societies to absorb modern scientific and technical knowledge in a manner compatible with Muslim ideals.

The intellectual substance of "Islamic science" requires definition and elaboration. If Islamic science means that certain areas of research should be emphasized and others neglected—that emphasis should be on rural development, appropriate technology, and basic human needs— then there is no cause for concern. Such thinking is consonant with existing scholarship on modernization and development. Yet, if Islamic science means rejecting modern scientific conceptions of knowledge and replacing them with an epistemology based on assumptions about the nature of knowledge and man's place in the universe, involving restrictions on intellectual freedom, then one must question the future of education and research in societies that accept such a paradigm.

Islamic fundamentalism affects education in two other ways as well. First, policies towards women's education will undoubtedly change if conservative Muslims gain political influence, for their ideas about the role of women in society and the nature and content of their education differ greatly from those held by such leaders as Bourguiba and Atatürk. Second, for scientific progress to occur, a society must value the activities of science and must be supportive of them. An educational system trapped into static moral norms rather than scientific and technological ones, can not produce the technical manpower that is required for progress. Nor can it disseminate the kinds of values essential to the kind of technological development to which the successor states aspire.

MIGRATION AND THE BRAIN DRAIN

The brain drain to the West has traditionally siphoned off a significant percentage of the region's skilled manpower. PhDs in the social sciences and the sciences as well as engineers, doctors, and technicians have moved in large numbers (an estimated 150,000 between 1950 and 1975) to Canada, the United States, and Europe. Turkey, Egypt, Jordan, Lebanon, and Syria have been the biggest losers. And, in recent years, the oil-rich, manpower-short Gulf states have proven to be a powerful magnet for skilled personnel of all types. The overall number of foreign workers there stood at 1.6 million in 1975 and was expected to increase to 4.3 million by 1985. Egypt accounts for over 20 percent of the total stock and Jordan, for 9 percent. Though Egypt possesses a surplus in many fields, skilled workers are in short supply. And, if all its nationals were to return, Jordan would be confronted with a labor surplus.

The shortages that exist in many exporting states are being met, to some extent, by replacement migration. Push factors are also involved. Many persons are alienated by the degree of political control or by the importance of political connections and seek an environment of academic freedom. Others leave because of a lack of opportunities or dissatisfaction with working conditions. Some governments, such as Tunisia, encourage scholars in various fields to accept assignments abroad in order to alleviate its surplus.

These flows have already had important consequences for both the exporting states (inflation and shortages of skills) and the receiving states (the establishment of large immigrant communities). These consequences will continue to be felt in the future. Such flows tend to reduce educational standards as many of the migrants are the most qualified teachers, especially those with vocational and technical skills; they are urgently needed not only to teach students but to prepare others to be teachers of these vital subjects. Thus, shortages that limit economic development are further aggravated. Schooling is affected in another way. The attraction of working abroad is so strong that many persons are making educational decisions on the basis of their potential for migration. Hence, there is pressure to prepare students in careers for which no domestic need exists, whereas other careers are neglected. Even though this bias is already evident, the training that is available is of such quality that many graduates find that they have not acquired the skills necessary to gain employment abroad. To deal with the problems of education in a relatively closed system is difficult enough, but when one has to do so under these conditions, it becomes even more of a challenge.

INTERNATIONAL COMPARISONS

Although all the successor states continue to confront serious educational weaknesses, the progress achieved in building modern educational systems and in diffusing modern knowledge is impressive, especially within an international context. Since World War II, educational opportunities throughout the world have increased markedly at all levels and in all countries. But enrollments in this region have grown at a much faster rate than in most other parts of the globe. Independence from colonial rule led to a major growth in education. World Bank figures indicate that, whereas in the 1960s a smaller percentage of male students (6 to 11 years old) were enrolled in school than in any other region, except for Africa, by the mid-1970s these enrollment ratios had surpassed even those in South Asia and East Asia as well.

The trend at the secondary level is similar; the increase in enrollments is also among the fastest in the world. By the mid-1970s, the enrollment ratios were at about the same level as in Latin America and higher than South Asia, East Asia, and Africa. Women have also participated in this trend. The percentage of female students attending primary schools has risen dramatically and become higher than in South Asia and Africa. Enrollment ratios for women, however, remained much lower than in East Asia and Latin America. At the secondary level, as well, Latin America has surpassed the region's female enrollment ratios. UNESCO data indicate a growth in student enrollments at all levels and in all regions, but the rate of increase for the Arab states (4.8 percent) remains the highest in the world. This rate of increase has, however, slowed in the 1980s.

Everywhere the state has come to play a prominent role, increasing its control over curricula, examinations, textbooks, and degree requirements while also strictly regulating minority and religious schools. This new role and the concomitant expansion have led to vast increases in the amount of resources allocated to education. The Middle East has invested very heavily in education. In the mid-1970s, with per student expenditures in higher education of $3,100, it ranked second only to Africa ($3,800) and well above the industrialized countries ($2,300), the U.S.S.R. and Eastern Europe ($1,000), Latin America ($735), East Asia ($470), and South Asia ($120). In elementary education, the Middle East ranked third ($180), behind the industrialized countries ($1,160) and the U.S.S.R. and Eastern Europe ($540), but above Latin America ($90), East Asia ($54), Africa)$40), and South Asia ($13).

Unfortunately, even these large investments have failed to keep pace with ever-growing demands, and, at present, education in the successor states as in all the developing countries suffers, to a greater or lesser degree, from inadequate facilities and shortages of qualified teachers, high wastage rates, limited relevance to personal and national needs, and a lack of equity. Moreover, the huge efforts and the allocation of vast amounts of resources have not yielded the hoped-for results because the outputs of the educational system do not match economic and social requirements.

The attraction of an academic training has increased everywhere so that in all the regions of the world (except for Eastern Europe and Asia) the proportion of secondary school students attending vocational schools has declined dramatically since 1950. Overall, this figure has dropped by about a third, but significant regional variations exists—Africa has witnessed the sharpest decline, followed by the Middle East and Latin America. As a result, schools everywhere are graduating large numbers of students who do not possess the necessary skills to find adequate employment and to lead productive lives; at the same time, manpower shortages, especially of midlevel manpower and technical workers, are commonplace.

CONCLUSION

Although it is now widely accepted that the relationship between education and development is not as simple as was once assumed, governments in the successor states and elsewhere continue to strive to build systems that can produce the required manpower while functioning at an intellectual level that would satisfy individual aspirations and make possible the achievement of societal goals. Hence, policymakers have sought to reform their educational systems, in some cases to transform them. They have attempted to bring educational opportunities to neglected groups and to improve the quality of education through curricular reforms, the introduction of new materials and instructional methods, and through measures to raise the numbers and quality of teachers. Many problems remain, however, and numerous suggestions for reform continue to be presented. These include limiting access to universities, formulating more sophisticated manpower analyses and better planning, emphasizing primary instead of higher education, using emigrants for short-term courses, and emphasizing nonformal education.

Educational reform must be viewed within a broad context. Education not only affects but is profoundly affected by such features in its environment as incentive structures, dominant values, and, above all, the nature of the political order. Hence, the nature of the state as well as the orientation and capabilities of its political elites become critical variables that determine the character of a society's educational system. A strong state with a regime that is committed to societal transformation is essential, but such a commitment does not suffice. The leadership must also possess the skill and the resources to implement an appropriate package of policies in a coherent and systematic fashion. This is a difficult challenge, but only those states that possess the ability to confront it successfully can achieve their national aspirations.

CHAPTER FIFTEEN

Conclusion

DISJUNCTIVE DEVELOPMENT IS perhaps the best term to characterize the modernization of states emerging from the Ottoman Empire. On the one hand, many changes in virtually all aspects of society, polity, and economy have occurred since the First World War. Moreover, in most cases the pace of change has accelerated over the past seven decades, especially during the last three decades. To the extent that one can measure modernization quantitatively, the Middle East can be said to be modernizing at a fast pace. Indeed, the quantitatively measurable amount of modernization in the Middle East is well above the average for the Third World. On the other hand, the integrative and institution-building effectiveness of these massive and accelerating changes seems less assured.

The question of how best to explain this phenomenon of disjunctive development takes us back to an issue raised in the Introduction. This book is one in a series of comparative modernization studies of which three have already appeared—*The Modernization of Japan and Russia*, *The Modernization of China*, and *The Modernization of Inner Asia*. Unlike the first three books, our study deals with an area that was once, indeed for an impressively long time span, a single state (the Ottoman Empire) but has since been divided into many (of which we selected eight for study: Egypt, Iraq, Israel, Jordan, Lebanon, Syria, Tunisia, and Turkey). The lack of state continuity stands out as a major causal factor in explaining the modernization experience of the Middle East.

At the same time, fluctuations in the political and territorial units of analysis are matched by other disjunctions in the economy, in social structure, and in knowledge and education. Altogether, this persistently disjunctive pattern stands out as a major obstacle to effective modernization. This is not to suggest that modernization is ever a smooth, linear progression anywhere in the world. Modernization is never without crises, often of system-destroying, revolutionary magnitude. Nor do we assume that, other things being equal, a relatively flat developmental curve may be more effective or less painful to the several generations of individuals involved. Rather, the image we seek to convey in interpreting Middle Eastern modernization is one of fits and starts. Breakdowns and break-

311

throughs have both been avoided. So, too, has a process of steady, incremental change.

This distinctive modernization pattern will now be briefly discussed by reference to the different chapter rubrics used in Parts One and Two.

INTERNATIONAL CONTEXT

The eight states studied here are located in a region that perhaps more than any other in the world has been shaped by the actions of international diplomacy. This pattern of international politics began roughly two centuries ago and continued even after the end of the Ottoman Empire following the First World War. It became, instead, even more pronounced, especially after the Second World War. Indeed, over the past forty years, the Middle East (particularly the Fertile Crescent and Egypt) has played the role in global politics assumed by the Balkans in the nineteenth century. The Middle East is an area in which complex, multipolar regional political disputes both attract and are provoked by outside powers.

The resulting diplomatic context in which politics at the local, state, and global levels becomes closely intertwined has profoundly shaped the modernization process in several ways. First, a fluctuating pattern of alliance making-and-breaking tends to produce a kind of stability in which diplomatic problems are not resolved but simply kept in abeyance. This is because the loser in the ongoing balance-of-power diplomacy can readily find counterbalancing allies either within the region or among the Great Powers.

With diplomatic problems thus held in abeyance, two variant patterns of regional conflict can be discerned. One, as seen from the perspective of the Great Powers, is that of "proxy wars" in which the Great Powers (chiefly the United States and the former Soviet Union since the Second World War) contend with each other by supporting their regional clients. This pattern has characterized the Arab-Israeli confrontation as well as the inter-Arab regional power struggles. This is for most of the time a matter of struggles short of war, but, when war does break out, it tends to be short (although viciously intense as with the October 1973 Arab-Israeli War); this is because the contending superpowers (and arms suppliers) seek to avoid being dragged into the conflict. This explains the effective superpower "hot-line" diplomacy in times of Middle Eastern wars.

The other conflict pattern is one in which the superpowers lose their ability (or perhaps the will) to restrain their clients and at least one of the belligerents depicts the struggle in primordial or inflexibly rigid ideological terms. Examples are the long Iran-Iraq War, the civil war that has raged in Lebanon since 1975, and the Palestinian Intifada against Israeli occupation that began in December 1987.

It is noteworthy that in both patterns diplomatic power balances do not change sufficiently to provoke systemic change. Two extreme examples make the point. The crushing Israeli defeat of its Arab opponents in the June 1967 War did not really change the "rules of the game." And the Iran-Iraq War ended with a cease fire deadlock—favorable, it is true, to Iraq but not sufficiently so to reverse preexisting power balances.

Second, this pattern is exacerbated by a full-blown Middle Eastern arms race. In recent years, the Middle Eastern expenditure on arms as a percentage of gross national product has been roughly two-and-a-half times the developing world average. Only Tunisia and Turkey are close to the developing-world average of about $45 in 1985. Syria spends almost 10 times, and Israel almost 20 times, the developing-world average. The developing-world average of military personnel per 1,000 inhabitants is 4.9. The figures for Iraq, Israel, and Syria are 49.9, 47.8, and 38.8, respectively. Only Tunisia, with 6.2 per 1000, approaches the developing-world average. (The Lebanese figure in present circumstances of civil war is meaningless.) These comparative figures indicate the extent to which international relations in the Middle East divert resources from development. This is even more the case in that, with the partial exception of Israel (a major arms exporter, especially for its small population), expenditures for military hardware go overwhelmingly for imports of finished equipment with little development of local industry and equally limited exposure to high technology on the part of the importing countries.

Third, the resulting diplomatic system is burdensome to all, yet little is done to change it. Political inertia favors more of the same.

Fourth, existing political leaders risk losing domestic support if they do not appear to match the efforts of potential or actual regional enemies. Given the tenuous legitimacy of many of the Middle Eastern regimes, this adds up to yet more pressure to concentrate on foreign policy (where little can be gained) at the expense of domestic concerns (where developmental gains might well be realized).

Two successor states would seem to have avoided the worst of the foregoing—Tunisia and Turkey. Moreover, Egypt since its 1979 peace treaty with Israel and its diminished Nasserist ambitions to be a regional leader may be embarked on a similar path. As for the five states of the

Fertile Crescent (plus those Fertile Crescent groups, such as the Palestinians, who aspire to statehood), their inability to escape a diplomatic system that concentrates enormous human and material resources on foreign policy issues that, even so, do not get resolved clearly impedes their efforts to modernize.

POLITICAL STRUCTURE

Here the theme of disjunctive development looms especially large. In the seven decades since the end of the First World War, the three political units studied in Part One (Egypt, Tunisia, and the central Ottoman Empire) have become eight sovereign states. Nor have the intervening seven decades been a period of reasonably uniform development among those eight states. One (Turkey) was never subjected to outright Western colonial rule. All others were, but in different forms and for different time periods and with different colonial overlords, Britain or France.

Yet, except possibly for Tunisia, the period of Western colonial rule for each was marked by disjunctures. A few examples indicate the overall pattern. Egypt was under British military occupation (never further regularized for reasons that have everything to do with European diplomacy and little with Middle Eastern realities) from 1882 to 1914. Then, for a short period from 1914 to 1922 (four during the First World War), Egypt was a British Protectorate. There followed, from 1922 on, a pattern of what can best be described as indirect British rule that maintained the dubious fiction of Egyptian independence. France had a strong position among the Maronite Christians of Lebanon but never really got firmly established in Syria. British rule in Jordan (then Transjordan) and Iraq was, by comparison, relatively effortless and efficient. But the very opposite colonizer/colonized relationship prevailed in Palestine.

Independence for these states came at different times and in different ways. The political records since independence are equally diverse, ranging from military interventions to restore a threatened system (Turkey) to system-changing coups (Egypt, Iraq, Syria) with the peaceful move by a military man in Tunisia (Ben Ali's replacement of Bourguiba in 1987) being perhaps somewhere in between the two but leaning toward the Turkish pattern.

Three states have relatively well-institutionalized democratic systems (Israel, Lebanon, and Turkey), but Lebanon's has been destroyed—perhaps beyond restoration—by the civil war. Israel's democratic system, ironically, has come to be threatened by a military victory, that of June 1967. With the ensuing military occupation of the West Bank and Gaza Strip (with their 1.5 million Palestinian Arabs), an Israel intent on keeping the "spoils" of its 1967 victory faces tough choices. It can continue to rule over conquered territories while denying their people citizenship rights, or it can drive the Palestinians out while annexing the land— neither option being justified by democratic principles. Alternatively, Israel could annex the territories and grant the Palestinians living there full citizenship rights. But this would eventually lead to an Arab majority in the would-be Jewish state.

The foregoing indicates that the successor states are not easily analyzed as a single entity. They are also, given the systemic multilateral and fluctuating diplomatic rivalries noted earlier, less likely to cooperate and to learn from each other or from others. To this extent, the potential advantages accruing to late modernizers (by adapting the experiences not only of early modernizers but also of neighboring late modernizers possessing similar sociopolitical structures) are reduced.

For all their diversity, many of these states share a number of characteristics. In most of them, the legitimacy of the existing political institutions is weak. In most of them, the majority of the people are still only weakly politicized; they are, accordingly, inclined to approach government with varying combinations of acquiescence and avoidance. Such weak political legitimacy and a low politicization make for uncertain modernizing possibilities. On the one hand, those holding political pwoer face fewer political demands from the ruled and are freer to make policies without facing the domestic opposition that would be the case in more thoroughly politicized societies. On the other hand, to the extent that policies adopted require active participation by the ruled, the rulers face difficulties exceeding those in more modernized societies.

Again, however, it is difficult to generalize. Greater political legitimacy (or, more accurately, greater national legitimacy) characterizes Egypt, Israel, Tunisia, and Turkey. In all four a consensus exists concerning the legitimacy of the existing state.

But for the post-1967 Israeli rule over West Bank and Gaza, it could be argued that Israel possesses the highest political (and national) legitimacy of any state in the region. It is a state whose Jewish citizens chose to come from elsewhere and were motivated by a system-challenging political ideology (Zionism) that was buttressed by a special interpretation of a religion (Judaism). Moreover, the land chosen for immigration has a powerful historical-religious attraction (Eretz Israel, the Biblical Promised Land). And, finally, the political crises attending the rise of Zionism (European anti-Semitism) added urgency to the enterprise, at least from a Zionist point of view. Much of this hard-earned political legitimacy and cohesion is now threatened by the post-1967 de facto reality of a "Greater Israel," with a large and growing minority of unassimilable Palestinian Arabs.

Turkey offers an example of a state growing out of a period of crisis and evolving in a system-challenging fashion, in this case largely under the aegis of a single charismatic leader, Kemal Atatürk. In both Turkey and Israel, the ability of political leadership to create new facts based on new ideologies has been impressive. Both states face unassimilated and possibly unassimilable minorities (e.g., the Kurds and Islamic fundamentalists in Turkey; the Palestinians in Israel), but in each state political adjustments are available. For Israel, this would mean eschewing the fatal attraction of a "Greater Israel" in order to avoid the perils of a de facto Jewish-Arab state, binational in fact if not in name. For Turkey, giving the Kurdish minority limited linguistic and cultural autonomy while improving living conditions in impoverished areas of Eastern Turkey where the Kurds live would seem feasible. The Kurds do share the religion of Islam with their Turkish compatriots, and culturally the two groups are not dissimilar.

As for Egypt and Tunisia, history and geography have combined to produce political communities that have existed for centuries (indeed, in the case of Egypt, for millennia). The sense of identification as Egyptians or as Tunisians is accordingly well established. No special effort is required to inculcate national loyalty. Yet, both states (especially Egypt) began modern times confronting a popular disinclination to view government as a positive force. Government since has had mixed results in its efforts to politicize its citizenry. Since the First World War, neither the era of the Wafd nor of Nasserist Arabism left in place institutionalized political participation. The political leadership of post-Nasser and post-Sadat Egypt has been more cautious in encouraging political participation; such slower politicization may, on balance, prove more effective.

Tunisia seemed embarked on a near-ideal staged development under the leadership of the Neo-Destour party. The party founder and leader, Habib Bourguiba, could rightly be dubbed the Tunisian Atatürk. Unlike Atatürk, however, Bourguiba lived long after independence was restored in 1956, and his autocratic tendencies came into full play. Tunisia, thus, did not experience the active political party life that developed in Turkey from 1950 on. Instead, even the organizations outside of the single, Destourian party (trade unions, students, women, business associations, and the like) that showed promise at the time of independence were stripped of their autonomy and made subservient to party and state. After making laudable progress toward modernizing political institutionalization, Tunisia lost momentum in the latter years of Bourguiba's long rule. It is too soon to determine if the peaceful overthrow of Bourguiba in November 1987 has been able to change the political climate and move that state toward political pluralism.

Of the Fertile Crescent Arab states, only Lebanon has experienced political pluralism within a democratic framework, but the brutal and long-lived civil war (since 1975) puts in doubt the very viability of the state. Syria and Iraq have developed in recent years authoritarian single-party systems that manage to remain in control after years of political instability. Both Ba'thist regimes (although archrivals) share a populist and secularist modernizing orientation. Top leadership in both countries is controlled by tightly organized regional minorities. Both countries possess huge military establishments. Can a modernizing but authoritarian political leadership, possessing a fragile political legitimacy and demonstrating both the capacity and the will to use violence in imposing obedience, institutionalize political participation? This is a major question still facing Syria and Iraq.

Jordan's monarchic government is characterized by a traditional pattern of dynastic authoritarianism. It has managed a high level of political stability in a possibly less favorable situation than any of the other eight states. Even so, whether this record has produced increased loyalty to the political system remains questionable.

The above review of political structures presents a bleak picture, but one can also offer a positive interpretation. In every state (save Lebanon) strong central governments possessing the personnel and the means to control the country and set integrative political goals have been established. Moreover, although governmental bureaucracies are in many cases unnecessarily swollen (with resulting inefficient use of human resources), such bureaucracies do constitute organized groups. They are also among the most modernized members of their society in terms of education, technical experience, and life-styles. Because of this, they have the potential for effective organized action.

Some of the themes stressed here are not peculiar to the Ottoman successor states. Indeed, the tradition of an overpowering central state largely autonomous from civil society is also seen in such diverse regions of the world as Russia, Japan, China, and, to some extent, in Latin

America. This strong "state tradition" distinguishes them from Britain and North America (having weak or decentralized states) and from some Western European countries (whose states, though strong, have roots in a feudal tradition). The Ottoman sipahis (fief-holders) more nearly resembled the Japanese samurai and the Russian gentry as a state-service class in a political system that stressed duties to the state rather than rights against it. This Ottoman class had less in common with the feudal aristocracy of Western Europe. The later emergence of a class of local notables (ayan) parallel to the decline of central administration in the eighteenth century can, in turn, be compared to warlordism in China and *caciquismo* in Latin America. In none of these cases did such local chieftains possess the status, power, and, more importantly, the legitimacy of Western European feudal lords.

Such unrivalled supremacy of the state vis-à-vis civil society made it possible for the Ottoman sultans and their equivalents in autonomous Egypt and Tunisia to embark upon policies of modernization from above, defensively at first but gradually extending into other fields, at a quite early stage. If the rule of Selim III (1789–1807) is taken as the beginning of Ottoman modernization, it is clear that the Ottoman Empire entered its modernization process somewhat later than Russia but earlier than Japan and much earlier than China. Yet, the empire and its successor states were considerably less successful in attaining modernity than were Japan and Russia. One reason may have been the ethnic, linguistic, religious, and cultural heterogeneity of the Ottoman population.

By contrast, the relatively small size and geographical isolation of Japan together with its cultural homogeneity and the numerical and cultural superiority of the Great Russians in the Russian Empire gave these two societies greater cultural unity and an early sense of national identity. This, in turn, seems to have fostered in them a kind of developmental ideology that enabled them to better mobilize social resources at the service of modernization than was possible for the Ottoman Empire. To this must be added the military-strategic vulnerability of the Ottoman state and its constant wars with its neighbors, compared to the relatively insulated position of Russia and especially of Japan. Moreover, Japan and Russia developed in the fringes of older cultural areas—China and Byzantium—and borrowed heavily from them in the more distant past. Because of this, they were receptive to cultural borrowings, whereas China and the Ottoman Empire had a strong belief in the ethical and cultural superiority of their own system and were resistant to such change. Ottoman culture, whose foundations were based on divine revelation, was reluctant to borrow from the Christian West.

Furthermore, the Ottoman successor states also differ in other ways from other late modernizing, postcolonial nations. For the latter, the problem has been to create a state (in most cases a nation as well) almost from scratch. By contrast, the Ottoman successor states—notably republican Turkey, but in varying degrees others as well—inherited indigenous administrative cadres highly experienced in running a state. This helps to explain the unbalanced development of the "output" (administrative) functions of the contemporary Middle Eastern states compared to the weak "input" institutions representing civil society. It also helps to explain the remarkable staying power of the post-Ottoman (especially Arab) states, in view of the often-made claim that most of them are artificial and alien creations designed to serve the interests of former colonial powers.

ECONOMIC STRUCTURE AND GROWTH

The economic revolution of the region also shows sharp disjunctures. Its overall growth compares favorably with that of most Third World countries. However, as regards the structural changes required to ensure sustained growth in the future, it has done less well. Part of the explanation lies in the political factors analyzed in the foregoing section and in the effects the oil boom has had in the Gulf.

National income figures show that the rate of growth in the region was relatively high (see Chapter 12, Table II) and that consumption rose correspondingly. That this is not a statistical illusion is shown by figures on such basic indices of economic activity as steel and energy consumption and of mass consumption items such as food, textiles, and radio sets. At the same time, considerable progress has been made in developing the region's human resources. Health standards have improved considerably, and mass education has been greatly extended. The stock of technical skills available has also been enormously expanded, but the region started from a very low level and still lags behind many developing countries, not to mention Russia and Japan at their earlier stages of modernization. And in one very important field the region has made very little progress: the reduction of birth rates to a level characteristic of modern societies.

An appreciable proportion of the rise in income is due to the rapid expansion of services, particularly government. The productive sectors grew much more slowly. Agriculture has been lagging, a feature that the region has shared with other developing countries, as well as with Russia, but not with Japan or China. Turkey, Israel, and Syria have done somewhat better in this respect than their neighbors. Industry has expanded rather fast, but much of the increase in this sector is illusory, since it is due to misuse of resources made possible only by high protection. Few industries are capable of competing in world markets, but in this, too, the region is not unique. Conditions may be expected to improve with greater experience.

More serious is the failure to raise the savings rate or balance the current account in the balance of payments. The two, of course, are intimately linked. The region has been able to have high rates of investment coupled with increasing consumption and huge expenditures on armaments only because it has been receiving huge amounts of foreign aid.

These resources have come, first, from the superpowers and their allies—from the United States to Israel, Egypt, Turkey, Jordan, and Tunisia, from the former Soviet Union to Syria, Iraq, Egypt, and Turkey. The connection between this aid and superpower rivalries in the region is obvious. The other source of funds was the Arab oil states of the Gulf, most of which were also motivated by the regional political rivalries. Funds have also been generated by remittances from expatriate Arab workers in the Gulf and from purchases of goods and services by nationals of the oil-rich countries in the rest of the region.

In this dependence on outside forces for its economic growth, the region is continuing a pattern that is 150 years old and that differentiates it sharply from Russia, Japan, and China. In those countries, the main impulse for modernization was internal. To varying degrees and in various ways, it was their governments and their people that conducted the process of modernization, relying mostly on domestic resources. In the Middle East, however, the initiative generally came from outside, and foreign enterprise and capital played a predominating role in economic development.

Starting around the First World War, nationals wrested control of economic activity from foreign and minority business interests. In the last few decades, however, caught up in their regional conflicts and in superpower rivalries, they have once more become greatly dependent on outside funds to meet their rapidly escalating military expenditures, sustain a level of consumption high enough to prevent internal unrest, and secure an investment rate that ensures adequate growth. This dependence on foreign aid—and the ensuing mounting indebtedness—casts a dark shadow over the progress achieved and raises serious doubts about the region's future.

Another characteristic of the region may be noted: the role of government in economic activity. In Japan, government played a secondary, but pivotal, role; it created favorable conditions for growth and pioneered certain key industries, which were then privatized, but left the main initiative to private enterprise. In Russia and China, government took over almost all fields of economic activity. Government's role in this region was far greater than in Japan but much less than in Russia or China. In all countries, agriculture, housing, and construction and most services have remained in private hands. In some, however, significant portions of industry, transport, hauling, and insurance have been nationalized. On the whole, nationalization seems to have retarded growth, and, in most countries, measures are now being taken to extend the private sector.

SOCIAL INTERDEPENDENCE

Disjunctive development or a pattern of "fits and starts" that has characterized Ottoman Afro-Asia since 1800 is perhaps nowhere clearer than in social interdependence. Between 1800 and 1914, those patterns included relatively slow demographic growth and dramatic external and internal migration, uneven economic changes, the persistence of family and religious-communal bonds, and an increasingly powerful state that met increased public resistance and foreign interference.

First, a relatively slow rate of demographic growth before 1800 kept the region's population within Malthusian limits, with cities and towns constituting roughly 20 percent of the total population. The gradual process of eliminating these Malthusian constraints, from about the middle of the nineteenth century on, led to a rough doubling of Ottoman Afro-Asia's population between 1800 and 1914. Coastal cities and towns involved in international trade were the beneficiaries; interior towns grew much more slowly because they suffered from competition by imported European goods. As a result, the overall urbanization rate on balance showed relatively little change between 1800 and 1914.

Second, internal and external migration had a profound impact on Ottoman society as a whole. The influx of Muslims from areas lost to imperial Russia in particular was matched by internal migration of Ottoman Christians and, toward the end of the nineteenth century, the emigration of significant numbers of Christians to the Americas and West

Africa. As a result, the proportion of Muslims in the population as a whole increased, with important political consequences, particularly the sponsorshp by Sultan Abdulhamid II of Pan-Islamic ideas and the increasingly vocal demands of some non-Muslim communities for national self-determination.

Third, economic change, particularly the gradual subordination of Ottoman Afro-Asia's foreign trade to the European system and in particular the fiscal collapse of the Tunisian, Egyptian, and Ottoman states, slowed the region's industrialization. Significant industrial growth did not begin until after the First World War, because of a shortage of capital, skilled management, and relatively low per capita income. As the international trade balance continued to shift in Europe's favor, traditional urban crafts declined, the export of agricultural commodities and raw materials rose, and those segments of the population (primarily non-Muslim) with commercial and cultural ties to Europe benefited as compared with their Muslim compatriots. All this exacerbated social and communal tensions.

Fourth, perhaps the most profound disjunctive development was the persistence of religious-communal identification in an age of nationalism, state-sponsored reform, and social change. The dissolution of the old order, both at the hands of the Ottoman reformers and through economic and social changes, did not have uniform results. The extended family, along with religious-communal identity, continued to exercise a powerful influence well into this century, indeed down to the present. Slow change in the status of women contrasted with rapid change in the world of work, where the beginnings of industrial unrest made their appearance by the end of the nineteenth century.

Fifth, state-sponsored change was the most spectacular of all, particularly for political institutions and land tenure. New legislative and municipal institutions made a halting start; but the autocratic sponsorship of reform met with resistance from a social order that sought legitimacy in other forms of political organization, whether nationalist or pan-Islamic. Land-tenure reform substituted modern notions of private property for the customary one of state land, resulting in the creation of a class of absentee landlords and the loss by peasants of many of their customary rights.

Sixth, social mobility took place among those who had modern skills, education, and cultural and economic links to Europe. Because non-Muslim communities tended to have these advantages to a significantly greater degree than those of Muslims, this differential social mobility had grave political consequences. Thus communal and ethnic-national ties grew in importance just as economic and political relationships changed. Whereas the state insisted on the legal and social equality of individuals under the ruler's sovereignty, the social order rejected that formulation. The disjunction between political development, on the one hand, and economic and social change, on the other, was devastating; it contributed to the occupation of Egypt and Tunisia in the 1880s and to the dissolution of the Ottoman Empire after World War I.

These same disjunctive transformations persisted, often becoming sharper in subsequent decades of the twentieth century. They are apparent in distinctive demographic features obstructing development and socioeconomic mobilization. Despite substantial progress made in standards of public health, literacy, and nutrition—and the consequent decline in mortality and incidence of early marriage—the successor states continue to suffer from mounting population pressure. Comparatively high fertility, youthfulness of the population, and dependency ratios are doubtless a reflection of the survival of pronatalist norms. Unless these sentiments and their supportive values change, prospects for any appreciable reductions in fertility through family-planning programs and other means of population control are unlikely. The repeated failure of such programs, and the lack of public enthusiasm for them, attest to the dissonance between conditions conducive to the reduction of mortality and those encouraging high fertility.

Equally disruptive are dislocations associated with massive population shifts and the changing pattern of migration. Two world wars, Arab-Israeli hostilities, protracted civil unrest, and other regional and local conflicts continue to be destabilizing sources of population dislocation and relocation. They also exacerbate problems of political management inherent in the factional tensions of plural and divided societies. Recently, these imbalances have been compounded by the displacement of large numbers of Arab migrant labor from the Arabian Peninsula and Europe. Embittered returnees, particularly in countries like Egypt, are swelling the ranks of militant and fundamentalist movements. The loss in remittances is critical since several of the successor states are in dire need of such capital inflow to meet mounting foreign debts and other public expenditures.

The magnitude and pattern of urbanization have also had disruptive consequences for the character of socioeconomic and cultural transformations. On the whole, the rates of urban growth in the successor states are almost four times higher than those observed in the more developed metropolitan regions of the world. Such swift and accelerated growth has accentuated the disjunction between "urbanization" as a physical phenomenon and "urbanism" as a qualitative and sociocultural attribute. Among other things, it has obstructed urban planning, aggravated problems of adaptation to urban life-styles, and marginalized a growing segment of the already disenfranchised rural migrants.

Such discrepant transformations are also visible in changes in labor-force distribution. Here as well the successor states depart from the commonly observed three-stage pattern of labor mobilization: from agrarian to industrial to services. By and large, processes of development have by-passed the intermediate stage of industrialization. Concomitant with these trends, indeed because of them, rapid urbanization and primate cities are characterized by a bloated or overcrowded service sector and its twin feature, high rates of underemployment.

Another disjunctive feature with serious implications for socio-economic mobilization is the persistence of the cultural syndrome of female segregation or of the exclusion of women from public life. It is curious that the greater accessibility to educational opportunities women enjoyed during the past three decades, and their alleged liberalization and emancipation, have had negligible impact on the relaxation of these restrictive taboos. Indeed, recent evidence appears to suggest that a growing segment of Arab women who had earlier espoused emancipatory causes are now sanctioning the return to a more cautious form of feminism.

Despite the differences, the successor states share an underlying concern for correcting some of the imbalances and dislocations generated by sweeping structural transformations, residues of feudalism, colonialism, and the dismemberment of the Ottoman Empire. Hence they all, as we have seen, experimented with different redistributive strategies —often dramatically shifting from centralized planning to economic liberalization—to achieve a more egalitarian society.

These efforts have had varying consequences, particularly when differences between so-called revolutionary and nonrevolutionary regimes are considered. The interplay, for example, between state intervention and private initiative has influenced in contradictory fashion the extent of economic and political participation by formerly excluded and powerless groups. What is unambiguous, however, is the impact of such measures on the size, composition, and sociopolitical importance of the nascent middle class. This fairly new social stratum, largely a result of newly acquired skills and occupational opportunities, differs strikingly from the older and more conventional status groups of small merchants, bureaucrats, and clerics.

Although relatively diminutive in size and lacking in cohesion and self-consciousness, this diffuse and heterogeneous social category has had, nonetheless, a profound impact as carriers of new values and life-styles. Perhaps because they are drawn from groups not too deeply anchored in society, they have been more venturesome than other comparable vectors of sociocultural and political mobilization.

KNOWLEDGE AND EDUCATION

After millennia of cultural elitism, Middle Eastern societies began democratizing education in the nineteenth century. Initially conceived in terms of elite formation, the change unintentionally launched one part of the mass mobilization that accompanies modernization. At first, different religious communities moved at different rates, a fact evidenced in the nineteenth century by the initial superiority of minority and foreign schools, which Muslims were for a long time reluctant to patronize. Differential rates of cultural change widened existing cleavages between subject and dominant communities, exacerbating nationalist resentments of Ottoman rule and creating or magnifying regional differentials in literacy and intellectual achievement, especially in localities like Lebanon, where non-Muslims were most numerous.

By the late twentieth century, the age of mass literacy had arrived for the Muslim majority. By then, democratizing education had long since become a consciously espoused goal of nationalist leaders. Ironically, however, just as this effort approached realization, it ran into massive obstacles created by the unprecedented twentieth-century population explosion. Increasingly a fact since about the 1930s, this was recognized as a critical issue by the 1960s.

Trying to expand education in the midst of explosive demographic growth has created an unmanageable cost-quality squeeze. Especially for poor, newly independent states still suffering the aftereffects of colonial educational policy, success in educational reform has proved a matter of realizing quantitatively, rather than qualitatively, defined goals. Outside observers have been quick to note the qualitative shortcomings of modern education in the Middle East, without recognizing the significance of achieving mass literacy in the face of such obstacles, both historical and contemporary.

The traditional Islamic world of knowledge can be understood in terms of four intellectual strands: religious studies (*ilm*), mysticism (*tasaw-wuf*), the worldly literary culture (*adab*), and the philosophy-science-mathematics continuum (*falsafah*). The growth of knowledge about the outside world began essentially as an expansion of adab culture toward the West. Nineteenth-century westernizers, beginning with members of governmental elites, emerged from an adab background as generalists and popularizers of Western culture. Sultans and statesmen would have found such a westward expansion in the falsafah culture even more desirable, especially in terms of military technology. In the scientific and technical (as opposed to the belletristic) fields, however, cultural westernization faced exceptional obstacles. Such obstacles were due to the decline of Islamic science and the higher costs and technical requirements of acquiring modern science and technology. In addition, the Islamic world's integration into a European-dominated global system served, through the capitulations and free trade as well as through military defeats, to undermine its technical and manufacturing capabilities. Under the circumstances, the acquisition of modern science and technology remained—after the aborted efforts of Muhammad Ali Pasha and his heirs, the Bey of Tunis and the Ottoman sultans—a goal for the twentieth century.

Meanwhile the cultural westernization that did occur created a profound and debilitating sense of cultural dualism. Islamic activists countered with vigorous responses but were held back by disputes among themselves over the acceptability in sharia terms of prevalent forms of popular religion and mysticism. Throughout the nineteenth and early twentieth centuries, with religious activists divided by internecine conflict over these issues, westernization seemed to carry the day. "Islamic resurgence" could not become a dominant theme in Middle Eastern cultural life until the victory of the sharia activists had resolved this conflict.

Education reform began, in the nineteenth century, to display common rhythms in the major centers of the Mediterranean Islamic world. Especially important milestones include the founding of the first modern military schools, then the first modern civil schools, the beginnings of a generalized system of public schools, and attempts at medrese reform. Schools for girls were founded late and lagged, except for missionary schools; the Turkish Republic pioneered in making coeducation an official policy. In general, the development of minority and foreign schools preceded and helped stimulate that of government schools.

The growth of literacy, a new interest in the outside world, and a sense of threat felt by Islamic activists all helped stimulate new developments in publishing. As governments began trying to reach their constituencies through mass diffusion, as moden print media emerged, and translation movements gave rise to new genres and messages, the Gutenberg Age at last arrived for the Middle East, bringing with it all the cultural baggage of nineteenth-century Europe. By the late nineteenth century, a publishing industry, and writers supported by their readers rather than by patrons, had begun to appear. Among the Ottomans, these innovations produced reform movements oriented chiefly at preserving the state; among Arabs, it was oriented toward a revival of Islam. Muslims everywhere, however, were agitated by a sense of conflict between Islamic and Western culture. This only yielded to a more confident outlook with the waning of European imperialism. But this confidence later ebbed as the performance of most postindependence states appeared inadequate to the tasks. Compared with China or Japan, the Middle East is a region of exceptional cultural complexity, with three major Islamic high-cultural languages not related to each other. The Middle East had the kind of ethnic heterogeneity seen in the Russian Empire and suffered much more from it because of the precocity of non-Muslim communities (as opposed to the politically dominant Muslims) in responding to modern innovations such as nationalism. In Russia, by contrast, political and cultural dominance more nearly coincided.

Japan was exceptionally well favored in being essentially a nation-state to start with. Moreover, it lacked a traditional religious elite, with vested interests in maintaining a traditional educational system, and no traditional orthodoxy existed to block or channel cultural change in the way Islamic law did. Japan's ethnic homogeneity spared it from the "pariah entrepreneurship" problem that the Ottomans faced with their non-Muslim commercial elites. Japan's population was also quicker to interest itself in Western forms of production rather than of consumption. This may well be linked to the fact that indigenous traditions of technology and manufacturing survived into the nineteenth century.

Japan also spent the shortest time of any major Asian country in subjection to the unequal trade regimes represented by capitulations in the Middle East, Britain's free-trade policy in India, or the Unequal Treaty System in East Asia. The ethnic and cultural homogeneity of the nation-state ideal, lack of any entrenched elite or ideology opposing cultural change, minimal rather than maximal exposure to Western encroachment and its technological, entrepreneurial, and cultural consequences—Japan's advantages merge in a mirror image of the Ottoman world's liabilities as it entered its era of modern cultural change.

A comparison of the growth of education and knowledge in the successor states reveals certain important commonalities. Modern schools were introduced into the Ottoman Empire, Egypt, and Tunisia by elites who came to realize that the traditional educational system could not provide the state with the kind of trained manpower needed to cope with powerful, external challenges. Since the most obvious need was for military reform, the first schools were designed to train military officers to lead the modern armies being established. Soon these schools proliferated, for it became clear that a modern military requires officers with a variety of specialized skills.

The state also required a modern bureaucracy because military power is dependent upon a modern infrastructure. Hence, a second stage of educational reform was initiated that involved opening schools wherein administrators could learn foreign languages and European techniques. It proved, however, difficult to produce modern officers and administrators from those who had received a traditional education. Moreover, an effective bureaucracy, like a powerful military, could not be based on a small number of well-trained officials at the top. Large numbers of persons with a modern education at all levels were required. Accordingly, the need for lower-level schools came to be recognized, and, in time, a network of modern civilian and military schools was created that stretched from the primary to the university. Concomitantly, missionaries and minorities opened schools to serve their respective communities. By the time of World War I, the region possessed a significant number of modern schools of different types coexisting with the traditional religious educational system.

The emergence of the successor states did not necessarily lead to a dramatic change in this pattern even though the importance of a modern education was, by then, widely recognized. Many of these states came under the rule of Britain and France. These foreign powers sought primarily to maintain the status quo; educational expansion was not one of their priorities. Only Turkey remained independent. There, Atatürk embarked upon a sweeping program of modernization in which education was accorded an important role. The kinds of reforms that he adopted—nationalizing the system, expanding and equalizing educational opportunities, integrating the religious and secular schools, relating the schools to economic needs—could not be implemented in the other states until they achieved their independence. Until then, only modest change took place; the modern systems remained small, fragmented, and elitist.

Independence was a necessary but not a sufficient condition, and only a few of the new states, such as Tunisia under Bourguiba and Egypt under Nasser, had a leadership that was able to develop and implement a coherent policy of modernization. Elsewhere, leaders tried to deal with the growing demands for education on an ad-hoc basis within a short-term framework. The importance of the state in shaping the pattern and pace of educational developments cannot be slighted. Strong states with a commitment to modernization and an effective leadership were able to carry through important reforms. Only Israel, Egypt, Tunisia, and Turkey, however, fit into this category. For an extended period of time and in the latter three countries, subsequent developments brought different regimes to power, thus exemplifying the "disjunctive modernization" pattern.

Whatever the regime, the demand for academic training proved insatiable, and every government had to devise means of accommodating all those who wished to acquire it. And, despite attempts at planning and the allocation of large amounts of resources, the constraints proved to be so severe that no government was able to maintain quality; shortages of facilities and teachers became commonplace. In such a context, educational reforms could lead only to incremental improvements in various parts of the system. It was not possible to enact the kind of program that would transform education so that it would function efficiently or be harmonized with the requirements of modernization. Nevertheless, these reforms did produce important structural changes and enabled large numbers of persons, including women, to acquire a modern education. Processes of diversification, differentiation, integration, and centralization continued, and modern educational systems were created, although important variations in the rate, scope, and intensity of these developments can be identified owing to differences in the nature of the society and polity.

These developments affected the course of modernization within the societies in many ways. Their impact, however, depended upon particular historical and other conditions. Nevertheless, it is obvious that the modern schools have been major channels for the diffusion of knowledge, ideas, and ideologies and their graduates played, and continue to play, important roles within their countries. In some cases, university students have also been active politically. Certainly, educational qualifications have become ever more significant in determining status, though the precise connection between social background and education varies from society to society. Still, one can not assume that the spread of modern education will inevitably lead to higher rates of mobility for persons from lower- and middle-class backgrounds. Specific policies of sponsorship are required. Otherwise, children of upper- and upper-middle class backgrounds will tend, because of the advantages they possess, to cluster in high-status institutions.

Traditional patterns and values have continued to retain their importance in these states; they coexist, more or less uneasily, with the modern institutions (as in the case of religious schools) or have influenced the way new schools function. Islamic customs have been resistant to innovation, as have the practices of former colonial rulers. The power of the Islamic revival and the continuing appeal of religious education illustrate the degree to which traditional practices remain important in the successor states.

CONCLUSIONS

A few general findings concerning modernization in the Ottoman Empire and those successor states selected for study here may now be restated in summary form by way of conclusion.

Such disjunctive regional development, emphasized in the preceding pages, can itself be attributed in large measure to the continuing problem of determining the boundaries of the state. From an Ottoman Empire that before World War I constituted de jure a single unit but de facto more nearly three polities of vastly different size and resources (the central Ottoman Empire ruled from Istanbul, plus autonomous Egypt and Tunisia), that portion of the Middle East examined in this book is now divided into eight different political units. Moreover, these eight polities not only continue to be characterized by vastly different size (whether measured in territory or people) and different resources, but even greater variations separate them when measured by the extent to which they are accepted as legitimate by their own peoples.

All of which is to suggest the great importance of institutional continuity represented by the state as a positive factor in modernization. The Ottoman Empire was not the first, nor the last imperial system, to break up into smaller states (witness developments in the Soviet Union at present). But few imperial breakups have consumed as much time, and the process is not yet completed. Indeed, the entire period of Middle Eastern modernization, or roughly the last two centuries, has evolved in the context of the slow dismemberment of a centuries-old imperial political system and the still incomplete transitional period toward some new political pattern. This amounts to a phenomenon radically different from that faced by the first modernizing nations or by such states as Japan or Russia. To a large extent, the time as well as the intellectual and material resources devoted to the not-yet resolved question of the size and nature of the state and of its undergirding civil society must be listed on the debit side of the Middle Eastern modernizing ledger.

Nor did Western colonial rule, which existed in all successor states considered except Turkey, offer a continuity of experience. Different colonizing powers, different forms of colonial rule, and different periods of colonialism only added to the disparity and diversity.

Both economically and strategically the Middle East has been in modern times especially attractive to outside powers. From early in the nineteenth century with such primary products as cotton and, later, petroleum, the Middle East has been a source of needed raw materials for finished products from the industrialized world (the Middle East being the only Third World region sharing a border with Europe). Such slogans as "lifeline to India" or the "bridge to three continents" serve to emphasize the way in which the Middle East has become in modern times, more—it can be argued—than any other world region, the most convenient arena for proxy battles waged by clients of the Great Powers. The lineup of the Great Powers most directly involved has changed more than once since Napoleon landed in Egypt as long ago as 1798, but the Middle Eastern variant of the "great game in Asia" continues apace. Thus far, neither the outside powers nor the political leaders of the area have shown a capacity completely to break out of this bind of squandering resources and diverting attention away from basic infrastructural development.

In the early phase of modernization—while the old imperial system was being slowly torn asunder—Middle Eastern political leaders sought salvation in terms of military modernization. Alas for the region, the efforts of Egypt's Muhammad Ali (not to mention the later Khedive Ismail), Tunisia's Ahmad Bey plus the even more sustained endeavors of the Ottomans from Selim III until the end of empire prefigured a strategic syndrome that exists to this day. Indeed, the total proportion of societal resources devoted to the military has increased to grotesque proportions.

The inability of these states to reach acceptable and stable decisions on their national borders is thus to be seen as necessarily linked to a complex network of mutual reinforcing causal factors, including the weak political legitimacy of most of the existing political units, excessive emphasis on military build-up with a corresponding role for the military in politics, and uninterrupted regional involvement in the politics of the Great Powers.

Middle Eastern social organizations on the eve of modern times meshed in a way that had long provided for considerable stability and certainly for institutional longevity. Compounding the problem of those who would opt for modernization, however, was that the very strength of premodern social institutions proved often to be obstacles in the way of needed change. A state system that restricted its function to providing minimal security and collecting taxes necessary for maintaining usually quite small governmental cadres left the basic modern tasks of health, education, and welfare to the smaller units of society organized according to some combination of religion, tribe, locality, and family. Middle Eastern peoples being neither yoked together by the state for shared goals nor encouraged by nongovernmental institutions or ideologies to achieve the aims of a single civil society necessarily brought to the experience of modernization a legacy of fissiparous resistance. Why, indeed, would a people accustomed to living close to the lower limits of physical security and material well-being choose to exchange all the old defenses to be found in family, clan, and religion for a nebulous and alien notion of a centralizing nation-state?

Moreover, the would-be initiators of change have usually acted against the religious establishment, Muslim or non-Muslim. Or, at best, such modernizers have been able, for a time, to co-opt certain spokesmen from within the religious establishments in a way that has risked undermining their status as legitimate interpreters of ultimate values. Put differently, the Middle East was denied the Western temporal sequence of ideological preparation (Reformation, Renaissance, moves toward secularization) followed later by material modernization (commercial and industrial revolutions). So, too, were the rest of the world, but here again the Middle Eastern inability to settle the issue of the extent and nature of the different political communities largely frustrated what might otherwise have emerged as growing alliances of governmental and nongovernmental forces.

In the same way, all too many nongovernmental forces for modernization, such as the small entrepreneurial class, were to be found outside the majority community (a disproportionate number being non-Muslim) and had neither the desire nor the ability to be co-opted to modernizing state-building groups. At this point, yet again, the Middle East as an arena of international political maneuvering in modern times looms large. There was no lack of outside powers willing to enlist the minorities (including the minority entrepreneurs) as clients. Such actions, in turn, only decreased further the likelihood that minorities would be accepted and integrated into future political systems.

The same variegated and disjunctive approach to modernization was to be found in education. Potentially, no institutional network can more effectively change the orientation of an entire society than a coherent system of formal education. Instead, for all of the area during most of modern times, and for most of the area even to this day, the pattern has been one of diverse educational approaches (religious versus state, public versus private, indigenous versus foreign, traditional and rote versus modern and flexible).

Finally, the Middle Eastern demographic explosion that has taken place during the past several generations (which in certain countries has hardly begun to slacken) is forcing those who would work to foster modernization to, indeed, run even faster if only to stay in the same place.

A confused and rather bleak picture, yes. Still, major societal change even in the best of circumstances is rather like a battle with many armies involved. Not even the leaders can have an adequate image of developments. The contest is usually won by those generals who make the fewest mistakes. In the Middle East, as for that matter in most of the Third World, the battle of modernization continues. The Middle East studied in this book has changed enormously in the past two centuries. The many negative elements hampering the effective integration of these massive changes into stable and dynamic systems are not to be wished away. They grow out of the confrontation of Middle Eastern culture with modern times. But certain positive elements should not be ignored, including, by Third World standards, impressive numbers of educated cadres, an economic resource base and existing per capita income and quality of life indices above much of Asia and Africa, and elements of a cultural legacy that can—more than has been done in the immediate past—be adapted to the creation of an ideology of pragmatic dynamism.

Bibliographical Essay*

CONSISTENT WITH THE approach adopted by the other books in this modernization series, the authors of *Modernization in the Middle East: The Ottoman Empire and its Afro-Asian Successors* have sought to produce a coherent work of synthesis that the educated lay person can follow without the distraction of references and notes that would be meaningful only to specialists. At the same time, acknowledging the sources relied on in producing this book is essential, and such is the first aim of this bibliography.

A second aim is to provide guidance to those seeking additional readings on selected subjects. Certain contributors have produced quite detailed bibliographies. Listings of sources and suggested readings for other chapters are much more limited. To hammer all chapter bibliographies into a consistency of breadth and depth would be to sacrifice the useful detail offered by some without gaining any offsetting advantage.

The variation in bibliographies is also a function of the subject treated in the different chapters. Certain chapters lend themselves more to statistical and quantifiable approaches, e.g., the chapters treating economics, society, and knowledge and education, and the sources of such data must be indicated. Others address subjects that are covered to some extent, and often to a considerable extent, in virtually every work on the modern Middle East. This is more nearly the case for the chapters on the international context and on politics. It thus makes sense to have more detailed bibliographies for the former group, but a more selective indication of sources consulted or suggested additional readings for the latter.

The bibliographical chapter offers first a brief note on the basic reference works on the modern Middle East. This is followed by bibliographies keyed to the appropriate chapters.

Basic Reference Works

The standard multivolume encyclopedia is the *Encyclopaedia of Islam*. The second edition, much less "Orientalist" than the first edition, is still being written, with 7 volumes and fascicules up to the letter M (Mifrash-Mirwaha) having already appeared. The *Encyclopaedia of Islam* covers the entire Muslim world and the whole period of Muslim history, not just the Middle East and modern times. It is also quite detailed and specialized. Nevertheless, many of the articles can be useful to nonspecialists,

---

*A complete list of works cited arranged alphabetically by author is to be found beginning on p. 357.

e.g., those on specific countries or public figures. Thorough cross referencing and bibliographies for the separate articles add to its utility.

A single volume handbook is *The Middle East and North Africa*. The fifth edition (Oxford University Press, 1980) was edited by Peter Mansfield. This would cover all countries treated in *Modernization in the Middle East: The Ottoman Empire and its Afro-Asian Successors* except for Tunisia. For this country consult the companion volume edited by Wilfrid Knapp, *Northwest Africa: A Political and Economic Survey* (3rd edition, Oxford University Press, 1977).

More recent is *The Cambridge Encyclopedia of the Middle East and North Africa*, executive editor, Trevor Moystn; advisory editor, Albert Hourani, Cambridge University Press, 1988, which is quite successful as a short single-volume encyclopedia. It is also well illustrated.

Yet another handbook that offers the advantage of annual updating is *The Middle and North Africa*, one in a series of annual handbooks published by Europa Publications. This is strong on updated statistical data and narration of recent political and economic events, but it lacks interpretive explanation, and the historical background is scant.

Most general readers would surely prefer to consult, first, not an encyclopedia or handbook but a single work that provides a clearly delineated interpretive framework. Several such books will be cited in the separate chapter bibliographies, but a few titles can be listed here.

Two studies treating the Ottoman Empire and then (after the First World War) the Republic of Turkey can probably be classified as "modernization studies." They are Niyazi Berkes, *The Development of Secularism in Turkey* (McGill University Press, 1964), and Bernard Lewis, *The Emergence of Modern Turkey* (Oxford University Press, 1961, with later paperback editions). Volume Two of the two-volume *History of the Ottoman Empire and Modern Turkey*, entitled *Reform, Revolution and Republic: The Rise of Modern Turkey, 1808–1975*, by Stanford J. Shaw and Ezel Kural Shaw (Cambridge University Press, 1977), is a detailed narrative of political and institutional history.

All three concentrate on the central Ottoman Empire (those lands ruled directly from Istanbul) and then, after the First World War, restrict their coverage to the Republic of Turkey. (Shaw and Shaw do, however, provide more coverage than the other two on the Arab lands under Ottoman rule.) To get the basic political and institutional history of modernization in the Arab portions of the Empire one must look elsewhere, often to histories of individual countries. Certain of these will be cited in the chapter bibliographies. More complete listings can be found in the encyclopedias and handbooks listed above. For present purposes one highly acclaimed general study is recommended. This is *A History of the Arab Peoples* by Albert Hourani (Harvard University Press, 1991). Somewhat more than half of this work treats the Arab world during the Ottoman and then the modern period. Moreover, while the subject is clearly the Arab world, Hourani is able to depict that world since the sixteenth century in its proper Ottoman context. He avoids the error found in many earlier general accounts of assuming anachronistically an Arab nationalism before it emerged (just as some other accounts assume a Turkish nationalism prematurely).

CHAPTER THREE
International Context

The standard account of "Eastern Question" diplomacy is M. S. Anderson, *The Eastern Question, 1774–1923: A Study in International Relations* (London, 1966, with later paperback editions). This supersedes earlier works such as J. A. R. Marriott, *The Eastern Question: An Historical Study in European Diplomacy* (Oxford University Press, four editions between 1917 and 1940). The problem with these works, however, for present purposes is that the Eastern Question has long been perceived as a theme in modern European history, and the approach taken is decidedly Eurocentric. Marriott's subtitle makes that point quite explicitly. Anderson gives much more attention to the Middle Eastern side of the story, but even he is writing essentially from a European perspective.

International Politics and the Middle East: Old Rules, Dangerous Game (Princeton University Press, 1984) by L. Carl Brown seeks to interpret Eastern Question diplomatic history as seen from the Middle East. It also argues that if one accepts to view the Eastern Question as an example of intensive involvement among the Great Powers and the Middle East then the Eastern Question did not go out of existence with the demise of the Ottoman Empire. It continues to this day as a distinctive pattern of diplomacy or what political scientists would call an "international relations subsystem." This book also has a bibliographical essay that can introduce readers to other works on the general subject.

The Middle East and North Africa in World Politics: A Documentary Record, edited by J. C. Hurewitz, offers not just the texts of treaties and other diplomatic documents but prefaces each entry with a succinct explanation of the historical context followed by suggestions for further readings. Volume one, *European Expansion, 1535–1914* (Yale University Press, 1975) is relevant to this chapter.

CHAPTER FOUR
Political Structure

The books by Berkes, Lewis, and Shaw & Shaw, cited before, cover this subject, concentrating on the central Ottoman Empire with less coverage of the Arab lands treated in this book and virtually none on Tunisia. A short book by Norman Itzkowitz, *Ottoman Empire and Islamic Tradition* (New York, 1972), offers an effective overview of Ottoman institutions up to roughly the beginning of the modernization period.

For political history of the Arab countries treated in this book, the foregoing works can be supplemented by a number of single-country studies. Only a few will be noted here. Others can be found in the standard bibliographical listings.

For Egypt:
Lufti al Sayyid Marsot, *A Short History of Modern Egypt* (Cambridge University Press, 1985) and P. J. Vatikiotis *The History of Egypt From Muhammad Ali to Mubarak* (3rd edition, Johns Hopkins University Press, 1985).

For the Fertile Crescent:
A good general overview concentrating on political history is Peter M. Holt, *Egypt and the Fertile Crescent, 1516–1922: A Political History* (Cornell University Press, 1966). See also the more recent M. E. Yapp, *The Making of the Modern Near East, 1792–1923* (Longman, London & New York, 1987), which includes a useful annotated bibliography.

There are several good works on the smallest country, Lebanon, and certain of these deserve mention not only for the light they shed on that country in the pre-World War I period but also because the themes they raise are relevant to other countries studied in this book. It is perhaps most useful to view Lebanon not as a "typical" but rather as an "extreme" case that illuminates sharply developments that occurred, but less clearly, in many other Middle Eastern countries. Three books will be mentioned: Iliya Harik, *Politics and Change in a Traditional Society: Lebanon, 1711–1845* (Princeton University Press, 1968); Samir Khalaf, *Lebanon's Predicament*

(Columbia University Press, 1987); and Kamal Salibi, *The Modern History of Lebanon* (Praeger, 1965). A good single-country study on Iraq is Phebe Marr, *The Modern History of Iraq* (Westview Press, 1985); for Syria plus Lebanon and Palestine, A. L. Tibawi, *A Modern History of Syria Including Lebanon and Palestine* (London, 1969). Other single-country studies could be cited, but they can be found in standard sources (e.g., *The Cambridge Encyclopedia of the Middle East and North Africa* or the Yapp book noted before). It may be more useful here to mention a few more specialized works that touch in part on the subject matter of this chapter. Several chapters in *Beginnings of Modernization in the Middle East*, edited by William R. Polk and Richard L. Chambers (University of Chicago Press, 1968), are relevant, including "Some Aspects of the Aims and Achievements of the Nineteenth-Century Ottoman Reformers" by Stanford Jay Shaw; "The Modernization of Syria: Problems and Solutions in the Early Period of Abdulhamid" by Shimon Shamir; and "The Advent of the Principle of Representation in the Government of the Ottoman Empire" by Roderic H. Davison.

Two important political/institutional studies are both by Carter Vaughn Findley—*Bureaucratic Reform in the Ottoman Empire: The Sublime Porte, 1789–1922* (Princeton University Press, 1980) and *Ottoman Civil Officialdom: A Social History* (Princeton University Press, 1989). A similarly focused study for Egypt is *Egypt Under the Khedives, 1805–1879: From Household government to Modern Bureaucracy* (University of Pittsburgh Press, 1984), by F. Robert Hunter.

See also the references to Albert Hourani, Hanna Batatu, Philip Khoury, and Moshe Ma'oz in the bibliography for Chapter Six.

For Tunisia, *The Tunisia of Ahmad Bey* by L. Carl Brown (Princeton University Press, 1974) has the advantage of being explicitly a modernization study. It situates the activities associated with Ahmad Bey, who reigned from 1835 to 1857, in a comparative context with Egypt in the time of Muhammad Ali and the Ottoman Empire under the modernizing sultans Selim III and Mahmud II. This can be followed by a solid monograph that deserves to be better known: *Relations Internationales et Sous-developpement: La Tunisie, 1857–1864* (Acta Universitatis Upsaliensis, Studia Historica Upsaliensia 102, Uppsala, 1978), by Mezri Bdira.

CHAPTER FIVE
Economic Structure and Growth

There are two general economic histories of the region, Charles Issawi, *An Economic History of the Middle East and North Africa* (Columbia University Press, 1982) and E. R. J. Owen, *The Middle East in the World Economy, 1800–1914* (Methuen, 1981); both contain extensive bibliographies. Charles Issawi, *The Economic History of the Middle East* (University of Chicago Press, 1966), is a collection of documents dealing with some aspects of the economies of the various countries in the period 1800–1914. A very good study of the foreign trade and balance of payments of the Ottoman Empire, and of the movement of foreign capital into it, is Şevket Pamuk, *The Ottoman Empire and European Capitalism, 1820–1913* (Cambridge University Press, 1987). A valuable collection of available Ottoman statistics is Justin McCarthy, *The Arab World, Turkey and the Balkans (1878–1914)* (Boston, 1982).

The coverage of the individual countries varies widely. Egypt has been studied most intensively. A. E. Crouchley, *The Economic Development of Modern Egypt* (London, 1938), although somewhat dated, is a useful introduction. A. E. Abd al-Maqsud Hamza, *The Public Debt of Egypt, 1854–1867* (Cairo, 1934) is still authoritative, as is A. E. Croughley, *The Investment of Foreign Capital in Egyptian Companies and Public Debt* (Cairo, 1934). E. R. J. Owen, *Cotton and the Egyptian Economy* (Oxford University Press, 1969) is a thorough study of what was by far the leading sector of the economy. Some articles and unpublished papers by Bent Hansen have pioneered the quantitative study of various aspects of the Egyptian economy in the late nineteenth and early twentieth centuries; e.g., Bent Hansen and Michael Wattleworth, "Agricultural Output and Consumption of Basic Foods," *International Journal of Middle Eastern Studies*, November 1978.

A comprehensive documentary history of Turkey is Charles Issawi, *The Economic History of Turkey* (University of Chicago Press, 1980). Reşat Kasaba, *The Ottoman Empire and the World Economy, The Nineteenth Century*, (State University of New York Press, 1988), focuses on trade and investment in Western Anatolia. The Ottoman Public Debt has been the subject of a large literature, the best book still being Donald Blaisdall, *European Financial Capital in the Ottoman Empire* (New York, 1929). Similarly, the best study in English of the Baghdad Railway is Edward Meade Earle, *Turkey, The Great Powers and the Baghdad Railway* (New York, 1923).

Charles Issawi's *The Fertile Crescent, 1800–1914* (Oxford University Press, 1988) is a documentary history covering Iraq, Syria, Lebanon, Palestine, and Jordan in 1800–1914. Two symposia on Palestine contain valuable economic studies: Gad Gilbar, editor, *Ottoman Palestine, 1800–1914* (Leiden, 1990) and David Kushner, editor, *Palestine in the Late Ottoman Period* (Jerusalem–Leiden, 1986). A valuable study on Lebanon, focussing on silk and foreign trade, is Boutros Labaki, *Introduction à l'histoire économique du Liban* (Beirut, 1984).

Little is available in English on the economic history of Tunisia. The best book is Lucette Valensi, *Tunisian Peasants in the Eighteenth and Nineteenth Centuries* (Cambridge University Press, 1985). The literature in French is extensive. Mention may be made of Jean Ganiage, *Les origines du Protectorat français en Tunisie* (Paris, 1959), and Jean Poncet, *La colonisation et l'agriculture européennes en Tunisie* (Paris, 1962).

CHAPTER SIX
Social Interdependence

Premodern trends are examined broadly in Halil Inalcik, "Military and Fiscal Transformation in the Ottoman Empire," *Archivum Ottomanicum*, 5 (1980), 283–307. A useful collection of essays, most of which are pertinent to Ottoman Afro-Asia, is *Studies in Eighteenth Century Islamic History*, ed. Thomas Naff and E. R. J. Owen (Southern Illinois University Press, 1978). Implications of the premodern trends for nineteenth and early twentieth century history in the region are succinctly and elegantly discussed by Albert Hourani, "The Ottoman Background of the Modern Middle East," in *The Emergence of the Modern Middle East* (Berkeley: University of California Press, 1981).

The case for urban spatial and commercial growth during the Ottoman period is made by Andre Raymond, *The Great Arab Cities in the 16th–18th Centuries* (New York University Press, 1984). Urban-rural relations in Damascus province are discussed by Abdul-Karim Rafeq, "Economic Relations Between Damascus and the Dependent Countryside, 1743–1771," in *The Islamic Middle East*, ed. A. L. Udovitch (Princeton: Darwin Press, 1981), 653–685.

Shifts in trade patterns are analyzed in Thomas Philipp, *The Syrians in Egypt, 1725–1975* (Stuttgart, 1985). See also Amnon Cohen, *Palestine in the Eighteenth Century: Patterns of Government and Administration* (Hebrew University Press, 1973), and, more recently, Bruce Masters, *The Origins of Western Economic Dominance in the Middle East: Mercantilism and the Islamic Economy in Aleppo, 1600–1750* (New York University Press, 1988). Thomas Philipp, *The Syrians in Egypt*, also discusses the demographic shift among Syrian Christians during the eighteenth century and beyond.

In addition to the lengthier studies of Berkes and Lewis, previously cited, and that of Roderic H. Davison, *Reform in the Ottoman Empire, 1856–1876* (Princeton University Press, 1963), an excellent treatment of Ottoman reform pertinent to a discussion of social interdependence is Halil Inalcik, "Application of the Tanzimat and its Social Effects," *Archivum Ottomanicum*, 5 (1973), 97–127. For the role of the "notables" in mediating the reform program, or resisting it, see the classic article by Albert Hourani, "Ottoman Reform and the Politics of Notables," in *Beginnings of Modernization in the Middle East: the Nineteenth Century*, ed. William R. Polk and Richard Chambers (University of Chicago Press, 1966), 41–68. A study of Damascene notables' adaptation to change is Philip S. Khoury, *Urban Notables and Arab Nationalism; the Politics of Damascus, 1860–1920* (Cambridge University Press, 1983), which is also pertinent to an understanding of the notables elsewhere in the region.

Patterns of settlement and demographic data for the period considered are contained in a number of recent works. For cities in the premodern period, see Raymond, *Great Arab Cities*. Charles Issawi, in *An Economic History of the Middle East and North Africa*, provides statistics for the nineteenth and twentieth centuries. Further data for different regions are contained in Justin McCarthy, "The Population of Ottoman Syria and Iraq, 1878–1914," *Asian and African Studies*, 15 (1981), and in his *Muslims and Minorities: the Population of Ottoman Anatolia and the End of the Empire* (New York University Press, 1983). Statistics for Tunisia may be consulted in Lucette Valensi, *Tunisian Peasants in the Eighteenth and Nineteenth Centuries*, and in Nancy E. Gallagher, *Medicine and Power in Tunisia, 1780–1900* (Cambridge University Press, 1983). An extensive collection of Ottoman statistics, and a discussion thereof, is Kemal Karpat, *Ottoman Population, 1830–1914: Demographic and Social Characteristics* (University of Wisconsin Press, 1985).

The growth of coastal towns is discussed by Issawi, *An Economic History*, passim; and, for Beirut, by Leila Fawaz, *Merchants and Migrants in Nineteenth-Century Beirut* (Harvard University Press, 1983).

Studies of religious-communal organization or the millet system may be consulted in *Christians and Jews in the Ottoman Empire: The Functioning of a Plural Society*, ed. Benjamin Braude and Bernard Lewis (2 vols.; New York, 1982). The impact of the Tanzimat on the Syrian provinces is examined by Moshe Maoz, *Ottoman Reform in Syria and Palestine, 1840–1861: The Impact of the Tanzimat on Politics and Society* (Oxford University Press, 1968). An important and useful discussion of the millet system within the context of the Ottoman empire's social organization as a whole is Kemal Karpat, *An Inquiry into the Social Foundations of Nationalism in the Ottoman State: From Social Estates to Classes, From Millets to Nations* (Princeton: Center for International Studies Monograph No. 39, 1973). Karpat's analysis adds ideological and economic elements to the usual discussion of religious identity and intercommunal conflict, and, for that reason, it has served to inform the discussion of social interdependence in this chapter.

For the status of women see the pioneering study by Judith Tucker, *Women in Nineteenth-Century Egypt* (Cambridge University Press, 1985). The impact of economic change on the work force in one part of Ottoman Afro-Asia is treated by Donald Quataert in *Social Disintegration and Popular Resistance in the Ottoman Empire, 1881–1908: Reactions to European Economic Penetration* (New York University Press, 1983). Religious-communal tensions resulting in part from economic change are discussed by Linda Schatkowski-Schilcher, *Families in Politics: Damascene Factions and Estates of the 18th and 19th Centuries* (Stuttgart, 1985).

The transformation of the Sufi life or way is vividly portrayed by Albert Hourani in two papers, "Sufism and Modern Islam: Mawlana Khalid and the Naqshbandi Order," and "Sufism and Modern Islam: Rashid Rida," in *The Emergence of the Modern Middle East* (University of California Press, 1981).

The evolution of municipal institutions is discussed by Gabriel Baer, "The Beginnings of Municipal Government," in *Studies in the Social History of Modern Egypt* (University of Chicago Press, 1969), and by William L. Cleveland, "The Municipal Council of Tunis, 1858–1870: a Study in Urban Institutional Change," *International Journal of Middle East Studies*, 9 (1978). See also the article "Baladiyya" in the *Encyclopaedia of Islam* (New edition). For the provincial councils, see Stanford J. Shaw, "The Origins of Representative Government in the Ottoman Empire: an Introduction to the Provincial Councils, 1839–1876," in *Near Eastern Roundtable, 1967–68*, ed. R. Bayly Winder (New York University, 1969), pp. 53–142. The case of Mount Lebanon's council is discussed by Samir Khalaf in *Persistence and Change in Nineteenth-Century Lebanon* (American University of Beirut Press, 1979).

Discussions of the region's economy are contained in the standard histories by Charles Issawi and E. R. J. Owen, to which may be added Bruce Masters, *The Origins of Western Economic Dominance in the Middle East,* and Sevket Pamuk, *The Ottoman Empire and World Capitalism, 1820–1913*, both cited earlier. Changes in land tenure are discussed by Kemal Karpat, "The Land Regime, Social Structure, and Modernization in the Ottoman Empire," in *Beginnings of Modernization in the Middle East: The Nineteenth Century*, ed. William R. Polk and Richard Chambers.

CHAPTER SEVEN
Knowledge and Education

The conceptualization of the general state of knowledge and education (pp. 1–5) draws primarily on Marshall G. S. Hodgson, *The Venture of Islam: Conscience and History in a World Civilization* (University of Chicago Press, 1974); Fazlur Rahman, *Islam and Modernity: Transformation of an Intellectual Tradition* (University of Chicago Press, 1982); Bernard Lewis, *The Emergence of Modern Turkey*; id., *The Muslim Discovery of Europe* (New York, 1982); Ibrahim Abu-Lughod, *Arab Rediscovery of Europe: A Study in Cultural Encounters* (Princeton University Press, 1963); Madeline C. Zilfi, *The Politics of Piety: The Ottoman Ulema in the Postclassical Age (1600–1800)* (Minneapolis, 1988); Abdülhak Adnan Adivar, *Osmanli Türklerinde Ilim* (Istanbul, 1943); and id., *La science chez les turcs ottomans* (Paris, 1939). The idea of the "tangled magic garden" mentality comes from Michael Gilsenan, *Saint and Sufi in Modern Egypt: An Essay in the Sociology of Religion* (Oxford University Press, 1973). The broader background on these subjects appears in Carter Vaughn Findley, *Bureaucratic Reform in the Ottoman Empire: The Sublime Porte, 1789–1922* (Princeton University Press, 1989), especially chapters 4–5; and id., "Knowledge and Education in the Modern Middle East: A Comparative View," in *The Modern Economic and Social History of the Middle East in its World Context*, ed. Georges Sabagh (Cambridge University Press, 1989). For a comprehensive bibliography on education and related topics in all lands, and among all communities, that were under Ottoman rule, see the relevant headings in the *Turkologischer Anzeiger*, Vienna, published annually from 1973 on, initially as a supplement in the *Wiener Zeitschrift für die Kunde des Morgenlandes* and, from 1975 on, as separate yearly volumes; this series is under the general editorship of Andreas Tietze. To some degree, the same kind of bibliographical coverage can be extended back, prior to 1973, by consulting Hans-Jürgen Kornrumpf, *Osmanische Bibliographie mit besonderer Be-*

rücksichtigung der Türkei in Europa (Leiden, 1973) (*Handbuch der Orientalistik, Ergänzungsband VIII*) and James D. Pearson, *Index Islamicus: A Catalogue of Articles of Islamic Subjects in Periodicals and Other Collective Publications* (London, 1958–).

On the development of schools in Turkey, the still-indispensable source is Osman Ergin, *Istanbul Mektepleri ve Ilim, Terbiye ve San'at Müesseseleri Dolayisile Türkiye Maarif Tarihi* (referred to below as *Türkiye Maarif Tarihi*), 5 vols. (Istanbul, 1939–1943). Ergin also includes valuable information on minority and missionary schools. See also Yahya Akyüz, *Türk Egitim Tarihi* (Ankara, 1982); Hasan Ali Koçer, *Türkiye 'de Modern Egitimin Dogusu ve Gelisimi (1773–1923)* (Istanbul, 1970); Reşat Özalp, *Milli Egitimle Ilgili Mevzuat (1857–1923)* (Istanbul, 1982); Bayram Kodaman, *Abdülhamid Devri Egitim Sistemi* (Istanbul, 1980); Faik Resit Unat, *Türkiye Egitim Sisteminin Gelismesine Tarihi bir Bakis* (Ankara, 1964); Joseph Szyliowicz, *Education and Modernization in the Middle East* (Cornell University Press, 1973), and Andreas M. Kazamias, *Education and the Quest for Modernity in Turkey* (London, 1966).

On Egyptian schools (pp. 7–9, 14–19), see J. Heyworth-Dunne, *An Introduction to the History of Education in Modern Egypt* (London, n.d.: c. 1938); Afaf Lutfi al-Sayyid Marsot, *Egypt in the Reign of Muhammad Ali* (Cambridge University Press, 1984); F. Robert Hunter, *Egypt under the Khedives, 1805–1879: From Household Government to Modern Bureaucracy*; Robert L. Tignor, *Modernization and British Colonial Rule in Egypt, 1992–1914* (Princeton University Press, 1966); P. J. Vatikiotis, *The History of Egypt from Muhammad Ali to Mubarak*; Ahmad 'Izzat 'Abd al-Karim, *Ta'rikh al-Ta'lim fi 'Asr Muhammad 'Ali* (Cairo, 1938); Sa'id Isma'il 'Ali, *Ta'rikh al-Tarbiyah wa al-Ta'lim fi Misr* (Cairo, 1985); Bayard Dodge, *Al-Azhar: A Millennium of Muslim Learning* (Washington, 1961, 1974).

On Tunisia (pp. 9–10, 19–20), see L. Carl Brown, *The Tunisia of Ahmad Bey, 1837–1855* (Princeton University Press, 1974).

Information on the Greek, Jewish, and Armenian schools (pp. 22–24) comes from Ergin, *Türkiye Maarif Tarihi*, which summarizes a number of original sources not otherwise readily available, and from A. Synvet, *Les grecs de l'Empire ottoman* (Istanbul, 1878); Avedis K. Sanjian, *The Armenian Communities in Syria under Ottoman Dominion* (Harvard University Press, 1965); Avram Galanti, *Türk Harsi ve Türk Tahudisi: Tarihî, Siyasî, Ictimaî Tetkik* (Istanbul, 1953); id., *Türkler ve Yahudiler: Tarihî, Siyasî, Tetkik*, (Istanbul, 1947); and Paul Dumont, "Jewish Communities in Turkey during the Last Decades of the Nineteenth Century in the Light of the Archives of the Alliance Israélite Universelle," in *Christians and Jews in the Ottoman*

Empire:- The Functioning of a Plural Society, ed. Benjamin Braude and Bernard Lewis (New York, 1982), vol. I, pp. 209–42. The same volumes, edited by Braude and Lewis, also contain extensive bibliographies on the non-Muslim communities in vol. II, pp. 207–223.

On non-Muslim schools in the Arab lands and also Muslim schools in Syria and Lebanon, see K. S. Salibi, *The Modern History of Lebanon*; Abdul Latif Tibawi, *Arabic and Islamic Themes: Historical, Educational and Literary Studies*, London, 1976; id., *Islamic Education: Its Traditions and Modernization into the Arab National Systems* (London, 1972); id., *A Modern History of Syria, including Lebanon and Palestine*; and Doris Behrens-Abouseif, "The Political Situation of the Copts, 1798–1923," in Benjamin Braude and Bernard Lewis, eds., *Christians and Jews in the Ottoman Empire: The Functioning of a Plural Society*, vol. II.

For additional information on missionary schools, see Joseph L. Grabill, *Protestant Diplomacy and the Near East: Missionary Influence on American Policy, 1810–1927* (Minneapolis, 1971); Robert L. Daniel, *American Philanthropy in the Near East, 1820–1960* (Athens, Ohio, 1970); Abdul Latif Tibawi, *American Interests in Syria, 1800–1901* (Oxford University Press, 1966); David H. Finnie, *Pioneers East: The Early American Experience in the Middle East* (Harvard University Press, 1967); and Derek Hopwood, *The Russian Presence in Syria and Palestine, 1843–1914: Church and Politics in the Near East* (Oxford University Press, 1969).

The literacy statistics cited on p. 29 derive from Charles Issawi, *An Economic History of the Middle East and North Africa*, p. 14 (Egypt, Syria) and Stanford J. Shaw and Ezel Kural Shaw, *History of the Ottoman Empire and Modern Turkey*, vol. II: *Reform, Revolution, and Republic: The Rise of Modern Turkey, 1808–1975*, p. 387 (Turkey). On the early history of publication, see William J. Watson, "Ibrahim Müteferrika and Turkish Incunabula," *Journal of the American Oriental Society*, LXXXVIII (1968), and Richard N. Verdery, "The Publications of the Bulaq Press under Muhammad 'Ali of Egypt," *Journal of the American Oriental Society*, XCI (1971), 129–32.

On new trends in thought among Ottoman Turks, see Fatma Müge Göçek, *East Encounters West: France and the Ottoman Empire in the Eighteenth Century* (New York, 1987); Stanford J. Shaw, *Between Old and New: The Ottoman Empire under Sultan Selim III (1789–1807)* (Harvard University Press, 1971); Uriel Heyd, "The Ottoman 'Ulema and Westernization in the Time of Selim III and Mahmud II," *Scripta Hierosalymitana*, IX: *Studies in Islamic History and Civilization* (1961), pp. 63–96; Serif Mardin, "Some Notes on an Early Phase in the Modernization of Communications in

Turkey," *Comparative Studies in Society and History,* III (1961), pp. 250—71; id., *The Genesis of Young Ottoman Thought: A Study in the Modernization of Turkish Political Ideas* (Princeton University Press, 1962); Niyazi Berkes, *The Development of Secularism in Turkey;* Richard L. Chambers, "The Education of a Nineteenth-Century Ottoman *Alim,* Ahmed Cevdet Pasa," *International Journal of Middle Eastern Studies,* IV (1973); Uriel Heyd, *Foundations of Turkish Nationalism: The Life and Teachings of Ziya Gökalp* (London, 1950); and Tarik Zafer Tunaya, *Islâmcilik Cereyani: Ikinci Mesrutiyetin Siyasi Hayati Boyunca Gelixmesi ve Bugüne Biraktigi Meseleler* (Istanbul, 1962). On intellectual trends among the Arabs (primarily), see Gilbert Delanoue, *Moralistes et politiques musulmans dans l'Egypte du XIXᵉ siècle,* 2 vols. (Cairo, 1982); Albert Hourani, *Arabic Thought in the Liberal Age, 1798–1939* (Oxford University Press, 1962); Charles Wendell, *The Evolution of the Egyptian National Image: From Its Origins to Ahmad Lutfi al-Sayyid* (University of California Press, 1972); Nikki Keddie, *Jamal al-Din "al-Afghani": A Political Biography* (University of California Press, 1972); Malcolm Kerr, *Islamic Reform: The Political and Legal Theories of Muhammad 'Abduh and Rashid Rida* (University of California Press, 1966); and Hamid Enayat, *Modern Islamic Political Thought: The Response of the Shi'i and Sunni Muslims to the Twentieth Century* (University of Texas Press, 1982).

With specific reference to science and technology, see Fahim Qubain, *Education and Science in the Arab World* (Johns Hopkins University Press, 1966); Antoine B. Zahlan, "Established Patterns of Technology Acquisition in the Arab World," in *Technology Transfer and Change in the Arab World,* ed. Antoine B. Zahlan, Oxford, 1978; Ziauddin Sardar, *Science and Technology in the Middle East: A Guide to Issues, Organizations, and Institutions* (London, 1982); Edward C. Clark, "The Ottoman Industrial Revolution," *International Journal of Middle Eastern Studies,* V (1974); Ekmeleddin Ihsanoglu, ed., *Osmanli Ilmî ve Meslekî Cemiyetleri: 1. Millî Türk Tarihi Sempozyumu, 3–5 Nisan 1987* (Istanbul, 1987).

For international comparisons, see James R. Bartholomew, *The Formation of Science in Japan: Building a Research Tradition* (Yale University Press, 1989); Ronald P. Dore, *Education in Tokugawa Japan* (University of California Press, 1965); Wen-yuan Qian, *The Great Inertia: Scientific Stagnation in Traditional China* (London, 1985); Evelyn Rawski, *Education and Popular Literacy in Ch'ing China* (Ann Arbor, 1979); Claude A. Alvares, *Homo Faber: Technology and Culture in India, China and the West, 1500 to the Present* (New Delhi, 1979); Alun M. Anderson, *Science and Technology in Japan* (London, 1984); Tong B. Tang, *Science and Technology in China* (London, 1984).

CHAPTER TEN
International Context

An interpretive overview and a bibliographical essay is provided in Brown, *International Politics and the Middle East*, cited before.

Volume Two of the already cited Hurewitz book is entitled "British-French Supremacy, 1914–1945" (Yale University Press, 1979). A third volume continuing the documentary record beyond 1945 is in preparation.

A standard diplomatic history text is George Lenczowski, *The Middle East in World Affairs*, now in its fourth edition and available in paperback (Cornell University Press, 1980).

There is a wealth of material on the international relations of the modern and contemporary Middle East. They are listed in the bibliographies of the works noted above. Since the emphasis in this chapter is rather on the underlying system of international relations, the books cited here will be selective in that sense.

Three books treating an overlapping subject are recommended. They are Malcolm Kerr, *The Arab Cold War: Gamal Abd Al Nasir and His Rivals, 1958–1970* (3rd edition, Oxford University Press, 1965); Patrick Seale, *The Struggle for Syria: A Study of Post-War Arab Politics* (Oxford University Press, 1965, reissued by Yale University Press, 1987 available in paperback); and Nadav Safran, *Saudi Arabia: The Ceaseless Quest for Security* (Harvard University Press, 1985, reissued by Cornell University Press, 1988, available in paperback). All three are quite detailed books, and all but Kerr's (slightly more than 150 pages) are long. The nonspecialist may find it tedious to keep all the names and dates in order. Read them instead to get the sense of the underlying pattern of politics and diplomacy in the Middle East.

The Origins of Alliances by Stephen M. Walt (Cornell University Press, 1987) is an in-depth study of alliance making and breaking in the Middle East from the mid-1950s to the end of the 1970s. Walt is concerned to test whether these states are more likely to line up ("balance") against a threatening state or seek to join such a state in good time ("bandwagon").

The works on individual countries and specific Middle Eastern wars or crises are legion. Even a summary listing of such sources on just one major issue—the Arab-Israeli confrontation—would require pages. Better to refer the reader to the bibliographies following each article in the Hurewitz volumes or to the bibliographical essay in Brown, *International Politics and the Middle East*.

CHAPTER ELEVEN
Political Structure

For an analysis of the question of legitimacy in the Arab world, see especially Michael C. Hudson, *Arab Politics: The Search for Legitimacy* (Yale University Press, 1977). The characteristics of "command politics" encountered in many post-Ottoman successor states have been inspired by Ellen Kay Trimberger, *Revolution from Above: Military Bureaucrats and Development in Japan, Turkey, Egypt, and Peru* (New Brunswick: Transaction Books, 1978). The statistics on the expenditure of central government as a percentage of GNP are taken from Bruce M. Russett et al., *World Handbook of Political and Social Indicators* (Yale University Press, 1964), 60–61. The statistics on the changes in such percentages from the 1960s to the 1970s are based on Hudson, *Arab Politics,* 155–56. The percentage of the Egyptian work force on the public payroll is taken from John Waterbury, *The Egypt of Nasser and Sadat: The Political Economy of Two Regimes* (Princeton University Press, 1978), 242. Public sector employment figures on Iraq are taken from Joe Stork, "State Power and Economic Structure: Class Determination and State Formation in Contemporary Iraq," in Tim Niblock, ed., *Iraq: The Contemporary State* (London, 1982), 36, 39. Figures on public investment in Iraq are based on Rodney Wilson, "Western, Soviet and Egyptian Influences on Iraq's Development Planning," in Niblock, *Iraq,* 237.

Bernard Lewis's *The Emergence of Modern Turkey* in addition to being the best book on the modern history of the Ottoman Empire and the Turkish Republic provides extremely valuable insights into the political structures of both. Serif Mardin, in his two important articles, "Power, Civil Society and Culture in the Ottoman Empire," *Comparative Studies in Society and History,* vol. 11 (June 1969), and "Center-Periphery Relations: A Key to Turkish Politics?" *Daedalus* (Winter 1973) describes in both some of the essential characteristics of the Ottoman political structures and their continuing impact on the Turkish Republic. Also stressing the elements of continuity, as well as those of change, between the two is Dankwart A. Rustow, "Turkey: The Modernity of Tradition," in Lucian W. Pye and Sidney Verba, eds., *Political Culture and Political Development* (Princeton University Press, 1965). Similarly, Ergün Ozbudun, in his *Social Change and Political Participation in Turkey* (Princeton University Press, 1976) discusses continuity and change in social cleavages and political alignments in the Ottoman Empire and the Republic of Turkey. Frederick

W. Frey, in his detailed and comprehensive study, *The Turkish Political Elite* (MIT Press, 1965) describes the changes in the composition of the Turkish Grand National Assembly membership from 1920 to 1957. Studies comparing political institutions in the Arab world and the Republic of Turkey are practically nonexistent, and this is one of the major failures of contemporary Middle Eastern studies. Turkey has been compared to Japan (Robert E. Ward and Dankwart A. Rustow, eds., *Political Modernization in Japan and Turkey*, Princeton University Press, 1964) and Mexico (Ergün Ozbudun, "Established Revolution Versus Unfinished Revolution: Contrasting Patterns of Democratization in Mexico and Turkey," in Samuel P. Huntington and Clement H. Moore, eds., *Authoritarian Politics in Modern Society: The Dynamics of Established One-Party Systems*, (New York 1970), but hardly ever to an Arab (or other) successor state. A partial exception is *Electoral Politics in the Middle East*, edited by Jacob M. Landau, Ergün Ozbudun, and Frank Tachau (London 1980), which compares electoral issues, voting behavior, and parliamentary elites in Turkey, Lebanon, Israel; hardly the most fertile area of comparison among the Ottoman successor states and hardly a representative sample of them! The late Cyril E. Black provided valuable insights into the Ottoman modernization process by comparing it mainly with Russia, Japan, and China, but again without extending his analysis into a comparison between Turkey and the Arab successor states: "A Comparative Approach to the Preconditions of Ottoman Modernization," *International Journal of Turkish Studies*, Vol. I, No. 2 (Autumn 1980), pp. 25–37.

Among comparative studies of the political institutions of Arab states, two have been particularly influential and of great analytical value: Manfred Halpern, *The Politics of Social Change in the Middle East and North Africa* (Princeton University Press, 1963), and Michael C. Hudson, *Arab Politics: The Search for Legitimacy* (Yale University Press, 1977). For the former, the most potent explanatory factor in modern Middle Eastern politics is the emergence of a new (salaried) middle class; for the latter, the lack of legitimacy and of participatory mechanisms in contemporary Middle Eastern states.

Most of the works on the political institutions of these states are, as expected, single-country studies. But some of them have been written with good comparative insights and a keen awareness of broader comparative issues. One outstanding example of this genre is John Waterbury's *The Egypt of Nasser and Sadat: The Political Economy of Two Regimes* (Princeton University Press, 1983).

Parallel to the recent tendency in political science to "bring the state back in" as an independent and autonomous political factor, some of the most recent writings have explicitly focused on the state in the Middle East. Among the good examples of this category is the four-volume study on the Arab state, sponsored by the Istituto Affari Internazionali. Two volumes of this study are particularly germane to our present discussion: Ghassan Salamé, ed., *The Foundations of the Arab State* (London, 1987) and Adeed Dawisha and I. William Zartman, eds., *Beyond Coercion: The Durability of the Arab State* (London, 1988). Also in the same category are Gabriel Ben-Dor, *State and Conflict in the Middle East: Emergence of the Postcolonial State* (New York, 1983) and Metin Heper, *The State Tradition in Turkey* (Beverley, North Humberside, 1985).

Finally, no analysis of the Ottoman legacy can neglect the closely intertwined Islamic legacy. Clearly, there is a vast amount of literature on the Islamic theory of government. Two recent and important books on the subject are P. J. Vatikiotis, *Islam and the State* (London, 1987) and Leonard Binder, *Islamic Liberalism: A Critique of Development Ideologies* (University of Chicago Press, 1988). While the former is closer to the classical orientalistic tradition, the latter is considerably more sympathetic toward the somewhat elusive notion of Islamic liberalism. Also relevant is James P. Piscatori, *Islam in a World of Nation-States* (Cambridge University Press, 1986).

CHAPTER TWELVE
Economic Growth and Development

The data for this chapter was obtained from: World Bank, *World Development Report* (annual), *Food and Agriculture Organization, Production Yearbook* (annual), *United Nations, Statistical Yearbook* (annual), and International Monetary Fund, *Balance of Payments Yearbook* (annual).

Charles Issawi, *Economic History of the Middle East and North Africa* (New York, 1982).

Yujiro Hayami and Vernon Ruttan, *Agricultural Development an International Perspective* (Baltimore, 1971).

Ergün Ozbudun and Aydin Ulusan (eds.) *The Political Economy of Income Distribution in Turkey* (New York, 1980).

Gouda Abdel-Khalek and Robert Tignor (eds.), *The Political Economy of Income Distribution in Egypt* (New York, 1982).

Atif Kubursi, "Arab Agricultural Productivity" in Ibrahim Ibrahim (ed.) *Arab Resources* (London, 1983).

The best general economic survey of the region is Alan Richards and John Waterbury, *A Political Economy of the Middle East* (Westview Press, Boulder, Colo., 1990), which has an extensive bibliography.

On the individual countries, see: William Hale, *The Political and Economic Development of Modern Turkey* (London, 1981); Z. Y. Hershlay, *The Contemporary Turkish Economy* (London, 1988); Ibrahim Oweiss, *The Political Economy of Egypt* (CAS) (Georgetown University, Washington, 1990); John Waterbury, *The Egypt of Nasser and Sadat* (Princeton University Press, 1983); Robert Mabro, *The Egyptian Economy, 1952–1972* (Oxford University Press, 1973); Edith and E. F. Penrose, *Iraq* (Boulder, Colo., 1978); Tim Niblock, ed., *Iraq: The Contemporary State* (London, 1982); André Raymond, ed., *La Syrie d'aujourd'hui* (CNRS, Paris, 1980); Jean Hannoyer and Michel Seurat, *Etat et Secteur publique industriel en Syrie* (CERMOC, Lyon, 1980); Yoram Ben-Porath, *The Israeli Economy: Maturing through Crises* (Harvard University Press, 1986); Nadav Halevi and Ruther Klinot-Malul, *The Economic Development of Israel* (New York, 1968); Bichara Khader and Adnan Badran, eds. *The Economic Development of Jordan* (London, 1987); Michael Mazur, *Economic Growth and Development in Jordan* (Boulder, Colo., 1979); Harold Nelson, *Tunisia: A Country Study* (American University Press, 1979).

CHAPTER THIRTEEN
Social Interdependence

For an overview of some of the distinctive demographic features and changing trends and patterns in specific countries, United Nations *Demographic Yearbooks, Selected World Demographic Indicators, World Population Prospects* along with the World Bank's *World Development Reports* and *World Tables* are essential. One may also wish to consult several of the more analytical and comparative studies. The following are particularly instructive: J. I. Clarke, and W. B. Fisher (eds.), *The Populations of the Middle East and North Africa* (University of London Press, 1972); Allan Hill, "Population Growth in the Middle East since 1945 with Special Reference to the Arab Countries in West Asia," in John Clarke and Howard Bowen-Jones (eds.), *Change and Development in the Middle East* (London, 1981); D.

Kirk, "Factors Affecting 'Muslim Natality'," in UN Department of Economic and Social Affairs, *Proceedings of the World Population Conference* (Belgrade, 1969), 149–154; J. Allman (ed.), *Women's Status and Fertility of the Muslim World* (N. Y., 1978); E. T. Prothro and Lutfi Diab, *Changing Family Patterns in the Arab East* (American University of Beirut, 1974). An overall assessment of population policies and programs can be found in R. Lapham in the *MESA (Middle East Studies Association) Bulletin* (1977) 11 (2): 1–30. On population shifts, manpower migration and their impact on socioeconomic and political development, two chapters in Charles Issawi's *An Economic History of the Middle East and North Africa*, 77–117 offer a comprehensive analysis of changing patterns and trends. A special issue of *The Middle East Journal*, vol. 38, No. 4 (August, 1984) is devoted to a discussion of manpower migration. J. S. Birks and C. A. Sinclair in *Arab Manpower* (New York, 1980) and their essay in *The Journal of International Affairs* (Fall/Winter, 1979) also provide useful comparative analysis of the impact of migration on the poorer Arab countries. Saad Eddin Ibrahim in *The New Arab Order* (Boulder, Colo., 1982) focuses specifically on the impact of oil wealth on redistribution and sociocultural transformations.

Conceptual overviews and perspectives on the nature of urbanization and urbanism on the distinctive spatial character of the "Islamic city" can be found in A. Hourani and S. M. Stern, *The Islamic City* (University of Pennsylvania Press, 1970); Janet Abu-Lughod, "The Islamic City—Historical Myth, Islamic Essence, and Contemporary Relevance," in *International Journal of Middle East Studies* (1987), vol. 19, 155–176; Michael Bonine, "From Uruk to Casablanca," *Journal of Urban History* (Feb. 1977), vol. 3, No. 2, 141–180; Paul Wheatly, "Levels of Space Awareness in the Traditional Islamic City," *Ekistics*, vol. 42, no. 253 (December 1976), 354–66, and Francisco Benet, "The Ideology of Islamic Urbanism," in Nels Anderson (ed.), *Urbanism and Urbanization* (Leiden, 1964), 211–226. Case studies of contemporary transformations in some of the prominent cities of the successor states can be consulted in L. C. Brown (ed.), *From Madina to Metropolis* (Darwin Press, Princeton, N.J., 1972); Leila Fawaz, *Merchants and Migrants in Nineteenth Century Beirut* (Harvard University Press, 1983); Charles Issawi, "Economic Change and Urbanization in the Middle East," in Ira Lapidus (eds.), *Middle Eastern Cities* (University of California Press, 1969), 102–121; S. Khalaf and Per Kongstad, *Hamra of Beirut* (E. J. Brill, 1973); Gilsenan, M., *Recognizing Islam* (Pantheon, 1982), chaps. 8 and 9; Janet Abu-Lughod, *Cairo* (Princeton University Press, 1971); Ellen Micaud, "Urbanization, Urbanism and the Medina of Tunis," *International Journal of Middle East* (November 1978), vol. 9, N.Y.; Blake, G. H., and R. I. Lawless (eds.), *The Changing Middle Eastern City* (London, 1980); Khuri, Fuad, *From Village to Suburbs* (University of Chicago Press, 1975).

Lapham, Hill, and Kelly in Ann Mayer (ed.), *Property, Social Structure and Law in the Modern Middle East* (State University of N.Y. Press, 1985) 153–83, offer an excellent analytical study of international migration, particularly the disparity between individual goals and government policies, and their impact on property and social structure. The entire volume, in fact, includes concrete case studies (Egypt, Jordan, Lebanon, Tunisia) for a better understanding of property as an idiom of social relationships and its impact on power and socioeconomic mobility.

Many of the previously cited volumes, particularly Issawi (1982), UN and World Banks reports, Polk and Chambers (1968), include trends and analyses of various dimensions of social mobilization. The more recent work by Allan Richards and John Waterbury, *A Political Economy of the Middle East*, offers substantive updated analysis of manpower and human resources, the impact of education on social mobility, agriculture, and class formation. This, however should not detract from the merit of earlier groundbreaking studies such as Hanna Batatu's *The Old Social Classes and the Revolutionary Movements of Iraq* (Princeton University Press, 1978). Of note in this regard are also the following: John Waterbury, "The Socio-Economic Stratification of Middle Eastern Economies," in Waterbury and el-Mallakh, *The Middle East in the Coming Decade* (New York, 1978); Saad Eddin Ibrahim, *The New Arab Social Order* (Boulder, Colo., 1982); Nicholas Hopkins, "The Emergence of Class in a Tunisian Town," *International Journal of Middle East Studies* (October, 1977) 8 (4); E. Longueness, "The Class Nature in the State in Syria," *MERIP* (May 1979); Ishaq Qutub, "The Rise of the Middle Class in a Traditional Society," in M. B. Kiraz (ed.), *Social Stratification and Development* (The Hague, 1973); J. A. Bill, "Class Analysis and the Dialectics of Modernization in the Middle East," *International Journal of Middle East Studies* (1972) 3 (4): 417–434.

In recent years there has been an impressive amount of writing, mostly by Arab women themselves, on perceptions and images of the changing status of women and the sociocultural and psychological consequences of their growing participation in public life. Of special note are the following: S. Altarki and C. El-Solh (eds.), *Arab Women in the Field: Studying Your Own Society* (Syracuse University Press, 1988); Azizah al-Hibri (ed.), *Women and Islam* (Pergamon, 1982); Lila Abu-Lughod, *Veiled*

Sentiments (University of California Press, 1986); N. El-Saadawi, *The Hidden Face of Eve* (Zed Press, 1980); Amal Rassam in UNESCO, *Social Science Research and Women in the Arab World* (Frances Pinter, 1984): 1–13, 122–138; Nadia Youssef, *Women and Work in Developing Countries* (University of California Press, 1974); H. Zurayk, "Women's Economic Participation," in I. Sharter and H. Zurayk (eds.), *Population Factors in Development Planning in the Middle East* (Little, Brown, Co., 1985): 3–58; N. Hijab, *Womanpower: The Arab Debate on Women at Work* (Cambridge University Press, 1988); L. Beck and N. Keddie (eds.), *Women in the Muslim World* (Harvard University Press, 1980); E. Fernea (ed.), *Women and the Family in the Middle East* (University of Texas Press, 1989); E. Fernea and Bezirgan, B. (eds.), *Middle Eastern Muslim Women Speak* (University of Texas Press, 1977).

CHAPTER FOURTEEN
Knowledge and Education

Despite the importance of this topic, the literature dealing with education in the successor states is relatively sparse and tends to be descriptive rather than related to larger theoretical concerns. Most studies deal with single countries; only a few look at education from a regional perspective. Roderic Mathews and Matta Akrawi, *Education in Arab Countries of the Near East* (Washington, D.C.: American Council on Education, 1949), provide important data on the development of national education systems in the Arab world during the interwar period; Joseph S. Szyliowicz, in *Education and Modernization in the Middle East*, analyzes, from a comparative and historical perspective, the role of education as an object of change and as an agent of change, with special emphasis on Turkey, Egypt, and Iran; Byron G. Massialas and Samir A. Jarrar, *Education in the Arab World* (New York, 1983) present the most recent analysis of educational conditions in the region. Two specialized, though somewhat dated, studies also contain useful information. Fahim Qubain, *Education and Science in the Arab World* (Johns Hopkins University Press, 1966) and J. J. Waardenburg, *Les Universités dans le Monde Arabe Actuel* (The Hague, 1966), 2 vols.

Surprisingly, the educational systems of many countries have also been largely ignored; apart from descriptive studies by the American Association of Collegiate Registrars and Admissions Officers (AACRAO), there are no books in English dealing with Syria, Iraq, Lebanon, and

Algeria, and only one on Tunisia: James Allman, *Social Mobility, Education, and Development in Tunisia* (Leiden, 1979). Several important works deal with Turkey, however, including the recent OECD report, *Turkey* (Paris, 1989); A. Kazamias, *Education and the Quest for Modernity in Turkey* (University of Chicago Press, 1966); and I. Basgoz and H. E. Wilson, *Educational Problems in Turkey: 1920–1940* (Indiana University Press, 1968). Egypt too has been the subject of several recent studies including Judith Cochran, *Education in Egypt* (London, 1986); Georgie D. M. Hyde, *Education in Modern Egypt* (London, 1978); and Hagai Erlich, *Students and University in 20th Century Egyptian Politics* (London, 1989). The Israeli scene has been analyzed from many perspectives. A. F. Kleinberg, *Society, Schools and Progress in Israel* (Oxford: Pergamon Press, 1969) is a useful introduction. More specialized studies include A. Minkowich, D. Davis, and J. Bashi, *Success and Failure in Israeli Elementary Education* (New Brunswick: Transaction Books, 1982), and M. Spiro, *Children of the Kibbutz* (Harvard University Press, 1958).

Some national bodies carry out important research; sometimes these studies are reported in works published by UNESCO, which is an important source of information (e.g., Conference of Ministers of Education and Ministers Responsible for Economic Planning in the Arab States, *New Prospects in Education for Development in the Arab Countries*, Paris: UNESCO, 1977). Its *Statistical Year Book* is a valuable source of quantitative data.

Specialized studies are to be found most often in the periodical literature, but the topic of migration has been analyzed in depth by I. Serageldin et al, *Manpower and International Labor Migration in the Middle East and North Africa* (Oxford University Press, 1983). Discussions of the role of students in many countries, including Turkey and Israel, are to be found in Phillip Altbach, ed., *Student Political Activism: An International Reference Handbook* (New York, 1989).

Bibliography

[The number or numbers in parentheses following the entry refer to the chapter(s) for which the work cited is most relevant. Basic works relevant to most of the chapters are marked (B).]

ABD AL-KARIM, AHMAD 'IZZAT. *Ta'rikh Al-Ta'lim Fi 'Asr Muhammad 'Ali.* Cairo, 1938. (7)

ABDEL-KHALEK, GOUDA and TIGNOR, ROBERT (eds.). *The Political Economy of Income Distribution in Egypt.* New York, 1982. (12)

ABU-LUGHOD, IBRAHIM. *Arab Rediscovery of Europe: A Study in Cultural Encounters.* Princeton University Press, 1963. (7)

ABU-LUGHOD, JANET. *Cairo: 1001 Years of the City Victorious.* Princeton University Press, 1971. (13)

—————. "The Islamic City—Historical Myth, Islamic Essence, and Contemporary Relevance," *International Journal of Middle East Studies,* Vol. 19, No. 2, May 1987. (13)

ABU-LUGHOD, LILA. *Veiled Sentiments.* University of California Press, 1986. (13)

ADIVAR, ABDÜLHAK ADNAN. *La Science Chez Les Turcs Ottomans.* Paris, 1939. (7)

—————. *Osmanli Türklerinde Ilim.* Istanbul, 1943. (7)

AKYÜZ, YAHYA. *Turk Egitim Tarihi.* Ankara, 1982. (7)

AL-HAMAMSY, LEILA SHUKRY. "Belief Systems and Family Planning in Peasant Societies," *Are Our Descendants Doomed?* New York, 1972. (13)

AL-HIBRI, AZIZAH (ed.). *Women and Islam.* New York, 1982. (13)

'ALI, SA'ID ISMA'IL. *Ta'rikh al'Tabiyah Wa Al-Ta'lim Fi Misr.* Cairo, 1985. (7)

ALLMAN, JAMES. *Social Mobility, Education, and Development in Tunisia.* Leiden, 1979. (14)

ALLMAN, J. (ed.). *Women's Status and Fertility of the Muslim World.* New York, 1978. (13)

ALTARKI, S. and EL-SOLH, C. (eds.). *Arab Women in the Field: Studying Your Own Society.* Syracuse University Press, 1988. (13)

ALTBACH, PHILLIP (ed.). *Student Political Activism: An International Reference Book.* New York, 1989. (14)

ALVARES, CLAUDE A. *Homo Faber: Technology and Culture in India, China and the West, 1500 to the Present.* New Delhi, 1979. (7)

ANDERSON, ALUN M. *Science and Technology in Japan.* London, 1984. (7)

ANDERSON, M. S. *The Eastern Question, 1774–1923: A Study in International Relations.* London, 1966 (with later paperback editions). (3)

BAER, GABRIEL. "The Beginnings of Municipal Government," in his *Studies in the Social History of Modern Egypt*. University of Chicago Press, 1969. (6)

BARTHOLOMEW, JAMES R. *The Formation of Science in Japan: Building a Research Tradition*. Yale University Press, 1989. (7)

BASGOZ, I. and WILSON, H. E. *Educational Problems in Turkey: 1920–1940*. Indiana University Press, 1968. (14)

BATATU, HANNA. *The Old Social Classes and the Revolutionary Movements of Iraq*. Princeton University Press, 1978. (13)

BDIRA, MEZRI. *Relations Internationales et Sous-Developpement: La Tunisie, 1857–1864*. Acta Universitatis Upsaliensis, Uppsala, 1978. (4)

BECK, LOIS and KEDDIE, NIKKI (eds.). *Women in the Muslim World*. Harvard University Press, 1980. (13)

BEELEY, BRIAN. "Migration and Planning: The Turkish Case," *Urbanization in the Developing World*. London, 1986. (13)

BEHRENS-ABOUSEIF, DORIS. "The Political Situation of the Copts, 1798–1923," in Benjamin Braude and Bernard Lewis (eds.), *Christians and Jews in the Ottoman Empire: The Functioning of a Plural Society*. New York, 1982. (7)

BEN-DOR, GABRIEL. *State and Conflict in the Middle East: Emergence of the Postcolonial State*. New York, 1983. (11)

BENET, FRANCISCO. "The Ideology of Islamic Urbanism" in Nels Anderson (ed.), *Urbanism and Urbanization*. Leiden, 1964. (13)

BEN-PORATH, YORAM. *The Israeli Economy: Maturing Through Crises*. Harvard University Press, 1986. (12)

BERKES, NIYAZI. *The Development of Secularism in Turkey*. McGill University Press, 1964. (B) (4) (6) (7)

BILL, JAMES A. "Class Analysis and the Dialectics of Modernization in the Middle East," *International Journal of Middle East Studies*, Vol. 3, No. 4, October 1972. (13)

BINDER, LEONARD. *Islamic Liberalism: A Critique of Development Ideologies*. University of Chicago Press, 1988. (11)

BIRKS, J. S. and SINCLAIR, C. A. *Arab Manpower*. New York, 1980. (13)

BLACK, CYRIL E. "A Comparative Approach to the Preconditions of Ottoman Modernization," *International Journal of Turkish Studies*, Vol. I, No. 2, Autumn 1980. (11)

BLAISDELL, DONALD. *European Financial Capital in the Ottoman Empire*. New York, 1929. (5)

BLAKE, G. H. "Israel: Immigration and Dispersal of Population," *Populations of the Middle East and North Africa*. London University Press, 1972. (13)

BLAKE, G. H. and LAWLESS, R. I. (eds.). *The Changing Middle Eastern City.* London, 1980. (13)

BONINE, MICHAEL. "From Uruk to Casablanca," *Journal of Urban History,* Vol. 3, No. 2, February 1977. (13)

BRAUDE, BENJAMIN and LEWIS, BERNARD (eds.). *Christians and Jews in the Ottoman Empire: The Functioning of a Plural Society.* New York, 1982. (6)

BROWN, L. CARL (ed.). *From Madina to Metropolis: Heritage and Change in the Near Eastern City.* Darwin Press, Princeton, N.J., 1972. (13)

——————. *International Politics and the Middle East: Old Rules, Dangerous Game.* Princeton University Press, 1984. (3) (10)

——————. *The Tunisia of Ahmad Bey, 1837–1855.* Princeton University Press, 1974. (4) (7)

CHAMBERS, RICHARD L. "The Education of a Nineteenth-Century Ottoman Alim, Ahmed Çevdet Pasa," *International Journal of Middle East Studies,* Vol. 4, No. 4, October 1973. (7)

CLARK, EDWARD C. "The Ottoman Industrial Revolution," *International Journal of Middle East Studies,* Vol. 5, No. 1, January 1974. (7)

CLARK, J. I. and FISHER, W. B. (eds.). *The Populations of the Middle East and North Africa.* London University Press, 1972. (13)

CLEVELAND, WILLIAM L. "The Municipal Council of Tunis, 1858–1870: A Study in Urban Institutional Change," *International Journal of Middle East Studies,* Vol. 9, No. 1, February 1978. (6)

COCHRAN, JUDITH. *Education in Egypt.* London, 1986. (14)

COHEN, AMNON. *Palestine in the Eighteenth Century: Patterns of Government and Administration.* Hebrew University Press, 1973. (6)

COLEMAN, JAMES S. *Education and Political Development.* Princeton University Press, 1965. (14)

CROUCHLEY, A. E. *The Economic Development of Modern Egypt.* London, 1938. (5)

——————. *The Investment of Foreign Capital in Egyptian Companies and Public Debt.* Cairo, 1934. (5)

DANIEL, ROBERT L. *American Philanthropy in the Near East, 1820–1960.* Athens, Ohio, 1970. (7)

DAVISON, RODERIC H. *Reform in the Ottoman Empire, 1856–1876.* Princeton University Press, 1963. (6)

——————. "The Advent of the Principle of Representation in the Government of the Ottoman Empire," in William R. Polk and Richard L. Chambers (eds.), *Beginnings of Modernization in the Middle East.* University of Chicago Press, 1968. (4)

DAWISHA, ADEED and ZARTMAN, I. WILLIAM (eds.). *Beyond Coercion: The Durability of the Arab State*. London, 1988. (11)

DELANOUE, GILBERT. *Moralistes et Politiques Musulmans Dans l'Egypte du XIXe Siecle*. Cairo, 1982. (7)

DODGE, BAYARD. *Al-Azhar: A Millennium of Muslim Learning*. Washington, 1961, 1974. (7)

DORE, RONALD P. *Education in Tokugawa Japan*. University of California Press, 1965. (7)

DUMONT, PAUL. "Jewish Communities in Turkey during the Last Decades of the Nineteenth Century in the Light of the Archives of the Alliance Israelite Universelle," in Benjamin Braude and Bernard Lewis (eds.), *Christians and Jews in the Ottoman Empire: The Functioning of a Plural Society*. New York, 1982. (7)

EARLE, EDWARD MEADE. *Turkey, the Great Powers and the Baghdad Railway*. New York, 1923. (5)

EL-SAADAWI, N. *The Hidden Face of Eve*. New York, 1980. (13)

ENAYAT, HAMID. *Modern Islamic Political Thought: The Response of the Shi'i and Sunni Muslims to the Twentieth Century*. University of Texas Press, 1982. (7)

ERGIN, OSMAN. *Istanbul Mektepleri ve Ilim, Terbiye ve San'at Müesseseleri Dolayisile Türkiye Maarif Tarihi*. Istanbul, 1939–1943. (7)

ERLICH, HAGAI. *Students and University in 20th Century Egyptian Politics*. London, 1989. (14)

ESPOSITO, JOHN L. *Islam and Politics*. Syracuse University Press, 1984. (11)

FAWAZ, LEILA. *Merchants and Migrants in Nineteenth-Century Beirut*. Harvard University Press, 1983. (6) (13)

FERNEA, ELIZABETH (ed.). *Women and the Family in the Middle East*. University of Texas Press, 1989. (13)

FINDLEY, CARTER V. *Bureaucratic Reform in the Ottoman Empire: The Sublime Porte, 1789–1922*. Princeton University Press, 1980. (4) (7)

——————. "Knowledge and Education in the Modern Middle East: A Comparative View," in Georges Sabagh (ed.), *The Modern Economic and Social History of the Middle East in its World Context*. Cambridge University Press, 1989. (7)

——————. *Ottoman Civil Officialdom: A Social History*. Princeton University Press, 1989. (4) (7)

FINNIE, DAVID H. *Pioneers East: The Early American Experience in the Middle East*. Harvard University Press, 1967. (7)

FREY, FREDERICK W. *The Turkish Political Elite*. Massachusetts Institute of Technology Press, 1965. (11)

GALANTI, AVRAM. *Turk Harsi ve Turk Tahudisi: Tarihi, Siyasi, Ictimai, Tetkik.* Istanbul, 1953. (7)

————. *Turkler ve Yahudiler: Tarihi, Siyasi, Tetkik.* Istanbul, 1947. (7)

GALLAGHER, NANCY E. *Medicine and Power in Tunisia, 1780–1900.* Cambridge University Press, 1983. (6)

GANIAGE, JEAN. *Les Origines du Protectorat Francais en Tunisie.* Paris, 1959. (5)

GILBAR, GAD (ed.). *Ottoman Palestine, 1800–1914.* Leiden, 1990. (5)

GILSENAN, MICHAEL. *Recognizing Islam.* New York, 1982. (13)

GOÇEK, FATMA MUGE. *East Encounters West: France and the Ottoman Empire in the Eighteenth Century.* New York, 1987. (7)

GRABILL, JOSEPH, L. *Protestant Diplomacy and the Near East: Missionary Influence on American Policy, 1810–1927.* Minneapolis, 1971. (7)

HALE, WILLIAM. *The Political and Economic Development of Modern Turkey.* London, 1981. (12)

HALEVI, NADAV and KLINOT-MALUL, RUTHER. *The Economic Development of Israel.* New York, 1968. (12)

HALPERN, MANFRED. *The Politics of Social Change in the Middle East and North Africa.* Princeton University Press, 1963. (11)

HAMZA, ABD al-MAQSUD. *The Public Debt of Egypt, 1854–1867.* Cairo, 1944. (5)

HANNOYER, JEAN and SEURAT, MICHEL. *Etat et Secteur Publique Industriel en Syrie.* Lyon, 1980. (12)

HANSEN, BENT and WATTLEWORTH, MICHAEL. "Agricultural Output and Consumption of Basic Foods," *International Journal of Middle East Studies,* Vol. 9, No. 4, November 1978. (5)

HARIK, ILIYA. *Politics and Change in a Traditional Society: Lebanon, 1711–1845.* Princeton University Press, 1968. (4)

HAYAMI, YUJIRO and RUTTAN, VERNON. *Agricultural Development, An International Perspective.* Baltimore, 1971. (12)

HEPER, METIN. *The State Tradition in Turkey.* Beverly, North Humberside, 1985. (11)

HERSHLAY, Z. Y. *The Contemporary Turkish Economy.* Routledge, 1988. (12)

HEYD, URIEL. *Foundations of Turkish Nationalism: The Life and Teachings of Ziya Gokalp.* London, 1950. (7)

————. "The Ottoman 'Ulema and Westernization in the Time of Selim III and Mahmud II," *Scripta Hierosalymitana, IX: Studies in Islamic History and Civilization,* 1961. (7)

HEYWORTH-DUNNE, J. *An Introduction to the History of Education in Modern Egypt.* London, 1938. (7)

HIJAB, N. *Womanpower: The Arab Debate on Women at Work.* Cambridge University Press, 1988. (13)

HILL, ALLAN. "Population Growth in the Middle East," in John Clarke and Howard Bowen-Jones (eds.), *Change and Development in the Middle East.* London, 1981. (13)

HODGSON, MARSHALL G. S. *The Venture of Islam: Conscience and History in a World Civilization.* University of Chicago Press, 1974. (7)

HOLT, PETER M. *Egypt and the Fertile Crescent, 1516–1922: A Political History.* Cornell University Press, 1966. (4)

HOPKINS, NICHOLAS. "The Emergence of Class in a Tunisian Town," *International Journal of Middle East Studies,* Vol. 8, No. 4, October 1977. (13)

HOPWOOD, DEREK. *The Russian Presence in Syria and Palestine, 1843–1914: Church and Politics in the Near East.* Oxford University Press, 1969. (7)

HOURANI, ALBERT. *A History of the Arab Peoples.* Harvard University Press, 1991. (B)

—————. *Arabic Thought in the Liberal Age, 1798–1939.* Oxford University Press, 1962. (7)

—————. "Ottoman Reform and the Politics of Notables," in William R. Polk and Richard L. Chambers (eds.), *Beginnings of Modernization in the Middle East: The Nineteenth Century.* University of Chicago Press, 1966. (6)

—————. "The Ottoman Background of the Modern Middle East," in his *The Emergence of the Modern Middle East.* University of California Press, 1981. (4) (6)

—————. "Sufism and Modern Islam: Mawlana Khalid and the Naqshbandi Order," in his *The Emergence of the Modern Middle East.* University of California Press, 1981. (6)

—————. "Sufism and Modern Islam: Rashid Rida," in IBID.

HOURANI, ALBERT and STERN, S. M. (eds.). *The Islamic City.* University of Pennsylvania Press, 1970. (13)

HUDSON, MICHAEL C. *Arab Politics: The Search for Legitimacy.* Yale Univesity Press, 1977. (11)

HUNTER, F. ROBERT. *Egypt Under the Khedives, 1805–1879: From Household Government to Modern Bureaucracy.* University of Pittsburgh Press, 1984. (4) (7)

HUREWITZ, J. C. *The Middle East and North Africa in World Politics: A Documentary Record.* Volume One, "European Expansion, 1535–1914." Yale University Press, 1975. (3) (10)

—————. *The Middle East and North Africa in World Politics: A Documentary*

Record. Volume Two, "British-French Supremacy, 1914–1945." Yale University Press, 1979. (10)

HYDE, GEORGIE D. M. *Education in Modern Egypt*. London, 1978. (14)

IBRAHIM, SAAD EDDIN. "Oil, Migration and the Arab Social Order," in Malcolm H. Kerr and El Sayed Yassin (eds.), *Rich and Poor States in the Middle East*. American University in Cairo Press, 1982. (13)

——————. *The New Arab Social Order*. Boulder, 1982. (13)

IHSANOGLU, EKMELEDDIN. *Osmanli Ilmi ve Mesleki Cemiyetleri: 1. Milli Turk Tarihi Sempozyumu, 3–5 Nisan 1987*. Istanbul, 1987. (7)

INALCIK, HALIL. "Application of the Tanzimat and its Social Effects," *Archivum Ottomanicum*. Vol. 5, 1973. (6)

——————. "Military and Fiscal Transformation in the Ottoman Empire," *Archivum Ottomanicum*. Vol. 6, 1980. (6)

INTERNATIONAL MONETARY FUND. *Balance of Payments Yearbook*. Annual. (12)

ISSAWI, CHARLES. *An Economic History of the Middle East and North Africa*. Columbia University Press, 1982. (5) (6) (7) (12) (13)

——————. "Economic Change and Urbanization in the Middle East," in Ira M. Lapidus (ed.), *Middle Eastern Cities*. University of California Press, 1969. (13)

——————. *The Economic History of the Middle East, 1800–1914*. University of Chicago Press, 1966. (5) (6)

——————. *The Economic History of Turkey*. University of Chicago Press, 1980. (5) (6)

——————. *The Fertile Crescent, 1800–1914*. Oxford University Press, 1988. (5) (6)

ITZKOWITZ, NORMAN. *Ottoman Empire and Islamic Tradition*. New York, 1972. (4)

KARPAT, KEMAL. *An Inquiry into the Social Foundations of Nationalism in the Ottoman State: From Social Estates to Classes, from Millets to Nations*. Princeton University Center of International Studies Monograph No. 39, 1973. (6)

——————. *Ottoman Population, 1830–1914: Demographic and Social characteristics*. University of Wisconsin Press, 1985. (6)

——————. "The Land Regime, Social Structure, and Modernization in the Ottoman Empire," in William R. Polk and Richard L. Chambers (eds.), *Beginnings of Modernization in the Middle East: The Nineteenth Century*. University of Chicago Press, 1966. (6)

KASABA, RESAT. *The Ottoman Empire and the World Economy, the Nineteenth Century*. State University of New York Press, 1988. (5)

KAZAMIAS, ANDREAS M. *Education and the Quest for Modernity in Turkey.* London, 1966. (7) (14)

KEDDIE, NIKKI. *Jamal al-Din "Al-Afghani": A Political Biography.* University of California Press, 1972. (7)

KERR, MALCOLM. *Islamic Reform: The Political and Legal Theories of Muhammad 'Abduh and Rashid Rida.* University of California Press, 1966. (7)

——————. *The Arab Cold War: Gamal Abd Al Nasir and His Rivals, 1958–1970.* Oxford University Press, 1971 (3rd edition). (10)

KHADER, BICHARA and BADRAN, ADNAN. *The Economic Development of Jordan.* London, 1987. (12)

KHALAF, SAMIR. *Lebanon's Predicament.* Columbia University Press, 1987. (4)

——————. *Persistence and Change in Nineteenth-Century Lebanon.* American University of Beirut, 1979. (6)

KHALAF, SAMIR and KONGSTAD, PER. *Hamra of Beirut.* Leiden, 1973. (13)

KHOURY, PHILIP. *Urban Notables and Arab Nationalism; The Politics of Damascus, 1860–1920.* Cambridge Unviersity Press, 1983. (6)

KHURI, FUAD. *From Village to Suburbs.* University of Chicago Press, 1975. (13)

KIRK, D. "Factors Affecting Muslim Natality," in UN Department of Economic and Social Affairs, *Proceedings of the World Population Conference.* Belgrade, 1969. (13)

KLEINBERG, A. F. *Society, Schools and Progress in Israel.* Oxford, 1969. (14)

KNAPP, WILFRID (ed.). *Northwest Africa: A Political and Economic Survey.* Oxford University Press, 1977 (Third edition). (B)

KOÇER, HASAN ALI. *Türkiye 'De Modern Egitimin Dogusu ve Gilisimi, 1773–1923.* Istanbul, 1970. (7)

KODAMAN, BAYRAM. *Abdulhamid Devri Egitim Sistemi.* Istanbul, 1980. (7)

KORNRUMPF, HANS-JÜRGEN. *Osmanische Bibliographie Mit Besonderer Berücksichtigung der Türkei in Europa.* Leiden, 1973. (7)

KUBURSI, ATIF. "Arab Agricultural Productivity," *Arab Resources.* London, 1983. (12)

KUSHNER, DAVID (ed.). *Palestine in the Late Ottoman Period.* Jerusalem-Leiden, 1986. (5)

LABAKI, BOUTROS. *Introduction à l'Histoire Économique du Liban.* Beirut, 1984. (5)

LANDAU, JACOB M., OZBUDUN, ERGÜN and TACHAU, FRANK. *Electoral Politics in the Middle East.* London, 1980. (11)

LAPHAM, ROBERT J. "Population Policies in the Middle East and North Africa," *Middle East Studies Association Bulletin*, Vol. 11, No. 2, May 1977. (13)

LAPHAM, ROBERT J., HILL, ALLAN G. and LINTNER, CHARLES F. "International Migration in the Middle East: Effects on Property and Socieal Structure," in Ann Mayer (ed.), etc. (13)

LENCZOWSKI, GEORGE. *The Middle East in World Affairs*. Cornell University Press, 1980 (4th edition, available in paperback). (10)

LEWIS, BERNARD. *The Emergence of Modern Turkey*. Oxford University Press, 1961 (with later paperback editions). (B) (4) (6) (7) (11)

—————. *The Muslim Discovery of Europe*. New York, 1982. (7)

LONGUENESS, E. "The Class Nature of the State in Syria," MERIP (Middle East Research and Information Project). May 1979. (13)

MABRO ROBERT. *The Egyptian Economy, 1952–1972*. Oxford University Press, 1974. (12)

MANSFIELD, PETER (ed.). *The Middle East and North Africa*. Oxford University Press, 1980. (Fifth edition). (B)

MAOZ, MOSHE. *Ottoman Reform in Syria and Palestine, 1840–1861: The Impact of the Tanzimat on Politics and Society*. Oxford University Press, 1968. (6)

MARDIN, SERIF. "Center-Periphery Relations: A Key to Turkish Politics?" *Daedalus*. 1973. (11)

—————. "Power, Civil Society and Culture in the Ottoman Empire," *Comparative Studies in Society and History*. 1969.)11)

—————. "Some Notes on an Early Phase in the Modernization of Communications in Turkey," *Comparative Studies in Society and History*, Vol. 3, No. 3, April 1961. (7)

—————. *The Genesis of Young Ottoman Thought: A Study in the Modernization of Turkish Political Ideas*. Princeton University Press, 1962. (7)

MARR, PHEBE. *The Modern History of Iraq*. Boulder, Colo., 1985. (4)

MARRIOTT, J. A. R. *The Eastern Question: An Historical Study in European Diplomacy*. Oxford University Press, four editions between 1917 and 1940. (3)

MARSOT, AFAF LUFTI al SAYYID. *A Short History of Modern Egypt*. Cambridge University Press, 1985. (4)

—————. *Egypt in the Reign of Muhammad Ali*. Cambridge University Press, 1984. (7)

MASSIALAS, B. G. and JARRAR, S. A. *Education in the Arab World*. New York, 1983. (13) (14)

MASTERS, BRUCE. *The Origins of Western Economic Dominance in the Middle East: Mercantilism and the Islamic Economy in Aleppo, 1600–1750*. New York University Press, 1988. (6)

MATHEWS, RODERIC and AKRAWI, MATTA. *Education in Arab Countries of the Near East.* Washington, D.C., 1949. (14)

MAYER, ANN (ed.). *Property, Social Structure and Law in the Modern Middle East.* State University of New York Press, 1985.)13)

MAZUR, MICHAEL. *Economic Growth and Development in Jordan.* Boulder, Colo., 1979. (12)

MCCARTHY, JUSTIN. *Muslims and Minorities: The Population of Ottoman Anatolia and the End of the Empire.* New York University Press, 1983. (6)

——————. *The Arab World, Turkey and the Balkans (1878–1914).* Boston, 1982. (5)

——————. "The Population of Ottoman Syria and Iraq, 1878–1914," *Asian and African Studies,* 15, 1981. (6)

MICAUD, ELLEN. "Urbanization, Urbanism and the Medina of Tunis." *International Journal of Middle East Studies,* Vol. 9, No. 4, November 1978. (13)

MINKOWICH, A., DAVIS, D. and BASHI, J. *Success and Failure in Israeli Elementary Education.* New Brunswick, 1982. (14)

MORTIMER, EDWARD. *Faith and Power: The Politics of Islam.* New York, 1982. (11)

MOYSTN, TREVOR and HOURANI, ALBERT. *The Cambridge Encyclopedia of the Middle East and North Africa.* Cambridge University Press, 1988. (B) (4)

NAFF, THOMAS and OWEN, E. R. J. *Studies in Eighteenth Century Islamic History.* Southern Illinois University Press, 1978. (6)

NELSON, HAROLD. *Tunisia: A Country Study.* American University Press, 1979. (12)

NIBLOCK, TIM (ed.). *Iraq: The Contemporary State.* London, 1982. (12)

OWEISS, IBRAHIM. *The Political Economy of Egypt.* Center for Contemporary Arab Studies, Georgetown University, 1990. (12)

OWEN, E. R. J. *Cotton and the Egyptian Economy.* Oxford University Press, 1969. (5) (6)

——————. *The Middle East in the World Economy, 1800–1914.* Oxford University Press, 1981. (5) (6)

ÖZALP, RESAT. *Milli Egitimle Ilgili Mevzuat, 1957–1923.* Istanbul, 1982. (7)

OZBUDUN, ERGÜN. "Established Revolution Versus Unfinished Revolution: Contrasting Patterns of Democratization in Mexico and Turkey," Samuel P. Huntington and Clement H. Moore (eds.), *Authoritarian Politics in Modern Society: The Dynamics of Established One-Party Systems.* New York, 1970. (11)

—————. *Social Change and Political Participation in Turkey.* Princeton University Press, 1976. (11)

OZBUDUN, ERGÜN and ULUSAN, AYDIN. *The Political Economy of Income Distribution in Turkey.* New York, 1980. (12)

PAMUK, SEVKET. *The Ottoman Empire and European Capitalism, 1820–1913.* Cambridge University Press, 1987. (5) (6)

—————. *The Ottoman Empire and World Capitalism, 1820–1913.* Cambridge University Press, 1987. (6)

PEARSON, JAMES D. *Index Islamicus: A Catalogue of Articles of Islamic Subjects in Periodicals and Other Collective Publications.* London, 1958– . (7)

PENROSE, EDITH and E. F. *Iraq: International Relations and National Development.* Boulder, 1978. (12)

PHILIPP, THOMAS. *The Syrians in Egypt, 1725–1975.* Stuttgart, 1985. (6)

PISCATORI, JAMES P. *Islam in a World of Nation-States.* Cambridge University Press, 1986. (11)

POLK, WILLIAM R. and CHAMBERS, RICHARD L. (eds.). *Beginnings of Modernization in the Middle East.* University of Chicago Press, 1968. (4)

PONCET, JEAN. *La Colonisation et l'Agriculture Européennes en Tunisie.* Paris, 1962. (5)

PROTHRO, E. T. and DIAB, LUTFI. *Changing Family Patterns in the Arab East.* American University of Beirut Press, 1974. (13)

QIAN, WEN-YUAN. *The Great Inertia: Scientific Stagnation in Traditional China.* London, 1985. (7)

QUATAERT, DONALD. *Social Disintegration and Popular Resistance in the Ottoman Empire, 1881–1908: Reactions to European Economic Penetration.* New York University Press, 1983. (6)

QUBAIN, FAHIM. *Education and Science in the Arab World.* John Hopkins University Press, 1966. (7) (14)

RAFEQ, ABDUL-KARIM. "Economic Relations Between Damascus and the Dependent Countryside, 1743–1771" in A. L. Udovitch (ed.), *The Islamic Middle East.* Darwin Press, Princeton, N.J., 1981. (6)

RAHMAN, FAZLUR. *Islam and Modernity: Transformation of an Intellectual Tradition.* University of Chicago Press, 1982. (7)

RASSAM, AMAL. *Social Science Research and Women in the Arab World.* UNESCO, 1984. (13)

RAWSKI, EVELYN. *Education and Popular Literacy in Ch'ing China.* Ann Arbor, 1979. (7)

RAYMOND, ANDRE (ed.). *La Syrie d'Aujourd'hui.* Paris 1980. (12)
—————. *The Great Arab Cities in the 16th–18th Centuries.* New York University Press, 1984. (6)
REID, DONALD M. *Cairo University and the Making of Modern Egypt.* Cambridge University Press, 1990. (14)
RICHARDS, ALAN and WATERBURY, JOHN. *A Political Economy of the Middle East.* Boulder, Colo., 1990. (12) (13)
RUSSETT, BRUCE M., et al. *World Handbook of Political and Social Indicators.* Yale University Press, 1964. (11)
RUSTOW, DANKWART A. "Turkey: The Modernity of Tradition," in Lucian W. Pye and Sidney Verba (eds.), *Political Culture and Political Development.* Princeton University Press, 1965. (11)
SAFRAN, NADAV. *Saudi Arabia: The Ceaseless Quest for Security.* Harvard University Press, 1978 reissued by Cornell Univeristy Press, 1988 (available in paperback). (10)
SALAMÉ, GHASSAN (ed.). *The Foundations of the Arab State.* London, 1987. (11)
SALIBI, KAMAL. *The Modern History of Lebanon.* New York, 1965. (4) (7)
SANJIAN, AVEDIS K. *The Armenian Communities in Syria Under Ottoman Dominion.* Harvard University Press, 1965. (7)
SARDAR, ZIAUDDIN. *Science and Technology in the Middle East: A Guide to Issues, Organizations, and Institutions.* London, 1982. (7)
SCHATKOWSKI-SCHILCHER, LINDA. *Families in Politics: Damascene Factions and Estates of the 18th and 19th Centuries.* Stuttgart, 1985. (6)
SEALE, PATRICK. *The Struggle for Syria: A Study of Post-War Arab Politics, 1945–1958.* Oxford University Press, 1965, reissued by Yale University Press, 1987 (available in paperback). (10)
SERAGELDIN, ISMAIL (ed.). *Manpower and International Labor Migration in the Middle East and North Africa.* Oxford University Press, 1983. (14)
SHAMIR, SHIMON. "The Modernization of Syria: Problems and Solutions in the Early Period of Abdulhamid" in William R. Polk and Richard L. Chambers (eds.), *Beginnings of Modernization in the Middle East.* University of Chicago Press, 1968. (4)
SHAW, STANFORD J. *Between Old and New: The Ottoman Empire Under Sultan Selim III, 1789–1807.* Harvard University Press, 1971. (7)
—————. "Some Aspects of the Aims and Achievements of the Nineteenth-Century Ottoman Reformers" in William R. Polk and Richard L. Chambers (eds.), *Beginnings of Modernization in the Middle East.* University of Chicago Press, 1968. (4)

—————. "The Origins of Representative Government in the Ottoman Empire: An Introduction to the Provincial Councils, 1839–1876," in R. Bayly Winder (ed.), *Near Eastern Roundtable, 1967–68.* New York University Press, 1969. (6)

SHAW, STANFORD J. and SHAW, EZEL KURAL. *Reform, Revolution and Republic: The Rise of Modern Turkey, 1808–1975.* Cambridge University Press, 1977 (Volume two of the two volume *History of the Ottoman Empire and Modern Turkey*). (B) (4) (7)

SHORTER, FREDERICK C. and ZURAYK, HUDO (eds.). *Population Factors in Development Planning in the Middle East.* Boston, 1985. (13)

SPIRO, M. *Children of the Kibbutz.* Harvard University Press, 1958. (14)

STORK, JOE. "State Power and Economic Structure: Class Determination and State Formation in Contemporary Iraq," in Tim Niblock (ed.), *Iraq: The Contemporary State.* London, 1982. (11)

SYNVET, A. *Les Grecs de l'Empire Ottoman.* Istanbul, 1878. (7)

SZYLIOWICZ, JOSEPH. *Education and Modernization in the Middle East.* Cornell University Press, 1973. (7) (14)

TANG, TONG B. *Science and Technology in China.* London, 1984. (7)

TIBAWI, ABDUL LATIF. *American Interests in Syria, 1800–1901.* Oxford University Press, 1966. (7)

—————. *A Modern History of Syria Including Lebanon and Palestine.* London, 1969. (4) (7)

—————. *Arabic and Islamic Themes: Historical, Educational and Literary Studies.* London, 1976. (7)

—————. *Islamic Education: Its Traditions and Modernization into the Arab National Systems.* London, 1972. (7)

TIGNOR, ROBERT L. *Modernization and British Colonial Rule in Egypt, 1892–1914.* Princeton University Press, 1966. (7)

TRIMBERGER, ELLEN KAY. *Revolution From Above: Military Bureaucrats and Development in Japan, Turkey, Egypt, and Peru.* New Brunswick, 1978. (11)

TUCKER, JUDITH. *Women in Nineteenth-Century Egypt.* Cambridge University Press, 1985. (6)

TUNAYA, TARIK ZAFER. *Islamcilik Cereyani: Ikinci Mesrutiyetin Siyasi Hayati Boyunca Gelixmesi Ve Bugune Biraktigi Meseleler.* Istanbul, 1962. (7)

UNAT, FAIK RESIT. *Turkiye Egitim Sisteminin Gelismesine Tarihi Bir Bakis.* Ankara, 1964. (7)

UNITED NATIONS. Preliminary Report on the *World Social Situation.* New York, 1952. (13)

VALENSI, LUCETTE. *Tunisian Peasants in the Eighteenth and Nineteenth Centuries.* Cambridge University Press, 1985. (5) (6)

VATIKIOTIS, P. J. *Islam and the State.* London, 1987. (11)

————. *The History of Egypt from Muhammad Ali to Mubarak.* Johns Hopkins University Press, 1985 (3rd edition). (4) (7)

VERDERY, RICHARD N. "The Publications of the Bulaq Press under Muhammad 'Ali of Egypt," *Journal of the American Oriental Society.* XCI, 1971. (7)

WAARDENBURG, J. J. *Les Universités Dans Le Monde Arabe Actuel.* 2 vols. The Hague, 1966. (14)

WALT, STEPHEN M. *The Origins of Alliances.* Cornell University Press, 1987. (10)

WARD, ROBERT E. and RUSTOW, DANKWART A. *Political Modernization in Japan and Turkey.* Princeton University Press, 1964. (11)

WATERBURY, JOHN. *The Egypt of Nasser and Sadat: The Political Economy of Two Regimes.* Princeton University Press, 1983. (11) (12) (13)

————. "The Socio-Economic Stratification of Middle Eastern Economies," in John Waterbury and R. El-Mallakh, *The Middle East in the Coming Decade.* New York, 1978. (13)

WATSON, WILLIAM J. "Ibrahim Muteferrika and Turkish Incunabula," *Journal of the American Oriental Society.* LXXXVIII, 1968. (7)

WENDELL, CHARLES. *The Evolution of the Egyptian National Image: From Its Origins to Ahmad Lutfi Al-Sayyid.* University of California Press, 1972. (7)

WHEATLY, PAUL. "Levels of Space Awareness in the Traditional Islamic City," *Ekistics*, Vol. 42, No. 253. December 1976. (13)

WILSON, RODNEY. "Western, Soviet and Egyptian Influences on Iraq's Development Planning," *Iraq: The Contemporary State.* London, 1982. (11)

WORLD BANK. *Food and Agriculture Organization, Production Yearbook.* Annual (12)

————. *United Nations, Statistical Yearbook.* Annual (12)

————. *World Development Report.* Annual (12)

YAPP, M. E., *The Making of the Modern Near East, 1792–1923.* London and New York, 1987. (4)

YOUSSEF, NADIA. *Women and Work in Developing Countries.* University of California Press, 1974. (13)

ZAHLAN, ANTOINE B. "Established Patterns of Technology Acquisition in the Arab World," in Antoine R. Zahlan (ed.), *Technology Transfer and Change in the Arab World*. Oxford, 1978. (7)

ZILFI, MADELINE C. *The Politics of Piety: The Ottoman Ulema in the Post-classical Age, 1600–1800*. Minneapolis, 1988. (7)

Chronology

1529	First Ottoman siege of Vienna (peak Ottoman penetration into Europe)
late 1500s	European powers establish permanent resident embassies in Istanbul
	End of Ottoman expansion
1683	Second Ottoman siege of Vienna
1699	Treaty of Carlowitz
late 1600s–early 1700s	New World silver floods Ottoman lands contributing to inflation
1705	Advent of autonomous Husaynid Dynasty in Tunisia (continued de jure until 1957)
1718–30	"Tulip Period" of Westernization in Ottoman Empire
1727	First Turkish printing press established in Istanbul by European convert to Islam (in operation until 1742)
1734	Military engineering school established in Istanbul
1773	Naval Engineering Academy established in Istanbul
1774	Treaty of Kuçuk Kaynarca (loss of Crimea; end of Russo-Ottoman War)
1789–1807	Rule of Sultan Selim III in Istanbul marked by reformist trends
1793	Ottoman Empire established a permanent resident embassy in London
	Army Engineering Academy established in Istanbul
1798	Napoleonic invasion of Syria
late 1700s–early 1800s	Plague and cholera rampant
1805–48	Muhammad 'Ali, viceroy of Egypt, ushered in reformist period in Egypt; state factories started in Egypt under Muhammad 'Ali
1807	British invasion of Alexandria (failed)
	Sultan Selim III deposed by Janissaries and ulema
	Nizam-i Cedid (reform of Sultan Selim III) disbanded
1808	*Sened Ittifak* marks peak Ottoman decentralization
1809–39	Reforms of Selim III continued by Mahmud II

1811	Destruction of Mamluks in Egypt
1816	Bey of Tunis put down a revolt of Turkish *jund* (army)
1820	End of plague in Tunisia
1820s	Muhammad 'Ali conquers Sudan
1821	Establishment of Translation Office of Sublime Porte in Istanbul
1822	First Arabic printing press under Muslim control
1826	Destruction of Janissary corps by Mahmud II
1827	Foundation of schools of medicine in Istanbul and Cairo
1830	Beginning of French conquest of Algeria
1830s	Muhammad 'Ali conquered Greater Syria
	Increased reliance by Bey of Tunis on troops levied locally
	Advent of steamboats and tugs on Nile
1831	Abolition of timars in Ottoman Empire
1833	Treaty of Unkiar Skelessi (between Russia and Ottoman Empire)
1835	Ottomans reestablish direct control over Tripolitania
1836	School of Languages founded in Cairo
1837–55	Rule of westernizing Ahmad Bey in Tunis
1838	Anglo-Ottoman Commercial Convention
1839	Hatt-i Sherif of Gulhane (Ottoman reform edict)
1839–76	Period of the Tanzimat
1840	Bardo Military Academy founded in Tunisia
1840s	Attempt to start state factories in Ottoman Empire and Tunisia
1843	End of plague in Syria
1845	Councils established in Mount Lebanon
1849	Most state factories abandoned in Ottoman Empire and Tunisia
1849–54	Rule of Abbas I in Egypt
1850s–1860s	Civil war in Mount Lebanon
1851	Beginning of railway construction in Egypt
1854–63	Rule of Said in Egypt
1856	Hatt-i Humayun (Ottoman reform edict)
	Railways begun in Ottoman domains financed by European powers
	Treaty of Paris terminates Crimean War

1858	Land Law passed in Egypt
	Ottoman land law passed
	Municipal coundil of Tunis founded
	First intermediate level school for girls opened in Turkey
1859	School of Civil Administration opened in Istanbul
1860	Napoleon III sent French troops to Lebanon to quell disorders between Maronites and Druze; Mount Lebanon subsequently created special autonomous province
	First Turkish newspaper started; al-Jawa'ib started by al-Shidyaq in Arabic
1860s	Advent of steamboats and tugs on Tigris-Euphrates
1861	Tunisian constitution
	Ottoman Scientific Society established
	Introduction of telegraph to the area
1861–62	Import duties raised and export duties lowered at Ottoman request
1861–65	Cotton boom in Egypt (period of American Civil War)
1863	Precursor of Robert College founded in Istanbul by Americans
1863–79	Rule of Ismail in Egypt
1864	Ottoman Law of vilayets
	Revolt in Tunisia
	Tunisian constitution suspended after revolt
1866	Syrian Protestant College founded (later American University of Beirut)
	Establishment of a parliament in Egypt
1867	Egyptian law on education
1869	Opening of the Suez Canal
	State bankruptcy in Tunisia
	Ottoman education law established five-tier education system
	Religious communities required to establish primary schools
1873–77	Ministry of reformist Khayr al-Din in Tunisia
1875	Establishment of Mixed Courts in Egypt
	al-Ahram founded
	Sadiqi College founded in Tunis

1876	State bankruptcy in Egypt and Ottoman Empire
	Establishment of European Caisse de la Dette to
	service Egyptian debt
	Ottoman constitution and parliament created
	Tunisian railways begun
1876–1909	Reign of Sultan Abdul Hamid; Abdul Hamid
	champions Pan-Islam
1877	Ottoman constitution and parliament suspended
	End of Plague in Iraq
1877–78	Ottoman-Russian War
1878	Ismail decrees cabinet government and ministerial
	responsibility in Egypt
1879	Sultan deposes Ismail at behest of European powers
1879–92	Khedive Tawfiq in Egypt
1881	First aliyah (immigration) to Palestine by European
	Jews
	Beginning of French Protectorate in Tunisia (until
	1956)
	Construction of modern port begun in Tunis
1881–82	'Urabi Pasha revolt in Egypt
1882	British occupation of Egypt
	First Jewish vocational school established in
	Palestine
1885	Land Registration Act in Tunisia
1888	Beginning of Baghdad Railroad project
	Vienna-Istanbul railway line completed
1896	Reforms undertaken at al-Azhar
1898	Royal Agricultural Society founded in Egypt
1900	Istanbul University founded
1901	Beginning of Hijaz railway
1902	Aswan dam built
1907	Import duties raised in Ottoman Empire
1908	Young Turk Revolution
	Egyptian University founded
1912	Building of Technion (Israel Institute of Tech-
	nology) begun
1913	Eleventh Zionist Congress passes resolution to
	establish a Hebrew University in Jerusalem
	Konya and Hindiyya dams completed

1914	Declaration of British Protectorate of Egypt
	Import duties raised in Ottoman Empire
	Public debt of Ottoman Empire equaled $600 million (excluding Egypt and Tunis); foreign private investment $500 million
	⅕ of cultivated land in Tunisia in French hands
	Internal combustion engine introduced to area
1916–16	Husayn-MacMahon Correspondence
1916	Sykes-Picot Agreement
1917	Balfour Declaration
	Capture of Baghdad by British
1918	Allied capture of Damascus
1919	Emir-Faisal proclaims Syrian state
	Atatürk's landing in Samsun
1920	San Remo Conference
	Mandates assigned (Syrian and Lebanese mandates to France, Mandate of Palestine and Transjordan to Great Britain, Mandate of Iraq to Great Britain)
	France creates Greater Lebanon
	Revolt in Iraq
	College of Law reopened in Iraq
	Bank Misr founded in Egypt
	Opening of Turkish Grand National Assembly
1921	Faisal declared King of Iraq
	Adoption of Turkish Constitution
	Turkish-Soviet Friendship Treaty
1922	End of Ottoman sultanate
	Unilateral British declaration of Egyptian independence (subject to major restrictions)
1923	Transjordan organized as autonomous state
	Syrian (later Damascus) University opened
	End of Capitulations in Turkey
1924	Law for the Unification of Education passed in Turkey
	Abolition of Caliphate by Turkish government
1925	Egyptian University organized as state institution
	Hebrew University in Jerusalem dedicated
	Closing of Progressive Republican Party in Turkey

1926	Adoption of Swiss Civil Code by Turkish government
1928	Principle of secularism incorporated into Turkish constitution
	Latin alphabet adopted by Turkish government
	Muslim Brethren founded in Egypt by Hassan al-Banna
late 1920s	Sharp fall in agriculture prices
1930	Anglo-Iraqi Treaty—Iraq to have nominal independence
1930s	New waves of educational reforms initiated in Turkey
	Formal municipalities introduced in Cairo
	Output in manufacturing and mining increase
1932	Iraq admitted to League of Nations (Iraq receives formal independence under King Faisal)
1933	Istanbul University established in place of the Darulfunun
1934	Foreign language schools in Egypt brought under governmental control
	Voting rights and eligibility to parliament granted to women in Turkey
	Precursor of Weitzman Institute of Science opened in Jerusalem
	Opening of oil pipelines to Mediterranean in Iraq
	Tunisian Neo-Destour Party founded by Habib Bourguiba
1936	Anglo-Egyptian Treaty
	French-Syrian Treaty signed but never ratified
1937	Peel Commission recommends partition of Palestine
	Ankara University established
	End of Capitulations in Egypt
1938	Alexandria University in Egypt established
	Death of Kemal Atatürk
1939–45	Industrial output increased; agriculture severly disrupted
1941	British and Free French defeat Vichy French in Syria
	British defeat Iraqi Army and oust Rashid Ali government
1943	Tuition fees for universities in Egypt abolished
	Pact made between Maronites and Muslims in Lebanon

1945	Land Reform Law in Turkey
1945–50	Transition to competitive multiparty politics in Turkey
1946	First organized attempt at educational planning in Iraq
	Syria and Lebanon achieve independence
	Anglo-Jordanian Treaty recognizes Jordanian independence
1947	Turkish universities granted autonomy by the state
	UN resolution to partition Palestine
1948	Establishment of State of Israel, followed by first Arab-Israeli war
1949	National Cultural Committee for the Organization of Education established in Syria
	Free and compulsory education for all children over five years of age mandated in Israel
	Textbooks standardized in Syria
1950	First Educational Plan organized in Tunisia
	Council for Higher Education established in Israel
	Higher education reorganized in Syria
	Land Reform Law in Syria and Iraq
	English language instruction offered at al-Azhar
	Lebanese Civil War
	Revolution overthrowing monarchy in Iraq
1958–61	United Arab Republic (linking Egypt and Syria)
1959	Education planning initiated in Tunisia
1960	Egyptian government established first Five Year Plan for Education
	Military intervention in Turkey
1960s	Vast extension of state ownership in Arab states
	Comprehensive national planning initiated in Turkey
1961	Reform law for al-Azhar
	Ministry of Higher Education in Egypt established
	University of Tunis established
1962	University of Jordan opened
	All public education made free in Egypt
1964	Nationalization Law (of European-owned land) in Tunisia
1965	Family Planning Law in Turkey
1966	Ministry of Higher Education organized in Syria
	Supreme Council on Family Planning established in Egypt
1967	Second Arab-Israeli war

1968–70	War of attrition in Suez Canal Zone
1970	Ministry of Higher Education and Scientific Research established in Iraq
1971	Iraq began reform of secondary agricultural schools
1972	Population education program begun in Tunisia
	Science Curriculum Improvement Study initiated in Lebanon
1973	Third Arab-Israeli war
1974	Turkish occupation of Cyprus
1975	Lebanese civil war begins
1976	Beginning of Syrian occupation of Lebanon
1978	Higher Literacy Council established in Iraq and literacy campaign launched
1979	Egyptian-Israeli Peace Treaty
1980	Military takeover in Turkey; abolition of political parties
	Iran-Iraq War begins
1981	Compulsory education in Egypt increased from six to nine years
	Turkish universities placed under the control of the Council of Higher Education
1982	Ten new universities, including "Open University," established in Turkey
	Council for Higher Education established in Jordan
	Israel invades Lebanon
1983	Turgut Ozal and Motherland Party take power in Turkey
1984	World Bank initiates projects to reform vocation and technical education in Turkey
	Free and compulsory education extended to children three years of age and older in Israel
1987	Peaceful overthrow of Bourguiba in Tunisia
	Palestinian Intifada erupts in the West Bank and Gaza
1990	World Bank funds National Education Development Project in Turkey
1990–91	Iraqi invasion of Kuwait
	Gulf War

INDEX